TRADITION AND MODERN JAPAN

TRADITION AND MODERN
JAPAN

EDITED BY
P. G. O'Neill

Paul Norbury Publications Limited
Tenterden, Kent

TRADITION AND MODERN JAPAN

PAUL NORBURY PUBLICATIONS LTD
Caxton House, High Street, Tenterden, Kent, England

First published 1981
© European Association for Japanese Studies

ISBN 0 904404 36 6

This book has been set in Journal Roman 10 on 11.
Printed in Scotland by Bookmag, Inverness.

Contents

Preface

The thirty-four articles contained in this book derive from papers given at the Second International Japanese Studies Conference organized by the European Association for Japanese Studies, which was held in Florence, 20-22 September 1979. The Association received help in this from a number of sources and, on its behalf, I should here like to thank the Japan Foundation for invaluable support before and during the conference, particularly by arranging for the participation of scholars from Japan and eastern Europe; and the City Council of Florence and the Regional Government of Tuscany for their cooperation and hospitality. Special thanks are also due to the Italian Association for Japanese Studies, in particular to Professor Fosco Maraini of the University of Florence, for all the time and work which went into the excellent arrangements made for the conference.

The publication of this book has been made possible by a generous grant from the Japan Foundation, and the European Association is most grateful for this further support, enabling it to achieve a lasting result from the conference.

The editing of the contributions has been limited as far as possible, in order to preserve their individuality, but it has of course sought to standardize spellings etc. in the usual way: the romanization of Japanese words follows the 'amended Hepburn' system as used in Kenyûsha's *New Japanese-English dictionary* (although, except for one article, the long vowel has been indicated by a circumflex accent instead of a macron, for ease of printing); long vowels have not been shown for Tokyo, Kyoto and Osaka, except where they form part of a Japanese name or phrase; and the names of Japanese have been given in the Japanese order of family name followed by personal name, except when they are quoted as the authors of works in western languages.

London, 1981   P. G. O'NEILL

Contributors

BOSCARO, Adriana	University of Venice, Italy
BRANDGAARD, Mette	University of Copenhagen, Denmark
CHAPMAN, John W.M.	University of Sussex, U.K.
DANIELS, Gordon	University of Sheffield, U.K.
DE LUCA, Maria	University of Urbino, Italy
FRIESE, Eberhard	University of the Ruhr, West Germany
GAMÔ, Masao	Meiji University, Japan
HAYES, Michael	University of Sheffield, U.K.
HENDRY, Joy	University of Oxford, U.K.
HIJIYA-KIRSCHNEREIT, Irmela	University of the Ruhr, West Germany
KIDD, John B.	University of Aston, U.K.
KLOPFENSTEIN, Eduard	University of Zürich, Switzerland
KOVALIO, Jacob	Hebrew University of Jerusalem, Israel
KRACHT, Klaus	University of the Ruhr, West Germany
KUNO Takeshi	National Research Institute of Cultural Properties, Japan
LEE Sang-Kyong	University of Vienna, Austria
LE NESTOUR, Patrick	University of Paris, France
MAY, Ekkehard	University of the Ruhr, West Germany
MELANOWICZ, Mikolaj	University of Warsaw, Poland
MORAN, Brian D.	University of London, S.O.A.S., U.K.
NEUSS, Margret	Philipps University, Marburg, West Germany
NISH, Ian	University of London, L.S.E., U.K.
PARINI, Milena	University of Venice, Italy
PICONE, Mary J.	University of Oxford, U.K.
RAVERI, Massimo	University of Oxford, U.K.
SCHAMONI, Wolfgang	University of Munich, West Germany
SHELDON, Charles D.	University of Cambridge, U.K.
SHILLONY, Ben-Ami	Hebrew University of Jerusalem, Israel
SLUIMERS, Laszlo	University of Amsterdam, The Netherlands
STANZEL, Volker	University of Bonn, West Germany
TOLLINI, Aldo	University of Novara, Italy
URAGUCHI-DOCHERTY, Miyoko	University of London, S.O.A.S., U.K.
VAN OPSTALL, Margaretha	Algemeen Rijksarchief, The Netherlands
VON ERDBERG, Eleanor	Aachen, West Germany

SECTION 1

People
and
Society

1

Tradition in Modern Japan

MARIA CONSTANZA DE LUCA

A highly developed technology has allowed Japan to take off economically and to become one of the greatest industrial powers in the world. It grew out of the Japanese people's traditional skills in arts and crafts and their ability to accept the stimulus of the West, and was helped by their capacity to select the most advanced technical achievements and to improve on them by using totally new and more efficient means.

If Japan's enthusiasm for modernization dates back to the final decades of the nineteenth century, one must not be led to think that every aspect of it has always been agreeable and well suited to Japanese sensitivity. It must always have been difficult for it to accept the coexistence of traditional values, even though they were already to some extent set aside, with achievements from the West which, though useful, were essentially alien. The tremendous shock of defeat in World War II caused, on the one hand, the complete failure of some traditional but by then meaningless beliefs, such as militarism and the virtues of obedience, because they were too closely linked to the dishonoured past; and it raised, on the other hand, the question of what principle should then be followed for the nation's proper growth—full modernization, or a, for many reasons improbable, return to a 'True Japan'.

The problems of this ambivalence, not resolved even today, are the psychological cause of the identity crisis deeply felt by Japanese youth, and of the country's sometimes dramatic quest for its true place in the world. As Ezra Vogel said, comparing the responses of the two major countries defeated in World War II: '...whereas Germans responded to defeat by reasserting their pre-war values without seriously re-examining them, most Japanese responded by questioning their view of life and submitting it to an agonizing reappraisal from which it never recovered.' (1)

Young Japanese feel it is impossible to turn away from the process of modernization, but wonder how long a traditional way of life can last in the presence of a technically highly developed civilization. It is necessary for them to reduce the negative effects and avoid the lack of spiritual values inherent in imported materialism. This operation is made easier for them by the presence, in their way

1

of life, of tenets which cannot painlessly be removed and which are, moreover, steadily kept alive by older people. Such ideas, free from fanaticism or formalism, are bound to appear as pure and authentic as they wish them to be.

The yearning after inner purity, typical of young people all over the world, has created in Japanese youth three different ways of facing the above problem. Some of them, seeking self-improvement and self-realization, see in transformation the only means to free themselves from both 'monopoly capitalism' and 'stagnant bureaucratism', as R.J. Lifton points out. (2) The Japanese heritage is, in contrast, the basis of the convictions of a second group, who turn to the restoration of the past as the only hope for putting Japan's future on a correct course.

The last of these politically articulated attitudes looks more inclined towards accommodation, and ends up by stressing a personal and private way of considering life and possibilities in the country. Its wide occurrence in contemporary Japan is made easier because it allows 'the vertical principle', as Nakane Chie defines it (3), to be preserved. In particular, it makes it possible to keep alive 'the intense, reciprocal emotional attachment between superior (*oyabun*) and subordinates (*kobun*)' which 'promotes highly shared goals, rapid internal communications and extraordinary harmony within a group' (4)—a successful way of using sound tradition to further modernity all over the country.

I must nevertheless point out that this social rule, which has deep roots in Japanese life based upon conscientiousness in work, a sense of duty, and diligence in using time to the full, usually prevents Japan from adapting completely to western trade-union practices. Japanese who know the West often point out that the strike weapon is used differently in Japan: there the attachment to the factory is too strong for workers to ignore the damage a strike would cause and, when faced with a strike situation, they may well simply continue to work without claiming any salary, making it clear in this way that they are in sympathy with the aims of a strike.

What is the education situation in the country? The normal generation gap has caused a deep change within the school system: moral behaviour has undergone an important transformation, the word *shûshin* ('morals, moral training') is not used any more, and the teaching of morals has either been abolished or changed. For many young people, it is difficult to find employment even though most of them have a degree, and they have no choice but to take up their father's work even though they may dislike it. Growing more and more impatient of an oppressive authority, they end up by envying western teenagers.

If we now turn to consider the causes of the present crisis in Japan, one might say that they arise from the indiscriminate way

2

in which people accepted the values brought by the Americans after World War II. Some of them were indeed probably not congenial to Japanese feelings, and others more suited to them may have been neglected or distorted. Among these latter, I would point out the lack of a deep sense of democratic principles, for their complete fulfilment was prevented by the too near feudal past, the values of which, typical of a privileged society, were meant to teach submission rather than to foster sound civil growth.

Tradition claims its rights more in the private sphere of inner, familiar feelings. A Japanese can recover and realize himself anew as a person only when he is again in contact with the reassuring steadfastness of what is worthwhile in the past of himself and his ancestors. This can be seen in the survival of ceremonies that may have lost their importance for people with different experiences, but fully maintain their meaning for those who are involved in them. I am referring to such well known arts as the tea ceremony, ikebana and bonsai, which are related to Zen spirituality. All of them help concentration and offer the possibility to their practitioners, even abroad, of regaining their own inner harmony. On a different level, since they involve the training and control of the body, such pursuits as jûdô and karate maintain their traditional importance, while kendô brings to life again the military tradition of the samurai.

It must be added that all these spare-time activities have particular features in Japan where they are part of a characteristic ceremonial, although purposes and goals may differ among those concerned, and that they have been exported, at least in a simplified form, all over the world.

A characteristic blend of local elements with western ones is to be seen in the forms of Japanese advertising. There the tradition does not really come out diminished since, as Katsumie Masaru says: 'We don't wish to be too conscious about our tradition, because this attitude easily leads to the flattering of western exoticism. We appreciate the universal visual language, begun and created by the twentieth-century Modern Movement, rather than the dead tradition of Japanese design. We actually think true tradition continues to live when, in spite of the widespread design pattern, there comes out spontaneously in our works that particular way of feeling which can but reveal itself just because we are Japanese.' (5) In these advertisements the writing is usually provided by tradition, while their figurative section is largely influenced by the western way of designing and by the widely spread values of modern life.

The most glamorous, though enigmatic, examples of ties with tradition are certainly represented by the survival of the *kanji*, the Chinese ideographic way of writing, and of the Japanese classical theatre. The former, together with the use of a large number of standard polite phrases in the language, is no mere relic of the past for a

3

Japanese. It really means something, rather like the spirit of the nation, which people would fear to lose. The particularly rich store of polite phrases deeply affects the sensibilities of the Japanese, and encourages a behaviour which they themselves admit to losing when they speak a foreign language. How kind, gentle and ceremonial they can be when speaking Japanese, and how hurried and informal when speaking English!

Finally, even though it is not clear to me whether modern Japanese find in their traditional theatre the responses to help them achieve their catharsis, I suppose that the Nô theatre, with its representation of inner and mostly unconscious feelings, may well still be a useful means of freeing their personal emotions.

On the whole, the image today's Japan offered me and the idea which was strengthened by my interviews when I was there, are those of a country searching for a new equilibrium which may require a spiritual adjustment. Its people have in fact somehow rejected the traditional eastern non-problematic unity between man and nature, and yet they have, on the other hand, been deceived by American humanistic beliefs, which are based on individualism and competition and can therefore hardly be fully realised.

If this equilibrium was not to be found in American culture, is it perhaps Europe with its long traditions of philosophy, art and religion, that can provide useful responses?

2

The Traditional Social Structure of Japan and Changes in it

MASAO GAMÔ

Since the Second World War, Japan has been making efforts to reform its social system, at first under the authority of the U.S. Occupation Forces, by such measures as the establishment of a new constitution, and by farmland reform. Nobody can deny that post-war Japan has experienced the following process of transition: innovation made by borrowing and invention, the social acceptance of this, the selective elimination of the traditional systems, and then the formation of a new system based on their integration. Post-war Japan has acquired some political freedom that had not existed before the war and has effected a remarkably high growth of the economy, but have the national characteristics and the social structure of Japan also been changed? Here, I shall consider the following two problems: first, how the social transition over the thirty-five years since the end of the war has influenced the traditional social structure, which was taken over from the pre-war society and still exists in rural communities; and second, how the traditional social structure has survived modern society.

There are many different points of view about the characteristics of Japan's traditional social system, but my aim here is to indicate what they are through an analysis of family, marriage, kinship and rural communities.

I take the view that the traditional Japanese social structure is based on the fact that there exists a regional variation. For example, the average size of a household in Japan was 4.52 persons in 1960, but in the north-eastern part of Japan, including Niigata, Tochigi and Ibaragi, it was more than 5.0. In the census of 1920, when the average was 4.99, the same kind of regional variation in the size of households in the north-eastern and south-western parts of the country can be seen. Since 1960, the size of a household has been substantially declining; nevertheless, the census in 1975 (with an average of 3.47 persons) shows that this trend has not yet disappeared.

A family is different from a household, but the same thing can be said about a family. If we examine the proportion of nuclear families, comparing the situation in Yamagata prefecture in the north-eastern part of the main island with that of Kagoshima prefecture in the southern part of Kyûshû, we find that in Yamagata,

48.6 per cent of the families were nuclear in 1955, and 49.6 per cent in 1975. On the other hand, in Kagoshima the proportion of nuclear families was 64.9 per cent in 1955 and 67.5 per cent in 1975. Although the same high economic growth rate has taken place in both of these prefectures, these statistics show that the proportion of nuclear families is high in a region where it used to be high and vice versa.

There have probably been various conditions which brought about the variation in family size mentioned above, but one of the main conditions must have been related to the traditional family system. Although succession of the oldest son has been the dominant pattern throughout the country both in the pre-war and post-war periods, there were variant forms. For example, traditionally there have also existed *ane-sôzoku* 'eldest (sister) inheritance' in which the oldest child, regardless of sex, was expected to remain with the parents, and *masshi-sôzoku* 'youngest-child inheritance' in which the youngest son succeeded, while older children moved out. *Ane-sôzoku* could be seen only in a section of the north-eastern part of Japan, and *masshi-sôzoku* was limited to a part of central Japan and western Japan. It is obvious that the function of *ane-sôzoku* consists in successfully securing labour in a family and that this, in turn, will help somewhat to extend the size of the family. On the other hand, *masshi-sôzoku*, in which the youngest son parts from the oldest son, may lead to a reduction in the family size.

There was also the *inkyo* 'retirement' system: in this, married children live away from their parents. As long as this system remains, it is obvious that the proportion of nuclear families will increase. This system has not existed north of Fukushima prefecture and has mainly been seen in a part of west Japan.

We may conclude that though the so-called 'stem family' (which links the family of procreation of one married child to his family orientation in a common household) is great in number and can be seen in every part, it does not typify the traditional Japanese family. It may therefore be necessary to classify the following three types as mechanical models.

(1) Extended family type:
    (i) *Ane-sôzoku* or living together of several married siblings.
    (ii) Living together of parents and a married couple or two.
(2) Preservative family type:
    (i) Succession by the oldest son.
    (ii) The living together of parents and one married couple.
(3) Contracted family type:
    (i) Succession by the youngest son or *inkyo* system.

There are certainly numerous reasons for the regional variations in household size which have existed for thirty-five years since World War II. Generally speaking, however, it can be said that eastern Japan has been associated with the extended family, and western Japan with the contractive family.

I now propose to take up the marriage system as an approach to the traditional Japanese social structure. Many people have pointed out that the Japanese traditional marriage system consists of *mukoiri* and *yomeiri*. Their characteristics can be shown as follows:

(1) *Mukoiri* marriage system:

(i) This is a kind of bilocal residence: that is, at first the husband visits his wife's residence and then, after some time, she moves into his home.

(ii) The premarital sexual relationship is socially accepted in the communities which have this marriage system. The young people can choose their spouse for themselves.

(iii) A *nakôdo* 'go-between' arranges a marriage ceremony, but only perfunctorily.

(iv) After marriage a woman never becomes a daughter-in-law or a mother-in-law in a household, but only a wife and a mother.

(2) *Yomeiri* marriage system:

(i) Virilocal residence.

(ii) The premarital sexual relationship is not socially accepted in communities which have this marriage system. There is a strong tendency to ask a third person to choose the spouse.

(iii) A *nakôdo* 'go-between' plays the main role in the marriage tie.

(iv) After marriage a woman becomes a wife and a mother, and at the same time a daughter-in-law, and eventually a mother-in-law, in the household.

The distribution of the first of these, the *mukoiri* marriage system, is limited only to a region located in a part of western Japan. The differences between these two marriage systems lie not only in the question of the rule of residence, but also in the fact that a woman in the *yomeiri* marriage system becomes a daughter-in-law and a mother-in-law without choice, while the *mukoiri* marriage system avoids this kind of situation. That is, these marriage systems are closely connected with the types of traditional family. In the *mukoiri* marriage system, the period before the wife moved into her husband's residence was not fixed. On the other hand, the period when her parents were alive and she was living with them was not considered a good time to move into her husband's residence. In other words, the *mukoiri* marriage system functionally corresponds to the contracted family type in some respects. It means that a man and wife do not cohabit with his parents. On the other hand, it can be said that the *yomeiri* marriage system functionally corresponds to the preservative or extended family type.

Thus, in observing the types of traditional families and marriages in Japan, we cannot help thinking that two different ideologies exist.

In one, the foundation of family life is based on the parent-child relationship regardless of the latter's marriage, as we can see in the type of extended or preservative family and the *yomeiri* marriage system. The other is the ideology in which a post-marital family life is centred on the conjugal relationship and a married couple living within the framework of their family of procreation. I should like to call the former the 'invariable-situation ideology' because it aims to preserve and continue the family of orientation throughout life. The latter ideology considers the family of procreation as important after marriage and I should like to call this the 'variable-situation ideology'.

Now we move on to another topic, the traditional Japanese kinship organization. It is generally said that there are two ways to organize kinship: a descent group organized on the ancestor-base, and a kindred group organized on the ego-base. Both of these have existed in traditional Japanese society. On the assumption that there have been various types within the traditional Japanese kinship organization. I should now like to classify them as follows:

(1) The kinship organization in which the descent group and the kindred coexist.
   (a) The type formed through the so-called *dôzoku*.
   (b) The type without forming the *dôzoku*.
(2) The kinship organization composed only of the kindred.
   (a) The tendency to the patrilateral agnatic type.
   (b) The remarkable tendency of the bilateral type.

The *dôzoku* is a hierarchical corporate group which consists of a main family and its branches, sub-branches and the like, and is characterized by the main family having priority over its branches and sub-branches. The constituent element of a *dôzoku* is not an individual but a family. The branches have usually been established by junior sons of the main family, but sometimes by non-kin.

Therefore, as the *dôzoku* is different in many ethnographic characteristics from a descent group, there is some opinion that it is not a descent group. But I have a different opinion, namely that the *dôzoku* is an ancestor-based kinship organization even if the family is the direct constituent element of the *dôzoku*; and that the principle of the unity of the family group, where the family is the constituent element, is a particular aspect of Japanese kinship.

This is to say, the woman becomes a member of a family as a result of her marriage; and, at the same time as becoming the man's wife, she becomes his parents' daughter-in-law.

This is symbolized by the fact that the relationship between a woman entering a family by marriage and her husband's parents was an important ritual in the marriage ceremonies performed in many rural communities in north-eastern Japan until around 1930. Furthermore, it must be wrong to say that a group which accepts

8

non-kin as its members can be called a 'descent group' just through a broad interpretation of that term. This can be said because we find similar cases in ethnographies in which such acceptance of non-kin has been made through certain ritual processes.

The descent group is characterized by unilineality and corporateness. The *dôzoku* is principally characterized by patrilinearity, but it must be potentially ambilineal, because some families take a son-in-law in order to have a successor, being willing to accept such a person in this role. We are not here concerned with the problem of kinship organization, but we would like to draw attention to the ideologies of people who have established their own specific kinship organization. For example, the *dôzoku* is based on the 'invariable-situation' ideology in which the hierarchical relationships between the main family and its branches or sub-branches are always pre-established and in which these relationships are invariable throughout life. On the other hand, the main family-branch group which does not expand to form the *dôzoku* and various types of ego-based kinship are connected with the 'variable-situation ideology', in which kin are linked in terms of different circumstances, or in which their hierarchical relationships will vary. Therefore, it can be supposed that a relationship exists between a specific kinship organization and a specific type of family and marriage.

It can be clearly said that the formation of the *dôzoku* has been limited to families of extended or preservation type and the *yomeiri* marriage-system. In contrast, it is obvious that such a kinship organization as the *dôzoku* has never existed in rural communities which have had the contracted type of family and *mukoiri* marriage-system.

Lastly, in order to deepen the understanding of the traditional Japanese social structure, I propose to study rural communities: there are many types of traditional Japanese rural communities. Here I should like to consider the following four:

(1) The rural community with the *dôzoku* system—the community consisting of one or two *dôzoku*.

(2) The rural community with the age-grade system—the community organized according to the age-grade system.

(3) The rural community with the *tôya* system—where households of the community take it in turns to be in charge of funerals, religious rituals, the construction of public roads, etc.

(4) The community other than those mentioned above.

The basis underlying the standard of this classification is the distinction between the one in which social status in a rural community is based on the origin of a particular authority (types (1) and (2)), and the one in which the origin of authority is not clear (types (3) and (4)). In type (1), whether an individual is born into the main family or into one of its branches, or whether his ascribed status is a

9

junior son or not, will not in principle affect or change his social status throughout his life. In type (2), as an individual gets older he will be able to acquire a status of authority. In type (3), the rotation system in a joint enterprise is not emphasized. In type (4), the community itself does not have the strong characteristic of a corporation, so that the origin of authority is not fixed and works are not actively carried out in the community. From the viewpoint of ideology, it can be said that type (1) belongs to the 'invariable-situation' ideology, and that types (2), (3) and (4) belong to the 'variable-situation' ideology.

We have so far discussed some problems which are necessary in considering traditional Japanese social structure. As I pointed out before, we have to emphasize once again that there were variable patterns in the social structure. The first pattern has 'the extended' or 'the preservative' family with the *yomeiri* marriage-system and forms a *dôzoku*. This social structure, in which the status order is respected, is supported by the 'invariable-situation' ideology. I should like to call it the *dôzoku* type of social organization. The second pattern, directly opposed to the first, has the 'contracted' family and the *mukoiri* marriage-system: its kinship organization consists only of kindred; and its rural community has the age-grade system. This pattern respects the seniority of age and is supported by the 'variable-situation' ideology. I should like to call this the 'age-grade' type of social system.

Therefore these two patterns, that is, the *dôzoku* type and the age-grade type, form the two extremes of traditional Japanese social structure. There are also various in-between patterns: some resemble the *dôzoku* type, some look like the age-grade type, and others resemble neither of the two extremes.

On the basis of these assumptions, I should like to mention how changes have occurred in Japanese rural communities during the thirty or so years since World War II. First of all, all the communities which could be regarded as typical examples of the *dôzoku* type or the age-grade type of social structure disappeared in the 1950s. The biggest element which hastened their disappearance was the changes in economic conditions in the rural communities, one being the farmland reform which began in 1945.

In the landholding situation as it was before World War II, almost half the farmland was cultivated by independent farmers and the rest by peasants, but after the land reform, more than 90 per cent of farmland was owned by the farmers themselves. This decidedly threatened the existence of the *dôzoku*. In this organization, it was common for the main family not only to build a house for or give furnishings or food to a branch family, but also to give or lend it a piece of land. Furthermore, without the help of the main family, branch families could not make a living at all. The main family of a *dôzoku* owned enough farmland to have such branch families, but after the land reform a farmer could not have more land than his family could manage. Therefore, the economic conditions necessary for the existence of *dôzoku* were taken away.

Another change is the improvement in farming techniques. Generally speaking, in eastern Japan, and especially in the north-eastern part, Hokuriku area, or the northern Kantô area, the size of the land a farm family would work was relatively larger than in western Japan. One of the reasons was that eastern Japan had only a short history of development; but the more essential background was that the techniques were too immature to overcome the natural conditions and, thus, productivity was relatively low. This was also the background for the formation of the 'extended' type of family. Remarkable progress was made in the 1950s in the improvement of rice and fertilizers, development of mechanization, and improvement in other techniques, so that productivity was raised in the areas of previous low productivity. There were at least two conditions for the existence of *dôzoku*: one was that farmlands were owned by a few landlords, and the other was the low productivity of the land itself. The land reform and the technical improvements in farming have prompted the dissolution of *dôzoku*.

The third characteristic change for us to point out is connected with the decrease in the number of workers in primary industry: that is, there has been a great outflow of the farming population into the cities, and the number of farmers with a side job has increased considerably. It can be said that this decreased the peasant's dependence on his farmland and also facilitated the extinction or relaxation of the traditional regimes in rural society. Such increased demand for labour in the cities stimulated especially the communities which had suffered from low productivity and, as a result, the population outflow was accelerated. This is a typical example of a rural community which has an age-grade type of social structure. This kind of community was mainly found in western Japan, where productivity was not relatively high, the area faced the sea and lacked sufficient farmland, and each person was forced to be a farmer as well as a fisherman because of low productivity.

Thus, in the rural communities with the age-grade type of social structure, the population outflow was significant, especially among young people. As a result, the age-grade system supported by young people just collapsed, and those villages became communities for the aged. Those communities forming a *dôzoku* organization based on the hierarchical order, and the age-grade system based on the age order, found themselves in a common situation in which neither could make a living without the co-operation and help of many people outside the family but within the same community. Under

11

these adverse economic conditions, in which they had to cultivate tenant land or their own insufficient arable land, it was difficult for each family to be economically independent. Among the points of difference, however, was the fact that, whereas the *dôzoku* was characterized by a considerable amount of farmland but a high dependance on tenancy, the age-grade system was characterized by a lack of farmland which caused a dependence on income from other than farming, mainly fishing.

Until 1940 the *dôzoku* organization and the age-grade system were an integral part of the Japanese rural community. It can be said that some Japanese had chosen them as a sort of 'strategic organization' in which they could attempt to live under the economically bad conditions of relatively low productivity. A hundred years have passed since the foundation of modern Japan and during this time the government did not legally urge the people to establish such regimes. Nevertheless, the people in a particular community chose this sort of severe heirarchical order due to a lack of any other way to live. Therefore, this can be properly called 'strategic organization'.

It is well-known that post-war Japan has achieved remarkable economic progress. Almost all tenant lands have come to be the farmers' own lands, productivity has increased thanks to technical improvements and, because of the surprisingly rapid economic growth, cities have demanded more labour. As a result, the conditions accounting for low productivity in rural communities have been eliminated. It can be said that this resulted in the dissolution of the strategic organization that had traditionally existed in rural communities.

Communities belonging to neither the *dôzoku* organization nor the age-grade system have not always enjoyed the best economic conditions in which each family could be independent, and in this kind of community co-operation beyond the family unit was sometimes necessary. But a family would choose to have assistance from kin or non-kin only when it was necessary. In other words, it was not necessary to have a strategic organization to fulfil economic purposes. Therefore, the members of a community would unite together mainly in magico-religious rather than economic activities. Needless to say, various economic innovations after the war influenced this kind of community but it is independent by nature. Thus, it is more appropriate to say that the characteristic of economic independence has been strengthened than to say that this kind of community was drastically changed to be independent after the war. The typical example of this kind is the *tôya*-type community. In this, people still jointly carry out funerals and other magico-religious activities, following traditional ways, but economically each family is as independent as it always was.

As already mentioned, the *dôzoku* organization and the age-grade system were dissolved in the post-war rural Japanese communities. The dissolution was not concerned with only the extinction of *dôzoku* and age-grade system but also with the extinction of the 'extended family type' and the *mukoiri* marriage-system. The extinction of the 'extended family type' was caused both by the disappearance of the economic condition of low productivity which had forced the extension of family size, and by the idea that it was very desirable for each couple to form an independent family. According to the statistics, it is not necessarily true to say that the number of nuclear families dramatically increased after the Second World War, for 54.0 per cent of Japanese families were nuclear in 1920, 59.6 per cent in 1955 and 64.0 per cent in 1975.

But the families have been firmly maintaining the tradition of preservative or stem family type. It is true to say that the extended or lineal family changed not to be nuclear but to be of the stem type; and temporary expedients such as *ane-sôzoku* to overcome low productivity have already disappeared in rural Japanese communities.

In the *mukoiri* marriage-system, a woman remained in her residence without living with her husband after marriage. This was because there existed conditions accounting for low productivity in which her family could not help being very dependent on her productive labour. Consequently the young generation rapidly moved as workers to the cities from rural communities where the *mukoiri* system had been maintained, because of an increasing demand for labour there arising from the high economic growth. The young people must have wondered why a newly-married couple should have to live separately, one in the city, one in the country, in spite of a socially accepted marriage. By 1950 the *mukoiri* had already disappeared completely as a marriage system in a community.

Then how about the *inkyo* and the *masshi-sôzoku* systems which have caused the formation of a traditional type of contracted family?

The traditional *inkyo* system, in which even an eldest son lived separately from his parents after marriage, was accepted by many Japanese as a modern progressive family system which fitted the new epoch. But the number of nuclear families has not necessarily increased rapidly, although it was accepted: not always by farming families but by white-collar or blue-collar workers living in the city.

Some rural communities still preserve the tradition of the *masshi-sôzoku* system. As already pointed out, the rural communities where this system was maintained have been limited to western Japan, especially because of insufficient farmland. In spite of the higher productivity after the war, the lack of farmland could not be solved and the outflow of population was inevitable.

13

The system of inheritance in post-war Japan changed considerably in two respects: first, the inheritance by the eldest son became no longer morally required and, second, all the children could legally succeed to their parents' estate. In fact, however, there are very many farming families in which the eldest son does inherit, and the custom by which younger sons abandon their legally accepted succession, at least to the land, has been taking root. Neither the *dôzoku* nor the age-grade systems were legally demanded or expected by the government, but they have been preserved from necessity. Thus, the inheritance system among the post-war Japanese farmers does not necessarily correspond to the legal order.

The strategic organization or system is effective in a critical situation, but it will necessarily be dissolved or relaxed as that situation disappears. Although the dangerous situation concerning productivity which had been observed in some parts of rural Japan still remained after World War II, it has been gradually resolved since the 1950s. During this period, the strategic systems of the *dôzoku*, the age-grade, *ane-sôzoku*, the living together of two or more married siblings, and *mukoiri* marriage came to be almost extinct. On the other hand, the *masshi-sôzoku* and the *inkyo* systems still remain in a somewhat loose form, adjusting themselves to the new world. The *masshi-sôzoku* is now alive, not as a system in which the heir must be the youngest son, but as a system which does not give the eldest son the exclusive right to be the only successor. In the communities which had the *inkyo* system, it was traditionally thought culturally normal that a son and his wife should live separately from his parents. However, at present, this system has turned out to be one where parents and children will live separately only if it is desirable and possible for each family.

Thus far we have discussed two big subjects: one is how we should understand the traditional Japanese social structure before World War II through observing family, marriage, kinship organisation and rural community organization; the other is how this structure has been altered by economic changes in Japanese society since World War II.

The *dôzoku* organization and the age-grade system have disappeared from rural Japan. This organization and this system had existed due to the dangerous situation caused by low productivity. It is for this reason that they became extinct as the severe situation of low productivity was lifted from rural Japan after World War II. Although the status principle regarded as the 'invariable-situation' ideology in the hierarchical order of the *dôzoku* organization and the age principle regarded as the 'variable-situation' ideology in the hierarchical order in the age-grade system are different in character, the Japanese people would follow either or both

14

of these two principles to form their societies when they were in a difficult situation.

Incidentally, the reason why the emperor system of Japan has lasted for so long might have something to do with the fact that this system and the *dôzoku* organization are based on the same ideology.

In Japan, at present, the mechanism of the government office or the organizations of many major companies are fairly characteristic of the status and age principles. For example, if a young student takes examinations for entry into the civil service, the results decide his future as a government official. On the other hand, there is a seniority wage-system in which the salary of any person increases as he gets older. Both government service and many big companies realized the shortcomings of this wage system, but there is no tendency to do away with it. Moreover, as far as companies are concerned, the status principle—such as what university an applicant has graduated from and what marks he might have gained—plays an important role in deciding his social status. It is for this reason that some famous universities are flooded with examinees and great efforts are being made to enter a good high-school that has produced many successful candidates.

The two traditional principles of social structure, that is, the status principle and the age principle, do not operate in an observable form in present-day rural Japan. If in the future, however, some dangerous situation appears again, it is probable that the status and the age principles will be made use of in some way. These two principles are preserved in a considerable manner in urban societies and have been the bases for many organizations and social structures which have supported the rapid economic growth after the war. The time of rapid economic growth is over. At present the Japanese people are about to take leave for the time being of the traditional principles of social structure, the principles of status and age.

3

The Rice Ecosystem and Folk Religion in Japan

MASSIMO RAVERI

It is difficult to determine the relative importance of the several factors which contribute to the formation of a cultural configuration and the effect of their interaction. My point of departure is an analysis of the relation between the agricultural ecosystem and certain religious concepts. There are two ways in which cultural behaviour can be related to environmental phenomena: 'Either showing that items of cultural behaviour function as parts of systems that also included the ecosystem, or else, showing that the environmental phenomena are responsible in some manner for the origin or development of the cultural behaviour under investigation.' (1)

Material conditions are a good starting point if only because they are basic and inescapable. It is also possible to quantify material data with a relatively high degree of precision. The influence of the ecosystem is constant and its modifications can be reconstructed.

A narrowly deterministic approach, however, would be misleading. The debate on the limits of applicability (when not on the validity) of the systems analysis, is still open. (2) The related problem of cultural 'adaptation' is not solved. (3) For the moment, it is only possible to say that the interaction of certain sets of conditions favours the development of certain social and religious forms of behaviour.

I analyse two basically different modes of cultivation in Japan: shifting or 'slash and burn', and the 'wet rice' or paddy field agriculture. I also consider, on the one hand, the annual cycle of rites: *ta-asobi*, *minaguchi*, *ta-ue*, *tanabata*, *mushi-okuri*, *niiname*; and, on the other, related by correlation and opposition, the *Shôgatsu* ritual complex.

In the tradition which started from the first hypothesis of Yanagita Kunio (4) and has subsequently been strengthened by the work of Oka Masao (5), the school of the University of Kyoto (Nakao Sasuke (6), Ueyama Shunpei (7) and Iwata Keiji (8)) has stressed the importance of the so-called *shôyôjurin* ('glossy-leaf forest') ecosystem.

This area generally features mountains of medium height and a humid but not completely tropical or monsoon climate. Here shifting agriculture is (or was) often practised. Here are found *konnyaku* 'devil's tongue root', *taro-imo*, *yama-imo* (two kinds of yam), *shiso* 'beefsteak plant', tea, bananas, and *mikan* (a citrus fruit). The *shôyô-jurin* ecosystem is practised in parts of the north of Vietnam, and of Laos and Burma, most of Assam, and the south-eastern slopes of the Himalayas; then northwards from the south of China, to Okinawa and Amami Ôshima to the tip of South Korea, Kyûshû and most of the Kansai. (9)

Shifting agriculture may be defined, in Conklin's terms, as 'always involving the impermanent agricultural use of land plots produced by the cutting back and burning off of vegetative cover'. (10)

To the distinctive features of this *yakihata* ('burned-field') type of cultivation it is possible to apply Gourou's outline:

1) It is practised on very poor soils.
2) It represents an elementary agricultural technique which utilizes no tool except the axe.
3) It is marked by a low density of population.
4) It involves a low level of consumption. (11)

It is also marked by a lack of tillage, and less labour input than other methods of cultivation. The productivity of a shifting agriculture can be only partially determined. (12)

Shifting agriculture integrates into the pre-existing natural eco-system. Wet rice cultivation, most strikingly of the terrace variety, displays the opposite characteristic, the prolonged effort to subdue the ecosystem in order to obtain complete control and increase the flow of energy to man. Shifting agriculture works through, as Geertz writes, 'a canny imitation' of nature rather than through its subversion. (13) The swiftness of the recycling process, that involves decay and rapid re-utilization, overcomes the apparent opposition of an abundance of flora and fauna supported on a poor soil.

The rites of folk religion connected with shifting agriculture in various societies of the *shôyôjurin* area fall into a coherent pattern, even if a certain amount of generalization may be necessary. There is one major rite, the most important of the year, which occurs in the winter after the end of the harvest and before the burning of the forest plots. This rite always includes a ritual representation of the nocturnal arrival of masked visitors. In Okinawa there are the *Ni-iru-pitu*, the *Akamata* and *Kuromata*, the *Maya* or *Mayu-ganashi*. (14) In Kagoshima appear the masked and straw-skirted *Toshi don* and the *Boze* of the Tokan archipelago. In Honshû there are the *Namahage* or the *Chase-go*, *Kase dori*, *To tataki*, *Kayu tsuri*, *Toro hei*, *Oiwaiso*: they are called with diverse names but they may be classified together because of their fundamental common features. (15) It is easy to connect them with the *oni*, who appear at the culmination of the ritual in the *Hana matsuri* of Aichi, in the *Shimotsuki matsuri* of Nagano, in the *Shujo oni o* of Oita. They can also be related to the *Tsuina* and the *oni* of *Setsubun*. They come to the village at night, mainly at *Koshôgatsu*. Announced by noise-making tools and shouts with animal-like voices, they appear wearing terrifying masks, straw coats and holding an axe. Often the duty (and the privilege) of impersonating the *oni* is restricted to young men, who threaten children and newly arrived members of the community. They are believed to come either from the near mountains or from the other world (*Niirasuku*) and there they return after being placated with the offering of *mochi*.

The rite represents not an exchange but a double theft. The manipulation of the ecological equilibrium of the forest to society's advantage with a minimum of direct work, implies that man is a thief of the products of nature. Thus, to re-establish the balance, man is robbed in his turn by uncontrollable forces. The masked creatures, whose very shape is uncertain, reveal latent capabilities of transformation; their fierce faces are frightening because the underlying resemblance to human features strengthens their basic and alien animality.

These excessive traits accentuate the uncertain status of the *oni* balanced, in Levistraussian terms, between nature and culture. *Oni* are created and remain a symbolic reflection of the 'loss of conscious personal identity'. (16) In this type of rite everything obeys a rigid scheme of correspondences: the ambiguity of the *oni* is related to that of the young men who, wearing the masks, are undergoing initiation. They will attack, in their turn, other socially non-integrated figures, that is, children and newly-arrived brides. It is not by chance that the rite is held during the night that marks the passage from the old to the new cycle of cultivation. On other occasions (in the *Tondo matsuri*, for example) ritual roles can be changed (the children will chase the evil spirits) without modifying the meaning of the performance.

The precariousness of shifting cultivation and the consequent difficulty in foretelling and planning the future, finds its religious expression in the importance given to the rites of ecstatic possession. Even with all the ritual precautions required by this type of religious experience, the village community believes that direct communication with the god must be established. The ideal form features a direct interrogation of the deity by the participants. No intermediary is required to codify the questions and decodify the answers. The types of answers obtained are potentially free and uncontrolled. The broken sentences and words uttered during the *kamigakari* 'spirit possession' in an unaccustomed juxtaposition may create a new way of seeing things. Because it can subvert all symbolic 'received knowledge', it can be adapted to all interpretations and satisfy all questions. If the *oni* express latent confusion, the *yoribito* 'medium', on the contrary, seems almost the realization of the ultimate ordinator.

18

This concept of divinity can be assimilated to the *hito-gami* complex, as defined by Hori Ichirô. (17) There can be no *Ubusuna* 'native place' *kami* in a society forced to move constantly by its own methods of cultivation, which abandons worn-out land to lie fallow while opening up new agricultural territory. In fact, the characteristic of the *yakihata* type of cultivation is the precarious equilibrium of its regime. With an increase of population the farmers must spread out widely in order to bring more land into cultivation. The decay process of the soil is irreversible. The only difficulty is to determine the period for which it must lie fallow before productive use. It seems to be somewhere between ten and twenty years. (18)

This ecosystemic property can explain, by analogy, the practice of shifting capitals before the Nara period, the complex 'journeys' of the sacred mirror (as described by Ponsonby Fane) and the belief still followed today that shrines should be rebuilt after a certain number of years because their sacredness will 'wear out'. The case of the cyclical rebuilding of Ise shrines is well known. It is not by chance that this occurs every twenty years. (19)

The burning of the plot is a technique of accelerating the process of decay and of directing it in such a fashion that the nutrients it releases are channelled into certain food-producing plants. To the agricultural effect (clearance-fertilization) of fire is connected its ritual significance:

1) *As a means of purification*   Among the *yamayaki* ('mountain-burning') rites, those of the Wakakusa Yama of Nara and the Daimonji of Kyoto are the most spectacular. Their equivalents, simpler but not less old, in the villages are, respectively, the *Tondo* or *Dondon-yaki* and the *okuri-bi* of the *Bon. Oni* are chased away with *taimatsu* 'torches', as in the widely-spread *Tsuina* rite or, among others, in the *Takiyama-dera sai* of Aichi, in the *Onbeyaki* of Kanagawa, in the *Oni yo* of Fukuoka, and in the *Onja Onja* of Shiga. During the *mushi-okuri* ('sending-away of insects') rite children use fire to expel noxious insects.

2) *As a symbol of fertility*   A great bonfire is the centre of the *Dôsojin matsuri* ('festival of the deities of sex, also patrons of travellers'). In other *hi-matsuri* ('fire festivals') such as those of Kuramadera in Kyoto and Kumano Nachi Taisha in Wakayama, the effort of carrying the great torches and the courage demonstrated in ignoring the falling sparks is an initiation ordeal for the young men. Only after having successfully undergone it will they be ready for adulthood and marriage.

Thus, conversely, water becomes a neutral or non-stressed symbol. During the preparation of the new fields on the mountain-side,

19

rituals are performed to exorcise rain. The water would ruin the chances of a good burning or wash away to the valley the fertilizing ashes.

To the *yakihata* system of agriculture, rice cultivation was added very early, prior to the Yayoi transformation. (20) In analysing the rice ecosystem, it must be said that 'the contrast between a terrace —an artificially and maximally specialized continuous cultivation, open field structure—and shifting plot, could hardly be more extreme'. (21) Stability, accompanied by continuity, is the most important feature of the integrated ecosystem of terrace cultivation. It can continue to produce virtually equal yields for an unlimited span of time: 'Soil fertility does affect its yield,' the geographer Murphey (22) has written, 'but it does not appear to exhaust the soil even over long periods without fertilization.' Rice cultivation produces a drastic change in the natural habitat. It necessitates collectively organized work and a continuous effort in the course of the year, accompanied by constant control of the water supply. The final results, however, are certain and, within limits, predictable. These systemic characteristics produce what is the sociologically most critical trait of rice cultivation: its ability to adapt to the needs of a rising population through intensification and to absorb an increased number of cultivators on a unit of land.

The cycle of rites that follow every moment of rice cultivation represents a symbolic sanction of the pact between god and the community. There is a symmetrical relationship between the agricultural mimes (*ta-asobi*) and divinatory rites (*uranai*) at the beginning of the cultivation and the harvest feast which ends it. The harvest *matsuri* of the *niiname* (23) in the imperial palace, as in the shrine of Izumo or in the village *omiya*, are all based on a communal banquet in which the first fruits of the harvest are shared. Rice and *sake* are offered to the *kami* and then eaten. The form of this ritual is also that of the marriage ceremony. We cannot go too far in affirming that the *niiname* is an actual marriage of the celebrant and the *kami* but, if marriage can be defined minimally as a social institution that, through the exchange of wives, establishes a continuous, ordered and pacific relationship between families or groups, then it is possible to understand, at least in part, why the same symbolism was chosen.

However the religious iconography has radically changed. When the *ta-no-kami* is represented, as in rough statues found in Kagoshima, he assumes human semblances or even phallic connotation. As a protecting deity, his image is placed at the margins of the rice fields or in each of the village houses in turn. He is also identified with Daikoku (or Ô-kuni-nushi), an 'order-inducing' *kami*. Finally he is worshipped as Inari, the god of rice, who is ambiguously identified in default of any definite iconography.

In this type of community, ecstatic experience becomes rarer and is relegated to the peripheral rites. In a stable economy in which the members of the community can predict the results of future crops, the unexpectedness of the *kami*'s directives in a shamanic seance are a source of potential social disruption. Since Japanese farming communities devoted to paddy-field cultivation are necessarily stable, the main *kami* is the *ubusuna-gami*, inextricably connected to the valley, rice field and hill. The *ubusuna-gami* is also the *uji* ('extended kinship') *kami*, and the adult men of the village his children, *ujiko*. This leads to the formation of the politico-religious organization of the *miyaza-tôya* institution. (24)

Because of its vital necessity for cultivation, water is a very important ritual element: *iwai-mizu* 'ceremonial water'; *ikioi-mizu* 'water that gives strength'; *waka-mizu* 'young water'. Water purifies, assuming the function of fire in the preceding system. The Nara *Omizutori*, the ritual offering of the purest water, marks the beginnings of spring and the opening of the sluices in the rice fields. In the zone of the *shôyôjurin*, rice cultivation was adopted slowly and, even to the present day, has not completely superseded the originally shifting agriculture, in a delicate balance of geo-economic factors. For example, when comparing settlement patterns in Nepal, Assam, Laos and Japan, we can see that Nepalese villages are built on the slopes of hills or mountains, higher than the rice fields which stretch to the valley floor. In Laos, the paddy fields reach the top of most mountains and human settlements are scattered amongst the fields half-way up the mountain side. In Japan, as in Assam, the preferred species of rice grows well on the valley floor. This is so even if the paddy fields in mountainous regions sometimes reach the mountain side. Japanese villages are mostly groups of houses on the valley near the banks of a river. (25) The village shrine is mostly half-way up the mountain, the point of transition not only of two agricultural ecosystems which have now mingled, but of two forms of ritual.

Only by noting how the two types of ecosystem have harmoniously intermingled is it possible to understand the formation of the *ta-no-kami* and *yama-no-kami* symbolic pattern, as delineated by Yanagita Kunio. The cyclic exchange between the mountain and the field systems is represented in ritual by the descent and subsequent return of the mountain god. In this light can be seen the meaning of the winter *okonai* rite which centres on the mimed copulation, at the beginning of the village forest, of the male *ta-no-kami* with the female *yama-no-kami*.

Rice cultivation, which slackens during the winter, has been enriched by the cycle of shifting agriculture which culminates in winter rites. These rites, at least in their outward form, have survived even though their symbolic content has sometimes changed only in meaning or the emphasis has been modified to suit society's material requirements in each period.

21

A central symbol of this process of combination is the *mochi*, the Japanese offering par excellence. These are made by pounding rice into a soft glutinous paste. Taro and manioc are also prepared in this way; in fact, this is the only way they are edible at all. *Mochi*, whether the great *kagami-mochi*, the *mochi-inu*, or the *mochibana*, are always offered in winter, the time when taro is harvested; but they also came to signify the continuity of the cycle of rice and the year, in the period of non-productivity of the paddy fields.

4

Aspects of Death Symbolism in Japanese Folk Religion

MARY J. PICONE

The relative dearth of folk-belief (*minkan shinkô*) studies within the field of Japanese religion has been partially offset in recent years. A few areas, however, seem to have been neglected. One of these is the investigation of the rites of death, often treated as a province of Buddhist studies. A division into Shinto and Buddhist 'spheres of influence' can be justified primarily on methodological grounds. At a more basic level, beyond regionalist polemics, the antithesis of foreign religions and a 'pure' autochthonous tradition has also been proved false as exemplified by Suzuki's critique of Yanagita's view of the ancestor cult. (1)

After R.J. Smith's authoritative work on ancestor worship, centred on family rites (2), there remains scope for further investigation of the collective rites of death and of the belief in *muen-botoke* ('unaffiliated spirits') or *gaki* ('hungry ghosts').

Nenjû gyôji ('annual ceremonies') and 'redundant' rituals
An ideal or model *nenjû gyôji* cycle (which could not parallel the actual practice of any present-day Japanese village), would include a series of rites implicitly or explicitly concerned with the spirits of the dead. The *reikon* are overtly conceived to be present at *Bon, Jizô-Bon* and the two *Higan* celebrations. In the Tôhoku area the annual contact takes a more striking form in the gatherings of the *itako* (blind female shamans).

Yanagita's concept of a year divided in two symmetric halves in which the *Bon* corresponds to *Shôgatsu, Koshôgatsu* to *Jizô-Bon* and the vernal *Higan* to that held in the autumn (3), is strengthened by other parallels: the December *Tsuina*, an exorcism, repeats the *mushi-okuri* 'sending-away of insects' which adopts the form of the *Tanabata* and the *Nebuta nagashi*.

The individual versus collective rite distinction is not always clearly drawn. The Tenjin and Gion festivals (*matsuri*) are interesting examples of rites for individual spirits of the dead that have become collective and cyclical. (For Yanagita, instead, the *Bon* rites were first individual then 'degenerated' into collective rites for all spirits.(4)) There are other less-known rites of this type such as the *Narihira ki* (memorial service) held in Kyoto at the end of May.

Following an official resumption of the ancient Japanese form of the rite, a *mitama matsuri* is celebrated each *Bon* at the Yasukuni Shrine in Tokyo. The souls of the war-dead are invoked collectively as *kami*, instead of following the usual pattern of family practice with an apotheosis as ancestors or *hotoke*. The New Year *Okina* performances and the *Tsuina* repeat the *Bon* ancestral visit and the various forms of exorcism in summer such as the Buddhist *Segaki-e*.

Rituals now spread out in the course of the year were once celebrated at the same period. The shift from a lunar to a solar calendar created an intermediary period and, if both the original and the new date are celebrated, redundant rituals. Regional peculiarities explain the lack of basic rites in some areas. The vernal *Higan* (equinox ceremony), for example, was celebrated instead of *Shôgatsu* in parts of central Honshû because the new year by custom began locally in February or even March. Temporal partition in ritual lends substance to the hypothesis of symbolic correlation.

Categories of the dead

The ultimate fate of the soul depends on its status in family and community and on the manner and time of death. The first is pre-eminent. Thus, the head of a lineage who has established his kin in reasonable prosperity and generated sons will rarely be excluded from veneration as an ancestor, whatever the circumstances of his decease. (5) The most feared category of the dead includes those who have been wronged in some way. These spirits are excluded from rebirth or the customary veneration, and return to revenge themselves upon the living. However, 'we must be on guard against identifying people dead in an abnormal way with the damned; they may equally well be considered the elect'. (6)

In Japan only exceptional people are deified after death. Even the comforting belief in the transformation of the family dead into *hotoke* at the end of the memorial rites cannot disguise the precariousness of this status: the extinction of the lineage will change them sooner or later into *muen-hotoke*.

Collective rites and insect symbolism

Only the 'un-affiliated' and harmful categories of the dead are thought to be present in the collective rites. The most frequently recurring symbol appears to be that of the life-cycle of moths and certain species of birds and flowers. These symbolic objects are perceived as homologous to various 'liminal' social categories: children, the blind, outcasts, who all assume the role of mediators. (7)

24

The first references to insects in this context appear in the *Kojiki*. (8) The corpse of Izanami is devoured by maggots and inhabited by eight 'thunders' probably in the form of snakes. According to Shiratorı Kurakichi these maggots had taken the form of snakes and were thought to be the spirits of the dead. (9)

The second episode in which insects have an important part is the account of the ordeals undergone by Opo-kuni-nushi to win his bride, Suseri-bime. Opo-kuni-nushi is placed for one night by Suseri-bime's father Susanowo in a 'chamber of snakes'. These he drives away with a 'snake-repelling scarf'. On the second night he is compelled to sleep in a 'chamber of centipedes and bees' which he also repels. Other trials follow until he finally carries off Suseri-bime, after impressing Susanowo with his courage in apparently biting in pieces the poisonous centipedes in the latter's hair. (10) This episode is also thought to take place in the underworld.

Insects, however, were not to be found only in the land of the dead; their malignant power extended to the earth, 'the central land of the reed plains' as well.

The land, badly ruled by Opo-kuni-nushi, is infested by firefly spirits and 'evil deities which buzzed like flies'. (11) The *Engishiki* also describes the gods who seethe like summer flies during the daytime and, at night, the gods 'who shine like fire pots'. (12) These passages, while perhaps losing in poetical effect, will make sense only if we understand that the myriads of evil deities *are* insects or insect spirits. The pacification of the earth takes several years; to accomplish it, Amaterasu sends several subordinate *kami* to the land of the reed plains. The first divine messenger does not return and the second fails to carry out his mission—apparently the insect spirits are too strong for them.

A summary of the pollutions listed in the *Ô-harae* and the *Nihongi* includes: 'cutting live flesh, cutting dead flesh, birth, menstruation, skin disease, incest prohibitions, attacks from "creeping things" or "calamities" from birds'. (13) Even the infestation by insects of a man's rice fields was felt to make him ritually impure.

All these offences imply contact with death or disease. Skin disease was thought to be particularly polluting and, through the contagious properties of impurity, even the owner of an insect-infested field was subjected to ritual avoidance. Insects, then, always thought to be evil and harmful, are associated with death and decomposition, inhabit the underworld and, before the rule of the heavenly *kami*, had overrun the earth itself.

'Insects are not good to think about'
At this point it would be useful to try to determine what an insect is.

25

In a rough outline of the Japanese classification of living things, *mushi* may be situated as follows: (14)

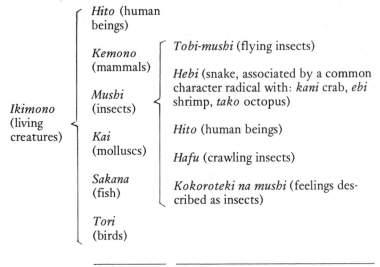

context free	context dependent

Insects harm by spreading disease and death. A common expression for stomach maladies is *mushi ke*. Other afflictions are called *mushi-ba* (a decayed tooth), and *mizu-mushi*, the name of a very common skin disease. A sickly, fretful child is said to have a *naki-mushi*. These children are exorcised in a special rite of the Nichiren sect. Often these illnesses are in no sense imaginary. Until recently, in some villages, intestinal parasites afflicted up to ninety per cent of the inhabitants. (15)

The *kokoroteki na* insect may, at times, influence a person's feelings: *mushi ga tsuku* is said of a woman who loves a man against the will of her family. Another expression, *mushi ga shiraseta*, is used to explain a presentiment of death or disaster.

All the idioms which include insects cannot be listed here but to be exact, a few refer also to pleasant feelings, for example, *gakumon no mushi*, i.e. the desire to learn. Elements common to all insects are an underground or underwater habitat, peculiar means of locomotion such as crawling or creeping and, *per extenso*, too many legs or none at all (octopus or snake). (16)

One type of insect, the moth, should be considered separately. The most destructive insect in Japan, thought by farmers to be 'the insect' par excellence is the *ine no gaichû* 'the rice-borer lava'. Such is the dread of insects in the countryside that villagers would often refuse to talk about them.

Another moth, a species of maggot, is also much feared. It lays its eggs in carrion or excrement. When the pupae hatch, they emerge as small white moths. The dust on their wings is thought to be poisonous.

The life of moths is seen as a negative metaphor for the human life and death cycle, in a society which has assimilated the idea of reincarnation. The larval period passed underground can be equated with burial, the period before rebirth and also with childhood. In the spring the moth appears from the chrysalis; in this overt phase its life (which approximately parallels the agricultural year) is a paradigm of evil since it consists of a series of oppositions to fundamental aspects of normal human existence: it feeds on carrion, it is airborne and nocturnal and it lives by destroying the food of mankind.

The most important ritual explicitly connected with insects is the *mushi-okuri*, their 'sending away'. It was once held in all parts of Japan, but now the introduction of insecticides has made it very rare. The use of pesticides will eradicate, paradoxically, the fear of even symbolic insects because it has been accompanied by the introduction of modern medicine and a consequent lowering of the death-rate. (A curious corollary of this phenomenon is the new, quasi-religious fear of chemical poisoning of the environment that has developed in most modern societies.)

A few isolated villages still perform *mushi-okuri*: in the evening the villagers form a procession and carrying torches, a large bell and a drum, they retrace the boundaries of their rice fields. Finally, they all gather around the bonfire in which a large straw figure in the shape of an insect or snake is burned. The drumbeats are the only means of reaching the insects under the earth: their purpose is to repel. The fires, in contrast, attract the moths, which throw themselves into the flames. (17)

Other rites centred on insects have disappeared. Up to the eighth century, before rice cultivation had spread to the whole of Japan, the taro was still a basic food crop and a cult of the *imo mushi* ('taro insect') was widespread.

In Okinawa, the *mushi-bare* ('insect eradication') rite is held on a day in which a general taboo on farming and fishing is observed. The *nuru* ('priestesses') gather on the beach and place insects, collected in the fields, in small boats made of leaves which are carried out to sea by the tide, thus paralleling the sending away of the dead at *Bon*. (18)

Insects, then, destroy the essential food, rice, attack man through diseases of the skin (which resemble the ravages of decomposition), and enter into the heart itself and direct man's feelings. After death, if not protected by the veneration of his descendants, a man's spirit will join the innumerable 'hungry ghosts' that, as insects, will return to devour the crops of the living.

Disease, one of the many associations of the word *mushi* (which, with increasing hesitation, I translate as 'insect'), led me to Japanese concepts of pathology and these, in turn, to Chinese medical texts. Chinese notions of science were diffused in Japan through many compilations such as the *Wakan sansai zue* and were available to me only from secondary sources, in particular De Visser's monograph on Ignes Fatui in China and Japan (19), Fujino Iwatomo on 'Chinese soul-inviting and firefly catching songs' (20), and D. Bodde's work on Chinese festivals. (21)

From 'ko' to 'oni' ('ku' to 'kuei')
The character *ko* (Nelson, no. 4201), meaning in modern Japanese a 'destructive rice-worm', is also translated as a poison, the ancient Chinese *ku*, that is the essence of venomous creatures (centipedes, snakes, spiders, grasshoppers) which have been buried together in a vessel. Poison accumulated in the body of the survivor, and was extracted and used in sorcery. (22)

The character appears already in Shang divinatory inscriptions. (23) A commentary on the *Spring and autumn annals* reports: 'vessels and worms make *ku*, caused by licentiousness. Those who have died violent deaths are also *ku*'. (24) *Ku*, therefore, is something more than poison; its malevolence is an active force: 'the *ku*' (after having killed its victim) 'flies about at night, appearing like a meteor'. This variety is called 'flitting *ku*'. When the light grows stronger, a shadow like a living man's is produced...it can have intercourse with women ...it can go wherever it desires, and spreads calamity through the countryside... (From a 17th-century description of the Miao Country). (25) In the *Tso Chuan* it is said that 'When a woman unsettles a man or wind brings down a mountain, that is called *ku*'. (26) (In the *Shuo Wen* (A.D. 100), it is explained that 'When the wind blows, worms generate'.) (27)

To summarise: the *ku*, as a poisonous insect (see also the Taoist theory of the 'three worms' *san chong*) (28), invades the body, it becomes or is identified with the unsettled and, thus, malignant souls of its victims (*oni* or *kuei*) and wanders about at night bringing calamities. *Ku* overcomes the natural order, it causes sexual irregularities, while as an evil 'worm-generating' wind, it is powerful enough to topple mountains.

Chinese texts furnish a vast quantity of material on conceptions of the soul or souls, seen in conjunction with the elements, according to 'chemical' rather than theological principles of analysis. The soul in various aspects (*hun* 'energy' which is male and positive, *yang*; and *p'o* 'terrestrial, or material' which is female and negative, *yin*) is identified with various organs such as the heart or stomach, and with elements such as fire, earth or air. (29) On historical grounds it is possible for Sinologists like Fujino to give priority to one interpretation (heart-fire) (30) but, from an anthropological point of view, all 'errors' can be as significant as orthodoxy.

In China and Japan the soul is associated with 'unnatural' fires, a category which includes our *ignes fatui* (called *shiranu-bi* and *oni-bi* in Japan), falling stars and fireflies. In China the annual Great Exorcism (in the *Tung Ching Fu*) expelled the 'roving lights'. (31) In villages children went into the fields singing *chao-hun*, soul-calling songs in which souls are explicitly referred to as fireflies. (32) In Japan, the *Tsuina* and children's songs such as the well known *Hotaru koi, achi no mizu wa nigai zo, kochi no mizu wa amai zo —Hotaru koi*, reflect the same belief.

Souls are also thought to manifest themselves without the help of natural agencies. The mobile, luminous *tama* soul is described with particular vividness in the *Wakan sansai zue*: 'The *hito-dama* has a round, flat head and a long tail like a ladle. Its colour is blue and white, with small red spots. It floats slowly thirty or forty feet from the ground. It is not possible to make out whether it is far or near...it falls and breaks... On the spot where it has come down there are many small black insects...we do not know what kind of beings they are. From time to time people themselves know that their soul has flown out of their body and say, "Something has gone out of my ear". Very soon...those people die'. (33)

The element *tama* in the word *hito-dama* brings together the idea of soul and that of jewel, both as something round and luminous and as a *maga-tama*, which has a round head and curved tail. (34) This shape recalls that of a comet and of a swarm of phosphorescent insects in flight. These unnatural fires, polluted and polluting, are ritually exorcized by the purifying properties of 'natural' fire in a long series of rites, from the *mushi-okuri* to the *yama-yaki*, the *hana matsuri*, and the *tôro-nagashi* in which lanterns representing the soul are floated away in the river or the sea.

Children as ritual mediators with the dead

Communication with the dead and various forms of exorcism are not always the province of religious specialists such as the Nichiren exorcist, the *shûgensha*, or the *itako*. Contact with the dead was also effected by social categories broadly defined as liminal: for example, children. In Suyemura the souls of children were said to be unstable until the 31st day (for a boy) or the 33rd day (for a girl) after birth. (35) I was told in the village of Tsuki in Aichi prefecture that the sound of a drum at its first *matsuri* put a soul into a child's body.

The sense of an imperfect and precarious achievement of human status clings to children even after infancy, as is shown by the necessity of periodical visits to the shrine (*shichi-go-san*). The practice of infanticide, referred to by the euphemism *ma-biki* ('thinning out'), was resorted to by the majority of Japanese villagers. (36) A limited number of children were chosen to live, like grains of rice stored after the harvest to 'live' again in the fields, or silkworms (the one beneficent insect) selected to breed. Cheated of life and of the veneration of descendants, the souls of children can be particularly dangerous.

At times children are associated with *mushi* directly (as in *naki-mushi*) or metaphorically, as in the divination of Kashima Shrine to which brides come and dig under a stone to foretell, by the number of insects discovered, the number of their future children. (37)

In many rituals the *chigo*, a child-participant in a ritual (who originally was in a state of trance), was thought to be in communication with the other world. Now only a few rituals such as the 'sleeping *chigo*' *matsuri* of Sone in October show traces of this idea. Children participate in most religious processions. In the *mushi-okuri* they carry the torches, and in the *Inoko* (ritual held on the day of the boar, *i*) they walk round the boundaries of the village beating the earth and chanting to drive away the *oni* and noxious insects.

Plants and disease

Death symbolism is also found in connection with several species of plants. Its most obvious form appears in the use of a long-stemmed flower as a resting place for the soul. When a corpse is laid out before the funeral, a vase containing a single flower is set beside it, and for this reason single-flower arrangements are avoided in traditional Ikebana. Offerings to the *kami* do not include flowers, while in Buddhist temples they are placed on all the altars. The *Hanagasa odori* held at the time of *Bon* is performed by dancers with flowered head-coverings, living *yorishiro* vessels for the returning souls of the dead.

To flowers is attributed the brevity of human life, as is told in the *Kojiki* in the story of Piko-po-no-ninigi-no-mikoto, on whom Opo-yama-tu-mi-no-kami bestows his daughters Ipa-naga-hime 'long as the rocks' and Ko-no-pana-no-saku-ya-bime 'tree-of-flower-of-blossom'. The *kami* cannot bear the ugliness of the former and sends her away. Her father then answers in anger that he has thrown away the chance for eternal life 'long as the rocks' for all mankind. (38) It is not by chance that until recently Japanese gardens had few flowers or none at all, while rocks formed the centre of aesthetic interest. The ritual use in Shinto of the evergreen *sakaki* is covertly contrasted with the quickly fading flowers offered to the Buddha.

The *Hana-shizume no matsuri* or *Chinka-sai* is held in April in Ōmiwa, Imamiya and Sai, all of which enshrine *kami* connected with epidemics. This rite is celebrated to 'pacify' the flowers so that, when the petals fall they will not spread disease. (39) The *Saigusa* and the *Yuri matsuri* have the same meaning.

Cherry blossoms scatter their petals with increasing frequency and preciosity in *haiku*, and nostalgic folk songs are sung on this theme; in April the annual reports of the precise moment of perfect bloom in famous cherry groves take precedence in the news, but few realize that this nation-wide cherry-viewing is the last trace of the ancient rite of exorcism.

The *Tanabata*, on the seventh day of the seventh month, incorporates several of the symbols discussed above. It is often seen as an anticipation or alternate form of *Bon*. (Around Kyoto it is called *Bon hajime*.) In view of the varying dates of *Bon* it appears probable that the whole of the seventh lunar month was dedicated to the cult of the dead.

Tanabata follows the ritual pattern of the *mushi-okuri*, a procession with a final casting-away of the decorated branches into the nearest river. Yearly meetings of star-crossed lovers, even if celebrated in Chinese legend, seem hardly enough to account for the nation-wide celebration of this rite. Instead of wishing for rain that, by flooding the 'River of Heaven', would allow the celestial lovers to meet again, villagers used to pray for cloudless skies. In the countryside it was thought that the union of the two stars would result in 'star children', the seeds of disease, which would then blight crops and infect men.

Notes on classification

What connects falling stars and cherry blossoms, bad feelings and Chinese poisons, worms and *hito-dama*?

Theories of 'folk' classification of natural species generally follow an ethno-scientific pattern and reveal an 'alternative zoology' or botany. Other theories, for example that of Mary Douglas in *Purity and danger*, focus on the so-called anomalies, that is, creatures which do not seem to fit the normative description of their species (for example, a wingless bird). For Mary Douglas the 'boundaries', the intellectual wilderness where categories overlap, are a centre for both positive or negative power.

It has been shown that these boundaries are eliminated by the application of polythetic (40) concepts of classification formed by family resemblances.

The negative connotation of *mushi* may be explained by the identification of a 'meta-category', a pole of inauspicious associations based on the metamorphic life cycle of insects and reptilia. Variations in form, in habitat and the larval period become a symbol for intermediate states of being and of rebirth. This ambiguity is extended to other related symbols, falling stars, clusters of flowers, through the mediation of 'liminal' social categories and identified with the ultimate negation: death and the formless multitude of 'un-affiliated' souls.

31

5

Tradition, The Past and The Ever-Changing Present in a Pottery Village

BRIAN D. MOERAN

Tradition can mean different things to different people. For some, its use is imbued with a sense of history; for others, it has a certain nostalgia; for yet others, it is a measurement of progress. Very often it is a concept that gains currency in the wake of change. Onta is a small hamlet of fourteen households situated in Ôita prefecture, Kyûshû. People living outside the community use the word 'tradition' to refer to the pottery made there; potters living in Onta itself, however, use it of the social organization of their community. Outsiders living in urban complexes of the Kantô and Kansai areas look to the country for 'tradition' in an attempt to define their 'Japaneseness' vis-à-vis the western world. Potters in Onta use the concept of 'tradition' to protect their community from changes stemming from contact with urban Japanese life. Thus both the content and the purpose of the use of 'tradition' differ within each group. In neither case, however, is the content of what is seen as 'traditional' actually 'traditional' at all.

The earliest mention of 'tradition' with reference to Onta was made when Yanagi Muneyoshi (1889-1961) 'discovered' the community and its pottery in 1931. Yanagi—scholar, philosopher and critic—was the first person in Japan to develop an aesthetic ideal for what came to be known as *mingei*, 'folk crafts'. From the early 1920s, he had been publishing various essays in which he argued that beauty was to be found not only in the 'higher' forms of art, but also in ordinary, hand-made objects in everyday use. He spent some time travelling round the countryside in search of such objects, and of the 'unknown craftsmen' who made them, and it was on one of these trips that he heard about and eventually visited Onta.

Yanagi was vividly impressed with the pottery and the people of the community. As he reported in a newspaper article a couple of months later, Onta perfectly fitted his folk craft ideal in that its pottery was functional, made by ordinary unknown craftsmen who worked in a centuries-old traditional manner. Types of pottery, their shapes and glazes, had hardly altered since the founding of the community in 1705. Potters used methods of production that were 'close to nature': clay was prepared with crushers powered by river water; glazes were made with natural materials only; pots were fired co-operatively in a wood-fired, climbing kiln. Modern technology was entirely ignored. (1)

At the time Yanagi first used the word 'tradition' of Onta, it is likely that many aspects of the hamlet's pottery and social organization were in fact 'traditional', in the sense that they had been handed down from one generation to the next over a long period of time. During the next forty years, however, things were to change considerably.

In the 1930s—and, indeed, until the mid-1960s—all potter households in Onta were also engaged in wet-rice agriculture; many of them worked at carpentering, stone-masonry or forestry as well. Pottery was only made by older men in their spare-time or when the weather was too bad for them to go out and work in the fields or mountains. While market demand was not sufficient to make full-time pottery financially worthwhile, production was also limited by technical aspects of clay, glaze and wood acquisition and preparation.

All households were linked in various kinds of labour co-operation. On the agricultural side, households pooled their labour for such activities as transplanting and harvesting rice, for growing crops on mountain land that had been cleared of timber and for cutting the grass for and thatching the hamlet's house-roofs. Potters also co-operated with one another in the acquisition and preparation of ball and slip clays, feldspar and iron oxide for glazes, and, occasionally, wood for firing their co-operative kiln.

In the 1950s, however, co-operation amongst potter households began to break down as a result of improved communications, on the one hand, and an increase in market demand, on the other. New roads to the hamlet made it possible for potters to order their wood from local lumber yards in the neighbouring town of Hita. They could now drive across country to get their supplies of slip clay or feldspar and iron oxide for glazes. Eventually they were able to hire a bulldozer to dig their rough stoneware clay. Tasks that had needed some 150 man-days per household in the 1950s were, by 1972, being completed in less than fifty days a year. Labour co-operation among households had almost entirely ceased.

Moreover, demand for folk-craft pottery from the mid-1950s meant that potters were having to devote more and more time to wheel-work in order to fill orders. As a result, agricultural tasks came to be carried out by women of the household, while the men—father and son—worked full-time at the wheel, except during the really busy farming seasons. By the mid-1960s, potters were able to give up agriculture entirely, encouraged to do so by the increasing demand for their work and by the government's rice curtailment policy. With the potters' decision to specialize, labour co-operation continued only amongst the remaining four non-potting households.

33

Such changes in social organization undoubtedly affected community solidarity, which was further weakened by the break-up of the co-operative kiln. Until after the end of the Pacific War, the kiln had worked according to a system of chamber rotation and kiln space was equally distributed amongst all those participating in a firing. As a result, potter households not only used the same amount of materials, but made and marketed the same number of pots. The co-operative kiln, therefore, gave rise both to mutual co-operation and to financial equality within the hamlet. With the increase in market demand, however, several potters found it more profitable to build and fire their own kilns. Freedom from the constraints of the co-operative kiln has led to considerable economic individualization amongst potter households, which are themselves for the most part very much better off than the remaining non-potting households in the community. There is, thus, no longer financial equality among households in the hamlet.

The community as a social group is also threatened by certain marketing practices. One of these is retail pricing. Wholesale buyers set their retail prices according to current market conditions and the quality of the pots that they are trying to sell. Although all potters sell at a standard wholesale price, shop-owners charge varying retail prices. But when a buyer differentiates the quality of one *pot* from another by pricing it higher or lower, he is in fact distinguishing between the quality of the *potters* who made those pots. That the buyer is aware of this may be seen in the fact that he often tries to promote an individual potter's name, rather than sell his work under the label of 'Onta pottery' (*Onta-yaki*). What he does not realize, however, is that, according to principles of social organization within the hamlet of Onta, all individuals should be equal if the hamlet is to function effectively. Individual talent, therefore, is only acceptable in so far as it reflects upon, and does not upset, the community as a whole. Thus, by promoting the names of certain individual potters and by pricing their work higher, buyers are in fact threatening the solidarity of the potters' community.

The same problem occurs as a result of the decision by some of the younger potters to participate in pottery exhibitions. Encouraged by the folk-craft organizations to contribute as individuals to annual exhibitions in Tokyo and Osaka, one or two potters have been awarded major national prizes. As a result, they receive considerable attention from the media and end up acting as spokesmen for the whole community. However, as the hamlet is 'traditionally' run according to an age-grade seniority system, elder potters resent the way in which their authority is encroached upon by outside forces.

The community has also been divided along a different axis, between households which make pottery and those which do not.

While some of the resentment between these two groups derives from unequal income differentials, much of it is exacerbated by the public appreciation of pottery. Both the media and the folk-craft organizations pay particular attention to the potters as a group, unaware that such attention may upset the principles on which the hamlet as a whole is organized.

Because community solidarity is threatened by the division between potting and non-potting households, on the one hand, and between elder and younger potters, on the other, two concepts are frequently referred to by residents of Onta. One of these is *mukashi* 'the past', and concerns the community as a whole. The other is *dentô* 'tradition', and affects potters in particular. By calling on the past, people living in Onta try to unite all households in the community and to stem resentment between potting and non-potting households. Potters, for their part, refer to tradition in an attempt to standardize their work and market a readily recognizable product known as Onta pottery, thereby counteracting the promotion of individual talent by outsiders. Both concepts, of the past and of tradition, involve a direct or indirect assumption that the way in which things used to be done was best.

The time span of 'the past' differs to some extent from one individual to another, but it is seen to apply in particular to the period immediately preceding the social changes outlined above. When talking to outsiders, all villagers tend to hark back to the way in which they used to lead their lives, to the hard times they had when there was not enough money with which to buy food or clothes, to the exhaustion they felt after working long hours from dawn to dusk in the fields or mountains. (2) The old way of life is viewed with a certain nostalgia, for villagers know that the good old days of 'community life' have gone forever. *Mukashi* is called upon, therefore, firstly to remind fellow residents not only of how things used to be in Onta, but how they should still be, and secondly to present a united front by the hamlet against the outside world.

The concept of 'tradition' is used by those living in Onta and by those living outside it. The potters' adoption of the term is very recent, and has two main functions. In the first place, it is used as a means of countering problems of talent and individualism that result from the marketing of pottery. Because individual stylistic talent is a permanent threat to the working of the community as a whole (3), potters actively discourage one another from experimenting too much with clay textures, glazes and designs. There is thus a remarkable uniformity about Onta pottery that is not to be found in other folk potteries such as Tanba, Mashiko or Koishiwara. Secondly, 'tradition' is called upon precisely because the community is in many ways no longer traditional. Now that the social organiz-

35

ation of the hamlet has fallen into disarray, it has become vital for potters to maintain a 'tradition' in pottery, since this serves to re-enforce a rapidly-fading community consciousness. The concept of a 'tradition' in pottery helps provide the whole community with an identity distinct from the outside world.

The idea of Onta's pottery 'tradition' is also used by the media and those connected with the folk-craft movement. Potters are praised because they continue to make 'traditional' old-style pots for rural farmhouses—large water containers, lidded jars for *miso* bean-paste and pickled vegetables, and pouring vessels for soy sauce and home-brewed wines. In fact, however, such pots no longer serve the functions for which they were originally made. Because they have come to be decorative rather than purely functional, 'traditional' Onta pots have changed in shape. They also constitute a very small percentage of a potter's total production, which now consists almost totally of small pots for urban domestic use. Still, the fact that thirty years ago potters had never made a coffee cup, tea bowl or flower vase in their lives, does not seem to deter outsiders' views of Onta pottery as 'traditional'. 'Tradition' in this sense, therefore, may be thought to refer not to the actual pottery itself so much as to tech-niques of pottery making—in particular to those that do not rely on modern technology and remain 'close to nature'.

It is not just Onta pottery that is praised for its 'tradition'. The Japanese are going through a phase of what has been called a 'tradition cult' (*dentô sûhai*), and National Cultural Treasures and the Folk Craft Movement are only two aspects of this reverence for the past and for a way of life that for the most part no longer exists. In one respect, people living in places like Tokyo and Osaka are attracted to Onta and its pottery because potters live in idyllic rural surroundings that are clean, quiet and uncrowded. In short, the yearning for the 'traditional' is a kind of nostalgia on the part of those who are surrounded by the noise and pollution of Japan's ugly, overcrowded cities.

Just as potters adopted the idea of 'tradition' after their com-munity had been profoundly influenced by contact with the out-side world, so have the Japanese as a nation turned to 'traditional' aspects of their past, following wide-reaching changes brought about by ever-increasing contact with the western world. Both the hamlet of Onta and the nation of Japan seek to assert their separate identities through the invocation of a 'traditional past'. Although the content of tradition and the past may differ, in both cases the concepts are adopted in an attempt to adapt to rapid social change. They deal with the ever-changing present.

6

Traditional Ultra-Nationalist Conceptions in Mishima Yukio's 'Manifesto'

VOLKER STANZEL

The frequency of rumours about co-operation between right-wing gangsters (*yakuza*), LDP politicians and industrialists makes it plain that ultra-nationalism is still a potent force in modern Japanese society. Mishima Yukio has been neither a *yakuza*, nor a politician, nor an industrialist, nor has his whole life been devoted to ultra-nationalism. He was, however, an ultra-nationalist among other things, and a very outspoken one at that. His last written statement, his 'Manifesto' (*geki*), was a kind of political testament.

The *geki* had been written by Mishima to be distributed as leaflets to the troops of the Self Defence Forces (SDF) present at Ichigaya base when Mishima made his speech there on 25 November 1970, to initiate a putsch. When his efforts miscarried, Mishima committed ritual suicide (*seppuku*). In the *geki*, Mishima calls upon the SDF to take over the government of Japan by force so as to save the country. Saving Japan has become necessary because it has 'forgotten itself'. The SDF are the only institution able to save Japan because only they still preserve the spirit of 'true' Japan. However, in view of the past behaviour of the SDF, Mishima doubts whether they will indeed be able to shoulder the responsibility of saving Japan. Hence Mishima's desperate clarion call directly to the soldiers at Ichigaya base.

The *geki* has four main topics: 1) present-day Japan, 2) true Japan, 3) the true (Japanese) man, 4) the Japanese army.

Present-day Japan is defiling itself, the soul of its people is 'lost', and the country is tumbling into an 'abyss of total emptiness'. The reason is that Japan has 'forgotten itself' during the period of its economic rise, as it has come to live for its economic interests only. Political decisions are left completely to the United States. As a result, the 'Japanese soul' is now morally degenerating, it has become rotten, and the government permits the country to 'sleep' instead of making it care for its foremost problems. While making economic headway, the country is a political opportunist.

One marginal point may be interesting here. Mishima does not create the image of some enemy outside the country, some scapegoat who is to blame for the whole misery. It is deplorable that Japan follows the political leadership of the US because it thus loses its independence, not because the US is a hostile nation. Other nations beside the US are not even mentioned. Mishima's main object of complaint is the domestic state of the nation, not any threat from outside on which one might project hostile feelings.

Directly opposite to present-day Japan stands 'true' Japan. This is a constantly present possibility of an ideal state of righteousness which may be actualized at any given time, contingent upon the correct action. 'True' Japan may be defined as an actualization of its own 'beloved history', its own culture and tradition. All its culture is centred around the emperor who is, in Mishima's language, the 'heart' of this 'true form' of a righteous Japan.

Those who are to realize 'true' Japan, are the 'true men' of whom the *geki* speaks. Mishima's 'true man'—'man' meaning not 'human' but 'male'—is necessarily a true Japanese and a true *samurai*. '*Samurai*' therefore is for Mishima not so much a social category but rather a moral category standing for the true Japanese in general. Rather than a soldier, he is a man able to act righteously and decisively, to whom only death is the end to his path of action. Death actually is the last resort of his action for righteousness. Righteousness at its highest level does not concern the life of an individual any more but the existence of the whole nation. Thus, to die for the righteous existence of Japan has, for the true Japanese, a much higher value than mere life. However, even higher than the lonely death of one *samurai*, Mishima values the death met in the company of like-minded comrades, a kind of communion in death.

This is what makes the army so important to Mishima. Here he finds—or would like to find—the cream of Japanese manhood together, trained to fight, act and die. Here all true *samurai* are—or should be—gathered together. The army should be the organization of true Japanese men with the purpose of saving the country. As true Japanese, the soldiers should not be serving the democratic or political order of present Japan, or liberty, but the ideal of true Japan. They thus carry the responsibility of actualizing through the very existence of the army the true Japan which as yet exists nowhere else. The army is predestined to be Japan's saviour: 'Japan will not wake up unless the SDF wakes up.' However, the kind of opportunist policies that structure the politics of Japan, misuse the army in the interest of those who control the country. Party politicians flatter and manipulate the army until it degenerates to the same level as the rest of the country. So the army is, for example, unconstitutional legally, but it refuses to deal with the problem arising from that fact. By cheating itself about the circumstances of its existence, the army is about to become a 'mercenary of America'.

The term 'ultra-nationalism' (*chôkokka-shugi*) is a convenient word to use. It is not as contested as the term 'fascism', for instance, and it is also firmly established in Japan. 'Nationalism' is an idea, tending to become an ideology, that develops together with the formation of national entities (hereafter 'nations', for the sake of simplicity) as a catalyzer of the in-group feelings and the consciousness of identity of the social group that regards itself as the creator of the nation. Depending on the reaction of the outside world, nationalism may or may not be hostile towards other nations. Ultra-nationalism would then be an extreme kind of nationalism, an ideology which aims at solidifying the concept of the nation in the consciousness of its citizens by falling back on ethnic and traditional components of a culture common to a majority and which tends to penetrate all aspects of the daily life of that nation.

Looking now at Mishima's *geki*, it seems to transmit three basic concepts. These are:

1) The miserable present state of Japan, characterized by impurity, opportunism and loss of identity, and tending towards self-destruction;

2) The actualization of a 'true' Japan, symbolized by the emperor, as a constantly present obligation;

3) The mediator between 1) and 2), the 'true' Japanese man, devoted to acting and sacrificing himself for the attainment of true Japan, who acts best in a body of like-minded men, namely the army.

The relationship of these three concepts to ultra-nationalism is quite obvious: the bleak picture of an impure present-day Japan serves as a centre onto which in-group feelings and the consciousness of national identity can focus; the definition of a 'true' Japan by its culture and the existence of the emperor—and also the *samurai* ethos—makes traditional images work as a kind of glue for the in-group consciousness that is, of course, threatened with fragmentation by modern democratic and pluralistic society. Finally, the concept of the modern *samurai* demands a subject who devotes his whole life and even himself totally to the national cause.

These basic ultra-nationalist concepts contain ideas as well as a character that one might term traditional. Regarding the content, a comparison with the traditional conception of *kokutai* might serve as an example for several other cases (Mishima also employs, for example, the traditional Confucian concept of *seimei*). *Kokutai* —translated as 'national polity' (R.T. Chang) or 'national essence' (Harootunian)—as it was understood from the *bakumatsu* period of the nineteenth century until at least the time of Japanese fascism, meant mainly the fundamental, unchangeable character of the Japanese nation which made it superior to the rest of the world. This character was thought to stem from the existence of a descendant of the Sun Goddess as emperor, who guaranteed a policy of righteousness, whose family had been ruling ever since the Age of the gods, and who acted as caretaker for the gods in Japan and as a representative of Japan to the gods. *Kokutai* also meant the obligation to realize a social and political system which would harmonize with this fundamental national character, and to pursue a policy which accorded with the principle of righteousness.

Up to this point the similarity to Mishima's concepts is clear; but *kokutai* did not necessarily mean that there would have to be a special body of loyalists who would be able to realize the demands of the national polity. The concept of *kokutai* was, however, created in the *bakumatsu* period when a large segment of the *samurai* class, the so-called *shishi*, regarded their own time as an insufficient actualization of the *kokutai*, and when these *shishi* regarded themselves as the mediators between miserable, impure reality and ideal national polity. Yoshida Shôin is certainly someone whom Mishima might have had in mind with his concept of the 'true' Japanese.

Not only the content but also the character of Mishima's concepts is traditional. None of the concepts can be reduced to a clear-cut statement about one specific idea. Rather, they all seem slippery and hard to grasp. On the other hand, while they contain only vague statements, they do contain certain signal words, like emperor (*tennô*), *samurai*, righteousness (*gi*), and truth (*shin*), which have broad connotations and thus permit almost any kind of concrete political interpretation, and almost any kind of policy to be drawn from them. This has always been exactly the character of the concepts of nationalist thinkers in post-Edo Japan, be it Inoue Kowashi (*kyôiku chokugo*) in the Meiji period (1868-1912), or the Amur Society in the Shôwa period (1926-   ).

In conclusion, then, the *geki*'s basic concepts are that:
— the degenerate and impure present-day Japan is on its way to self-destruction;
— a 'true' Japan exists in its culture and the person of the emperor, and thereby constantly demands its own actualization;
— the actualizator can only be a close-knit group of men who are morally righteous and willing to sacrifice themselves totally.

These typically ultra-nationalist concepts come right out of the tradition of nationalist thinking in Japan. They relate back to traditionalist categories. At the same time they employ signal words of vague contextual associations, and thus permit the understanding of a wide range of different policies.

40

7

The Modification of Tradition in Modern Japanese Weddings and Some Implications for the Social Structure

JOY HENDRY

A western visitor to a Japanese wedding could well be impressed by the degree to which tradition is apparently maintained. Indeed, an American scholar noted recently in a study of change in a Japanese village that 'weddings are still the occasion for the activation of much traditional behaviour'. (1) It is hoped to examine the nature of such tradition as observed recently in a number of weddings held in a provincial region of northern Kyûshû. (2) Many of these weddings involved farming families, who might be expected to be more traditional than urban workers, especially since their households are usually still three-generational, but there has also been a good deal of change. Some of the key elements of these marriages are studied to see how far and in what sense they could be described as 'traditional' (3), and, where there has been change, to see how this might be related to wider changes in the social structure.

Most of the marriages involved were initiated through a go-between who provided details of each of the families for the other and arranged a meeting known as a *miai* for the couple and possibly some other members of each family. Where the couple had independently decided to marry, they had usually sought the permission of their parents and the services of a go-between to arrange the details of the rites involved and to preside at the wedding itself. Once agreed, the decision to marry is clinched immediately by the dispatch of a gift of tea, *sake* and sea bream from the family who initiated the proposal to the other side. The proposal usually comes from the groom's family, although if a girl is to receive an adopted husband, who will inherit her father's home, these roles are reversed. This same initiating family later sends an expensive set of betrothal gifts including a number of symbolic items of otherwise purely decorative value, as well as a sum of money or a set of Japanese garments to help the other side prepare a trousseau. Locally these gifts are referred to as 'tea', or 'main tea' (*honcha*), while the first clinching gifts may be called *kimeja* ('decide-tea') or *kugicha* ('nail-tea') to indicate that the alliance has been secured. The trousseau, towards which part of the betrothal gifts are said to go, nowadays usually includes several large pieces of furniture such as wardrobes, chests of drawers, a dressing table and a sideboard, all complete with

41

contents, as well as equipment such as a washing machine, refrigerator, television, cooking-stove and bicycle. A boy going as an adopted son-in-law may take part of his family property, which is said to give him some of the status he would otherwise lose by taking up this rather inferior position in a family. One farming family in 1979 claimed to have received a million yen on betrothal to help their daughter prepare herself. Another, which received kimono from the groom's family, said they had spent three million on the goods their daughter was to take.

The wedding itself may take one of a number of forms, religious or secular, but certain elements appear to be common to all. Before a gathering of close relatives the bride and groom participate in an exchange of cups of *sake* known as a *san-san kudo*, after which they may well read a pledge and exchange rings. They then exchange cups with each other's parents and relatives, who will be formally introduced to one another. After this, there will be one or more receptions at which these and more distant relatives are entertained, along with neighbours, friends and work companions. The couple is almost always dressed in traditional Japanese kimono at first, but may well change into western dress during the course of the entertainment, perhaps after a second display of kimono by the bride. At the end of the day the couple usually leave for a honeymoon. If they are eventually to succeed to a household, they may well return to a room or rooms in the family home designed and newly constructed for their benefit.

Many elements of this procedure are quite traditional in that they appear to have ancient origins, but close examination reveals some interesting modifications and even alterations.

First of all, the *miai*, which is often described as the traditional way of arranging marriages, as opposed to the more modern *ren'ai* or 'love' match, actually appeared in this area during the lifetime of the older people, who themselves sometimes describe meeting their own spouses for the first time at their weddings. Indeed, the word is said to have developed from *me-ai*, literally, 'meeting the bride', originally a name of the principal marriage ceremony. (4) Many other older people married their first cousins, so there was usually no need for such a meeting, nor for the provision of information about the other family by the go-between. Earlier still, young people were said to have chosen each other in most rural areas, with the help of activities of the local youth group (5), or an institution such as *yobai* '(clandestine) night-visiting/-courting', which is remembered in this particular area.

The form of the *miai* has also changed completely during the time it has been in use, from a mere glimpse of the prospective spouse at some considerable distance, through a meeting at which the individuals were allowed to exchange a few words, to the most recent arrangement where the couple is expected to follow such a successful interview with one or more 'dates' (o-dêto) to be sure they will grow fond of one another. In the past, it was thought, at least in the country, to be extremely bad form to refuse a person one met in this way (6), whereas recently couples marry after an average of some two or three *miai* at least.

Elements of the betrothal gifts can be shown to have origins in many previous periods of Japanese history (7), if not always in rites having the same ostensible purpose. The chief and eponymous gift of tea is a local speciality, elsewhere thought to be inauspicious at this time, and thus probably the most truly traditional element, in that knowledge of its use has been passed down through the generations. Another apparent *sine qua non* of the gifts is also only found locally at this stage of the proceedings. That is a stand on which an old man and an old woman, referred to collectively as Takasago, are portrayed in front of a pine, bamboo and plum (*shôchikubai*) decoration further adorned with cranes and turtles. The pine, bamboo and plum are together said to symbolise happiness, and are used on other occasions of celebration, but according to Ema Tsutomu, their individual use dates back respectively to the Heian (794-1185), Kamakura (1185-1392) and Momoyama (1573-1615) periods. (8) The cranes and turtles represent longevity, and informants explained that the old couple also stand for long life and fidelity since they had sworn 'to grow grey together, until you are a hundred and I am ninety-nine' (*anata ga hyaku made, washa kyûjukyû made, tomo ni shiraga no haeru made*).

The tale behind this symbolism varies with the source used, but it seems to date back at least to the Heian period since there is reference to it in the tenth-century *Kokinshû*. (9) Elsewhere, however, rather than in the betrothal gifts, a stand of this description was apparently more commonly used as one of the chief decorations before which the wedding itself was held. (10) A Shintô priest's explanation of the old man and woman is that they used to represent Izanami and Izanagi, the mythical progenitors of the Japanese. The name Takasago appears again at weddings in this area since an extract from the Nô play of the same name is sung as part of the proceedings. Indeed it so specifically refers to weddings that a shop recently opened in the area to sell betrothal gifts and other wedding accessories calls itself Takasago-ya.

The bride's trousseau appears to be quite modern, with the western furniture and electrical equipment, and the expense is often explained as high because this represents the bride's (or the adopted son's) share of the family inheritance, which should be divided among all children to comply with the post-war constitution. However, the form of this part of the proceedings is perhaps one of the least changed. Previously the goods were carried by male relatives for all to see between the two houses to be united, the journey accompanied by the singing of special songs for the occasion. Now they are transported in a fleet of vans, but it is still the male relatives who do the loading and unloading, and it is still possible for people at both ends to examine the goods in some detail and assess the suitability of the match. The farewell party held for the bride is actually called an *ochami* or tea-viewing, in reference to the betrothal gifts on display, but it is held before the furniture is taken away so that this, too, may be seen.

The wedding itself usually appears rather traditional whether it is held in a Shintô or Buddhist place of worship, followed by a reception in a restaurant or wedding-hall, or whether it is held entirely in the home. Most commonly the guests sit on cushions on *tatami* mats, they eat Japanese food served in Japanese dishes, and many women wear Japanese dress. The Shintô wedding, which was the most popular during the 1975-6 period of research, includes offerings to the deities which used to form part of more ancient wedding ceremonies—rice, *sake*, fish, fowl and fruit (11)—and several other ancient elements. However, in its modern form before a Shintô shrine or altar, this is in fact rather a new type of marriage. The first was held in the Hibiya Shrine in 1898 (12), but the rise in popularity of such weddings seems largely to be a post-war phenomenon (13), and only popular in the area under consideration in the last ten years. It seems likely that this, and the Buddhist wedding preferred by members of some sects, have become popular as an indirect result of western influence, since the religious service, followed by a reception, coincides more closely with western procedure than do previous forms of marriage. (14) Indeed, the common elements referred to previously are by no means uniformly traditional. The exchange of rings, the western wedding dress and the honeymoon are undoubtedly western, although the *ironaoshi*, or change of clothes, during the reception, which provides the opportunity to wear a western dress, is an abbreviation of an ancient rite.

The separate living quarters also seem to be an innovative answer to the western-inspired expectations from young people of greater privacy and individuality than their parents enjoyed. The *san-san kudo* is another abbreviated version of an ancient ceremony (15), developed by the Ogasawara school of etiquette for samurai weddings but apparently relatively new in rural areas, where exchanges between the bride, the groom and each other's parents would have been more common if there were such exchanges at all. (16) This reflects the fact that the whole form of weddings was quite different. Within living memory in the area under consideration, the proceedings were divided into two parts: a reception for the groom into the bride's household called a *mukoiri*, and a further reception for the bride into the groom's house called a *yomeiri*. In some areas

44

these were separated by a period of uxorilocal residence (17), but, in the region under study, they would both take place on the same day. (18) The delivery of the betrothal gifts and the bride's trousseau seem often to have been part of the proceedings and, indeed, such an exchange, as well as the sharing of food, drink, and possibly fire, seem to be older ways than the *san-san kudo* for contracting marital alliances. (19)

During the Meiji period (1868-1912) the western idea of marriage as the union of individuals, rather than the reception of each into the other's household, is said to have been symbolised in the new type of joint reception called a *deai shûgi* or *yoriai-kon*. (20) The cost of this would often be divided between the two families since it replaced two separate functions. This type of joint reception has been practised only since the Second World War in the area under consideration, and recently use is often made of plush new wedding halls, which provide photographers, gifts, hire of garments and other services, as well as facilities for the marriage and reception. In 1975, families were said to share the cost of hiring such facilities, and it seemed likely that these halls did provide neutral ground as if to symbolise the union of individuals. This also seemed supported by the fact that the only two home weddings that year were of people who had moved away to live and would therefore not be concerned to emphasise their anyway obvious independence. By 1979, all weddings were being paid for entirely by the family receiving a bride or adopted son, even if the latter were subsequently to set up his own home. The other side was thus left to put all its resources into the trousseau and one or more farewell parties. One family even held an old-fashioned *mukoiri* for the prospective husband and family of their daughter, and this same family had also held the wedding of an older daughter, for whom they received an adopted son, entirely in their home.

When one considers the total scheme of exchange involved at this time, it is evident that one is still concerned with a union of families and the departure of an individual from one household to another, and from one community to another. The delivery of betrothal gifts and trousseau are usually accompanied by a reception of parents and other senior members of each family into the other, and the marriage ceremony includes the exchange of cups between, and the introduc- tion of, the two sets of relatives. The presentation of gifts which in- clude aid towards preparation for the needs of a lifetime, and the addition of enough goods to count as a share of the family inherit- ance, make clear that an individual is undergoing an important rite of separation from one family in order to be received by another. The farewell parties may also be seen as rites of separation from the old community, and the wedding receptions as rites of incorporation into the new one.

It is evidently pointless, then, to symbolise this event as an equal union merely of two individuals. Even at the wedding halls, boards announce the marriages as between households, X-*ke* and Y-*ke*, and the chief social function of these institutions seems to be to provide an outlet for the new affluence which abounds in the area. For the wedding itself, it seems as if so-called traditional features may be selected or rejected from the fund of Japanese and western stock, to suit the purse. This rite is referred to locally as the *go-shûgi*, the 'celebration' or 'congratulation', and it is probably better regarded as the culmination of events rather than the establishment of them. The more important aspects of the modern alliance must still be sought in the local rites which precede the wedding. The agreement to marry is clinched by the *kugicha* whose very name implies that the pact should not be broken, and I know of no cases where it has been. Once it has been delivered, no time is wasted and the wedding usually follows within a month or two. The main betrothal gifts must be delivered on an auspicious day, and it seems significant of their importance that they include one of the chief elements of the samurai marriage ceremony.

The bride's trousseau is modern precisely because of its importance. These rites vary only in detail from one marriage to another. The wedding has more possibilities for variety, and it seems less important now that it symbolises new aspects of the union. These have been conceded, in other ways. The part played by individuals in their choice of one another for marriage has increased immeasurably, although this may, in effect, be a return to an older state of affairs. The new and separate accommodation prepared for newly married couples gives them the privacy which they could not previously experience. Finally, the honeymoon sets a precedent for the young couple to spend time alone together, something which older people found laughable even to contemplate in their own early married life. Changes there have been, but they are more subtle than might at first have been expected.

8

Some Considerations of Individuals, Groups, and how Japanese Traditions may affect Decision-Making

JOHN B. KIDD

Although Japanese policies and trade have interacted with those of many countries of the world for some while, it is only since the late 1960s and especially during the last decade that the western world has become more conscious of the Japanese economy. It is not simply that it has changed from a rural structure to an industrialized urban one, thus enabling interaction with the international economic chain. Rather, it is the ease with which many Japanese firms have obtained world-wide dominance in some product-ranges and, in doing so, have demonstrated that their internal organizational structures appear able to cope with rapid changes, entrepreneurial developments, massive production facilitation and, finally, consolidation of effective and efficient production and marketing of their products. Quite naturally many studies have been undertaken on the Japanese management style looking towards its applicability in the West. Recently Kuwahara (1) compared the writings of a few scholars, namely R.T. Johnson, W.G. Ouchi, J.C. Abegglen and H. Ishida: he suggests

a) that management systems are the cultural and historic product of each society and that the Japanese system is congruent with the values and behaviour patterns of Japanese society;

b) that some aspects of the Japanese management structure contribute to the high productivity of Japanese companies working in the US, but that other aspects adversely affect productivity.

An attempt is made here to give very brief reviews of the decision-making process. On one side we have the Japanese model with its subtleties and ambiguities, whilst on the other side, the western model which is inclined towards openness and making explicit the preferences leading to the choice of some clearly stated policy. Finally, it is suggested as a working hypothesis that the individuals involved in decision-making may well process data using identical cognitive processes but externalize their answers as culture demands. Thus the investigation of the decision-making process must be considered not from the gross organizational behaviour viewpoint, but from the detail of the individual and his cognitive processing methods. Only after this comparison is made will it be possible to provide definitive answers to the role of tradition in Japanese decision-making.

Naturally we ought to take heed of the effects that emotion may have upon the decision-making process. After all, emotion is important as a determinant of behaviour. Toda (2) suggests that those who are interested in developing a model of empirical decisions should face the issue of emotions, the more so as practically anyone engaging in important actual decisions is not entirely free from emotions, especially as people tend to hide or distract the real content of their emotions by verbally rationalizing their emotion-guided decisions. Of course, psychologists and psychiatrists have studied emotions for many years. They are willing to predict the emotion likely to be displayed by persons in differing situations, and to do this, they rely upon the notion that emotions are said to be genetically pre-programmed. Thus, stimulus/response observations may be predicted, not only across people, but across species. Strongman (3) provides a comprehensive review of the relevant theories, and Okonogi (4) provides a psychiatrist's view of the role of emotion in the Japanese people in his recent papers upon the 'Ajase complex'. So we must admit that emotions are important and whilst at least one scholar, Toda, is attempting to integrate emotion with decision-making theories, we should accept this as a constraint and concentrate upon an Information Processing paradigm which will be used to study individual cognitive processes and thus to investigate possible inter-culture differences.

In the English-language literature, 'decision-making in Japan' refers to organizational mechanisms and is not concerned about the processes by which individuals come to the (same) decision when considering the facts appertaining to a problem. Quite often, therefore, we will find both Japanese and western authors citing (comparative) organizational studies which generally conclude, on the surface at least, that the Japanese methods of bureaucratic decision-making are fundamentally different from the western processes. (5-7)

A brief definition of the term *ringi-sei* suggests it means 'the system of reverential inquiry about a superior's intentions'. This is formalized in the organizational decision-making process as a document, the *ringi-sho*, which is circulated and given a stamp of approval by officials in turn if it obtains their agreement. The *ringi* process was formally referred to in the Meiji period (1868-1912) though it is believed to derive from early Chinese bureaucracy. It is said to possess the following attributes:

   a) The *ringi-sho* is initially drafted by a low-ranking official who has neither leadership nor status (in the sense that he alone cannot initiate procedures upon the topic in question, such as the modification of a production process).

   b) Following the drafting, the *ringi-sho* is discussed and examined by all relevant persons, officers, divisions, etc of the organization, with these approving the document officially by placing their seal upon it before the *ringi-sho* moves up to the next level of the organization.

c) In theory, the legal right to approve the *ringi-sho* rests with the chief executive. In practice, he generally gives a simple stamp of approval—expecting the long prior process of discussions and approvals to have made good any imperfections of the original draft.

Clearly this process has merit, insofar as all officials who may be concerned with the proposal become acquainted with its nature and its ramifications prior to approval being granted. However, as the *ringi-sho* must have all the required seals placed upon it, the discussion process will be lengthy and could easily be held up through an official being ill or by a divisional chief who, being politically disinclined to pass it, would delay it rather than say no, as that would cause friction. For a senior executive to by-pass the *ringi* system because of the need for expediency, or because he knows of the possibility of delayed seal-placing, would generally be foolhardy, as the mass of the organization would then revolt at his revocation of their right to discussion. (We should here exclude crisis decision-making.)

Tsuji (6) strongly criticizes the *ringi* process as a system of discussion which seems to be open but which, at any level, can only be as broad as the individuals have knowledge or experience. Furthermore, these individuals run the risk of being unduly influenced by outside pressures. Hence, he states that the *ringi-sho*, whilst having to be stamped by all levels of the organization, inevitably perpetrates a narrowness of organizational viewpoint dominated by old precedents. Similar arguments are presented by Arai (8) and, like Tsuji (6), he relates the acceptance of the acquired status of more senior ranks to the ancient patriarchal community that existed in the pre-Restoration eras. It is clearly argued that the organizational structure of urban business and industry depended upon the traditional behaviour patterns of workers arriving from the strongly feudal rural areas. Thus, the interests of the company come first, the company is thought of as a family, with the welfare and lifetime employment of the workers considered to be an act of benevolence on the part of the company president...to whom one owes allegiance...etc. Inevitably, the *ringi* process must nurture a strong company identity which could be beneficial to all concerned.

There is little doubt that Confucianism after it was adopted helped strengthen the 'family' concept, and other aspects of the Japanese tradition may be seen to boost this paternal or status-accepting aspect of the person within an organization. But *ringi*, if applied absolutely and with its full rigidity is, it seems, counter-productive and too great a stress is laid upon it being the sole decision-making device of the organization. Many organizational theorists would suggest that research be undertaken into the uses of the *ukagai* 'inquiry' process rather than the role-conscious process of *ringi*, or perhaps into how the administration selects the circulation routes of the *ringi-sho* documents. Furthermore, most studies of *ringi-sei* tend to assume a 'bottom-up' form of management in which the chief executive possesses the legal authority but the organization is the management powerhouse. A discrepancy can be seen to exist in this basic concept when one reviews the operations of the original *zaibatsu*-based organizations, or the post-war collectives, the *keiretsu*. In these organizations, often with very complex joint-stock ownership, the presidents wield tremendous power, and can take far-reaching decisions. Within these conglomerates, policy co-ordination takes place through the regular meetings of the presidents' clubs. In many instances it is possible to understand that some leaders may be required to push the organization in a given direction and thus they take a major decision, creating an *ato-ringi* system wherein the organization has to develop and approve the *ringi-sho* post hoc.

Perhaps, however, a more characteristic aspect of the Japanese management scene is the frequency of *nemawashi*, or consultation prior to decisions being taken. Much less appears to be cited upon this topic than the formalized *ringi* process, yet obviously it is a vital and unavoidable part of consensus-seeking prior to decision-making. Vogel (5) suggests that *nemawashi* can be undertaken upon broad issues or upon detail, but always it takes place with mutual confidence and support expressed by all parties to the discussion. This is the slow part of the *ringi* process, as executives are unwilling to act until a high degree of consensus is obtained (and this would even be true for *ato-ringi*). Vogel also suggests that the process of *nemawashi* operating in the senior levels of the *zaikai* would enable the companies to secure long-term goals. But this may cause some degree of *ato-ringi* to be practised. On the other hand, I would expect short-term goals to be generated through the normal *ringi-sei* by the strong bureaucracy of the organization acting, hopefully, for the good of the company.

I wish now to review one modern western approach to organizational decision-making and to consider how the eastern and western approaches seem to be similar at the level of the individual. It is known that senior Japanese executives express surprise when listening to the discussions of American executives: the American's arguments are detailed and the individuals involved seem to recognize their own responsibilities and their own authority both clearly and decisively, which is totally unlike the ambiguity which exists in the *ringi* process with which the Japanese are familiar. The western style of management requires that the decision maker's span of action is clearly defined and, within that domain, that his concepts of the subjective worth of the various attributes of the problem are publicly expressed. Perhaps this is overstating a normative approach to western senior-management technology, but in practice some senior groups of executives do make explicit all their subjective trade-offs of one attribute against another in order to allow an independent analyst to calculate a mathematical expression which could be used as a proxy of the decision maker. I must make it clear that we are not considering the day-by-day project management which goes on in complex engineering—in shipbuilding, for instance: western academics and engineers developed the methodology of Critical Path Techniques and PERT for project management, which the Japanese and others were quick to adopt and use. Rather, it is to show how complex policy decisions ought to be taken, such as energy generation, or environmental protection, through the use of Multi-Attribute Utility Theory. For this type of analysis the executive group must decide that it does require the aid of an analyst external to the group. His task would be to allow each executive in turn to express and externalize the variables which must be considered in the study, and these in total would thereafter exclude all other attributes. Once this limited list has been explicated, the analyst investigates the executives's preferences and trade-offs between the attributes he has listed in order to generate an equation which will adequately and completely describe the executives' preferences. By these means the westerners would make a completely explicit and open statement of their own preferences to the others in the decision-making group. The analyst's next task is effectively to merge the individuals' equations into one acceptable to the group, to generate an equation expressing the total group's feelings. An excellent exposition of this modelling process is contained in Keeney and Raiffa's book. (9) Other explicit decision-aiding models are clearly stated in Bell, Keeney and Raiffa. (10)

This process of making explicit one's preferences prior to deciding a policy, and then causing the implementation of the policy in a 'top-down' process is obviously unlike the generally quoted Japanese pattern. The *nemawashi* process would appear to be concerned with subtlety and ambiguity, and certainly no sharp definitions of preferences are mentioned in the citations. Even the use of the word 'lobbying' does not convey the subtlety within *nemawashi*.

Yet, if we were to pose the same major policy-evaluation problem to a group of Japanese and to a group of western executives, and accept for the moment that a decision must be taken, which for the Japanese group would lead to *ato-ringi*, is it unreasonable to assume that the Japanese *nemawashi* process has a fundamentally different purpose from that of the westerners' explicit externalisations – given that the same facts and data were presented to each group? If we can thus accept that the role of management, especially of large organizations, is one of goal-finding and achieving and that this is heavily dependent upon the persuasion of one's peers and others in the organization, then no matter what management style may be adopted by the executives, they as individuals must each appraise the facts, the data, and the arguments presented by colleagues and thereby come to some covert conclusion. The externalization of that conclusion may well be subject to strong traditional ties but, it will be argued below, whilst the internalization and the balancing of pertinent facts is a uniquely personal activity, the mechanisms by which this takes place may be completely open to generalization over all nations and peoples.

A theory of individual decision behaviour should explain and unify many phenomena. It should be able to explain what processes are performed during the task and what psychological mechanisms carry them out. Also, it should show how changes in the external conditions alter the decision-making behaviour. Tuggle and Hutton Barrow (11) state that their research objective is to understand the entire process of human decision-making. This includes problem finding and structuring, as well as the choice of a preferred alternative in the form of an explicitly encoded computer simulation of individual decision behaviour. Their research utilizes the Information Processing paradigm conceived first by Newell and Simon. (12) The IPS theory of decision-making seeks to explain the process in terms of information processing. That is, a theory linking our memories containing discrete symbols and symbolic expressions, our processes that manipulate these symbols, the receptors for sensing symbols in their environments, and the effectors for transmitting further symbols to the environment. In the paradigm, if a program for a particular decision situation exists, this program is said to constitute an explanation of the situation. It is the existence of such a program common to the Japanese and the westerner for which we are searching.

Within this theory we would attempt to construct macroprograms of elementary behaviours in order to explain the decision-making of an individual. If these programs adequately match the verbal, thinking-aloud protocol of the person coping with the situation, then it would be said that the macroprograms are an explanation of the person's behaviour. Given that there is some consistency observable in human behaviour, we postulate that some sub-routines or parts of one person's macroprogram will be a good descriptor of another person's behaviour. Thus it is expected that when presented with the same data, two persons of the same intelligence, etc, would use the same macroprograms. But as no two persons are exactly the same, exact macroprogam replication is not expected as individuality depends upon a personal utilization of the evaluative labels assigned to similar symbol structures. Tuggle and Hutton Barrow (11) have developed a series of decision tasks which were used by Surinder Kaur (13) in her exploratory work on cultural differences in decision-making. Respondents in her research were asked to imagine they were a chief executive of a marketing company which has eight new products, and that each product may result in one of four levels of demand yielding quoted profits (or losses). Given a table of 8 x 4 = 32 'profits', the decision demanded is to choose the best single product to introduce. This task is repeated for eight further tables of data with differing 'profit' structures supposedly representing further marketing areas. Naturally, the data in the tables have been carefully selected so that the subjective processes leading to the choice of one product may be linked to verbal protocols which, in turn, could be translated into computer based macroprograms. Tuggle and Hutton Barrow have developed an adequate simulator (macroprogram) for a set of US students—we consider that this program could be used to test the fundamental questions of the differences which are said to exist between cultures.

Earlier it was suggested that the *nemawashi* process and the western externalization process prior to decision-making ought to be the same isomorphic process, given the same task. But to simply investigate these two processes using the existing techniques of organizational behaviour analysis would lead to statements that the Japanese seem to use a different set of behaviours. That is, the western investigators would place too great an emphasis on the externalized observable process, as they have done earlier in writings upon *ringi-sei*. It is clearly better if we can investigate decision processes using the information processing paradigm so that we can compare the resulting macroprograms developed from a study of Japanese against the westerners' macroprograms. These macroprograms, if they were similar, may show that the internal processing of data is culture-free.

If that were not so, it would be quite reasonable to state that the externalized and observable decision-making process is a product of culture, and that these processes probably would not transfer easily. That is, the *ringi-sei* should not be used in the USA as a matter of course, nor should the explicit Multi-attribute Modelling be impressed upon unwilling Japanese executives. But, if the internal cognitive processes are the same, if the similarities of the macroprograms suggest that information-processing is culture-free, we could look forward to the development of an inter-cultural decision-making style which would accept externalized infra-national cultural differences.

9

Traditional and Modern Thought in Japan: Some Notes on the Problem of Continuity and its Meaning

KLAUS KRACHT

My thoughts on the problem of continuity centre on post-1945 studies of Japanese thought of the Tokugawa period (1615-1868). In raising the issue of 'traditional' and 'modern', we face a problem of perception with which both western and Japanese researchers have to grapple in their investigations of Japanese thought. I shall confine myself to three questions: 1. Can we detect an endogenous development of modernity out of the context of traditional culture in the Japanese history of thought? 2. What can a question like this tell us about the consciousness of the scholar who is searching for traces of modernity? 3. Is it advisable to continue the hunt for modernity in traditional Japanese thought? For a tentative answer to these questions I am going to propound four theses.

1) Conjectures on what might be considered 'traditional' or 'modern' are the result of a generalization of experience derived from within the context of the European and American consciousness of history.

As the question of 'modernity' has been the object of scholarly research from the times of Biondo (d. 1463) until today, we might have reason to assume that the various disciplines of scholarship, above all the social sciences and philosophy of history, are ready to give us some definite idea of the essence of modernity. But they are not. There are quite a number of disciplines and schools within each discipline struggling for a description and analysis of what we call 'modernity'.

On the other hand, it is true that there exists some understanding between bourgeois modernists and Marxists regarding their teleological understanding of history. Science, technology and capitalism are conceived to be the starting point of the One World as one of the ends of mankind. Further, they are considered to be the aim of global development until the time of their appearance. Thus science, technology and capitalism take the role of a central criterion for all historical phenomena before them as well as—and this is even more deplorable—for the evaluation of non-scientific, non-technological, non-capitalist societies. (1) From this point of view, change in history is looked upon as historical development, as the unfolding or

54

action of a universal principle, an entelechy implanted in history, causing mankind to develop towards modernity, the pre-condition for the One World.

In a way, it is fascinating to see to what degree the Hegelian interpretation of history has kept its appeal, not only by way of Marx, but along many other paths too. In this respect, the historian Reinhard Wittram speaks of the unchanged suggestive power of Hegel as the *hegelianische Zauber*. (2)

2) The quest by contemporary Japanese historians for continuity from 'Kinsei' to 'Kindai-Gendai', through the evidence of endogenous elements of modernity in pre-modern Japanese thought is the expression of their search for orientation in view of the Amero-European world and a form of articulation of their political beliefs.

In post-war Japan, modernity came to be a value in itself which could not be questioned. The maintenance of social and political values could only be successful by the evidence of their modern character. Generally speaking, he who wants to prove the rightness of his political persuasions tends to avail himself of the past to legitimize his convictions. He will find that his ideas were realized once in some ideal form or, at least, that they are implanted in principle in the history of his particular society.

In other words, the statements of Japanese studies of the history of thought concerning modern elements and developments out of traditional thought can hardly be understood correctly without reference to their extra-scholarly likings, their respective *leitendes Erkenntnisinteresse*. From that point of view, we may distinguish four main streams of intellectual historians.

First there is a group of scholars such as Nagata Hiroshi, Saegusa Hiroto, Hani Gorô and Fukumoto Kazuo, who saw themselves above all as Marxists. Their central motive was their wish to make use of and verify Marx's or Marxists' theory of history. To these historians we owe quite a lot of ingenious studies on the history of thought in the Tokugawa period, the most outstanding of which may be Nagata's *Nihon hôkensei ideorogii* and his *Nihon yuibutsuron shi* where he analyses the line from the bourgeois materialism of the period to Meiji enlightenment, or Saegusa's excellent *Nihon no yuibutsuronsha* and his studies on Miura Baien. (3) A very impressive study, in spite of all its weak points arising from its extreme parallelism, is Fukumoto's *Nihon runessansu shi ron*, where he treats the history of thought in the Tokugawa period as analogous to European renaissance thought. (4)

Secondly, we should mention the so-called 'modernists' (*kindaishugisha*), with Maruyama Masao once being their spiritual leader. Between Marxists and modernists there was agreement in their opposition to the scholars of *Kôkoku shigaku* and the 'overcoming of modernity' (*kindai no chôkoku*). (5) The modernists asked for modernity above all in respect of political thought. The reaction against modernity under the wartime regime had more or less strong anti-democratic elements. Behind their attitudes there was often the idea that the essentials of western modernity (a very diffuse concept in their thought) were fundamentally incompatible with the Japanese spirit. So their proximity to and, in a lot of cases, companionship with fascist thinking was evident.

What those who considered themselves as protectors of tradition held up as the strong points in Japanese thought, was considered to be the reason for the specific problems of Japanese political culture according to the judgement of Maruyama, as he explained in his article 'Chôkokka-shugi no ronri to shinri' in May 1946. (6) Nonetheless, in the years 1940-44, he had already undertaken the attempt to open the concept of tradition as held by its guardian angels, and to redefine it to find a way out of their cultural particularism. For Maruyama, the formation of Sorai's style of thought came to appear as an analogue to early modern western thought, whereas the supposed dissociation of *Shushigaku* seemed to be the symptom of the disintegration of the medieval world-outlook. Franz Borkenau had been the main sponsor of this interpretation. (7) While Maruyama himself had already mentioned some problematic points in his approach in his postscript to the 1952 edition of *Nihon seiji shisôshi kenkyû* (8), this view gave a considerable impetus to thought studies in the fifties and even sixties and, with good reason, is still held in high estimation for its ingenious approach.

Next, we should turn to the modernization theory (*kindaika ron*), the Japanese representatives of which appeared after the conference at Hakone in the summer of 1960, above all under the influence of E.O. Reischauer, J.W. Hall, the leading figure among modernization theorists concentrating on Japan, and R.N. Bellah. (9) Now the central question was no longer 'Why has Japan developed so late into a modern society?', as the Marxists wanted to know, or 'What modern political elements can be found in pre-modern Japan?', as the 'classical' modernists asked, but one that came from the functionalist approach: 'What were the economic, social, political and mental preconditions for the highly successful modernization of Japan since the Meiji Restoration?' This new approach had a considerable appeal in the sixties in face of the increasing economic power and the growing self-consciousness of the nation, and gave rise to a new, positive evaluation of the Tokugawa period in the formation of modern Japan.

The manifestly ideological character of the modernization theory, above all in its initial stage, its development out of the American tradition of missionary-type attitudes of superiority, its relation to

American crisis-consciousness in face of the advances of the Soviet Union after 1945, and its practical meaning for the Kennedy-Rostowian strategy towards the supposedly 'underdeveloped' states of the Third World, have given rise to so much criticism that we need not repeat it once more. (10) Among Japanese intellectuals, as among 'concerned Asian scholars' in the USA, it was above all the course of the war in Vietnam that opened many eyes to its ideological implications. Criticism towards the modernization theory in Japan is therefore primarily criticism of ideology and not so much of the underlying methodological assumptions.

Generally speaking, the ideological abuse of a given theoretical concept does not tell us anything about its true validity. The essentially weak points and inadequacies of modernization theories, which the historian will find more deplorable than the social scientist, may above all be found in the evolutionist convictions of their propagators and their combination with the methods of functionalism. Other shortcomings, such as their conceptual formalism and their fetishism of indicators, actually are not specific deficiencies of modernization theoretical thinking; but they do contribute to the dilemma of a discipline which is worming its way into the confidence of the humanities. The theoretical modernization approach does not in practice ask for the factual quality of pre-modern phenomena, but limits itself to the investigation of their functional value in respect to the social process since the Meiji period. Bellah's adaptation of the Weber-Parsonsian concept of 'rationalism' may be looked upon as a prominent example.

Last, I should like to mention the representatives of *minshûshi* 'plebeian-history' writing, such as the famous Irokawa Daikichi, Kano Masanao, Yasumaru Yoshio, and Haga Noboru. The *minshûshi* stream has been increasingly gaining appeal since the middle sixties. Their approach towards modernity is closely related to their critical attitude towards political change since the Meiji Restoration. Above all, they criticize the formation of a bureaucratic elite, and it gives a good impression of their political persuasions to notice their co-operation with the *jûmin tôsô* ('residents' struggle') movements. What they particularly want to know when studying pre-modern thought is the answer to the question: 'Does there exist in the pre-western thought of the Japanese a modern, alternative tradition of liberal thought, which is different from the system immanent in the ideologies of the "great thinkers"?' Of course they have already given a positive answer, and in doing so have found the historical basis and justification for an attempt which can be described as an endeavour to revive the autonomous individual as the actor of historical change. The best pre-conditions for this they hope to find in the villages of the countryside, which they hold in high esteem and make the object of their studies. So it is above all peasants' thought that they mean when they speak of *minshû shisô* 'plebeian thought'.

3) Statements concerning 'modern' elements and developments in pre-western Japanese thought are based on analogies, formed out of morphological similarities of isolated phenomena.

The analysis of a single idea cannot be undertaken without regard to the whole context of which it is an integral part. Its interpretation can only adequately tell something about its factual quality if it is done *in toto*. Actually this is a platitude, but a truism which rather often is not respected, for the simple reason that we want to prove something which is only possible through a selective perception of the object. It would be easy to give a lot of examples, such as Nakamura Hajime's 'parallel developments', Minamoto Ryôen's studies in 'empirical rationalism', Saegusa's conjectures on 'materialism', Bitô Masahide's detection of 'autonomy' in Arai Hakuseki as 'one face of modernization', or Matsumoto Sannosuke's analysis of 'natural right' in Itô Jinsai; but let us confine ourselves to one famous case of presumptive 'modernity'.

Ogyû Sorai has been an attractive target of modernist interest for about four decades. Especially in respect of Maruyama's 'from nature to invention' (*shizen yori sakui e*), Sorai was in the past often looked upon as 'modern'. Recently, R.N. Bellah once more followed Maruyama, stating that Sorai had, 'we almost might say single-handedly created "modern philosophy" in Japan'. (12) Indeed, in regard to the criterion of *sakui* or 'conceptional consciousness', as Bellah says (13), Sorai may remind us of a lot of thinkers we usually count among the demiurges of western modernity. One might think, for example, of Vico's idea that man could only gain full orientation when he lived in 'the constructed' (= *sakui*). (14) Conceptual consciousness, poietic subjectivism, gnostic immanentism or whatever we may call the phenomenon, may, it is true, be looked upon as one of the central characteristics of modern man. But while we have the dichotomy of man and the outer world as subject and object in both cases, the subject is very different in respect of its aims of creation. To put it in a very simple way, Sorai's 'subject' is a subject in a less radical and autonomous sense than we have in western tradition. It is a commonplace that the modern concepts of man in the West as the 'subject' of history can be understood as the secularized Christian concepts of God as the creator of the world and almighty father. 'Creativity' is the specific quality of the *creator mundi* and at the same time the foremost aspiration of modern western man, the projection of the Christian God. So we simply cannot understand Sorai's concept of 'invention' or western poietic subjectivism without looking at the whole context, the particular relationships to the specific concepts of God, man, time, etc.

4) Western studies of the Japanese history of thought (and, in due course, also the Japanese study of the history of thought) should attempt to approach pre-western Japanese thought primarily as an alternative to western traditions. Japanese traditional thought should not be understood a priori—in regard to a presumptive continuity —as an abortive development towards modern thinking.

The analysis of pre-western Japanese thought under the aspect of modernity is pure Euro-centrism. To clarify the problem we should try to imagine a situation in which western humanities took their categories and patterns of thought for the analysis of our own culture almost exclusively from the context of Chinese and Japanese tradition. Western thinking has first and above all gained a consciousness of itself by the adaption and refinement of its own, that is, Judaeo-Christian and Greek, conceptual tradition. It is self-evident that this means a confinement of cognition and is a good reason for the principal necessity of comparative studies. But to declare the very opposite, namely, the interpretation of a particular culture by means of the supposedly universal categories of a presumptively superior culture, as a principle of interpretation, is much more problematic from the viewpoint of cognition.

From time to time it may be useful to give some thought to the significance of one's own pursuits. In my view, the specific significance of investigating a given alien culture lies in the acquirement and transmission of experience. To acquire new experience is a difficult undertaking. The psychology of the individual tells us that already, at an early stage, we tend to perceive those parts of reality which are likely to correspond to and legitimize given assumptions and judgements and that, as far as possible, we try not to notice those things which do not fit with our received worldview. Transcultural comparative studies in a way have the same problems. Scholars engaging in them seem to be rather inclined to confirm given worldviews through their selective perception of the object culture, thereby neglecting one of their greatest opportunities. It is a commonplace that the so-called 'advanced' societies are today in an unprecedented crisis of orientation, and this at a time when traditional western beliefs are gaining more and more attraction in countries of the Third World. At a time like this, it might be reasonable to bring our minds to bear on alternative forms of thought, which we can experience in traditions other than those of Europe and America. I should therefore like to suggest that we take Japanese traditional thought seriously, not in its presumptive function as a now obsolete stage towards modern Japanese thought, but as one of many possible alternatives which we should consider.

SECTION 2

Early Western
and
Christian elements

10

The von Siebold Collection of the Ruhr University of Bochum: An Outline of its History and Problems

EBERHARD FRIESE

When Philipp Franz von Siebold died in 1866, the results of his scientific work were dispersed in half a dozen countries. Siebold had lived a cosmopolitan life in several parts of the world. Born in 1796 in Wurzburg, Franconia (now a part of northern Bavaria) and educated there, he spent many years in the Netherlands and her colonies, in Japan, in Prussia and in Bavaria. He also went for some weeks to Russia as counsellor of the Czarist Government as well as to Paris in a similar post, before he went back for a second time to east Asia (China and Japan) almost at the end of his life, working in the service of the Netherlands Trading Company (NHM).

In nearly all of these countries he left the marks of his immense works, in the form of numerous projects and scientific collections which, in some cases, became the nucleus of important museums. As a result, until now no one has been able to plan a complete edition of all his written works, his letters (that is, his correspondence with scores of scholars and scientific societies), his projects and petitions (he wrote to the governments of several states on behalf of Japan), and all the essays in different periodicals and series.

Great parts of Siebold's collections of ethnological and natural scientific materials, his libraries, original manuscripts, and botanical and zoological drawings can now be found in London, Leiden, The Hague, Ghent, Munich, Leningrad, Vienna, Berlin and—last but not least—in Japan, in Nagasaki and Tokyo. The material which is still the private property of some branches of his family consists mainly of hundreds of papers (in letter and other handwritten forms) of his European scientific periods (1830-59 and 1862-6), and is collected in family archives in Mittelbiberach (Württemberg, southern Germany) and in Castle Brandenstein (Hesse, near Frankfurt-on-Main). It must be said that they are still little known to scholars. Perhaps Hans Körner, who wrote about the members of the von Siebold family of Wurzburg (1), is the only living scholar who has worked for a long time on both archives.

As a result of the great inflation which Germany suffered between 1920 and 1923, a granddaughter of von Siebold, Frau Erika von Erhardt-Siebold (1890-1965), decided to sell some of the 600 items of von Siebold's personal papers and other documents. The lady, a professor of English literature, chose mainly matters of scientific interest and she avoided the loss of souvenirs concerning her family. She took care that the material became public property: at first the collection was loaned to the Ethnological Museum in Berlin, where it attracted the attention of the Director, F.W.K. Müller, who published a first short description of the formerly virtually unknown documents. (2) Kure Shûzo, the great biographer of Siebold, was perhaps the only one to have known about these papers but he did not examine them. (3)

In 1927 the collection was finally sold to the Japan Institute in Berlin, an independent research institute not connected with Berlin University. It was supervised and financed by Government cultural authorities and by the Kaiser-Wilhelm-Gesellschaft, the National Research Society of Germany in those days. It had been established just one year before, and according to the financial situation—as one can see from the records of the meetings of the Directory Board—not everybody was interested in the purchase. But success rewarded the efforts of F.M. Trautz (4), who had formerly been assistant professor at the Ethnological Museum, where he had already arranged for the loan of the material, and who was then one of the Scientific Directors of the Institute. When Frau Clara Sielcken-Schwarz (1879-1970), a well-known Maecenas in her residence in Baden-Baden (Baden-Württemberg), gave the sum of US$500, the deal was closed.

The collection was then analysed and catalogued, presumably by the Japanese Scientific Director, Kuroda Genji, and Herta von Schulz, a student working there. It was enlarged later on by some other smaller purchases, mostly of printed material. It was possible, for example, to get a copy of the first four-volume edition of von Siebold's *Nippon: Archiv zur Beschreibung von Japan...*, large folio size and hand-coloured, from the private library of the Austrian Emperor Franz I (1769-1835). (5)

It is still not known exactly how many items the collection contained: the highest number I have been able to find is 612, but there is no complete catalogue to be found (6). The whole collection (the so-called 'Sieboldiana') was complemented by an original oil painting (7) and old photographs and was arranged in a special room, the 'Siebold-Zimmer'.

How was the collection used? In 1930 Trautz published an enlarged edition of *Nippon: Archiv zur Beschreibung von Japan...*, the fifth volume of which was mainly based on studies of the manuscripts. In this edition was printed Siebold's diary of his voyage to the Court of Edo (No. 271), and some letters were shown in facsimile (8). Two years later Kuroda and von Schulz wrote about the letters of the collection (9). In the same year (1932) the Japan Institute loaned exhibits to the von Siebold Exposition at the University of Leiden. (10)

In the beginning of 1934 about 250 of the most remarkable items went to Tokyo, to be shown in an exhibition in memory of Siebold's work in Japan, as can be seen from the catalogue prepared for it. (11) At that time a facsimile reprint of nine of the so-called 'dissertations' of Siebold's Japanese scholars and some letters were published in Japan. I would say that these reproductions are so excellent that they can hardly be distinguished from the originals (12). Furthermore, the Sieboldiana were photographed and duplicated (as photostats) in Tokyo, and these copies are now kept in the Tôyô Bunko ('The Oriental Library'). (13)

Because of the bomb attacks on Berlin during World War II, the Japan Institute began in 1943 to evacuate great parts of its library to several places in central Germany. One year later, in March 1944, the material in the Siebold Room (or the most important parts of it) was brought to Chateau Weissenburg in the Saale Valley in Thuringia, together with about fifty boxes of books of the library, each box marked with the initials 'A.A.' ('Auswärtiges Amt': Foreign Ministry). When the U.S. Army conquered Thuringia in the spring of 1945, they confiscated the material they found and shipped it to the United States, where it was placed in the Washington Document Center in 1946. (14)

For about ten years the last Scientific Director of the Japan Institute, Martin Ramming, and other scholars tried to arrange for it to be brought back. Finally (in 1957?) they were successful in getting the Sieboldiana transferred to the Public Record Office of the Federal Republic of Germany at Koblenz, presumably given back by the Department of State, Washington. The circumstances of the return are still unknown, as I have not yet been able to find any record of it, either in Germany or in the States.

The Foreign Ministry of the Federal Republic of Germany then gave the material to the Max-Planck-Gesellschaft, the successor to the Kaiser-Wilhelm-Gesellschaft, after the legal liquidation of the Japan Institute in the beginning of 1966, according to its statutes. In the same year the Board of the Max-Planck-Gesellschaft decided to give the property of the former Japan Institute, which could be rescued for the Federal Republic of Germany, to the East Asian Institute of the newly established Ruhr University of Bochum. About 3,000 books, captured at Chateau Weissenburg in 1945 and given back to Germany in about 1957, have formed the nucleus of the Japanese Library of the Institute since 1966. The von Siebold collection itself was brought to Bochum in 1970. We have to say, however, that less than half of the Berlin Sieboldiana was left.

When Numata Jirô, Tokyo University expert on the history of Euro-Japanese relations, spent a year in Bochum (1974-5) as guest professor, the Department of East Asian Studies (until 1970 the East Asian Institute) was able to gain his help. He catalogued material according to the original Berlin registration numbers, although the catalogue itself seemed to be lost at that time. (15) In 1978, however, we succeeded in finding a copy of the Berlin catalogue in the Tôyô Bunko, and this was microfilmed by courtesy of the Librarian, Watanabe Kanenobu. Because of this, our institution is now able to plan a detailed description of the Bochum Collection, listing also the lost items. It must be said here that the catalogue, in type-written form, does not cover the complete collection but goes up to No. 609. (16)

As I mentioned above, 230 of formerly more than 612 items are left. Lost are many of the remarkable manuscripts, such as the original of von Siebold's *Journal während meiner Riese nach dem Kaiserlichen Hofe Jedo im Jahre 1826* ('Diary of my voyage to the Court of Jedo 1826', No. 271, published 1930-31 by F.M. Trautz, as I mentioned above) as well as all of Siebold's diplomas (Nos. 463 to 508) given to him by nearly fifty scientific societies between 1822 and 1865. Unfortunately his doctor's diploma (No. 462; two copies) from 1820 is also missing. (17)

The same must be said about the paintings, photographs, and decoration medals of the Siebold Room. Furthermore, all the famous geographical maps and views of Japanese landscapes (No. 101 to No. 133) are missing, but not two interpretations of the lost maps, written in Dutch in Siebold's hand (Nos. 113, 118). Siebold was interested in old descriptions of east Asia, and had copied hundreds of pages from the records of the Dutch East India Company of the seventeenth century (No. 362). These are now lost, as are the copies of the journal of the ship in which he sailed, the Drie Gezusters, from 1821 to 1826 (No. 361).

Missing also are a lot of printed essays and books on Siebold written in the nineteenth and early twentieth centuries and, last but not least, many of Siebold's printed works too (mostly first editions). It can therefore be said that not only items whose representative character could have impressed amateurs but also some of the most important manuscripts have been lost. Which items, then, have been saved?

The most important group are the original manuscripts of von Siebold's pupils, famous names in the history of Japanese sciences, like Katsuragawa Hoken, Itô Keisuke, Oka Kenkai, Takano Chôei and many others.(18) Eighteen essays, written in Dutch by Japanese scientists specified by name, are collected in Bochum—in Berlin there were twenty-two. (Unfortunately No. 297, *An atlas of the natural sciences in Japan*, with proper names in the hand of Itô Keisuke, 2 pages and 40 plates, is lost.)

Twenty other essays in Japanese hands, without names but ident-ified in some cases, have been saved. It would be of general interest, when working on the history of Siebold's works, to compare all these 'dissertations' with the author's manuscripts and with the published texts themselves. About twenty original handwritten items of von Siebold's, concerning *Nippon: Archiv...*, *Flora Japonica*, *Fauna Japonica* and other works, are present in Bochum.

Inside a fascicle of some newspapers of the mid-nineteenth century (Nos. 63 and 65) we found the 1856 *Catalogue raisonné et prix-courant des plantes et graines du Japon, cultivées dans l'établissement de von Siebold et Comp. à Leide.* Günther Schmid, a botanist, who wrote a detailed description of the role von Siebold's plants and flowers have played in the gardens of Europe since the middle of the nineteenth century had to state in 1942: '...when Siebold moved to the Netherlands, he laid out a garden of acclimatization...in Leiden in the neighbourhood of his house. We would be happy to get to know more about it. But I had no success in finding one of the trade catalogues of the nursery 'Siebold Ltd.', which are hardly to be found...' (19)

In Bonn University, where the library and personal papers of F.M. Trautz (1877-1952) are kept, we have found a group of fourteen manuscripts (Nos. 216-28, and No. 369) concerning *Fauna Japonica*. (20) It can be assumed that Trautz borrowed them before 1944 and saw no chance of giving them back. When Trautz died the manuscripts were considered as a part of his library.

By courtesy of Dr Axel Held of the University Library of Cologne, we were able to acquire one of the illustrated volumes of the facsimile edition of *Nippon: Archiv...* with a copy number identical to that of a copy of the Japan Institute Library. (21) The missing *De historia naturalis in Japonia statu. Dissertatio...de Fauna Japonica* is catalogued as No. 11 of the Berlin Sieboldiana. It is one of the first printed analyses of nature in Japan, written by Siebold on Dejima and published in Batavia in 1824. We were happy to find all the pages of another copy of the essay, tied up sheet by sheet inside a folio of handwritten notes on Japanese mammals (No. 215). When our institution acquired another copy of the first edition of *Nippon: Archiv...*some years ago, we could not know that the first owner mistakenly tied up in it copies of the *Tsiän dsü wen*, *Lui ho* and *Wa nen kei*, all of them parts of the Bibliotheca Japonica. (22)

What will be done in the future? First, we shall publish a detailed history and description of the Bochum Collection, of which the first part should be printed in vol. 3 (1980) of the yearbook of our institution. (23) We hope the publication will lead scholars to work with the material. Then we intend to buy most works by and about von Siebold, but this will require a considerable amount of money and time and as yet there is only a faint prospect of achieving this. We hope, however, to find some more material after publishing this 'wanted' notice. (24) Later, we shall look for ways to rebuild the collection by using the photostats of the Tôyô Bunko, and to enlarge it by collecting microfilms of items in other von Siebold collections.

Addenda:

By courtesy of Mr Paul T. Heffron, Acting Chief of the Manuscript Division of the Library of Congress, Washington, I was informed (by letter of 6 December 1979) that at least 82 manuscripts of the von Siebold collection of the former Japan Institute are held now in his Division. The first item of these papers is No. 142 (*Meteorologie*), a companion-piece to No. 141 (*Meteorologie, Geologie*) in the Bochum Collection. The Library of Congress gave notice of its collection in 1962 (25), but until now it seems to have been unknown to Siebold research in Europe and Japan.

As can be seen from a draft contents list Mr Heffron sent to me, the most important parts are 41 manuscripts of Siebold's studies on Japanese flora, 32 writings on Japanese fauna, and a bundle of letters beginning in 1827, which cannot be estimated more precisely at the moment. But we know now that all the 46 manuscripts on fauna and 44 of the earlier 46 manuscripts on flora are still extant.

A letter of 9 January 1980 from Mrs Annette Melville, Reference Librarian of the Library of Congress, confirmed that the Prints and Photographs Division there holds two albums of approximately 250 photocopies of photos and prints (26), which were given to the Japan Institute as a present from the organizers of the great von Siebold Exposition of 1935 in Tokyo (accession stamp: Japaninstitut Bücherei, 9.7.36). In the private papers of the President of the Japan Institute, Dr Wilhelm Solf (1862-1936), then retired Ambassador to Japan, which are kept now in the National Public Record Office in Koblenz, I have found a translation of a letter from Professor Irisawa, then Chairman of the Organizing Committee of the Exposition, announcing the present. (27)

11

A Basis for Modern 'Rangaku' Studies — Dutch Archival Material

MARGARETHA VAN OPSTALL

In accordance with the Congress theme, I shall direct my paper about archival material relating to Japan in the Algemeen Rijksarchief at the Hague (1) to a traditional Japanese discipline, *Rangaku* 'Dutch learning'. This is typical of the Tokugawa period (1615-1868), when Japan isolated herself from the rest of the world. Only through contacts with the Dutch at Dejima did the Japanese obtain information about the development of science and the political situation in the western world. Interpreters and, later, scholars studied the Dutch language in order to be able to extend and deepen their knowledge.

At present, when Japan is an active participant in world affairs and scientific knowledge is widely available, specialists in the Dutch language are no longer required in the same way. Nevertheless, there are still a few people belonging to small specialist societies who study Dutch, but they concern themselves now essentially with historical studies, aimed at the examination of various aspects of the early contacts between Japan and Holland.

Three groups of scholars, working in their spare time, and a department of the Historiographical Institute of the University of Tokyo use Dutch for their research and publications. The first group, supervised by Ogata Tomio, is working on the development of science in Japan, like *Rangaku* scholars of former days; two other groups (2) under the guidance of Iwao Seiichi publish historical material, in Dutch as well as in Japanese translation. Thus, the Nichi-Ran Kôshôshi Kenkyûkai has edited the Dejima diaries of 1800-1857 (3), and is now translating them into Japanese in its weekly sessions; and the Hôsei Rangaku Kenkyûkai has published the *Fûsetsu-gaki* ('(Dutch) news reports') (4) in two volumes, partly in Japanese and partly in Dutch.

Kanai Madoka is head of the Department of Dutch Studies at the Historiographical Institute. So far it has published the Hirado diaries kept by the heads of the Dutch factory there, in nine volumes of Dutch texts and Japanese translations. (5) Most of the material relating to these works is in Holland, at the Algemeen Rijksarchief at the Hague, but to explain the origin and organisation of these archives, I must look back to the past, even at the risk of repeating ancient history.

The beginning of the seventeenth century saw the foundation of the Vereenigde Oost-Indische Compagnie (VOC) (6), which had the monopoly of Asian trade and possessed supreme authority in some fields. (7) The organization thus had two functions, firstly as a trading company, and secondly as a state within a state. Based on contracts (8) with Asian princes, although of a widely differing scope, it built a trading empire in Asia which reached from Persia to the Pacific and from Japan to Australia. Batavia was the centre, the seat of the Governor-General and the Council, which ruled as a board under the supervision of the Board of Directors in Holland, the Heren XVII. They gave instructions for overseas policy, fixed the imports and exports, and organized the shipping to and from Asia. The factory in Japan had its place within the VOC organization until 1795.

The factory at Hirado dates from 1609, after permission for free trade was received from the shôgun Ieyasu. (9) This freedom was limited in 1617 and almost reduced to nothing in 1642 with the removal to Dejima, just evacuated by the expelled Portuguese. The first head (*Opperhoofd*) of the Dutch factory at Hirado was Jacques Specx, who organised the administration and the archives. (10) The beginning of the factory is the beginning of the archives, the first item of the inventory being the shôgunate trading permit of 1609.

The history of Japanese-Dutch relations determines the character and the place where the records are kept. The history may be divided into three phases:

1) The VOC period, 1609-1795.

2) The period in which the government replaces the VOC, 1795-1857.

3) The modern period of free trade and normal diplomatic relations.

In the opening period, the factory is part of the VOC, which means in the first place the government in Batavia and, in the second, the Heren XVII in patria. They are the counterpart of the factory administration. In Batavia the Governor-General wanted to have a good survey of the dealings and actions of the outside offices to be able to report on them and to answer for them to the Heren XVII. The procedure was as follows: all the factory documents, in original or copy, were sent to Batavia. After being examined there, they were passed on to Holland with the exception of the financial papers, of which only a compilation was forwarded. Those letters were annexes to the Governor-General's yearly report, the 'General Letter' (*Generale Missive*). (12) This collection of very different material is compiled in a series, 'Letters and papers received' (*Overgekomen*

70

brieven en papieren) from Asia. (13) Ideally, all documents could be located in two places: in the files of the factory and in the series of *overgekomen brieven* or, if the letter originated in Batavia, in the register of letters from Batavia to the outer offices (*Bataviaas vitgaand briefboek*). The factory files and the Company files are the counterparts of each other, so to speak: if a letter was written in Japan, the original would be sent to Batavia, with the copy in the Japan register, and the other way round. In reality this is not always the case, because some papers were lost in shipwrecks or destroyed in later times. The Japan archives of the eighteenth century are the more complete.

What is to be found in these archives? (14) To begin with, one should realize that since these are company files, and in part even government files, they contain no personal data except those useful to the Company. Only last wills were made at the factory.

The contents can be divided in five groups:

1) *Dagregisters* ('Diaries'); a survey of daily activities, incoming letters, council meetings etc; often with a report of the *hofreis* to Edo.

2) Resolutions on government and legal decisions. Although the Dejima community was small (in quiet times no more than twelve men, and in busy times about a hundred), all sorts of things had to be looked after.

3) Registers of incoming and outgoing letters, the complement of the VOC archives as mentioned above.

4) Accountancy records, containing journals, ledgers and auxiliary books. As they were kept by merchants, they are very precise.

5) General documentation, reports on other offices, etc.

To give you an impression of the completeness of the material, I should like to present a case to you, namely that of the Shimabara rebellion, December 1637-April 1638.

The *Dagregister* mentions the rebellion for the first time on 17 December 1637 (16), as being a result of bad government and extortion. The Christians, already in a difficult position, join the rebels. The *daimyô* of the region are called to war and the Dutch are invited to serve the Japanese government with ships and ordnance. The correspondence with the Japanese can be found (in translation) in the register of incoming and outgoing letters (17), together with letters to and from the Governor-General at Batavia and the Governor of Taiwan. The Governor-General and Council discuss the report of the *Opperhoofd*, Captain Couckebacker, in March and April 1638, but no decisions are taken. (19) On 16 June 1638 (20) they express their regret that no mortar was available during the siege, but when Caron, the next *Opperhoofd*, arrives at Hirado, the rebellion has already been put down. In December 1638 a General

Letter (21) reports the case to the Heren XVII, but they react rather laconically. (22) They are amazed at the great number of victims, but pleased that the assistance took only a short time. The Governor-General and Council react to the reports from Japan with remarks on the Portuguese influence behind it and bring the affair into the political atmosphere of Dutch-Portuguese antagonism. One may observe in the documents how the socially-based rebellion turns into a dark Portuguese conspiracy. (23)

In addition to the archives of the factory and VOC, there is the collection of material from the High Government Batavia (*Hoge Regerung Batavia*) (24) containing mostly eighteenth-century documents with a few on Japan.

The second phase of Japanese-Dutch relations starts in 1795. By this time the VOC is gone and the government has taken its place, so that now the factories have a different counterpart, although the pattern is the same. The *Opperhoofd* corresponds with the government in Batavia and, via Batavia, with the government in Holland, in the form of a number of different organizations during the complex period of the Napoleonic wars, ending with the Ministry for the Colonies. (25) Up to 1840 the King's Secretariat (*Staatssecretarie*, 1813-40) is even more important, because colonial affairs were a royal prerogative. The Ministry of Education (26) provides a great deal of data on scientific research in Japan through the reports on research by von Siebold and Blume ordered by the government of the Dutch East Indies.

There is not only a change in counterpart, but also in the handling of the papers. No longer are all papers sent to Holland, as was the case in the VOC period. Only important business material is forwarded, routine affairs being dealt with in Batavia and the documents held there. However, these documents may also be found in the archives of the Japan factory, among incoming and outgoing letters.

The copper and camphor trade is still the reason why the Dutch come to Japan. From the seventeenth century, there existed two types of trade: the official or *Comps* trade, and the private or *kambang* trade by Dutch civil servants, a very profitable business. (27) The government tries to pass over the official trade to the Netherlands Trading Company (Nederlandsche Handel Maatschapij = NHM), but after a try-out in 1827, the company refuses: the *kambang* trade is in the way. (28) After an experiment to change private trade into trade run by a society consisting of civil servants at Dejima, called the Society of Private Trade in Japan (1826-30) (29), this trade is farmed out to private merchants in 1835. (30) In

72

1855 the last part of the trade is relinquished, because the government wants to be free to act according to the political situation of
the time. The abolition of the official government trade follows in
1857. (31)

In that year starts the third phase, the period of free trade with
Japan while, in the political field, an ordinary diplomatic and consular service is organized. Trade and government are separated, to
the benefit of both.

As the government now has only a diplomatic task, the Ministry
of Foreign Affairs (32) comes into the picture. From this period
data on Japan may also be found there, as well as in the documents
of Parliament.

Trade has been taken over by the NHM and some other firms.
The NHM is closely connected with the government and has a great
influence upon Dutch trade in Asia. In Japan she acts not only as a
trading company, but as bank as well. From 1857 until 1880 the
large NHM archives are rich in material about Japan.

With the NHM, we leave the field of government archives and
come to private archives, collections of persons or institutions
connected in one way or another with Japan. In the VOC period
there is only one such collection, that of Sweers en Van Vliet
(34), having documents on the first contacts with Japan. From the
second period there are more: I bring to your attention the collections of Doeff (35), Cock Blomhoff (36), Bezemer (37), Bik (38)
and Fabius. (39) Among the papers of Baud (40), former Minister
for the Colonies and Governor-General, are some interesting reports
on Japan.

Beside the Algemeen Rijksarchief there are several institutions
with collections rich in Japanese material; for example, the Museum
for Ethnology at Leiden. For a survey of archival material relating
to Japan in the Netherlands, I refer you to two archival guides to
be published in the near future under the auspices of the International Council of Archives and UNESCO. (41)

Summarizing, one may say that a lot of material is ready for use.
The only problem may be the language of the documents. But what
is to stop present-day scholars from following the brave and persistent example of the *Rangakusha* of former days to gain a treasure
of information?

12

The Landing in Japan of Giovanni Battista Sidotti in 1708

ALDO TOLLINI

The Christian faith was introduced into Japan by Francis Xavier in 1549. It had a certain degree of success during the second half of the sixteenth century and the first decade of the seventeenth, until the anti-Christian edicts were issued. (1) After that, terrible persecutions followed and missionaries were banned from Japan or martyred with horrible torture, especially after the adoption of the policy of isolation in 1639. Even so, there were still attempts by Catholic missionaries to steal into Japan; most of them, however, were immediately seized and put to death.

The last and most famous of these attempts was that of the Italian missionary G.B. Sidotti who arrived in Japan from Manila in 1708. This short essay outlines the facts relating to Sidotti's arrival in Japan, beginning with his departure from the bay of Manila in August 1708, and concluding with his departure from Nagasaki for Edo in October 1709.

The reason for the choice of this period of Sidotti's history is that, though many studies have been made concerning his attempts at the evangelization of Japan, the actual circumstances of his journey to Japan and of his landing are still relatively little known. In contrast, the following period, that spent in Edo, is described in the report of the cross-examination, called *Seiyô kibun*, written by Sidotti's questioner, the scholar Arai Hakuseki.

The present essay is an abridged version of a more extensive study carried out by me in Japan on the same subject and has the purpose of presenting the main results of my research. This study has developed on a comparative basis; that is to say, I examined both the western and Japanese sources which are available, and tried to put them together in order to have an exhaustive reconstruction of the facts. Now, before proceeding on to the body of this essay, it may be convenient to quote here the main sources used.

1) *Relacion del viage que hizo el Abad don Juan Bautista Sydot, desde Manila al Imperio del Japon, embiado por Nuestro Santissimo Padre Clemente XI*, written by Fray Agustin de Madrid, provincial of the Philippines, and published in Madrid in 1717. It is written in Spanish, and is a revised edition of the log-book of the journey of Sidotti's ship from Manila to Japan.

74

2) *Breve relazione estratta da varie lettere...sopra l'arrivo nella città di Manila, partenza per l'Impero del Giappone, arrivo e dimora in quello dell'Abbate D. Gio. Battista Sydoti*, a translation of the above-mentioned book published in Rome in 1718. The translation, however, is not faithful and in some parts is completely different.

3) The documents under *fascicolo 1635* ('file number 1635') preserved in the Casanatense Library of Rome.

They include a few versions of the log-book of Sidotti's journey, dated from 1708 to 1709, and the declarations of the members of the crew about the journey and the landing of the missionary. There is also an autograph letter by Sidotti.

It is highly probable that Fray Agustin de Madrid's book derived from the documents in the Casanatense Library. (2)

4) Among Japanese sources, the most interesting and useful are gathered in the *Nagasaki chûshin Rômajin no koto*. They contain the exchange of information on Sidotti between the authorities of Kagoshima and those of Nagasaki, and also his two cross-examinations.

Other sources are: *Dejima Rankan nisshi*, passages regarding Sidotti taken from the documents of the Dutch trading house in Dejima (Nagasaki); and the *Seiyô kibun*, Arai Hakuseki's account of Sidotti.

Short history of Sidotti until his departure from Manila.

Sidotti was born of a noble family in Palermo, the capital of the Italian island of Sicily, in 1668. He studied in Rome, where he showed a good disposition for literature, but he preferred to follow his vocation and, in 1702, he was commissioned by Pope Clemens XI to re-open the way of the faith in Japan.

In 1704 Sidotti reached Manila, where he served in the local hospital for four years while waiting for an opportunity to cross the sea to Japan.

During this period Sidotti also strove to learn the Japanese language, in order to make himself understood by the Japanese once he arrived in their country.

We know from Sidotti's own words that he had also studied Japanese for about three years before leaving Italy. (3) In Manila, according to Japanese scholars, he looked for Japanese who could teach him their language, but he found only descendants of banished converts who, by that time, could speak little Japanese. (4)

In many instances in the Japanese documents, on the other hand, it is clearly stated that Sidotti's knowledge of the language was very poor (5), which constituted a serious hindrance to his plan of evangelization.

His stay in Manila came to an end on 22 August 1708, when he left the Philippines bound for Japan.

The journey from Manila to the first Japanese islands.
The long-awaited opportunity had come for Sidotti. A ship called Santissima Trinidad (6) had been specially built in Manila at the expense of the Governor-General of the Philippines, don Domingo Zalbalburu Aecheverri. A general by the name of don Miguel de Eloriaga offered himself as captain of the ship.

They boarded the ship on 22 August at eight in the morning but, in the absence of a favourable wind, the actual departure had to be delayed until the 25th.

Before leaving Manila, Sidotti fixed his daily schedule, which he followed until he left the ship on the day of his landing. It is a very severe schedule which exemplifies the strong nature of Sidotti's character and the firm will to achieve the goal to which he devoted his whole life.

There are three versions of the schedule: the first, contained in the documents of the Casanatense Library is the *Instruction que diò el Abad Juan Bautista Sidotti de lo que se havria de hacer (?) en el viaje del Japon* ('Instructions given by the Abbot J.B. Sidotti as to what should be done during the journey to Japan').

This is probably the most reliable version and runs as follows:
'From 5.00 to 6.00 in the morning, meditation. From 6.45, examination of the meditation and devotions. From 7.00, first Mass. At 8.00, second Mass, thanksgiving prayers and breakfast. At 9.00, reading of spiritual books, confessions and lesson in the Japanese language. At 11.00, visit to the sick. At 12.00, dinner. At 1.00, rest. At 2.00, breviary. At 3.00, reading of spiritual books and lesson in the Japanese language. At 4.00, breviary and other devotions. At 6.00, Our Lady's Rosary. At 7.00, meditation. At 8.00, particular examination of the meditation and of the devotions of the whole day. At 9.00, supper and rest. At 10.00, general examination and particular prayers. At 11.00, go to bed.'

The second version of the schedule is that of the *Relacion del viage...*, which is very similar to the one quoted above, while the third, that of the Italian edition of 1718, is very different and rather unnatural in its disposition.

On Tuesday 9 October, after 48 days' voyage, at around two or three o'clock in the morning, the men on the ship could see Japan for the first time, in the form of the island of Yakushima (which they believed to be Tanegashima).

The first Japanese islands.
'Tuesday, 9th: At daybreak we were in view of four islands, of which we had already seen one around three in the morning...on three of them, there were volcanoes, two of which emitted fire. At midday, passing through these islands, we measured 30 degrees of

latitude...hence we can see another island, very high and long from one end to the other, and three more islets to the north of it. Having approached the said island, we can now also see other islands of Japan.

'Wednesday, 10th: We woke up in front of the island called Tanegashima which belongs to the Kingdom of Sacssuma (Satsuma). It lies at 30 degrees 48 minutes. It is very high and mountainous. On the southern part of it there is a wide plain, beside which we coasted at a distance of less than a league, so that we could see men angling on the rocks. There were houses on the said beach, but we did not see any inhabitant because they were frightened (by our presence). Then we saw ten or twelve headlands (?).

'The slope of the mountain is cultivated. This land extends from east to west for about nine leagues and from north to south for about three leagues. Its trees are for the most part pines.' (7)

This is the most detailed description we have of the first sight of Yakushima by the men on the Santissima Trinidad.

The four islands seen at three o'clock on the morning of 9 October are probably those of the Tokara archipelago: Kuchinoshima, Nakanoshima, Suwaseshima and Akusetikô, which are in fact of volcanic origin. The three islets seen to the north of Yakushima are probably the Ôsumi archipelago.

The houses seen on the coast may correspond to Yudomari, the westernmost village on the south coast. The mountain is Miyanoura-gadake, 1935 metres high, in the centre of the island.

The measurements given for Yakushima and its geographical position are not accurate. In fact, it has a circumference of thirty kilometres and lies at a latitude of 30 degrees 20 minutes north.

Sidotti's landing in Japan
On the morning of the day when Sidotti landed, there was an encounter in the sea off Yakushima between some Japanese fishermen and a few men sent off by Sidotti in a shallop.

Since Japanese nationals were involved, the authorities drew up a report, and this represents the earliest Japanese historical source related to Sidotti. From now on, therefore, Japanese sources can be used along with western ones. Indeed, the encounter is the only event in the history of Sidotti's landing in Japan to have the distinction of being reported by western and Japanese sources.

What follows is a synthesis of the facts of this encounter, gathered from various sources.

On Wednesday morning, 10 October, while sailing along the southern coast of Yakushima, off the village of Koidomari, about ten kilometres from the coast, the men on the ship saw two Japanese fishing-boats. They called them with various signals, but they did not approach, so Sidotti and the captain decided to send out a shallop with eleven armed men on board, one of them being a heathen Japanese brought from Manila who, for the occasion, put on Spanish clothes. The shallop approached one of the boats with seven men on board and, at a distance of about 18 metres, the Japanese began to speak with them. What happened during this encounter is not certain, because the sources give incomplete or different versions of the facts. According to Agustin de Madrid who relates the event in a most detailed way, the men sent by Sidotti, on the pretext of asking for water, learned that the policy followed by the shôgun was still strongly xenophobic. As to water, they should go to Nagasaki; in other places they could not disembark. They also learned that, in order to prevent a night landing, many sentries would be put on guard and bonfires lit all along the coast that same night.

At around eleven or twelve o'clock that morning, they returned to the ship. (8)

After the encounter with the Japanese boat, Sidotti continued his daily activities according to the schedule until, around five o'clock in the afternoon, he resolved to land that same night. Accordingly he had a long talk with the captain, and finally managed to persuade him to agree. After that, he set himself to write some letters. Later, he addressed the crew, thanking everybody, and finally performed the ceremony of Maundy.

Having finished this, he began to get ready to disembark. First of all, he prepared his luggage, which consisted of a small case trunk in which he put a picture of Our Lady, a missal, a breviary, a book on the Japanese language, everything necessary to say Mass, the holy oils, some devotional books, a small crucifix that belonged to Marcello Mastrilli (9), and two pairs of whips and three stiff cilices. To this, the general added some food and clothes. (10)

Sidotti wore a light blue kimono and a Japanese sword, and his head was shaved in the Japanese way. This he did—he explained to his questioners—to avoid being laughed at by Japanese not accustomed to seeing European attire, and in compliance with the trend of following the customs of the country where a missionary went to preach. (11)

All the preparations being finished, he boarded a shallop together with the general and other men. In strict silence they made towards the coast and went into an inlet. First, they tried one side of it, but the steep cliffs kept them from landing. So they rowed to the opposite side where they found other rocks which could be climbed. Sidotti decided to land there and, leaving a few men to guard the boat, had the rest accompany him up the slope. Eventually, they came to a plain where Sidotti said that he could now be left to go on alone. After all had prayed together, the general gave the missionary a bar of gold to be used to ensure that secrecy about him was maintained.

The place of landing is clearly stated in the Japanese sources: Matsushita, on the southern coast of Yakushima. Near Matsushita there is an inlet called Tônoura, which corresponds fairly well to the description given in the western sources. (12)

Though we know the events and the place of Sidotti's landing in a rather detailed way, there are still doubts about the hour when Sidotti left the ship.

According to most of the western sources, it was around eleven or twelve at night (13), but in the *Breve relazione...* it is stated that it was 4.45 in the morning of 11 October. (14)

There are scholars who uphold this theory, but my personal opinion is different. In fact, a few pages after the passage about the hour of departure, it is written that, going back to the ship, they got lost and '...they went on rowing until, the moon rising, they could see the ship. The moon appeared a little earlier than one hour before daybreak, but nothing could be seen...' (15)

Around 10 October, the sun rises a little before 6 o'clock and daybreak is about 30 minutes before it, that is, at 5.30.

According to the book, the moon must have risen at 4.30 and, in consequence, it is impossible for them to have departed at 4.45. On the other hand, the other theory seems to me to be much more acceptable. Considering the difficulties met with on landing, it is reasonable that this should have taken from midnight to 4.30 to accomplish. I therefore prefer to consider as the right version the one which states that the departure from the ship took place at midnight and the return to it at 8.30 a.m. The boat left Yakushima at midday (16) and arrived back in Manila on 29 October.

Sidotti in Japan.
The only sources available on the subject concerning Sidotti in Japan are Japanese.

When Sidotti was left alone on the plain, he probably walked toward the interior of the island until he came to a path which led to the village of Koidomari. There, on the path, he met a Japanese named Tôbei coming to get firewood.

When they met, Tôbei was afraid of the foreigner but gave him a little water to drink. After that, he went to inform two other peasants, Gojiuemon and Kiuemon of the village of Hiranai. They came to Matsushita and took Sidotti to Koidomari. Sidotti was lodged in Tôbei's house until the arrival of the officials who took him to Miyanoura, the main village of the island. (17)

From there, the authorities of Yakushima informed those of Kagoshima, under whose jurisdiction the island came. In their turn, they informed the Magistrate of Nagasaki who was in charge of matters concerning the foreigners in Japan. This Magistrate asked for the foreigner to be sent to him, but bad weather prevented the journey so, instead, four reports were sent, the last of which is dated 9 November.

Not much later, it was decided to set out on the journey notwithstanding the bad weather (18), and on 20 December 1708, Sidotti arrived in Nagasaki. (19) That same day he was cross-examined, but they could not understand each other. (20) Therefore, on 30 December, the Japanese summoned a Dutchman who was said to have studied some Latin many years before, and the cross-examination was able to proceed. Sidotti repeatedly expressed his wish to go to Edo, the capital, probably because he considered it the most suitable place for his preaching. Eventually, he was escorted there. It was 27 October 1709 when he left Nagasaki in a palanquin, and he arrived in Edo around the middle of December of the same year. (22)

13

The Meaning of Christianity in the Works of Endô Shûsaku

ADRIANA BOSCARO

'I, who am at the same time Christian, Japanese and a writer, am always conscious of the links between these factors in my life and, at the same time, of their various contrasting features. It saddens me that these three factors do not find unity or harmony within me, and that they often show their contradictions.' With these words, in 1963, Endô began his work *Nihonteki kansei no soko ni aru mono* 'The basis of Japanese sensibility'. (1)

My aim here is to see how Endô has succeeded in overcoming these difficulties and in giving a meaning to his literary works. And, in particular, to understand how on earth a Catholic writer should have become a best-seller in Japan, which he has been for years.

In order to do this, we must go back along the weary path which has brought Endô to his present position and follow the development of some of his themes. I think the best way of doing this is to present him through his own words in order to 'interpret' those words as little as possible even if, by so doing, I have to work through a double process of translation. I may, of course, say things which are obvious to those who know his works well, just as it will be necessary to repeat things which I have stated previously, but it is only by retracing step by step his tormented experience that we can arrive at a complete understanding of his works.

We all know about his early years and how he was christened while still a child. He himself always uses the passive voice of the verb when, as he does so often, he describes this event. This emphasizes his feeling that he had nothing to do with the event. And out of this come the allegoric expressions *yôfuku* and *wafuku*. Endô uses *yôfuku* 'western dress', to indicate Christianity, which was not made for him, in contrast to *wafuku* 'Japanese clothing'.

'...I put on, just as it was, western dress which was ready made and had been bought for me by my mother. But this clothing did not suit me: it was too big in some places, and too tight in others. The clothes and my body were not made for each other and, after a certain age, this made me feel uneasy.' (2)

For years this *yôfuku* was a kind of straitjacket or, even worse, a shirt of Nessus which Endô never managed to get off his back, even for a short time. In fact, it finally got into his blood. The young

Endô was perfectly aware that the problem lay in the fact that he had been christened in a non-Christian country, simply to please his mother. The logical consequence was that, in order to stay faithful to the words uttered at his christening, he took on a heavy burden: that of a foreigner in his own country. He tells us about events which marked his school life, when he was silent and afraid, feeling himself different from the others and yet unable to speak about it. (3) These were significant episodes in the double life the boy led: at school he pretended not to be Christian, while his home life was closely tied to the new faith. From this comes the dilemma of conscience which we find in many of his characters, as well as his inclination to be on the side of the weak, the humble, the fragile, the unsure, the traitors, those who give up easily. All these are characters in his novels, and he has a soft spot for them and defends them. From this, too, comes his sympathy for the psychology of Judas and of the crypto-Christians, whom he feels close to because of the torment of un-sureness. In fact, he interprets the 'treachery' of these people as a bitter cup to sip year after year in order to survive in surroundings which reject them. This is described vividly in *Haha naru mono* 'Mothers' (1969).

If Endô felt uneasy in his *yôfuku* when he was young, he felt even more uneasy when he realized that he had to come to terms not only with Christianity but also with western culture. This happened when he began to study French literature at Keiô University. He was reading the works of François Mauriac, Georges Bernaños and Julien Greene, and the gulf became wider and wider.

'I was reading their works and feeling conscious of an abyss. When I read about their conversions, I understood that they had returned to Christianity just as one returns to one's native land. But I, on the other hand, could not feel Christianity as a return home. And these writers never wrote about the torments of the foreigner. The more I read Christian literature, the more the gulf between them and me widened. This same sense of distance is naturally felt with regard to any foreign culture, but I felt the distance which separates me from the West even more keenly just because Christianity contains something which is com-pletely foreign to our minds.' (4)

If, on the one hand, this world which he wished to enter seemed ever more difficult to conquer, on the other, the crisis was made more acute by the fact that he did not agree with the way Christian-ity was being interpreted in Japan. In particular, with the way it was being presented to him by Yoshimitsu Yoshihiko, who was the director of his college in 1943. Endô did not share this philosopher's thoughts because they were too 'western' and were an attempt to apply the same criteria to the two worlds. Yoshimitsu described the modern world as 'an age which has lost the fullness of the Middle

Ages'. In *Watashi no bungaku* 'My literature' (1967), Endô asked a question:

'What sense do definitions such as 'the age which has lost the fullness of the Middle Ages' or 'the age which has lost sight of God' have for us Japanese? In Japanese history there were never Middle Ages in the sense meant by Jacques Maritain, nor was there a man-centred Renaissance. Thus our modern age should be quite different from that of the West. I am forever conscious of this question.' (5)

But Endô accepts the teachings of Christ and accepts them most of all at an emotional level as a necessity which cannot be renounced. The problem is how total acceptance can co-exist with the fact of being Japanese.

'But I was not born into a Catholic country. I was born in Japan, where neither the Christian tradition nor its culture or history existed. And I discovered something within my heart which is still not imbued with Christianity, a feeling which rejects Christianity... If you say that one can have faith without having such a history and such traditions, the argument would be over. But unfortunately the Japanese mind contains some element which makes it reject Christianity. I discovered a mysterious feeling of this kind both inside and outside myself during adolescence. I was bowled over by it.' (6)

In the work quoted at the beginning of this paper, we can read an account of what this 'feeling' consists of. In fact, it becomes a 'triple non-feeling': an insensibility towards God, towards sin, and towards death. And it is against this moral apathy, which is a basic component of the Japanese cultural identity, that Endô says he has to fight in order not to let himself be overcome by the subtle fascination of his own feelings.

'...in the world of Christianity, since man is not God, he accepts or rejects God, obeys him or resists him: in one way or another it is necessary to have either active acceptance or struggle, while for our pantheistic minds, which consider both the totality and the singular to be equal, there is no need to assume either a positive or a negative attitude. Our private aspiration is not the wish to surpass ourselves by struggling against earthly existence, or by painfully moaning or begging, but it is rather a certain tender nostalgia, and a desire to feel oneself reabsorbed... Up to now I have been speaking in broad terms of the difference between the western aesthetic sense, which possesses three fundamental characteristics (the sense of limitation, of tension, and of dynamism), and ours, which aspires to being absorbed just as it is because, in the last analysis, even after having been made a Catholic, Japanese sensibility seduces me and draws me into its world. Captured by the irresistible fascination of the poetry and art which are the fruits of this sensibility, I feel myself seized by panic. I am afraid because this world, which lulls me to sleep among the intangible veils of a transparent light and a subtle and delicate obscurity, is in reality the world of drowsiness, closed into a way with no exit, veiled by a melancholy nihilism. The sense of nothingness inherent in the Japanese sensibility at times makes me truly afraid.' (7)

This is what Endô calls the conflict between the pantheistic blood of the Japanese and the monotheistic blood of the Europeans. In order to become part of a world moulded by Christianity, he had to go through a renunciation which, in no sense paradoxical, was also a conquest.

He was able to overcome the moment of impasse only when he understood that it was not the *yôfuku* which was responsible for the uneasiness which oppressed him, but rather his resistance to admitting that such a *yôfuku* could *even* be good for him.

The critic Takeda Tomoju wrote in 1969: 'The fact that Endô admits there is no other life for him than that of accepting this "blood" is in effect an act of resignation... But it is just this resignation which makes Endô typically Japanese and has allowed him to produce such original literary works. For the first time there is a Catholic writer in Japan.' (8)

Endô's stay in France from 1950 to 1953 had a decisive effect on this. One has only to read *Nanji mo mata* 'And you too' (1964) (which, with *Rouen no natsu* 'Summer in Rouen' and *Ryûgakusei* 'Student abroad' now appears under the collective title *Ryûgaku* 'Studies abroad'), to perceive the linking thread of this transformation. The main character of *Nanji mo mata*, Takeda, a student of Sade, is nothing but an *alter ego* for Endô. Using transparent symbolism, Endô describes the process of the expulsion of Takeda's pantheistic blood in front of the castle of La Coste, which is surrounded by a snow storm and can be reached only after superhuman efforts. The 'castle' represents western culture. But while *Ryûgaku* presents us with these ideas in a narrative form, they had already been expressed by Endô in such works as 'Kamigami to kami to (H.N. sama)' 'Gods and God (to H.N.)' in 1955:

> For we who are the sons of gods, it is not possible, solely by means of an intellectual knowledge of Catholicism, to understand the psychology, language or way of life of those who are the sons of God. Even if there were no conflict between us and Catholicism and even if we accepted that faith, that does not mean that we would become Catholics, because Catholicism, like Marxism, is not just a simple *-ism*. In fact, what is most important lies beyond the *-ism*. If a young Frenchman lost his faith and then found it again after some intellectual

searching, it would be a question of repossessing his faith. Because, in this case, his traditional blood plays the main role. For us Japanese, the intellectual conquest of Catholicism is not transmitted immediately into an act of faith in the Absolute. In fact, at times, the more we enter into Catholicism, the more we feel our pantheistic blood resisting. We have to pass through the purification of blood and through suffering in order to reach conversion.' (9)

The stay in France, which could have been a second home for the Catholic Endô, served instead to lead him to the discovery of his own country, the country to which his blood was drawing him back. If it is true that literature deals with the innermost reality of man, when Endô discovered this reality within himself, he could no longer ignore his inner drama. He felt the necessity to make the beings in whose veins his own blood ran participate in his personal discovery of reality. The culminating moment of his decision to become a novelist came when he discovered this feeling of 'being Japanese' in the fullest sense of the word, with a total participation in the life of his compatriots—that is, in a life without God.

The 'double-foreignness' of Endô, that of being a Catholic in his own country and a Japanese outside it, places him in the best position to make a bridge between the two worlds, the monotheistic and the pantheistic, and to be a bearer of a God into a world without God. In my opinion, Endô's route over this bridge, a route which has brought him to his present success, and which treats openly of God in works destined for a wide public, runs along two parallel paths. From the idea expressed above of the engulfing, annihilating, nihilistic force of Japanese sensibility, come the two themes of the swamp and the *baka*. From the moment when one comes out of the swamp by means of the *baka*, the final link in arriving at an understanding of God is the 'maternal' concept of religion. It seems worth stopping for a moment to analyse these three points.

The swamp (*numa*) is more or less the state of passive non-action which characterizes the concave (*boko*) 'Japanese world', a world without boundaries or limits, which is seen in contrast to the convex (*deko*) 'western world' with its boundaries. The swamp is the daily refusal to face reality, a reality which would disturb the apparent superficial tranquility of each day. It is a state of somnolent submissiveness which covers a total indifference towards everything which does not affect us directly. The only one who can break this crust of indifference is the *baka*, the messenger of the love of God who is unconsciously accepted by the inhabitants of the swamp.

It is not easy to give a definition or, even less, a translation, of *baka*. His main characteristics are the total readiness to love his neighbour and to pay in person, but also in certain cases an irritating candour with regard to the facts of human life. A *baka* is a person who leads others only by example, without any personal ambition. Through his conduct and his words, the *baka* insinuates the doubt that a different ideal of life can exist, and he succeeds in provoking the necessary crack to let the message of love pass through.

Let us now look at two typical works in which the 'swamp' and the *baka* exemplify what was said above. These two works are *Obakasan* (1959) and *Menamugawa no Nipponjin* 'The Japanese of the Menam' (1973). In *Obakasan*, which Francis Mathy has translated neatly as 'Wonderful fool', the daily life of a brother and sister, Takamori and Tomoe, is described in all its banality and selfishness. The intervention from outside comes in the shape of Gaston Bonaparte, an awkward Frenchman, who plummets like a stone into the swamp where the two are vegetating. According to Endô, God needs this human tool because the minds of the inhabitants of the swamp are too sleepy and dull. They can only be aroused by actions which shake them. These are acts of love taken as far as the sacrifice of someone they can identify with. Once the mind has had this hard shock, it is ready to accept love and thus itself to love.

Fourteen years later, this same conflict which exists in *Obakasan* between a westerner and the Japanese can be found in *Menamugawa no Nipponjin* between two Japanese, although one of them wears a cassock. On the one side there is Yamada Nagamasa, the soldier; on the other, the priest, Pedro Kibe. This work, a drama in three acts which takes place in seventeenth-century Siam, has Nagamasa as its central character. The other two main characters, Pedro Kibe with whom he is in spiritual conflict, and Kunswat, the Grand Chamberlain of Siam with whom he is in conflict over territorial supremacy, revolve around him. Here, the 'swamp' spreads out and involves everyone to some extent, but in a different way from in the preceding work. It is *also* a necessary 'evil'—necessary to make the lotus flowers of truth and goodness blossom. *Menamugawa no Nipponjin* marks a step forward, for Endô no longer sees Japan as a 'swamp' which swallows up the seed of Christianity and makes it rot as in *Chinmoku* 'Silence' (1966), but as an entity which is capable of producing individuals who will fight for an ideal and sacrifice themselves for it. The figure of the *baka* Kibe personifies all Endô's hopes of finding a way of communicating with his fellow-Japanese.

The final obstacle between the Japanese and Christianity is something Endô defines as the 'paternal aspect' of that religion. According to him, it was this aspect of Christianity which the missionaries of the sixteenth century presented. That is why the Japanese have always thought of the Christian God as a vindictive and fearful deity. Endô discusses this in various works, and in particular in one dated 1967, which has the significant title *Chichi no shûkyô haha no shûkyô* 'Father-religion and mother-religion':

'Masamune Hakûcho wrote somewhere that he believed that

God was a fearful God and he was not alone in thinking this. Almost all the men of letters from the Meiji period onwards, when they thought of God in the abstract, imagined Him as a figure who judges and punishes the secrets of everyone's inner life, the things no one can know. Most of them considered Christianity to be the religion of condemnation rather than one of peace and love. In my view, the cause of the impatience which the Japanese felt unconsciously with regard to Christianity was not merely a result of a feeling of difference and distance, but of the mistaken way of approaching God and his doctrine.' (10)

This reference to Masamune Hakûcho could lead one to say something about the effect that the theories of Uchimura Kanzô (1861-1930) had on Meiji intellectuals and writers, and about the distorted view of Christianity which they held, but that would lead us too far away. However, one must not forget how much this contributed to the formation of an atmosphere which was openly hostile to the coupling of literature and religion. But let us go back to Endô's idea of a 'mother-religion'.

The I-protagonist of *Chûsana machi nite* 'In the little town' (1969) says:

'In the Japanese mind, there is a tendency to allow only the maternal aspect of religion to flourish. In other words, the religion which pardons rather than that which judges and punishes. For most Japanese, the Christian God is the unmoving Centre of Creation, the severe Highest who judges, punishes and gets angry like a father. For the Japanese, who preferred to imagine this supreme figure with maternal connotations, Christianity seemed to be a religion which was too severe and difficult to approach... The Japanese search for the figure of the mother in every religion.' (11)

The blind trust in a protecting divinity, typical of the Japanese mentality, is due to the fact that, in general, the Japanese are inclined to find help and security in the mercy of the divinity, rather than to make any personal efforts. But in Endô's case, there is also a very personal experience: this is the link with his own mother, whom he writes about so much. I shall not discuss this here, as it is very well known, and because it is closely linked to his idea of the *yôfuku*. However, Endô suggests a way to the purification of that 'pantheistic' blood which tends to be gently absorbed into the swamp where there is neither effort nor sin: this may be through the emotional relationship between a son whose behaviour makes his mother unhappy and a mother who forgives everything. According to what he wrote, it was the sight of an old *fumie* (a Christian tablet on which suspected believers were made to tread to prove their innocence), worn down by the thousands of feet which had sorrowfully trampled on it, which suddenly made him discover the 'maternal' side of Christ:

'I felt I had discovered something which closed the distance between me and Christianity, between Japan and Christianity —which has been my problem for so long. The face of Christ in the *fumie* which I saw after it had been stepped on by so many people was so worn down that it no longer retained the shape of the original majestic, noble and triumphant features, but was now a lean, tired and sad face. But this face was the only thing which was able to reduce the distance between Japan and Christianity... In my view, there are two types of religion. Borrowing Erich Fromm's definition, one is a paternal religion, the other maternal. In the paternal religion, God is to be feared: he is a God who judges and punishes the sins of man, and who gets angry. The maternal religion is different: God forgives in the same way that a mother forgives a naughty child. It is a religion in which God suffers alongside man.' (12)

This passage from a 'paternal religion' to a 'maternal religion' is the thematic thread of *Chinmoku*, the thesis clearly identified by Etô Jun when he says that 'the face of Jesus on the *fumie* is the maternal aspect of Japan.'

In order to make the figure of a friendly God more understandable to the Japanese, Endô interprets him in *Iesu no shôgai* 'The Life of Jesus' (1973) as 'companion Jesus' (*dôhansha Iesu*). In fact, after the experience of *Chinmoku* in 1966, he had declared that the only acceptable interpretation of Christ for the Japanese was that of a 'companion', just as a mother is a lifelong companion. (13) Not a new idea for the West (14), but this was the first time it had been so strongly presented to the Japanese. In *Iesu no shôgai*, we are shown the image of the God of Love on whose face there is always a shadow of sadness, and who destroys the image of a majestic and severe God once and forever.

But Endô also understands that it is difficult to make a God of Love acceptable to a daily reality which seems to reject him.

'It is easy to say "the Love of God" and "the God of Love". Men who live in an implacable reality feel only the cold silence of God, not His love. In the present severe reality, it is easier to think of a God of anger and punishment than to believe in a God of Love. In the Old Testament, although the love of God was often spoken about, the image of a God who inspired terror was stronger in people's minds. How can we aspire to God's love when there seems to be no reward for the person who weeps and who is spiritually poor?' (15)

For Endô, the saddest reality surrounding us is the lack of love. And at the basis of the teaching of Christianity, it is just this love which expresses itself in the capacity to share suffering and penetrate the sadness of others. This is why his Jesus should be described as 'weak' (the *muryoku naru Iesu*) in order to understand the weak, as 'suffering' to be able to understand the suffering. His Jesus knows only that 'men have need of an eternal friend. They need a companion who shares this suffering and sadness, and can weep together with them, like a mother.' (16)

One might object that such an appeal to love is universal and not exclusive to Christianity. But only in the figure of the historical Christ does Endô recover a capacity to suffer as well as to love, a need for sacrifice which goes as far as the giving of oneself. With this firm conviction, he can now write about very different subjects and situations. However, the linking thread is always the aridity of daily life which can only be redeemed by the disinterested love of an individual.

By now, Endô has fully realized what was proposed during his stay in France, when he guessed what his future work would be. Having set out in search of a second homeland where Catholicism reigned, he discovered instead the enormous gulf between himself and the foreign country he was in. This helped him to realize that his only hope was to try to find Christianity where it did not exist, in Japan. This meant creating it in the world of art, making himself a writer, and remaining both Christian and Japanese. This is what he calls 'his own theme': that of creating 'literature which will accompany men forever'.

'It is difficult to be a Christian writer in Japan because one is forever torn between monotheistic Christianity and the pantheistic world around one. The first problem to face, as Sako Jun'inchirô rightly says, is that of becoming a Christian in Japan, of discovering God in a pantheistic society.' (17)

Some years ago, the Catholic writer Takeda Tomoju, to whom we owe a careful analysis of Endô's work, wrote: 'One cannot understand the main theme of Endô's writing if one does not take into consideration the drama of his mind in relation to Catholicism. Catholicism, which occupies an enormous place in Endô's inner world, makes him clearly conscious of the difference between East and West. This consciousness of being doubly a stranger, of inhabiting a different space, gives rise to his cosmopolitanism. Spiritually he is western, and criticizes the Japanese, who are strangers to him, from this viewpoint. Having Japanese blood, however, he can also criticize the West, a foreign world. His position is clearly not one to be envied, for he should find his own country in one of the two, but in reality he will have to live as an exile in both of the two worlds he likes.' (18)

These words are true, but the reactions of the public are quite different. The thing which goes straight to the heart of the Japanese is the drama provoked in Endô by being both Catholic (that is, 'foreign') and Japanese, far more than simply the question of the faith of an observing Catholic. This has meant that, while his popularity increases on the one side, on the other, the gulf which separates him from the official line of the Church gets wider and wider. This led him to comment bitterly:

'I always feel a sense of loneliness which arises from the fact of not succeeding in doing anything but write what I write, and what I write does not enjoy the moral support of the theologians and priests.' (19)

It is enough to say that *Chinmoku* has been banned in the Tokyo diocese, while passages of *Shikai no hotori* 'Around the Dead Sea', (1973) and his view of Christ as an anti-hero in *Iesu no shôgai* have shocked a great many people.

However, Endô is not alone in Japan. As well as a strong group of other Christian writers (Miura Shumon, Sono Ayako, Sawako Ariyoshi, Miura Ayako, to mention a few) whose works appeal to the public, he gets theological support from the words and works of Father Inoue Yôji. These can be summed up under two headings: (a) the clear distinction which must exist between the Old and New Testaments, since it is the latter which can present a religious reality acceptable to the Japanese; and (b) the necessity to get to know God not by the traditional way of western Thomistic theology, but through experience and, above all, by personal experience. Inoue also suggests that the oriental attachment to the 'void' can be a way of reaching God. (20) Thus, in different ways, one through theology and the other through literature, they are both in search of truth.

After having overcome many obstacles and having written narrative works which stand as fixed points in the history of Christianity in Japan, Endô is now very near to the final stage: that of creating works which, as well as attracting a large non-Christian public through the message of love, may also serve as meeting point with the Church.

SECTION 3

Politics
and
War

14

On the Political Thinking of Yamaji Aizan (1864-1917)

MARGRET NEUSS

It must be admitted at the outset that Yamaji Aizan's political thought is of minor importance compared with his role as a historian during the Meiji (1868-1912) and Taishô (1912-1926) periods. Nor does Aizan rank among the major thinkers or important socialists of twentieth-century Japan. He was, however, respected as a gifted journalist and author of historical biographies and treatises in his time. As I have already published an article on Aizan's achievements in the field of historiography, I will not go into the details of this aspect here. (1) My intention is to treat Aizan, who was the first person in Japan to propagate 'state socialism' (*kokka shakaishugi*), on the basis of his political ideology, certainly the darker side of his thinking.

With regard to their theories on state socialism both Aizan and Kita Ikki based their respective theories on already-existing ideological concepts of the period around 1906, but their ideas should also be seen in connection with the state socialism as formulated twenty years later by Takabatake Motoyuki, who is said to be the originator of Japanese state socialism. Thus Aizan is in reality only one of the earliest exponents of state socialism in Japan. Nevertheless, I am treating him here as an individual thinker because of the limited space available. I shall first outline the main points of Aizan's conception of state socialism, and then contrast these roughly with the ideas of Kita Ikki and Takabatake Motoyuki, so as to evaluate their importance for Japanese state socialism. On the one hand, the common ground shared by the three of them must be investigated and, on the other, the specific differences be outlined, so as to show how Aizan was caught up—like many of his contemporaries—in the intellectual dilemma of the Meiji period, the choice between society or state and the individual.

The life and career of Aizan is not that of a typical Meiji period intellectual, who would attend the Imperial University in Tokyo, and then, automatically, enter on a career as a civil servant. Instead, Aizan's education was that of a self-taught man, and in his career he showed independence, always refusing to enter government service. He had been born into a samurai family of reduced circumstances, which had found itself on the side of the losers during the Meiji

Restoration of 1868. At the age of seventeen, Aizan had to accept work as an assistant teacher so as to earn the family's living. His mother had died young, and his father, who had been married off to her against his will, had become an alcoholic and was unable to hold down a job. Thus, Aizan grew up in an incomplete family and lacked emotional bonds during much of his youth. However, this does not seem to have caused obvious psychological problems for him in later life, as far as one can tell. Instead, he seems to have used these experiences in a positive way. Thus, at an early stage he was forced to come to independent decisions and to make up his own mind, a trait of character which he kept. In his obituary, Tokutomi Shohô emphasized Aizan's fighting and independent spirit of opposition all through his life. (2)

On the other hand, Aizan's experiences in his youth made him develop a special esteem for solidarity and for life in some kind of community. It was also very likely this search for community (*Gemeinschaft*) which caused him to turn to Christianity, for it was the community of the Christian church which he praised in 1900 in the following words: 'In making heaven its model, it (the church) is the best and highest community of life in this world.' (3)

In his response to Christianity, Aizan does not represent the type of career-conscious samurai as defined by Irwin Scheiner. (4) For him, Christianity and a hope for a spiritual reform of Japan were connected, as the latter meant overcoming the materialistic spirit of his age to which he objected.

Aizan came into contact with Christianity when learning English at a Methodist missionary school. In 1886 when he was twenty-two, he was baptized. In 1890 he went to Fukui prefecture as a missionary, and in 1891 he became editor-in-chief of the Methodist journal *Gokyô* 'Orthodoxy'. Yet he was not limited in his thinking to Christian dogma. Besides his work for *Gokyô* he contributed critical articles to *Kokumin no tomo* and *Kokumin shinbun*, and became a member of the Min'yûsha. In 1891 he received a prize for his article 'Eiyûron' 'On heroes' published in *Jogaku zasshi*. In 1899 he went to Nagano to become the editor of the *Shinano mainichi shinbun*, returning to Tokyo in 1903 to found his own journal, *Dokuritsu hyôron* 'Independent Criticism', which he ran, with only short breaks, until his death in 1917. From February until November 1904 he called the journal *Nichiro sensô jikki* 'True reports on the Russo-Japanese war', which accurately described its role as a kind of propaganda periodical, but in February 1905 he went back to the earlier name of *Dokuritsu hyôron*. Apart from his journalistic activities, Aizan's only active participation in politics was the founding of the *Kokka Shakai-tô* 'The State Socialist Party'. But according to Yamaizumi Susumu even his direct involvement with the party's foundation is not unambiguously proved. Aizan himself, looking back at a later date, was very noncommittal. (5)

The party ceased to exist in 1909, but even before that its activities were limited to participation in the *Fûsen Senkyo Rengôkai*, 'The League for General Elections', founded in 1905, and to joining in the demonstration against fare increases on the Tokyo tramways in March 1906. However, this activity did correspond with the party's principles, which demanded concentrating on communal and regional reforms, in an attempt to achieve self-government. The party's other aims, as defined in its manifesto, were in the nature of reforms as well. They definitely were not aimed at revolutionizing the system, which is why Akamatsu Katsumarô in his *Nihon shakai undôshi* will not accept the Kokka Shakai-tô as a socialist party. However, its goals were distinguished by an acceptance of the state in its dominant role as 'protector of the people's well-being, patron of the sciences and arts, protector of industry and patron of an international community'. (6)

Aizan's reluctance to involve himself in the party can be seen as an attempt to remain independent of outside political and social ties, a result of his disappointment in the development of the earlier People's Rights Movement, with which Aizan—as was shown by Oka Toshirô (7)—had some loose connections. Logically, he refused to stand for parliament: he said he preferred to remain among those who attacked the present abuses, without belonging to a political organization. This is also why he found himself most in agreement with the socialists' criticism of existing conditions, and consequently defended vehemently their right to a free expression of their opinions, in spite of the attacks on himself by some members of the Heiminsha group. Thus, in 1906 he said in answer to the conservative thinker Inoue Tetsujirô, who followed closely the official government line, 'Where there is no freedom of conscience, there is no truth. Where there is no truth, there is no humanity (*jô*); and where there is no humanity, how can there be loyalty and patriotism?' (8)

His openmindedness caused contemporary Christians like Uemura Masahisa to criticize him, as they expected more Christian dogmatism in his opinions. Of course, his demand for independence and freedom of thought did not keep him from following certain tendencies in the political thinking of his day. Thus, his interest in the Edo period, and in historical biography, was stimulated by the reassessment of this era of Japanese history and of the country's traditions, which was prevalent in the 1880s. Yet it was only Aizan who managed to break with the existing historiography and offered an alternative to it in his so-called *minkan shigaku* 'popular historiography'. No doubt influenced by Fukuzawa Yukichi and by the *heimin-shugi* 'plebeianism' of Tokutomi Sohô, Aizan attacked academic history, claiming it dealt only with the collection and philological treatment of source materials, and with the description of governments, neglecting completely the history of the people. Also new in his model of history was his view of the dynamics of the historical process as the interaction of developments in the material sphere, which followed natural laws, with the personal achievements of individuals. These achievements he treated in numerous biographies of historical personalities, but finally he attributed only relative weight to the roles of heroes in history when he said, for example, 'Heroes are only the bubbles on the wide ocean of history.' On the other hand, he wrote monographs like *Nihon no rekishi ni okeru jinken hattatsu no konseki* 'Vestiges of the development of man's rights in Japanese history' or *Gendai Nihon kinken-shi* 'The antecedents of present-day monetary power in Japan'. In emphasizing the historical conditioning of thought, Aizan was strongly influenced by Ogyû Sorai, whom he also treated in a lengthy biography.

Aizan's state socialism could be seen in connection with this 'materialistic' approach to history, as Hattori Shisô has called it, yet it is based less on historico-theoretical conclusions than on immediate causes like the Russo-Japanese war and the pacifism of the Heiminsha socialists. Aizan, being attacked by the socialists because of his approval of the Russo-Japanese war, found himself obliged to define his socialism from a defensive standpoint. This is why there are many inconsistencies in his expositions, the essential points of which I shall discuss in this paper.

Any understanding of Aizan's state socialism must be based on just four articles published in his own journal, the *Dokuritsu hyôron*, during 1905 and 1906, that is, in the period during which the Kokka Shakai-tô was founded. The titles of the relevant articles are: 'Shakai-shugi hyôron' (1905), 'Wareware no sosen no shakai seisaku' (1905), 'Kokka shakai-shugi kôgai' (1905), 'Kokka shakai-shugi to shakai-shugi' (1906); and they appeared together under the title 'Shakai-shugi kanken' in 1906. One further article, 'Genji shakai mondai oyobi shakai-shugisha' 'The present-day social problems and the socialists' was written in 1908. This is, however, only an outline of the development of the socialist movement in Japan up to that time, and does not advance any original thoughts on socialist theory.

Aizan begins his first article 'Shakai-shugi hyôron' 'Critique of socialism' by defending the idea of socialism against the government and the public, and shows in it that he had merely a vague concept to begin with. He argues that there is nothing new or particular in socialism, but that there have always existed equivalent ideologies. Socialism is just a new name for the idea which has been approved and lauded as the humane government (*jinsei*) of the Chinese emperors. Those who claim that socialism aims at dismantling the existing system (*genseido*) are treating socialists as mentally deranged, without seriously trying to discuss their position. This kind of defence is nothing original, as Kôtoku Shusui had already pointed out in 1902 in his *Shakai-shugi to kokutai* that there was no contradiction between *kokutai* ('national essence, polity') and socialism.

In his second article of 3 May 1905, Aizan considers in detail the thesis that in Japanese antiquity a socialist policy had already been applied. It becomes evident that, for Aizan, socialism is a sort of moral imperative which presupposes a tendency to communality. In this, Aizan is directed by a familistic concept of the state typical of the Meiji era, and by the Confucian idea of a humane government (*jinsei*) which, however, he ascribes only to the Japanese emperor. Devotion to the emperor, he says, is natural as it was he who saved the people from despotism and slavery. Considering the polity as a great family with the emperor as its head and all the other members equal, like brothers and sisters, Aizan claims that real estate and all other possessions, even when privately administered, used originally to be common property. A similar political concept of limited egalitarianism in which all the emperor's subjects are equal, was advanced by Kita Ikki in his *Nihon kaizô hôan taikô* 'Plan for the reorganization of Japan'. The objection that Japan's centralization of government under an emperor followed the Chinese example, Aizan answers chauvinistically by admitting that this was true, but that in Japan the humane government was realized much more thoroughly than in China itself. This idealization can be explained to some extent by Aizan's nationalism, and by the fact that for him at this point it was more important to elaborate the socialist principle and to eliminate the fear of it than to investigate the historical realities.

He recognizes quite adequately, however, the realities of his times: in his first article on socialism, for instance, he comments on the economic system, saying that it is a grave mistake to assume that there always has been, and still exists, unrestricted competition. For Aizan, this is possible only under circumstances of equitable distribution of property and a preponderance of private ownership. The contemporary inequalities of possession clearly show the disadvantages of such a system. Besides, there have always been areas which had to be protected by the state. Private ownership has never been fully realized. As the state has always been quite ready to claim from a citizen the supreme contribution, his life, it is not surprising that it should also have made claims on his real estate and other property as well.

Aizan sees one of the basic faults and major dangers in Japan as being the unequal relationship between landed owners and tenants. This, too, proves his above-average penetration of the contemporary social scene, but instead of demanding the overthrow of the existing economic order, as his contemporary socialists did, Aizan only

97

wanted the present system to be modified. He wanted, for example, to give the older, more influential members of a village a bigger share in the decisions, and his suggestions for the improvement of the infrastructure, forestry, and finance, all aim at breaking the monopoly held by a few rich people (*fûgô*), or at least holding it in check by government intervention.

It was this criticism of the existing system above all else which linked Aizan with the socialists. By 'system' he understood primarily capitalism and individualism. He thus says '...as a patriot, I too am of the opinion that the present-day individualistic system of capitalism presents rather a danger.' (9) Aizan saw this danger not so much in the system as such, but rather in its representatives, the capitalists themselves, who gained ever more influence in political decisions, and thus endangered the state: 'For a patriot (*aikokusha*), the first principle must remain the inviolability of political authority.' (10) In his *Gendai Nihon kinken-shi*, published later, he demonstrates in detail how the connection between the government and the capitalists or the rich was reversed to one in which the government was slowly dominated by the rich. As has already been mentioned, the point that isolated Aizan from the socialists of his time was the pacifism of the Heiminsha. In the article I am treating here, Aizan claims that the successes in the Russo-Japanese war prove wrong the assumption that the soldiers were not enthusiastically motivated by the Japanese war aims. On the contrary, their victories prove the soldiers' feeling of responsibility toward their own people. On the other hand, Aizan sees in the state's claim to the life of the individual a reason for the individual to claim participation in decisions by means of the franchise. This is the only way which can assure that the advantages gained by a victorious war do not accrue only to the upper classes of Japanese society. Warfare and universal suffrage are inseparable for Aizan, 'as it is an effrontery to demand that someone lay down his life for his country, but not be allowed to vote'. (11)

The specifically socialist conception of the state, by which he tries to set himself off against contemporary socialists, Aizan presents only in the last two articles. It is interesting to note that, here again, the national defence of the state plays a decisive role. It is this, I think, which distinguishes Aizan's state socialism, and which proves how much he depended in his thinking on the situation of his time, that is, on the Russo-Japanese war. As long as imperialism was rampant, if a weak nation like Japan was to maintain herself among the major powers, a strong government was imperative. This is not, however, his overt argument. Instead, he claims to be a scientific socialist in the Marxist sense, arguing from Japanese history.

The term *kokutai* 'national essence'—which Aizan, unlike other nationalists, uses only rarely—he defines in the dual manner typical of Meiji-nationalist thinking: it means the unbroken genealogy of the imperial house on the one hand and, on the other, which is the point here, it is defined as 'communality' (*kyôdô seikatsu*). 'Communality' (in German, *Gemeinschaft*) is both the origin and goal of a state. Origin, because a polity in its early phases of development comes into being through expansion and has at the same time to defend its realm. When it is well established, the same aims are paramount: possessions have to be protected from foreign intervention, and the country's riches to be distributed equitably among all its inhabitants. While Aizan accepts an absolute authority of the state (*sono ken'i wa zettai nari*) with regard to defence inasmuch as it can lay claim to the lives of its citizens, in practice the authority is limited, as the government must not without need interfere with an individual's occupation, such as owning land. (12)

'Humane government' (*jinsei*) consists of the obligation of the state to encourage the individual's development, and in this Aizan refers to the Confucian classics as well as to Ogyû Sorai. Yet, like Sorai, Aizan confines himself by subordinating the individual, in the last analysis, to the authority of the state; and, again like Sorai, he is unable to make the state into the object of investigation itself.

Aizan could not accept the socialist theory of a class struggle as this would have been contrary to the internal solidarity necessary for defence. Also, he saw the polity as a functional and organic grouping of three 'classes' (*jinmin* 'the people', *fûgô* 'the rich', and *kokka* 'the state'), one of which always acted as mediator between the other two. In the Japanese case, according to Aizan, this duty lay with the state or, more precisely, with emperor and government. It is the emperor who is to protect the weak from the strong: thus, in Aizan's Japan, the common people from a minority of influential plutocrats. However, Aizan's theory also allows for the possibility of a coalition of the common people (*jinmin*) and the rich (*fûgô*) against a government (*kokka*) grown too strong.

In this concept of state there are points in common between Aizan and Kita Ikki. Kita also wants to protect the state, that is, the emperor, from the influence of corrupt politicians. But while, for Aizan, there is at least theoretically a distinct possibility of conflict between state and society, which is not realized only because of the ascendancy of the defence of the nation, for Kita state and society are indivisible. Kita believes that state and individual are identical, the state having a truly existing personality (*jitsuzon no jinkaku*), resulting from the union of emperor and people. Whereas Aizan wanted to integrate the plutocrats into the system, Kita wanted to eliminate them.

Aizan was convinced of having created, with his theory of the three classes, an original Japanese form of socialism consistent with the imperial way of Japan. Kita Ikki expressly rejected this familistic interpretation of the national essence (*kotukai*) as being absurd. For him it was only the Meiji Restoration which, by legally establishing a 'social democracy', took the first step along the way towards state socialism as a system.

In contradistinction to Kita, Aizan developed no programme for a new society. Instead, he emphasized externally a strengthening of the state, and internally an amelioration of the position of the weak, by reform on the local level, by universal franchise, and by an acknowledgement of the role of the trade unions. These he considered prerequisites for gradual changes within the system. Kita on the other hand, as is well known, hoped for changes by way of a revolution.

In Aizan's nationalism and his commitment to a universal franchise, there are parallels with the position of Ferdinand Lasalle. But I hope that I have made it plain that his thoughts were very heterogeneous. This is particularly evident if one considers them from the aspect of modernity versus traditionalism. They might then be described as a mixture of modern and traditional forms of thought. For instance, his nationalism is typically romantic and traditional, as shown by his demand in 1892 that Japan enter the universal history and thereby fulfil an ancestral mission. On the other hand, he is not as xenophobically narrow in his outlook as some of his contemporaries. Foreign influences and impacts he considers basically positive, as they serve the inevitable progress of culture and civilization.

He is often critical of the narrow interpretation of *kokutai*, based on the edict on education. Even when he claims for Japan the role of model and instructor in Asia and shows racial prejudices against the Koreans or Russians, he does not approve of an expansionist Japan, unlike Tokutomi Sohô, for instance. He wanted Japan only to guard her independence in an age of the survival of the fittest. Aizan's idea of the state was familistic and influenced by Confucianism, conditionally assigning an absolute role to the state's authority, and was thus traditional. On the other hand, it was also modernistic and functional in not accepting familism as an absolute ethical value—he himself, influenced by his own bitter experiences, rejected severely the demand for absolute piety from children. For Aizan, familism was just an expression of the interdependence of the members of a family, which was to strengthen the community outside. On the national level, this was the role played by Aizan's form of state socialism.

If one considers functionalism a criterion of modern thought, then Aizan is more progressive than Kita, in at least beginning to distinguish between state, that is, government, and society. However, Kita too is quite capable of functionalist thought, as for instance in his theory of the emperor as an organ of the state. Influenced by the experiences of the Russo-Japanese war, both equally consider the state as primarily an instrument of warfare, and only secondarily as an instrument of social reform. Takabatake Motoyuki, who was the first to translate the whole of Marx's *Capital* and is said to be the originator of state socialism in Japan, is much more explicit and modern as regards the functionalistic approach to the state than either Aizan or Kita. But as he began to develop his state socialism only in 1919, he started from a rather different position, being influenced by the Russian revolution and the then Japanese socialist movement in which he had taken part. His starting point was the nation, not as one among many in an international context, but as an institution faced with the problems of modern mass society For him the necessity for a strong state arose not from military needs, but rather from human nature, which he saw as basically egoistical and profit-motivated. It is this egoism of the individual which is the base for all kinds of power, and the task of the state is to hold this society in check (*tôsei no kinô*), for as long as society exists, there exists within it the function of order and control, (*Shakai ga sonritsu suru ijô wa kanarazu soko ni chitsujo mata wa tôseijô no kinô ga sonzai suru*). This Takabatake himself calls his 'functionalist nationalism' (*kinô-teki kokka-shugi*).

If one remembers that Aizan, too, assigned to the state in its narrowest sense the function of a mediator between different social groups, some similarity to Takabatake can be seen. However, their starting points are completely different. Takabatake in 1919 had arrived at a pessimistic or even cynical world-view and saw the state primarily as an instrument of power. Aizan, on the contrary, never lost his optimistic belief in the feasibility of an organic system of society through a change in the morality of the rich and a strengthening of the authority of the state. Where Takabatake showed disappointment with man in general, Aizan and Ikki argued mainly from disillusionment with the existing political system and the influence of the new plutocratic aristocracy. But whereas Kita and Takabatake in their potentially totalitarian concept of the state clearly formulated fascist ideology and had considerable influence, Aizan's thinking, though plainly on the line of *kokka-shugi*, had not yet had any great influence on his contemporaries. The main reason, I think, is that his alternative to the contemporary political system was looked for in the past, whereas the situation after the Russo-Japanese war required a concept for the future. He also failed to foresee the possibility of a too powerful state, stressing, as he did, solely the detrimental influence of the economy.

15

The Personnel Policy of Army Minister Araki Sadao: the Tosa-Saga Theory Re-examined

JACOB KOVALIO

General Araki Sadao was the first Army Minister to be nominated in Japan after the Manchurian Incident. The Araki administration lasted from 12 December 1931 to 20 January 1934. Japanese and non-Japanese historians, after the Pacific War, have unanimously described the Araki ministership as a time of strife in the high ranks of the Army Ministry and the General Staff between two antagonistic groups: the Imperial Way faction (*kôdôha*) and the Control faction (*tôseiha*). (1) This approach has identified Araki Sadao as the head of the *kôdôha* and Major-General Nagata Tetsuzan as the leader of the *tôseiha*.

In the light of the *kôdôha-tôseiha* theory, the Araki period in the Army Ministry was one in which the Imperial Way faction had the upper hand in the high command, a situation that supposedly allowed Araki to try to implement what are considered to have been his main ideas and policies: a personnel policy based mostly on preference for officers hailing from the former feudal domains of Tosa and Saga (today's Kôchi and Saga prefectures); an aggressive foreign policy centered on rabid anti-Sovietism, both stemming from the ultra-nationalistic Imperial Way ideology that justified Japan's expansion into foreign lands due to its spiritual 'superiority' embodied in the imperial throne; preference for spiritual indoctrination over technological modernization in the training of the military; and support for all kinds of groups of radical Young Officers (*seinen shôkô*) aiming at a 'Shôwa Restoration' (*Shôwa ishin*). This was an amorphous idea, the main ingredient of which was to have been the return of direct rule to the emperor, a reality that had not existed in Japan for many hundreds of years. (2)

Following an extensive analysis of the Araki administration, I have reached the conclusion that the traditional *kôdôha-tôseiha* theory is an inadequate and inaccurate basis for explaining the state of affairs in the Japanese Army high command while Araki Sadao was Army Minister. (3) Therefore, I believe that it is necessary to attempt a new understanding of the Araki era in the Army Ministry. My aim here, then, is to make an accurate presentation of one major aspect of the Araki ministership: the personnel policy in the high command and its structure. The main thrust of my

102

contention is that Araki's policy in regard to high-rank appointments was not factionally oriented.

The personnel policies of Araki Sadao as Army Minister have been described until now as being influenced by his partiality for officers with a Tosa-Saga background and his antipathy for officers closely related to former Army Minister Ugaki Kazushige. (4) This approach is said to have been illustrated by Araki's appointment of Generals Mazaki Kanzaburô, Yanagawa Heisuke, Yamaoka Jûkô, Obata Binshirô, Furushô Motô and others to key positions, and his dismissal of officers like Generals Sugiyama Gen, Tatekawa Yoshitsugu, Koiso Kuniaki and others from the important posts they had held in central headquarters during the Ugaki and Minami administrations. This interpretation is a logical outcome of the basic perception by historians of the Araki ministership as characterized by conflict between the so-called Control faction composed of 'Ugaki people' —officers associated with the former Army Minister—and the Imperial Way faction whose main figure is considered to have been Araki.

Regarding Araki's bias for officers of Tosa-Saga origin, one point that is usually ignored or underestimated is that Araki himself hailed from neither of these regions. This fact should not be neglected by any writer aware of the phenomenon of Japanese cliquism based on common geographical origin. However, the idea of Araki's preference for Tosa-Saga officers in high-rank appointments appears weakest when the structure of the Araki administration and that of Army Minister Hayashi Senjûrô that followed it are examined.

In the first half of the Araki ministership, after the completion of all high-level appointments in August 1932, out of the 23 main posts in the Army Ministry, the General Staff and the command of the territorial armies, six positions (about 26 per cent) and these not the most important ones, were held by officers of Tosa-Saga origin: in the Army Ministry, General Yanagawa Heisuke was Vice-Army Minister, General Yamaoka Jûkô was Chief of the Bureau of Military Affairs and Colonel Yamashita Tomoyuki was Chief of the Department of Military Affairs (5); in the General Staff, General Mazaki Kanzaburô was Vice-Chief of Staff and General Obata Binshirô served as Chief of the Second Section; and General Mutô Nobuyoshi first served as Inspector-General of Education and then, as Commander of the Kwantung Army, he became the first head of the 'three positions, one system' structure in Manchukuo. This structure, which gave the Army a strong position in the newly-acquired Japanese satellite, provided that the holder of the Kwantung Army command would, at the same time, also be ambassador to Manchukuo and head of the Agency for Kwantung Affairs. It is important to note that Mutô and Mazaki, the senior members in this group, had served in high posts in the Ugaki and Minami administrations that preceded Araki's. Mutô was Inspector-General of Education and Mazaki held, among other positions, that of Commander of the Taiwan Army.

By August 1933, following the summer personnel shifts, the number of Tosa-Saga officers holding high ranks in the Army Ministry and General Staff dropped by 33 per cent, from six to four. However, Tosa-Saga influence in the high command, if there had been any, must have dropped much more because, among those who left the Araki administration were holders of important positions and intimate friends of Araki. General Mûtô died, General Mazaki was relieved from his post as Vice-Chief of Staff and 'kicked upstairs' to be a member of the Supreme War Council, and Major-General Obata Binshirô, Araki's closest adviser, was forced to leave his position as Chief of the Third Section of the General Staff. (6) General Matsui Iwane of Tosa was the only Tosa-Saga man who was given a post of some significance in the high command. He was named Commander of the Taiwan Army. (7)

Regarding Araki's supposedly antagonistic attitude towards officers who had been close to former Army Minister Ugaki and his successor and friend Minami Jirô, the Table in the Appendix shows that six officers of the Ugaki-Minami era continued in their central command posts for at least one more year under Araki. Two Ugaki-Minami protegés, Nagata Tetsuzan and Tôjô Hideki, were promoted to higher positions by Araki, while Koiso Kuniaki, the influential Chief of the Bureau of Military Affairs in the Ugaki-Minami era, served as Army Vice-Minister before being named Kwantung Army Chief of Staff, a position of importance under the new '3-1' structure in Manchuria. It is true that leading generals of the Ugaki-Minami era such as Abe Nobuyuki, Sugiyama Gen, Tatekawa Yoshitsugu and others lost their positions, but there is no evidence to attribute their removal to something other than the usual change that accompanies the switch to a new administration. Indeed, that is exactly the way the Japanese viewed the change of positions in the high ranks of the Army in late 1931. At that time, when the Araki administration was established, it was called 'the present leadership group' (genkanbu-ha) as opposed to Minami's which was labelled 'the former leadership group' (zenki no kanbu-ha). (8)

A look at the personnel changes undertaken by Araki's successor Hayashi Senjûrô, and the structure of his administration, is quite striking. It easily dispels the widely held view that Hayashi moved away from Araki's supposedly factionalistic personnel policies. Hayashi reappointed to high positions in the Army two generals who were relieved by Araki. One was Major-General Nagata Tetsuzan, a brilliant strategist, who was named Chief of the Section of Military Affairs. However, considering the circumstances under which Nagata was banished from the Araki administration—in which he was promoted to Major-General—one cannot say that he was brought back as a 'Hayashi man'; after all he was not dismissed for being an 'anti-Araki' officer. (9) The other reappointment of a former high-ranking officer of the Araki era made by Hayashi was that of General Mazaki, usually described as a leading member of the so-called *kôdôha* and well known as a personal friend of Araki Sadao. Mazaki was brought back from semi-retirement and made Inspector-General of Education, one of the three most important positions in the Army, together with those of Army Minister and Chief of the General Staff.

Examining the twenty-three positions in the Hayashi command, we realize that seven Araki-era officers remained in their positions. Four holders of high posts under Araki were reassigned within the central command. Thus, overall, former key officers in the Araki administration held no fewer than eleven out of twenty-three central posts in the Hayashi administration: Prince Kan'in, Chief of the General Staff; General Mazaki, Inspector-General of Education; General Hashimoto Toranosuke, Vice-Army Minister; General Matsuura Junrokurô, Chief of the Personnel Bureau; General Yamaoka Jûkô, Chief of the Bureau of Preparations; Colonel Yamashita Tomoyuki, Chief of the Department of Military Affairs; Colonel Uetsuki Yoshio, Chief of the Control Department; General Yamada Otozô, Chief of the General Affairs Section of the General Staff; General Isogai Rensuke, Chief of the Second Section of the General Staff; Colonel Suzuki Yorimichi, Chief of the Department of Operations of the General Staff; and General Ueda Kenkichi was named Commander of the Korea Army. (10) Three of these eleven officers—Mazaki, Yamaoka and Yamashita—were of Tosa-Saga origin.

The impression one gets is that the Hayashi administration was more of a continuation of the Araki command rather than the result of a 'factional' housecleaning. Indeed, no such operation was necessary, since there had been no factional strife in the Araki administration to begin with.

16
Some Traditional Factors Affecting Japanese Politics and Foreign Relations in Two Periods of Crisis: 1853-68 and 1931-41

CHARLES D. SHELDON

An analysis of Japanese perceptions of the world since 1868 as well as of Japanese behaviour towards other peoples reveals the strong influence of traditional concepts and practices drawn from the Tokugawa period (1615-1868), when contacts with the outside world were kept to a convenient and comfortable minimum. Diplomatic relations of a sort did exist between the *bakufu* ('the shogunate') and the semi-autonomous *han* ('domains'), but these were carried on within a very homogeneous culture and value system and within a strongly hierarchical political structure whose rules, although beginning to break down in the last years of the period (the *bakumatsu*), were well understood and followed by the governing classes throughout Japan. Such relationships would have been a poor guide to the management of the western powers or to the application by Japan of European ideas of imperialism to Asia.

There is much evidence of a tendency for the Japanese in the period 1868-1945 to see the external world as, potentially at least, an extension of their own society. The failures to convince other peoples of their good will as well as the fruitless efforts over long periods to 'Japanize' the Koreans and Taiwanese, suggest that this perception of the outside world has been notably inappropriate to Japan's foreign relations. The use externally of domestic political habits formed in a period when foreign relations were almost non-existent has proven perhaps equally inapplicable. In view of recent efforts to internationalize Japan, some consideration of these failures might be useful.

The first step in the opening of Japan to western trade and diplomatic intercourse was forced upon a reluctant *bakufu* in 1854. Until the old regime was replaced in 1868 by a structurally more national government, no really positive policy was pursued to solve the problems posed by the intrusion of the western powers. The *bakumatsu* period, 1853-68, can be seen as a period of crisis and confusion in which a struggle was going on to achieve a national consensus. In the process, both *bakufu* and *han*, as well as some Imperial court officials, carried on endless and sometimes bitter discussions, political activists (*shishi*) agitated and used terrorism to further their cause of Emperorism and the expulsion of the foreigners, institutional experiments were made, and different responses to the foreign threat, including force, were tried (unsuccessfully, by Satsuma and Chôshû). Gradually a consensus emerged which recognized the need to accept the treaties and to consolidate all political forces under the emperor, a solution advocated even by some *bakufu* officials, and by the last shôgun, Yoshinobu, when he resigned at the end of 1867. Between the defeat of the *bakufu* forces in 1866 by Chôshû's semi-modernized army and the end in 1869 of the suppression by the Imperial army of the adherents to the Tokugawa cause in the civil war, people began to think of the foreign threat more positively, as a challenge and an opportunity. (1)

In the Meiji period, Japan's remarkable progress toward modernizing and strengthening the country along western lines was seen by most European and American observers as a proof of their own Victorian certainty of western superiority as well as of the feasibility of transplanting in a non-western country many aspects of European civilization. Considering the degree of Japan's isolation in the mid-nineteenth century and the extremely insular, inward-looking nature of Tokugawa society, Japan's response was surprisingly positive and pragmatic. In fact, there was much in the Tokugawa heritage that contributed to the dynamism and ultimate success of Japan's effort (2), in Fukuzawa Yukichi's phrase, 'to join Europe and leave Asia behind.'

However, there were also negative factors in the tradition. For example, the anti-foreignism of the slogan *sonnô jôi* ('revere the emperor and expel the foreigners') did not necessarily disappear when the emperor ratified the treaties in 1865. It was always possible to exonerate the emperor and blame his advisers for any decision of the government considered to be wrong. For ultra-nationalists, the slogan remained very much alive. In 1888, Tôyama Mitsuru, speaking for the Gen'yôsha, asserted, 'From of old, our principle is *sonnô jôi.*' (3) For most Japanese, borrowing from the West was purely instrumental. It was a necessary expedient.

From the first, western techniques and organization were adopted and used in order to avoid foreign domination and to raise Japan to the status of a great power. The third and final goal, to replace western interests and influence in East Asia, although foreshadowed by such ideologists as Yoshida Shôin (1830-59), became a concrete policy only in response to later developments. It did not follow inevitably upon the first two objectives, but it was a natural extension of them. That it should be done by force was less inevitable, but in the crisis years 1931-41, caution was abandoned and an imperialism developed which had little real awareness of the psychology, or regard for the interests and feelings, of those peoples who suffered from Japanese rapaciousness and arrogance. Ways were found to clothe even the supression of the Chinese and other uncooperative foreigners in a perverse and unbelievable kind of moral benevolence, as may be seen in a speech made by General Araki in 1933: (4)

'Needless to say, the Imperial Army's spirit lies in exalting the Imperial Way and spreading the National Virtue. Every single bullet must be charged with the Imperial Way and the end of every bayonet must have the National Virtue burnt into it. If there are any who oppose the Imperial Way or the National Virtue, we shall give them an injection with this bullet and this bayonet.'

One should add that thought for the susceptibilities of 'the lesser breeds' was hardly a feature of western attitudes, at least in the nineteenth century. The tragedy in Japan's case was that this arrogance persisted. Despite the warnings, mostly voiced privately, by the more cautious, older, and wiser statemen, among whom was a scattering of party men and elders of the Navy, as well as the closest advisers of the emperor, and the emperor himself, Japan continued to pursue narrowly self-interested policies with self-righteous single-mindedness as the government slipped more and more under military domination.

Thus, one can see a degree of continuity of outlook and behaviour from the *bakumatsu* through to the 1940s aroused by the necessity to deal with a dangerous and imperialistic outer world. The danger to Japan, as it was perceived, and without doubt much exaggerated in Japanese minds, produced a strong, emotional, 'fearful' nationalism. (5) Until the Manchurian Incident, policies of national aggrandizement were on the whole pursued with caution and an understanding of Japan's limitations, but this changed when the more bellicose elements in the army succeeded in imposing their policies on the government, assisted by increasing numbers of bureaucrats and politicians who were in general agreement with them.

One of the similarities in the two periods under review was the domination, or near-domination, of policy by military men who tended to think in terms of power politics and military solutions. Linked to this was a general sense of malaise in both periods which seemed to demand action. In the *bakumatsu* period, samurai felt acutely the limitations of the rigid status system which required them to suppress their ambitions for position and prestige, to be content with *de facto* influence, and often to cater to what they saw as ill-informed and stupid superiors. There was also much discontent among the common people as well as among the poorer samurai, due to the maldistribution of wealth and uncomprehending irritation with the despised merchants who were enjoying a standard of living completely out of keeping with their 'proper', formal position at the bottom of the social pyramid. In the late Tokugawa period, political and economic power were out of phase. (6)

In the 1920s and 1930s, conflicts of interest were also becoming increasingly apparent, and there was a widening economic gap between the modernized and traditional industries and, in values and outlook, between the modernizing cities and the traditional countryside. There was a widespread feeling that there was something wrong with society, which was becoming disconcertingly pluralistic and was losing, in the view of many traditionalists, the sense of community (*kyōdōtai*) as well as the loyalties and virtues which had given Japan its unique moral strength.

Military men who, in the samurai tradition, had nothing but contempt for businessmen, were impatient with a system of representation which gave importance to taxpayers and business interests. They desired the national strength provided by industrialization and modernization but not the pluralism which had accompanied them, and were convinced that the political parties and big business were equally corrupt. In common with their counterparts in the *bakumatsu* period, they advocated a whole variety of radical changes to produce their own versions of utopia, or a return to an idealized, harmonious past, or a combination of the two. It was common to combine statist and collectivist proposals for reforms at home and military expansion on the continent to solve social and economic problems. Like the *bakumatsu* Confucianists and reformers, they were convinced of their absolute rectitude, and some were ready to force their solutions on others. Many of the terrorists of the 1930s modelled themselves consciously on the *shishi* of the *bakumatsu* period.

The values of internal order and hierarchy were given very high priority in the Tokugawa period, and remained strong throughout the pre-war years. This view was projected to the world in general, understood as a hierarchy of nations whose places depended on their economic, but above all, on their military strength. (7) The great goal was to place Japan as near the top of this world hierarchy as possible, to find and gain recognition of 'Japan's proper place in the world,' a phrase which echoes and re-echoes in the public statements made by the pre-war government.

The Confucian view of national harmony held in both periods under consideration included the need for political opinions and policies to be the result of a consensus of all sections of the ruling classes; if this was not possible, there should at least be the appearance of consensus. This system can work very well in ordinary times, when decisions are fairly routine. Although extraordinary efforts are made to involve everyone in an organization in the decision-making process, and this takes time, once decisions are made in this way, everyone is disposed to do their best to prove the decisions right by making them work. All members, including the younger ones, are made to feel that their ideas are important. But in times of crisis, when groups advocating alternative policies hold their convictions

109

with strength and emotion, real consensus becomes extremely difficult, and this was the case often in the 1930s as well as in the *bakumatsu* period.

Related to the need to achieve a consensus on any important decision, with maximum participation within the organization, faction, bureaucratic unit in business or government, and the like, are the techniques by which determined factions, sometimes becoming impatient with the slowness of the process of achieving a consensus, contrive to get their policies accepted. One is the use of the common procedure of drafting policies on the lower level to be circulated and approved (the *ringi-sei*). (8) A more extreme method is to confront the leadership with *faits accomplis*, having acted without authorization. (9) Both methods were common in the *bakumatsu* period, as can be seen in the relations between Saigô and the *daimyô* of Satsuma, for example. Saigô was relieved of his position and even exiled for a time for this kind of insubordination, when he and his followers despaired of getting approval for radical solutions. (10) Also, court nobles were known to forge Imperial orders when it suited their political ends. (11)

In 1931, when the army began prosecuting its own war in Manchuria, it came closer to being a law unto itself, but already in 1928 it had refused to discipline the murderers of Chang Tso-lin, and the Navy, for its part, resisted Cabinet control after the 1930 dispute over the London Naval Treaty. The most fateful and famous examples of the uses by army units on the continent of calculated insubordination and the *fait accompli* method were, of course, the Mukden Incident in 1931 and the Marco Polo Bridge Incident in 1937, which began the Manchurian and China 'incidents'.

The drafting of policies by lower echelon officers to be ratified by their superiors in military, government or business bureaucracies is a traditional practice. In a work called *Jikun teikô* written in the 1730s, the author states, 'Rough drafts should be made by lower officials and then polished by higher officials.' (12) When working well, this system makes use of the energy and new ideas of young officials and the experience of their seniors who are expected to 'tone down the final product.' (13) But at least in the 1930s, it often had the effect in government of favouring the less cautious, less realistic, more radical, aggressive, and 'patriotic' policies. Combined with widespread consultations and meetings, it both strengthened solidarity and spread the responsibility so thinly that critics like Maruyama Masao can charge the pre-war bureaucracy with a dangerous irresponsibility (14), with much justice.

Because the basic face-to-face groups which make up Japanese society have traditionally been organized along family lines, leaders are expected to take a paternalistic interest in all lesser members, to be responsible for them, to understand and support them.

Students of Japanese feudal relations and law have been struck by the extremely indulgent treatment of subordinates in the long feudal period in Japan, compared to the stricter attitudes and much greater reliance on law in Western European feudalism. (15) A rather indulgent paternalism has persisted, and proposals made by subordinates have generally been accepted by the time they reach the top, covered with the approving stamps of all in between, making substantive alterations difficult.

A recent study by Michael Blaker concludes that Japanese international negotiating behaviour is a reflection of domestic political habits such as a desire to minimize risk and avoid open confrontations. Blaker also finds an emphasis on prearranged agreements, informal contacts and on a personal style of negotiating which attempts to communicate sincerity, patience and a willingness to compromise. All these are calculated to produce harmony within the country and are expected to work similarly on the diplomatic scene. (16) The *ad hoc*, personal approach is preferred to an emphasis on principles and legalities, as seen in the last-minute attempt in 1941 by Konoe to arrange a personal meeting with President Roosevelt. The proposal was countered by a requirement for a prior agreement on basic principles because the Japanese gave no specific or substantial reasons for the meeting, nor any indication of possible concessions. (17)

In the 1930s, when difficulties were experienced in reaching consensus in times of crisis, a number of institutional experiments were made, such as the creation of the five-ministers' conference and the liaison conference, in an attempt to coordinate policy-making and foster agreements at the highest level, but with scant success. (18) To give an air of consensus to important decisions, Konoe resurrected the *Gozen Kaigi* (the conference in the presence of the emperor), as a formality to ratify prearranged agreements. But when Konoe wanted an agreement and formal ratification of his policy of presenting an ultimatum to China in January 1938 together with clearly unacceptable terms, he knew the General Staff was opposed to it. Perhaps to bring to bear the pressure of an apparent consensus to force the General Staff to retreat, he arranged for the conference, instructing the emperor not to speak, as the policy was one 'which had been decided by the government.' The announcement, made at the conference by Foreign Minister Hirota, was greeted with shocked silence. Prince Kan'in, Chief of the General Staff, could not bring himself to question the decision, only permitting himself to remark that the Chiang regime should not be treated as a totally defeated government. (19)

The desire for consensus among ruling groups is not by any means unique to Japan. An American social psychologist, Irving L. Janis, has made an interesting study of what he calls 'groupthink', applying it to examples of American foreign policy decisions. He defines 'groupthink' as a dangerous psychological drive for consensus at any cost that suppresses dissent and appraisal of alternatives in cohesive decision-making groups. This occurs when members prefer to be agreeable and be thought well of by others in the group than to dissent, ask awkward and penetrating questions, which could destroy the good working relations of the group, and even the euphoria sometimes experienced at a 'perfect' solution to some problem, such as the proposed Bay of Pigs invasion plan which proved to be a fiasco. The application of this idea to Japanese political history would no doubt produce interesting results. (21)

Another traditional practice which has had an unfavourable effect on Japan's foreign relations is that of the go-between That this entrenched tradition mixes rather badly with the role of diplomatic representation abroad has been demonstrated perhaps most strikingly by Colonel (later General) Ôshima Hiroshi, the Military Attaché and later Ambassador in Berlin, who worked quite independently, going far beyond his function as communicator between governments to bring Japan and Nazi Germany closer together. He did this by not communicating the real positions of either government to the other if he thought they risked rejection. He would modify them so as to make them more acceptable, causing consternation in Tokyo among those opposing his policies, but gaining the support of the army. The same methods, though used for a more approvable purpose, were used by Admiral Nomura Kichisaburô as Ambassador, to try to get some agreement in the crucial months before the Japanese attack on Pearl Harbour. The resulting confusions were in fact counterproductive. (22)

Japan's rather half-hearted propaganda efforts provide another example of faulty communications with foreign countries. As G.R. Storry pointed out at our Zurich Conference three years ago, the presentation in English of Japan's case in the China emergency was ineffective for many reasons. One was the application of *mokusatsu* ('killing by silence') in which, in the final analysis, it was considered beneath Japan's dignity to justify itself to the world. To quote Storry, 'We are near the heart of the matter if we suspect that *mokusatsu* has been at the bottom of Japan's chronic failure to make the best of even a good case, let alone one that happened to be doubtful.' (23)

Other examples could no doubt be cited to make the point that traditional attitudes and practices have had important effects on political behaviour in foreign relations as well as on domestic politics in the two periods of crisis reviewed briefly here. It is not at all surprising that this should have been so in the *bakumatsu* period, but that such traditions should have been as important as they were in the 1930s, to the detriment of Japan, suggests their remarkable staying power. It also suggests the shift in leadership from the better-informed and more international-minded statesmen of the Meiji period to much more narrowly nationalistic leaders like Tôjô Hideki, whose concerns seldom embraced more than those of the particular organizations they represented.

17

An Aspect of Tradition and Modernity: Matusoka and Japanese Diplomacy at Geneva, 1932-33

IAN NISH

Our story is one of the high points of Japan's diplomacy just prior to her leaving the League of Nations. At this point of crisis she chose to be represented by Matsuoka Yôsuke (1880-1946), who was sent specially from Tokyo to present Japan's case in Geneva. Matsuoka was himself a mixture of modernity and tradition; and the government's decision to send him reflected these two ingredients.

By any criterion, Matsuoka was a 'modern Japanese'. On the one hand, he had gone at the age of thirteen to the United States as a student and attended Oregon State University. He then joined the Foreign Ministry in 1904 and served in Russia, the United States and China. After attending the Paris peace conference as a sort of press attaché, he resigned from the ministry in 1921 at the age of forty-one and joined the staff of the South Manchurian Railway Company, becoming vice-president six years later. Restless and ambitious, he left the Railway and entered politics in 1930. At the same time, Matsuoka had a modern way of working. His prime quality was his knowledge of English. Using this, he worked diplomatically not only behind the scenes but also—and this was his hallmark—in open court.

Whereas Japan's method at previous international conferences had been to avoid publicity, Matsuoka became famous for his eloquent, not to say rhetorical, speeches at Geneva. This went against the grain for many of Japan's traditional diplomats. But there was a traditional side to Matsuoka also. He was not really an internationalist, sensitive to world opinion or the niceties of international law. He was temperamentally a nationalist, whose task was very often to defend and justify Japan's course of action, whether at the Kyoto conference of the Institute of Pacific Relations in 1929 or in his various writings in English for the Foreign Ministry or the South Manchurian Railway in the 1930s. (1) Matsuoka might indeed by summed up as one who placed 'Modern skills at the service of traditional interests'. It was not for nothing that he was raised in the heart of Chôshû territory.

On 11 October 1932 the Japanese Foreign Ministry appointed Matsuoka as its delegate to the Council and the Extraordinary General Assembly of the League of Nations which were due to be held in Geneva to consider the report of the Lytton Commission. In a telegram to its existing delegates, Nagaoka Shun'ichi, its ambassador in Paris, and Satô Naotake, its ambassador in Brussels, the Ministry stated that the appointment of Matsuoka was the wish of all sections of the Japanese people and that he was a fitting choice because he possessed a deep knowledge of the China problem and had recently been sent to inspect the situation in Manchukuo. It therefore asked that every cooperation should be offered to him as the focal point of the body of Japanese delegates. (2)

It comes as no surprise that there had been opposition to Matsuoka's appointment. There were doubts—not to use the undiplomatic word 'opposition'—on the part of the Japanese diplomatic body. Satô took the view that, because of the weighty matters for discussion, it would be inappropriate for a diplomat on the spot to have to assume responsibility and better for a prominent person to be sent from Tokyo. This suggestion amounted to recommending the adoption of the practice of 1919 when Japan had sent to the Paris peace conference, Count Makino and later Prince Saionji. Clearly Matsuoka could not be compared in stature to these eldest statesmen. Moreover, if one judges him by his place in the Japanese bureaucracy, he ranked behind both Nagaoka and Satô. There was, too, another objection. Nagaoka and Matsuoka both came from Chôshû; and Nagaoka was much the senior. This raised delicate issues. But after Satô had gone to Paris to talk it over with Nagaoka, they agreed to leave the task of being chief delegate—and its inevitable agonies—to Matsuoka. (3)

The decision to send Matsuoka had followed the decision of the Saitô cabinet to recognize the state of Manchukuo on 15 September. This had only been taken after a good deal of protest from established diplomats. Thus, Matsudaira Tsuneo in London had questioned whether Japan required to recognize Manchukuo so hurriedly at this time and whether there was anything wrong with recognizing China's suzerainty (sôshuken) there. (4)

A similar view was held by Yoshida Shigeru, who returned in the middle of September from his post as ambassador to Rome. Yoshida took the view that 'if Japan sends Matsuoka as plenipotentiary to the League and does not appoint some senior statesman over him as head of the delegation, he will not return with the issue finally decided. This is because Matsuoka and Satô are great fighters and seem to be intending to pick a quarrel from the start. Of course, it is the nature of the thing that the plenipotentiary should go not to argue but to get things settled.' Later, Yoshida met Matsuoka himself and suggested that he should take a senior statesman along with him. Matsuoka was furious and rejected the proposal out of hand though he had earlier proposed it himself. Since the situation became overheated, Yoshida told him to douse his head with water and only set off after he had calmed down a little. (5)

Despite these doubts about his qualifications, his seniority and

115

his temperament, the consensus was established and Matsuoka's appointment was ratified. His was not an orthodox appointment of the Foreign Ministry bureaucracy. It was the result of a compromise between the civilians and the military in the cabinet; and Matsuoka was sufficiently in the good books of the military to be its favoured candidate.

Matsuoka received instructions in the form of a memorandum of reply to the Lytton Report. The Japanese Observations were about the same size as the Report itself, that is, some hundred pages. Matsuoka, who travelled via Siberia, studied an advance copy on the way and sent back criticisms from Moscow and Geneva. The final version of the Observations was brought by another member of his delegation, Yoshida Isaburô, who attended in his capacity as the Japanese assessor on the Lytton Commission. Yoshida did not reach Geneva until 16 November.

Matsuoka had a tough mandate and by temperament chose to take a tough line. Passing through the Soviet Union, Poland and Germany en route, he asked the officials he met to grant early recognition to Manchukuo. He declined to meet the press in Paris, which he reached on 9 November, but he defended Japan's actions three days later, saying that 'Japanese action in Manchuria could not fail to be of advantage to all the European powers and the United States in the Far East' and called once again for recognition. After his first major press conference on 18 November, Matsuoka also held private discussions with Sir Eric Drummond, the Secretary-General of the League, and Sir John Simon leading the British delegation. The British were very disappointed by 'the very unyielding attitude adopted by Mr Matsuoka on his first arrival', though they later conceded that it was to a large extent bluff. (6)

The Manchurian issue came before the Council of the League which met from 21 to 24 November under the chairmanship of de Valera of Ireland. It was Matsuoka's objective to ensure that the issue stayed with the Council and was not referred to the Assembly, where the known hostility of the smaller powers to Japan would not help her cause. But after a sharp confrontation between him and the Chinese delegate, it became impossible for the Council to delay longer in referring the Report to the full Assembly.

Matsuoka's delegation, which contained a great deal of talent and diplomatic experience, considered that Japan ought to avoid a face to face clash with the League. On the other hand, now that Manchukuo had been recognized by the Japanese government, it was hard to see how a clash with the League could be avoided. (7) Matsuoka's awareness may have led him to take a more reasonable attitude after his disappointment over Japan's treatment at the hands of the League Council. It was at this point that Britain emerged as a force ready to work privily for a settlement when the matter came up before the Assembly on 6 December. Britain's conclusion was that 'the Japanese are prepared to make considerable concessions in order to reach a settlement by consent' and that they were 'anxious to avoid any open or final break with the League'. (8)

But Britain did not find it easy to steer the League towards a policy of conciliation. When the Assembly debate opened, it was soon clear that the representatives were generally critical of Japan and some were anxious to eject her from the world body without delay. Sir John Simon reported that the speeches made by the smaller powers were so universally hostile to Japan and so one-sided in their references to the Lytton Report that the Great Powers had to intervene. He considered that it was necessary, 'especially in view of ultimate possibilities, to take this corrective line' (9), in his own speech on 7 December. When the debate concluded, it was decided to refer the issue to a committee, the Committee of Nineteen, which duly met on 11 December and requested a smaller drafting committee to draw up proposals indicating a basis for conciliation. This was adopted four days later by the Committee of Nineteen, which laid down regulations for setting up a committee to conduct negotiations for a settlement on the principles in the Lytton Report, in conjunction with the parties, with the United States and Soviet Union being invited to take part. This became the basic League document. On 20 December, Matsuoka announced that the Japanese government had refused to give way on any point and expressed the pessimistic view that this meant the final breakdown of efforts at conciliation. The Secretary-General of the League, Sir Eric Drummond, took the line that negotiations could continue until 16 January, when the Committee of Nineteen would meet again after its adjournment. He hoped privately that the big powers might influence Japan to take a more reasonable attitude. (10)

Matsuoka, who had presumably accepted the assignment in the hope of advancing his political career, saw the prospects of settlement as bleak and felt that the failure was not of his making but the work of an incompetent government in Tokyo. On the one hand, there was the uncompromising attitude of Uchida, who seemed to be unbending. On the other, there was the capture by the Kwantung Army on 3 January of Shanhaikuan, the strategic point and railway junction inside the Great Wall. However it might be justified militarily and politically, this action was from Matsuoka's point of view chronologically inept. For a person who was seeking to keep Japan in the League, it made his diplomacy of conciliation most difficult. Whenever negotiations took place, Shanhaikuan was always mentioned to indicate that western nations were fully aware of the extent of military autonomy in Japan. It made Matsuoka, Nagaoka and Satô openly critical of the Tokyo government. Nonetheless, over the one month of the Christmas and New Year recess, there was a flurry of talks in the world capitals. But they were less consequential than happenings in Geneva. (11)

On 12-13 January, in preparation for the forthcoming meeting of the Committee of Nineteen, Sir Eric Drummond met Sugimura Yotarô, an assistant under-secretary on the League secretariat, described by Satô as an unofficial adviser to the Japanese delegation. Together they worked out a formula which would reconcile the views of Japan and the League and bring about a realistic settlement within the limits of the Lytton Report but divorced from the provisions of the League covenant. From this point onwards, the Matsuoka delegation treated the 'Drummond-Sugimura formula' as a breakthrough and pressed for it as the key to future negotiations. Tokyo would not accept the Committee of Nineteen's principles of 15 December but was in due course persuaded to endorse the Sugimura terms. Sir John Simon had to advise Matsuoka not to speak too complimentarily of 'the efforts which Sir Eric Drummond had made to assist in finding a formula which might be acceptable; I warned him that a false construction had been put upon these complimentary references and that the Secretary-General had been exposed to the unjust reproach that he was engaged in assisting one side at the expense of the other'. (12) In the end, however, the League Committee saw no reason to modify its statement of principles or to depart from them in favour of what was essentially a private arrangement, to which even Britain was not committed.

Though Matsuoka saw the Sugimura formula as a practical way of breaking the deadlock, the Committee tended to view it as a time-wasting device. For two months the League had held up consideration of the Lytton Report while it pursued the possibilities of conciliation. Meanwhile, the Japanese armies had become active in Jehol. It was incumbent on the League to proceed with its own findings on the Lytton Report, which were bound to be lengthy. Henceforth, conciliation would remain open while the drafting committee was devising its recommendations on the Report to the full Assembly. But, in finding some solution, the big issue which divided Tokyo and Geneva was the issue of admitting non-League members to any conciliation attempts. The Saitô government felt that Japan had been so insulted by America in 1932 that the Americans could not be a fair judge of the issues. (13)

On 17 January, the Committee of Nineteen found the revisions which the Japanese insisted on making to be unacceptable. Meanwhile, Drummond was attacked for his mediation efforts with the Japanese. Still, he indicated that the League would be ready to give up its suggestion that the United States and Soviet Union should take part in conciliation, provided Japan accepted its resolution of 15 December. While this was being mulled over in Tokyo, opinion was hardening in the League that Matsuoka and Tokyo were engaged in a time-spinning operation, while no progress was being made towards a settlement. The Committee of Nineteen, despite Matsuoka's objection that this would create tension with Tokyo, insisted on going ahead to draw up its report on the Lytton Commission's findings. After a meeting on 26 January, Simon remarked that Matsuoka adopted a more subdued attitude and 'both he and Mr Matsudaira felt that the Japanese Government really was making a mistake' which they regretted. (14)

On 1 February Matsuoka put forward a personal plan for settlement, in the name of the Japanese delegation. Japan would agree to the ten principles of Chapter Nine being made the basis of settlement 'taking into consideration the realities of the situation'. The intention behind this was to legitimize the state of Manchukuo and to exclude for the present China's sovereignty over Manchuria. The Committee of Nineteen on 4 February declared this to be unsatisfactory and told Japan that the only possible settlement was on the basis of their original principles of 15 December with only minor amendment.

Somewhat surprisingly, Matsuoka brought forward yet another formula, this time based on the December resolution. He was hopeful of a successful outcome but the Japanese terms still included a safeguard clause which implied that they did not propose to acknowledge China's sovereignty over Manchuria. The Japanese let it be known that this last-minute modification of policy was due to the influence of the imperial family and entourage who were admirers of the League. (15)

On 9 February, when the Committee of Nineteen met to consider the latest Japanese proposals, they found them to be a considerable advance on the attitude previously taken by the Matsuoka delegation. It was still thought, however, that the language used might veil Japan's true intentions over Manchuria if and when conciliation proceedings began. It was felt that the League could not permit any vagueness to exist over so fundamental a point as China's sovereignty over Manchuria. Matsuoka was therefore informed orally that this point must be cleared up and that, in any case, conciliation could not be started unless the attack on Jehol threatened by the Kwantung Army were to be abandoned. While the Japanese delegation replied soothingly, the Committee of Nineteen on 14 February decided that the reply was not satisfactory and that they could not recommend that the Assembly should embark on further conciliation proceedings. (16)

The Japanese representatives took the decision of the Committe of Nineteen to pass on their report and recommendations to the Assembly very badly. On the morning of 17 February, Matsuoka passed over a one-page telegram to Sawada Setsuzô, the head of

Japan's League of Nations office, saying 'since things have come to this pass, there is no room for indecision. If we do not take steps to leave the League of Nations, we shall inevitably invite the ridicule of the outside world'. Sawada was told to send off the telegram straight away but, when he saw its terms, he asked Matsuoka whether it had been shown to the other Japanese representatives, Satô and Nagaoka. When Matsuoka replied 'No', Sawada called together a meeting of the four (including himself, since he had the rank of deputy plenipotentiary). The meeting stretched from noon into the evening. Sawada took the view that it was a Tokyo decision whether Japan left the League or not, and that it was not wise for representatives on the spot to take action to influence Tokyo's ultimate decision. Persuaded by Matsuoka's eloquence, however, Nagaoka and Satô moved round to supporting him; and eventually Sawada sent off the telegram to Tokyo as it stood. It reached Japan at a time when cabinet opinion there was still undecided.

On 19 February, Prime Minister Admiral Saitô made a personal report to the elder statesman, Saionji. Saionji asked whether any views had been expressed from Geneva. When he was shown the telegram, he said only 'Is that so?'. (17) Nonetheless, the cabinet on the following day decided that, if the report was adopted by the Assembly, Japan would have to leave the League of Nations. When the Assembly met in Geneva on 21 February, its members received a Japanese document containing Observations and ending with an appeal to them to think twice before taking action. This was not the approach of conciliation any more but an open warning.

It is too much to deduce from this that Matsuoka alone was instrumental in influencing Tokyo to pull out of the League. That had been on the agenda of discussion since the start of the crisis, and many differing views had emerged. Nor should it be imagined that Matsuoka had thought this way all along. He now realized the failure of his mission and reacted accordingly at the eleventh hour.

The proceedings of the League Assembly on 24 February opened with statements by the delegates of China and Japan. China's representative accepted the report on the part of his government, while Matsuoka rejected it. His speech lasted over an hour; it adopted a stern tone; and it made the whole session tense. One observer remarked: 'It brought sweat to the hands of the Japanese delegates: in the face of overwhelming world opinion, we were not forlorn and crestfallen'. (18) It did not antagonize the other delegates. The vote was taken, and the Assembly adopted the report by forty-two votes to one (Japan), with Thailand abstaining. When the result was known, Matsuoka returned to the rostrum to announce that his government was forced to the conclusion 'that Japan and the other members of the League entertain different views on the manner of achieving peace in the Far East, and the Japanese government is obliged to feel that it has now reached the limit of its endeavours to cooperate with the League of Nations in regard to the Sino-Japanese differences'. As in all first-class dramatic performances, Matsuoka brought down the curtain without completely satisfying the curiosity of his hearers: he made no reference to whether Japan would stay within the League. Some of his British hearers described it as 'a speech of great dignity and sincerity which for the first time in seventeen months gained the sympathies of a League audience'. (19)

Matsuoka left the hall in silence, followed by Nagaoka and Satô. He was followed by the Japanese in the audience. It was a bizarre and dramatic occasion. It presented a picture of complete unity on the part of the Japanese. Yet Geneva gossip had it that this was an illusion:

'Japanese delegates then walked out in a body. They maintained the self-possession of their race to the last, but many of them are known to have been cleft in their emotions.' (20)

Most were indeed opposed to moving out of the hall symbolically.

On 25 February Matsuoka left Geneva. He was badly in need of a rest, having been engaged in almost continuous argument, debate and lobbying for over three months. He had had disagreements within the Japanese delegation. He had also had the increased tension which comes from being out of line with the policy laid down by his home government, declaring himself openly as an 'unwilling agent who would follow his mandate'. With all this anxiety he had been finding solace in heavy drinking. But there is no evidence that this affected his set-piece performances at the conference.

* * *

The Times wrote of his homecoming: 'Happier than various other Japanese delegates to international conferences, Matsuoka has no need to fear murderous attacks by disgruntled patriots'. (21) There was a tradition for those who went out to negotiate with foreigners to come back without popularity and with their reputations dented. Katô Tomosaburô, Saionji and Makino, Komura, Itô and Mutsu were all examples of this. They had not, so it was thought, argued strongly enough with foreigners and brought back to Japan what was her due. Matsuoka had not won a victory over foreigners. But by sticking to his guns, he had prevented a victory by the rest of the world.

So Matsuoka had broken with tradition. He had followed popular opinion. The journalist and critic, Kiyozawa Kiyoshi, criticized this kind of diplomacy for its lack of leadership, for 'not having the will to turn their backs on public opinion in order to save Japan at this critical juncture'. (22) But Kiyozawa's was a lone voice. Matsuoka

121

won popularity for his actions which, however much propaganda there was, appealed to the people.

The tradition that had developed in Japanese diplomacy in the *bakumatsu* and Meiji periods was that of submission to foreigners, and especially to westerners. Hence Matsuoka's break with tradition at Geneva was, in effect, a refusal to submit to international opinion and international pressure. We have in this paper made reservations about the conventional accounts of Matsuoka's role at Geneva, which have tended to be written with too much use of hindsight and to play up his strong, uncompromising stand; we have tried to suggest that he was until the eleventh hour ready to explore all possibilities of a settlement and was far from defiant. Yet in the final analysis Matsuoka—with a strong-willed and unyielding government behind him—failed to reach an accommodation with world opinion or world leaders, both of which were solidly against Japan over the Manchurian crisis. It we are to interpret a break with tradition as innovation, then innovation for Japan in this case was not so much a trend towards westernization or a move towards international opinion, as a trend towards national self-assertiveness and away from internationalism. It reflected a consciousness on the part of Japan that she was, by 1933, modern enough and strong enough not to have to accept a solution of her affairs which she considered to be wrong.

In the new and unfamiliar environment of the League of Nations, a body without precedent in world history and barely one decade old, Matsuoka had employed the modern skills of public speaking (in English), press conferences, press briefings, extensive publicity hand-outs and broadcasts for the sake of Japan's interests. But persuasiveness is not enough if it is not backed by some concessions.

18

Traditional Limitations on Dictatorships: the Bureaucracy vs. Tôjô Hideki

BEN-AMI SHILLONY

Pre-war Japan was run by an educated bureaucracy, recruited largely from the imperial universities. The bureaucrats were regarded as the cream of society, because they were representatives of the emperor rather than the servants of the people. They were responsible for many things that went on, and were entitled to interfere in most affairs. Their professed paternalistic outlook, combined with an arrogant awareness of their power, was reminiscent of the attitude of the samurai in feudal Japan, or the oligarchs of the Meiji period (1868-1912). Even when the politicians were accused of being selfish and corrupt, the bureaucrats kept their image of honesty and devotion to duty. Only the military officers, who sacrificed their lives for the country, were regarded as representing a higher kind of duty to the emperor.

The bureaucracy functioned on the basis of laws, and officials were usually graduates of the law departments of the universities. The Meiji constitution, which had established the rule of law in Japan, was never amended or abrogated. Unlike totalitarian countries, there was no constitutional break in Japan prior to 1945. Some laws, like the General Mobilization Law of 1938, could be regarded as violating the spirit of the constitution, but they were essentially emergency measures.

Constitutional continuity was paralleled by institutional stability. Most of the institutions that had functioned in the 1920s and 1930s continued to function throughout the war. However, their relative power changed. Cabinet positions which in the 1930s were held by party politicians, were held in the late 1930s by bureaucrats and military men. But despite the changes in policy, there were no major purges in Japan. The bureaucrats continued to serve the state in time of war with the same zeal they had evinced in time of peace.

The war strengthened the power of the bureaucracy, but that power was not concentrated in the hands of one individual or one institution. The cabinet remained a federation of ministries and agencies, each guarding scrupulously its privileges and autonomy. The prime minister was not the chief executive, but rather an imperial servant whose task was to ensure a united cabinet policy. He could not dictate to the other ministers or change them at will; and replacing a minister was a complicated task which required both pressure and persuasion.

Policies were not dictated by a single statesman, but were reached after consultations among various power elites like the general staffs of the army and navy, cabinet members, and palace officials. Decision-making remained, as it had always been, an exhausting process, even in time of war. Kishi Nobusuke, who served as Minister of Commerce and Industry and later as Vice-minister of Munitions in the Tôjô cabinet, told a newspaper reporter in 1944:

'It often takes two or three months for the Munitions Ministry to reach a decision on an important matter. Then the decision must be discussed at a meeting of the cabinet, which in turn issues an order to be executed at various government and industrial levels. Thus it may take half a year before the decision goes into effect. Even a wise decision is sometimes worthless by the time it is executed, for the situation by then has changed.' (1)

Hillis Lory, an American military expert who had spent several years in Japan, observed in 1943: 'Japan is not a one-man government. General Tôjô, the premier, has great power, but his authority in the Japanese government does not equal Roosevelt's in the United States nor Churchill's in England, to say nothing of Hitler's and Mussolini's dictatorships.' (2)

Tôjô was the first person to be Prime Minister and Army Minister concurrently. This combination of portfolios gave him great power in both military and civilian affairs. In addition, during the first four months of his cabinet, Tôjô was also Home Minister and, as such, in charge of internal security during the crucial first months of the war. He also held other portfolios for short periods, and from November 1943 he was Munitions Minister. This concentration of power made Tôjô into the strongest prime minister in Japan in the twentieth century, but it was not enough to make him into a dictator.

Tôjô was neither the head of state nor the commander-in-chief of the armed forces. The army and navy continued to enjoy their privileged status of being directly under the emperor's command. Tôjô was the first among equals, and he was expected to consult his colleagues on all important questions. Some of these colleagues were his seniors or his previous superiors. Generals Terauchi Hisaichi, Hata Shun'roku, and Sugiyama Hajime preceded him in rank and had been Army Ministers before him. (When Sugiyama was Army Minister in the First Konoe Cabinet, Tôjô was his deputy). Tôjô dismissed a few of his opponents, but not all of them. One of his main rivals, General Terauchi, remained Commander-in-Chief of the Southern Front, and in June 1943 was promoted, together with the army's Chief of Staff, General Sugiyama, and the commander of the expeditionary army in China, General Hata, to the rank of marshal, while Tôjô himself remained a general until the end of the war. (3)

Tôjô's status and popularity were much lower than those of the German, Italian, Russian or Chinese dictators of that time. He was not accorded any special title and no one pledged allegiance to him. There was no particular faction behind him, and no brains trust or personal coterie around him, and all expressions of loyalty had to be directed solely toward the emperor.

After the initial victories in the Pacific War, Tôjô took advantage of the jubilant mood to enhance his public position. He addressed rallies, inspected factories and schools, reviewed troops, chatted with people in the street, and drove in open cars. But he knew well that any attempt to build a personality cult would backfire. Therefore he took care to assure the public that he harboured no personal ambitions. Appearing before the House of Representatives' Committee on the Special Wartime Administration Bill in February 1943, he said:

'The interpellation has used the term "dictatorial government". This is a point on which I wish to make myself perfectly clear. Führer Adolf Hitler, Duce Benito Mussolini, Premier Joseph Stalin, President Franklin D. Roosevelt, and Prime Minister Winston Churchill have been mentioned. But my position in the Japanese state is essentially different from theirs. In my humble way, I am serving His Majesty, at His Majesty's August Command, as prime minister. In that capacity I am the leader of the nation, but as such that makes the prime minister of Japan entirely different from the European dictators.' (4)

Such expressions of humility and self-effacement might have been hypocritical, but the fact that Tôjô found it necessary to make them in the first place and to resort to the image of the humble servant, sets him apart from the European and Asian dictators of that time.

Although Tôjô was not a dictator, there was little freedom in Japan by the time he became Prime Minister and even less after the Pacific War broke out. Constant arrests of leftists and liberals were a sordid feature of the pre-war and wartime regime. From the first roundups of communists in 1928 until the outbreak of the Pacific War in 1941, about 74,000 persons were arrested on charges of violating the Peace Preservation Law, and during the Pacific War about 2,000 more people were arrested on these charges. But out of these, only about 5,000 people were prosecuted for violating the Peace Preservation Law during the seventeen years between 1928 and the end of the Pacific War, while most of the rest were released after interrogation. When the war ended, there were only about 2,500 political prisoners behind bars, including the leaders of the communist party and the spy suspects. (5)

The largest and most pervasive civilian branch of government was the Home Ministry (*Naimushô*). It was in charge of local government, police, internal security, public works, civil defence, rationing, publications, censorship, and Shintô shrines. It also supervised the neighbourhood associations, the IRAA and a host of other patriotic organizations. Its officials, policemen, and agents represented, more than anyone else, the government's authority in every locality, controlling the population and deciding about its essential needs. But, unlike the situation in totalitarian countries, no individual built for himself a power basis in the Home Ministry. Tôjô was Home Minister during the first two months of the war, and then turned the post over to a senior bureaucrat, Yuzawa Michio. Yuzawa, who orchestrated the general election of 1942, stayed in office for fourteen months. Altogether, five different men served as Home Minister during the war, but none of them became particularly powerful in that role.

As a corporate body the Home Ministry was strong and influential. It resented sharing power with other branches and prevented attempts to set up independent grass-roots organizations. For some time, the IRAA, backed by the military, constituted a threat, but in March 1941 the radical wing of that organization was suppressed and the IRAA came under the control of the Home Ministry. Once that organization was tamed, it was allowed to increase its authority. In May 1942 the IRAA was given control over most patriotic organizations, such as the Great Japan Industrial Patriotic Organization, the Agricultural Patriotic Association, and the Great Japan Women's Association. (6)

The *Dai Nihon Yokusan Sônen-dan* ("The Great Japan Imperial Rule Assistance Adults' Association'), which was established in January 1942, proved more difficult to curb. It enjoyed the support of the army and many of its leaders were reserve officers. Indeed, during the election campaign of April 1942, it criticized both the 'old-fashioned politicians' as well as the 'selfish bureaucrats', in its drive for a national revival. Its populist appeal, independence of action, and links with the army were resented by the Home Ministry, which feared this Nazi-model organization. But ultimately the Home Ministry was triumphant. In December 1943 Tôjô was prevailed upon to force the Association to reshuffle its leadership and accept the hegemony of the IRAA. (7)

The agency charged with the enforcement of the Peace Preservation Law and other laws of political nature was the Special Higher Police (*Tokubetsu Kôtô Keisatsu*, abbreviated as *Tokkô*), which was established in 1911 after the alleged attempt on the emperor's life by Kôtoku Shûsui and his fellow anarchists. During the 1920s and 1930s, the *Tokkô* carried out the arrests and interrogations of communists, socialists, suspicious Koreans, certain religious leaders and, occasionally, right-wing extremists. It had branches in all police precincts and was responsible to the Police Bureau of the Home Ministry. (8)

126

Another agent of political repression was the Military Police (*Kenpei*). This branch, which was basically in charge of police functions within the ranks, expanded its vigilance in the late 1930s to include anything which might endanger the war effort. Since pacifism, liberalism, and sympathy for the U.S. or Britain were considered to be obstacles to victory, the military police was determined to suppress them. (9) There were only about 7,500 *Kenpei* in Japan during the war, but they were dreaded everywhere. Tôjô had a special relation with the Military Police, dating from the time he had served as commander of the Kwangtung Army's *Kenpei*. In January 1942, he appointed his friend from Manchuria, General Katô Hakujirô, as Commander-in-Chief of the Military Police, and his former deputy, Colonel Shikata Ryôji, as chief of the Tokyo Military Police. The *Kenpei* remained Tôjô's most trusted instrument against dissenters and opponents, spying on politicians and officials, whom he suspected of disloyalty, and trying to intimidate them. (10)

Yet the *Tokkô* and the *Kenpei* could not suppress the opposition to Tôjô among politicians and senior statesmen. When the military setbacks increased and Tôjô lost the support of the emperor's advisers and some of his own peers, neither the Special Higher Police nor the Military Police could keep him in office.

Unlike totalitarian countries, there was no central, powerful and independent secret police in wartime Japan, on the model of the *Gestapo* or the NKVD. The *Tokkô* was subordinate to the Home Ministry and functioned as part of the metropolitan and local police. Yet the Home Minister who controlled it did not acquire extraordinary power, and Home Ministers were changed as often as other ministers. (11)

The *Kenpei* were subordinate to the Army Ministry (the navy had no military police of its own) and could not act independently of it. During the four years of Tôjô's term as Army Minister, six different officers held the post of Commander-in-Chief of the Military Police (*Kenpei Shireikan*), but none of them became particularly powerful in it. (12) The *Tokkô* and the *Kenpei* suppressed political dissent, but they did not owe allegiance to a single leader or chief.

The Justice Ministry cooperated with the Home Ministry in suppressing dissent. Its prosecutors prepared the trials and its judges passed the sentences. However, unlike the situation in some other countries in war, there was no state of emergency in Japan, and the police could not act arbitrarily. Those who were arrested had to be put on trial or freed. There were no special tribunals for wartime offenders and every defendant faced the same judicial system. Although the judges were government officials and together with other parts of the bureaucracy helped to maintain the oppressive system, they enjoyed a degree of freedom. They were appointed for life, could not be dismissed, and could not be shifted at will.

The tendency of Japanese judges was not to impose severe sentences, but to enable the offender to correct himself, according to the traditional policy of trying to bring the offenders back into the fold. Capital punishment was rare, and life imprisonment was imposed only in extreme cases. Although there were many criminal offences for which a person could be sentenced to death, such as murder, arson, treason, rebellion, and certain violations of the Peace Preservation Law, only fifty-seven people were executed during the war for all kinds of offences. This average of fifteen executions a year was considerably lower than the average of twenty-eight executions a year in the liberal 1920s, or the twenty executions a year in the 1930s. Only two people were executed for violating the Peace Preservation Law: the master spy Richard Sorge and his Japanese accomplice Ozaki Hotsumi. (13)

The government exerted pressure on the judges to be more severe. In February 1944, judges from all over Japan were summoned to Tokyo, where Prime Minister Tôjô and Justice Minister Iwamura Michio called on them to be strict and to impose 'extraordinary sentences' in view of the circumstances. But one of the judges present at that meeting, Hosono Nagao, president of the Hiroshima Court of Appeals, criticized the instruction, saying that it violated the autonomy of the judiciary; he was not punished for his outspokenness. Another judge, Okai Tôshirô of Yokohama, went so far as to send a letter to Tôjô urging him to resign. He was put on trial for misdemeanour and obliged to resign, but he was not arrested. (14)

The independence of the judges was also apparent in the legal repercussions of the general election of 1942. Ozaki Yukio, who was charged with *lèse majesté* during the election campaign, was defended by two prominent lawyers and was permitted, at his trial, to accuse Tôjô of violating the Constitution and of suppressing the freedom of the people. The verdict was given in December 1942. The 84-year old politician was found guilty and sentenced to two years in prison, but the judges ruled that the sentence be postponed for two years, apparently in the hope that he would die in the meantime. Ozaki appealed the case to the Supreme Court, where it remained for almost two years. Then, on 27 June 1944, the Supreme Court dismissed the verdict of the lower court and acquitted the defendant. Ozaki outlived the war-time leaders of Japan: he died in 1953, at the age of 95. (15)

Another trial that emanated from the 1942 elections was related to their very legality. Four unrecommended candidates from the second district in Kagoshima prefecture, who had lost the elections, appealed to the Supreme Court to nullify the election results in their district, on the grounds that there had been official interference. The plaintiffs, led by Tomiyoshi Eiji, a former Diet member from the Social Mass Party, claimed that the governor, Susukida Yoshitomo had urged teachers and policemen to help the semi-officially recommended candidates to be elected. Their attorney was Diet member Saitô Takao, who himself had been elected despite the government's efforts to suppress him. The Supreme Court treated the complaint seriously and appointed one of its members, Judge Yoshida Hisashi, to investigate it. The government tried to convince Yoshida to dismiss the case, but Yoshida did not succumb to the pressure He went to Kagoshima and after a long investigation, which lasted almost three years, he ruled on 1 March 1945 that the plaintiffs were right; the governor had interfered in the elections and therefore the election results in the district were null and void. Consequently, new elections were held in the district on 20 April. By this time the prefecture of Kagoshima was already subject to American air raids, and fewer people were concerned with the elections. The semi-officially recommended candidates were re-elected once again, but whereas in the 1942 election they had each received between 17,000 and 25,000 votes, this time they received only between 8,700 and 13,000 votes each. On the other hand, the unrecommended candidates, who had each received only about 4,000 votes in 1942, polled about 7,000 votes each in 1945. (16)

Thus the bureaucracy, which had constituted an obstacle for the development of democracy before the war, proved to be an important barrier to the development of dictatorship during the war. The regime was oppressive and narrow minded, but its inherent conservatism kept it confined within the previously established rules. In a society where teamwork, collective leadership, factional allegiance, consensus politics and loyalty to a passive imperial institution were the accepted rules, dictatorship by a prime minister or an army chief could not succeed.

19

Oil, Deviance and the Traditional World Order — Japanese and German Strategies for Violent Change 1931-41

JOHN W. M. CHAPMAN

In the past, peoples fought to get hold of gold.
Nowadays, it's all about such raw materials as
petroleum, tin and rubber. (1)

Though penned all of forty years ago from Washington by a German general observing Japan's struggle with the United States, the comment has a remarkably familiar ring to it. From the vantage point of the present day, it is possible to observe the historical development of the competing philosophies of Anglo-American economic liberalism and of national egalitarianism which have emerged with the international diffusion of industrial technology since the end of the eighteenth century. Both philosophies emphasise competition: the one advocates peaceful competition, the other physical struggle; both amount to different interpretations of self-help. The one is based on the myth of freedom of choice, the other on the myth of egalitarianism. Greater freedom of choice was possible before 1914 because the basic resources of industrialisation were more equally distributed among national societies and the rate of consumption of resources was so much lower than it has since become.

International relations in the post-1914 era have continued to be managed on the philosophical premisses of an economic and social structure that has largely disappeared. The Soviet Union and China have clung to Marxist-Leninist ideas long after any claims they could make to inequality and deprivation have ceased to be really credible, while the Anglo-American powers have presented themselves as exponents of the freedom of the individual and of human rights knowing full well that their freedom of choice has spelled a denial of choice for most of the rest of the world. Economic liberalism has long posited a necessary and sufficient linkage between peace and minimal regulation of economic activity: 'unhampered trade dovetailed with peace', Cordell Hull concluded, and averred that 'high tariffs, trade barriers, and unfair competition "dovetailed" with war.' (2) To see that economic liberalism is far from dead, one need only examine a recent discourse by William Bundy on international power, where he argues:

'If economic self-interest (as enlightened as possible) is a dominant guideline, and if nations feel at least broadly satisfied with their place in an overall economic system, then the possibilities of bargaining and constructive accommodation are at least far greater than if groups are driven by other motives.' (3)

Both tend to assume in a rather self-satisfied fashion that American economic arrangements were and are bound to confer universal benefits that all can tap in order to acquire an equal quotient of happiness. The dubious character of such premisses can be illustrated quite swiftly from recent events in Iran: if the Shah was unhappy with his place in the economic system, how can the system accommodate the anti-materialism of the Islamic nationalist movement?

The coexistence of large political or economic units with smaller ones in the international system is usually fraught with dangers for the smaller rather than the larger units and national aspirations to equality of treatment are constrained by the realities of economic and military disparity. The larger units tend to discipline or punish the smaller units which deviate from the rules. Since the larger units determine the rules, however, even those smaller states which claim to be operating under the approved rules are quite liable to be chastised for operating the rules to the disadvantage of the larger states, as was evident in the case of Czechoslovakia, of Britain and France over the Suez Canal, or of Japan in its trade relations with the United States up to the time of the Nixon 'shock'. The Soviet Union and China have a preference for emphasizing the politics of international relations and tend to employ short sharp armed shocks to their victims in most cases, while the Anglo-American powers have traditionally sought to shock the recalcitrant with economic cold douches, accompanied by liberal helpings of moral admonition. Economic self-interest for the national egalitarian state is usually achieved by political and military means; for the liberal-economic state, economic means are the favoured vehicles toward political ends. (4)

The inter-war economic and political system was very much a transitional one. The states of the system could not be broadly satisfied with their place in it because the whole economic system was undergoing a slow structural change whose principal engine can be identified, it is argued, in the shift from coal to oil as the dominant energy source. (5) This structural cause had both economic and military effects, already in evidence in 1914, which were far from devastating for those societies which had oil in abundance on their territory. But for those societies not in this favoured category, and these included most of the European states and Japan, varying degrees of deprivation were to prove of critical significance for their status in the existing hierarchy. Those states, such as Britain, the Netherlands and France, which could gain access to the fuel for the new technology that went with it, suffered less acutely because it could be tapped from areas within their existing spheres of control or influence. Such states as Germany, Italy and Japan, on the other hand, which already tended to be somewhat less favoured under the old system, found this deprivation especially acute because, as latecomers to the processes of industrial organization and technological innovation, they had also failed to secure an advantageous access to the world's raw materials commensurate with their demographic, economic and aspirational needs.

Their sensitivity to these structural changes gradually assumed a degree of vulnerability by 1919 that was manifestly alarming, because they were now painfully aware that that vulnerability could be exploited for political ends by states more geologically favoured but certainly not morally superior. Even before the outbreak of World War I, the relative paucity of indigenous resources was a factor in their levying of financial indemnities on France, China and Russia between 1871 and 1905, which seemed to confirm that imperialism by military means paid. The almost total lack of crude oil on their territories, coupled with the increasing use of internal combustion engines in the twentieth century, contrasted sharply with the near-monopoly of the oil industry by U.S. interests up to 1971. (6) Up to 1930, Germany's only stake in the world's oil industry was a twelve per cent share in the Mosul field in Iraq, while the Japanese finds on Karafuto provided only about three per cent of annual oil consumption. Eighty-five per cent of German imports of oil came from the United States, the Dutch West Indies, Venezuela and Mexico, while at least eighty per cent of Japanese imports came from California and, of a further ten per cent obtained from the Dutch East Indies, much of this was exported by Standard-Vacuum, the largest single U.S. investor in Asia. (7)

The strong U.S. trading position after World War I enabled the U.S. oil companies and other financial interests to obtain substantial stakes in the German and Japanese economies. U.S. investment capital was particularly large in Germany, whereas trade between the U.S. and Japan was high, accounting for forty per cent of all Japan's foreign trade. Japanese financial institutions were tied in with a consortium of western banks led by Wall Street during the 1920s, as Mitani Taichirô has shown. (8) U.S. penetration of the Japanese economy made it difficult for those groups in Japan which advocated independence from and rivalry with the U.S. in the period from 1917 to 1921 to get their way, and this in turn affected Germany's chances of obtaining Japanese loans in 1919, as well as of benefiting from selling arms to both sides in the anticipated Japanese-American war. The possibility of economic cooperation with Japan came up again during international economic discussions in 1930, following the Wall Street crash and internal division within the Japanese Navy about the maintenance of cooperation with the

132

United States over naval arms limitation. Admiral Katô Kanji, the Chief of Naval Staff in 1930, had been an opponent of the Washington Treaty in 1922 and had advocated close cooperation with Germany at that time. (9)

The fact that eighty per cent of Japan's earnings from exports to the United States in 1930 came from silk made the Japanese economy particularly vulnerable, especially when import dependence on the United States was also very high. As the German ambassador in Japan prophetically remarked at the time:

'Japan knows that it can, if it is lucky, win a battle against America, but not the war. Her policy must be guided by an avoidance of disputes with America rather than by trying to find allies for a very improbable and ultimately destructive war —allies whose reliability would remain doubtful to say the least.' (10)

At this stage, the likelihood of Germany allying itself against the U.S. was remote, not least because U.S. investments there were so high. But when these investments began to be repatriated steadily from 1930 to 1933 because of the uncertainties of German domestic politics in those years, and when the outflow became a dangerous torrent in the first two years of the Hitler administration, the incentive to remain friendly to the western capitalist powers declined. (11) Likewise, the effects of the recession on Japan's trade proved to be almost equally catastrophic until Japan left the gold standard. Both countries were hard put to it to maintain positive balances in their trade payments with the rest of the world: Hitler's insistence on eliminating trade with the Soviet Union had an almost fatal effect on the economy in 1934 and only the decision to barter arms and industrial goods for raw materials kept the economy going; Japan's colonial areas and their expansion in Manchuria after 1931 provided a buffer and a hope for the discovery of resources under Japanese control. The fact that Germany had suffered catastrophic inflation between 1919 and 1924 and that Japan had suffered from an immediate post-1919 recession and from the Kantô earthquake in 1923 made their populations all the more resentful and fearful when the evident collapse of the capitalist system threatened to ruin their national economies for a second time in a single decade.

Hitler was one of the few European politicians who spoke out in support of Japan's expansion in Manchuria and whose emulation of the Japanese example received private assurances of support, particularly when it became clear that the Weimar regime's links with the Soviet Union were to be explicitly repudiated. (12) The seizure of Manchuria provided no effective answer to the problem of raw material supply, especially not oil, but rather tended to engender hostility and international isolation, which in turn made the need for military security even more acute. The resort to rearmament in both countries, intimately linked to feelings of enforced inferiority and the desire for self-assertion, inevitably made dependence on foreign oil and other raw materials even greater when armed forces transported by oil-fired engines were expanded. To prevent these arms from becoming useless white elephants, time was needed to build up stockpiles and to earn hard currency with which to purchase these. Potential enemies had to be allayed or neutralized until the moment was ripe to seize the deficient resources.

Germany had the advantages of being able to supply about one-third of its oil requirements in the 1930s from the hydrogenation of coal and shales, while Japan's efforts in this direction produced only four per cent of total consumption in the best year, 1942. (13) Her stockpiles of oil grew steadily up to mid-1941, from an estimated 72,000 tons in 1931 to a nine to twelve months' supply by mid-1940, while German oil requirements continued to be met fully until the middle of 1941 when the requirements of the campaigns in Russia and Africa and the needs of occupied Europe began to stretch supply capabilities to breaking point. The different sorts and mixtures of fuels, however, often presented problems and bottlenecks: for example, diesel fuel was in such short supply for the German Navy from the spring of 1941 that it became virtually impossible to operate large surface warships for any length of time and fuel had to be conserved for the use of the U-boat fleet, while in Japan the limited refining capacity available to the Japanese Army left it short of aviation fuel following the U.S. embargo on aviation fuel exports on 1 August 1940. (14)

The oil factor played a highly significant role in foreign economic and military strategy. The fact that, apart from small amounts of oil available on Sakhalin, all fuel for Soviet forces in the Far East had to be brought thousands of miles from the Caucasus meant that the value of attacking the Soviet Union remained slight in economic terms. Added to that, the cost of catching up technically and numerically with the Soviet armed forces meant that the Japanese Navy, recalling the limited returns from the Russo-Japanese War and especially the Siberian intervention, positively refused to contemplate demands from the Army between 1932 and 1936 to support a pre-emptive attack on the Soviet Union. Japanese Navy spokesmen explained to Commander Wenneker, the German Naval Attaché in Tokyo, in the summer of 1936, that they were determined not to fall into a British trap to provoke Japan into fighting a war with Russia and argued:

'The Navy would view a war with Russia as a national disaster. Even if Japan emerged victorious from the war, she would be so weakened that she would be forced to submit to every dictate of England or America. What then would a victory have won for us? At most, prestige. The newly conquered bits of territory would represent more of a liability than advantages. We should not lose sight of our experiences with Manchuria.' (15)

From an early stage, the Japanese Navy set its sights on the oil resources of the Dutch East Indies which produced more than enough oil for Japan's annual requirements at this time. But until the Japanese Navy's fleet expansion programme was completed in 1941, the senior members of the naval officer corps felt it necessary to move southwards slowly and consolidate control over the East and South China Seas without provoking unified Anglo-American opposition either in the shape of sanctions or military alliances. From an observation of Anglo-American reactions to moves to bring the foreign-dominated oil industry in Japan under tighter control, it became clear that it was the British who played the more active role in trying to organize oil sanctions against Japan in the latter half of 1934. While Shell and Standard-Vacuum, based on the Dutch East Indies and Borneo, were prepared to cooperate in this, the producers of California crude who had extensive links with domestic Japanese oil interests refused to cooperate and the State Department could not cajole or coerce them into an embargo either in 1934 or later, in 1937, when a strict interpretation of the Neutrality Law could have prevented the supply of oil to belligerents in the Sino-Japanese War. (16) Consequently, supplies reached Japan unabated until 1940 when restrictions began to take effect slowly in the face of growing evidence of threats to U.S. interests in the Far East.

Until then, Japanese policy strove to minimise friction with the United States, while maximising pressure on China and Britain, just as in the period from 1932 to 1936 efforts were made to maintain tolerable coexistence with Britain and treat the United States as the principal enemy. Since only ten per cent of Japanese imports came from Anglo-Dutch sources, Anglo-Japanese antagonism could be afforded when Japanese-American hostility certainly could not. Ultimately, however, it was realized that the interests of Britain and the United States were too closely linked to be separated if seriously threatened and the close geographical proximity of British, Dutch and U.S. territories made for their strategic inseparability. As Admiral Kondô Nobutake and others emphasised, the occupation of these territories would only be the first shots in a conflict that could last a decade: even with the addition of the resources of South-East Asia, economic self-sufficiency was by no means assured and there were grave doubts about Japan's capacity to withstand a war of attrition with the United States. (17)

Whatever moves Japan made to secure oil by force, it had to be imported by sea and this made for vulnerability to hostile naval attack. By contrast, German access to continental sources of oil represented a real alternative not available to Japan. During the period of restrictions on the German armed forces, access to Soviet resources could not be assured by direct land links not liable to be cut, so that it became imperative for Germany to maintain good relations with the Anglo-American powers in order to assure imports of raw materials from overseas from the Atlantic and North Sea. Continuing British neutrality after 1933 could only be bought at a price: over the Abyssinian crisis, Britain demonstrated its preparedness to side with France and not Italy. British willingness to resort to sanctions heightened the sense of vulnerability in Germany and Japan as well as in Italy, but as with abortive consideration of sanctions against Japan in 1934, sanctions against Italy were bound to fail so long as Standard Oil and other U.S. suppliers refused to join in the League's sanctions and the State Department proved unwilling to enforce the Neutrality Law strictly. Like Japan and the threat that it could pose to the Dutch East Indies, so Italy could pose a threat to the Suez Canal which was credible in the context where, through deciphered Admiralty signals, the Italians knew that the Home Fleet had insufficient ammunition for an effective, sustained fleet engagement in the Mediterranean. Faced with enemies in three major sea areas, and with evidence of U.S. displays of economic power without political or military responsibilities, Britain's decision-makers felt stalemated, but hopeful that Japan's economic strength would be sapped in the vastness of China and Germany's economic isolation would make her leaders see reason at last. (18)

By 1938, the last of Germany's hard-currency reserves were being thrown into the completion of rearmament and Hitler waited for the moment to launch eastwards his last major asset, the armed forces. Austria and Poland added to the total of domestic oil production, Czechoslovakia to Germany's industrial strength, and the way was opened up in December 1939 to Rumanian supplies of oil. But the most significant step was, of course, the breakthrough in relations with the Soviet Union which netted nearly 900,000 tons of oil by the middle of 1941 in addition to 80,000 tons from Estonia and 746,000 tons from Rumania in the year ending 31 August 1940. Oil imports from the Americas which had averaged 4.6 million tons annually in the years 1936-38, fell to 3.1 millions in 1939, mainly from Mexico, where the oil industry had been nationalized. With the outbreak of war, oil from the Americas slowed to a trickle as a result of Anglo-French naval blockade measures.

Although the bulk of Germany's oil supply came from synthetic production and imports from Eastern Europe, small amounts of oil continued to reach the German Navy from Mexico, where German and chartered tankers were loaded with fuel to supply armed merchant raiders in the Pacific and Indian Oceans through the supply and provisioning service organized by the German Naval Attaché in

Japan. Tankers sent from the Mexican west-coast port of Manzanillo to Japan and others from the Caribbean port of Tampico to Teneriffe in the Canary Islands were organised with the assistance of Davis & Co., a small renegade oil company registered in New York and Mexico City and dealing in nationalised Mexican oil. W.R. Davis, its head, worked with Richard Eversbusch, a Mexican citizen of German origin in charge of the local organization of the German Navy's secret Supply Service (*Marine-Etappendienst*) since 1934 and also, after the outbreak of war, with J.G.A. Hertslet, a director of the Berlin-based tanker company Eurotank, who had served on the staff of Himmler and Goering, and was now the representative of Dr. Fetzer, the German Navy's senior oil expert. The link between Tampico and Teneriffe had been planned since 1934, when officers of the Supply Service in Berlin had made soundings of the possibilities for German warships and merchant ships to obtain bunkering facilities from companies other than Shell or Esso—a very early indication of the intention to provide German warships with supply facilities not controlled by the Anglo-American powers. After the Abyssinian crisis, these firms refused to accept payment from the German Navy in marks and demanded hard currency, which made it even more imperative, for financial reasons, to diversify suppliers of fuel. Eventually, the Navy secretly took the majority shareholding in the Spanish oil company CEPSA with its refinery at Teneriffe, from where fuel was taken on by German tankers located in various Spanish ports to carry out transfers of oil and provisions to U-boats in the central Atlantic until 1942, in spite of protests from the British Naval Attaché in Madrid. (19)

In view of the fact that Standard Oil had gone on supplying Japan and Italy with fuel during the wars in China and Ethiopia, Hertslet and Helmuth Wohlthat of Goering's economic staff believed that it might be possible, at a price, to persuade Standard Oil to sell oil to middlemen of the German Navy. After some of the assets of the international oil companies were taken over by the German forces of occupation in Scandinavia and the Low Countries, Hertslet tried to acquire some of their assets in neutral countries overseas in exchange for release of their sequestered funds in occupied Europe. All these ploys appear to have come to nothing, for all the oil majors seem to have fired all German employees by early 1940. Standard Oil, which owned twenty-seven modern tankers registered in Danzig with the Baltic-American Petroleum Co. and chartered them with German crews via the Waried Tanker Agency of Hamburg, swiftly transferred these to the Panamanian flag of convenience soon after the Munich crisis, when the German authorities had hoped to divert them and their cargoes to German use in the event of war. (20)

This was probably one of the few levers that German interests could exert on the U.S. oil industry, save for their affiliates and holdings in the occupied countries and Rumania, where over fifty-five per cent of the industry was owned by British, French, Dutch and U.S. stockholders. Davis and Co. was the only U.S. oil firm which would entertain German proposals, mainly because it handled nationalized Mexican oil seized from the big oil majors in early 1938. The German side suspected that German, Italian and Japanese dealings with Davis and the Mexican authorities were a very good reason for the U.S. oil majors rebuffing direct German approaches. Davis was one of those businessmen in the United States who supported the candidacy of Wendell Wilkie in 1940 to prevent Roosevelt from being elected to a third term. He was suspected of being a Nazi agent and ordered to give testimony to the House Committee on Un-American Activities in February 1941. He warned Hertslet not to make a payment of $157,000 direct to his New York office for chartering the tanker Laurent Meeus with oil for the German supply organization in Japan, because the FBI had been checking into business accounts with New York banks where unusually large sums of money were transacted. (21) In fact, Davis had had a meeting in person with Goering in late September 1939 when he had promised to supply fuel to Germany and also to support the campaign to prevent Roosevelt's re-election.

From the beginning of the war, there had been numerous signs of Anglo-American and Canadian-American cooperation to Germany's disadvantage. Consular and naval personnel reported on the movement of German shipping in the western hemisphere and this information found its way in due course to the various undercover British agencies in the United States. This attitude of benevolence toward Britain did not become more clearly manifest before the German Army's attacks in Scandinavia and the Low Countries. Until then the German side was content to note that U.S. orders warning its merchant marine not to enter the German-designated war zone in N.W. Europe would prevent the kind of unfortunate incident which had helped bring the United States into World War I. Hitler expressly forbade any kind of hostile attack on U.S. warships or merchant vessels by U-boats or surface raiders in the Atlantic in order to avoid all chance of a repetition of such incidents. By April 1940, the task of making improvements in economic relations with the United States had moved far enough to convince the ever-optimistic Hertslet that it might be possible to make arrangements which would permit raw materials to be sent indirectly to Germany from the United States. Certainly, some goods were arriving via such friendly neutrals as Japan, Italy and Spain in neutral vessels, but particularly when German ships tried to beat the Allied blockade from Latin American ports, from information received it was quite clear that U.S. warships and aircraft were maintaining a quiet surveillance about twenty miles offshore. (22)

Even before the German breakthrough in the west and Japanese pressure in the western Pacific, however, German agents with sabotage instructions were being despatched from late 1939 via Japan and South America to the United States, though there is plenty of evidence to prove that they had also been made to understand that they were not, under any circumstances, to initiate such activities until it became clear that the United States was likely to enter the war. (23) In Japan, meanwhile, German agents using U.S. passports or posing as Americans were being employed in ports in Japan, and subsequently in Shanghai and Bangkok, to mingle with Allied and American merchant seamen, picking up information about ship movements and encouraging seamen from the occupied European countries to defect, provide intelligence and collaborate with the German war effort. (24) Such enquiries tended to confirm growing Anglo-American collaboration just as Anglo-American agents in Japan and elsewhere could confirm collusion between Germany and Japan.

The U.S. denunciation of the trade treaty with Japan in July 1939, which terminated in January 1940, was the first serious move made by the United States against Japan. The Japanese Navy and Army, however, were far from prepared to contemplate the opening of hostilities with the Western Powers at this stage. Oil imports from the Dutch East Indies, particularly diesel and gas oil used by the fleet, rose from 4.8 per cent of Dutch oil exports in 1939 to 8.3 per cent in 1941, while imports, mainly of crude and diesel oil, from the United States, which had peaked in 1938 began to decline, though by no means steeply, until 1941. (25) Japanese stockpiles of oil by the end of 1939 were so high that, when the German Navy despatched a tanker with 10,000 tons of marine oil to Japan to supply German vessels and armed raiders in the Pacific, it could find no Japanese firm to store the oil and had to distribute the cargo among the numerous German merchant ships in Japanese ports. Several German tankers and merchant ships in Latin American west-coast ports escaped to Japan in 1940 and 1941, but by the spring of that year virtually all the loopholes that had enabled the German Navy to transfer funds from Switzerland to the Latin American oil-producing states and the United States to pay for oil and raw material purchases had been stopped, even before the U.S. Treasury froze Axis states' assets in June 1941. FBI and Treasury agents were known to be putting pressure on affiliates of U.S. banks operating in Latin America to prevent German funds from being transferred. Diplomatic pressure on Latin American governments to cooperate with the U.S. measures against the Axis states became increasingly intense after the signature of the Axis alliance in September 1940.

Japanese sensitivity to U.S. measures after the outbreak of the

European war was highly acute. When British warships appeared in the South China Sea and in the Straits of Shimonoseki to intercept German shipping, the possibility that neutral Japanese ships would be stopped and searched for German contraband or for German citizens of military age was raised by the contacts of the German Naval Attaché in Tokyo, Captain Leitzmann. (26) The actual search of the Japanese liner Asama Maru thirty-five miles from the Japanese coast at Nozimagaseki, not far from the naval base at Yokosuka, led to the removal of fifty-one Germans on 21 January 1940. These included a number of former employees of the Standard Oil Company's tanker fleet paid off in American ports, whose names were on a passenger list in the possession of the British officer commanding the armed boarding party. As no Japanese ships had been searched up to that point and as the U.S.-Japanese trade agreement was due to lapse in a few days, the Japanese press drew the conclusion that the two facts were closely interconnected. Whether or not that was true, the fact was that the incident played a significant part in stimulating widespread anti-British sentiment in Japan, reminiscent of the mass demonstrations that had accompanied the Tientsin crisis of the previous year. At this stage of the war, both the Japanese and German navies were convinced of the need to prevent the United States from participating in the European war. Rear-Admiral Wenneker, who arrived in Tokyo as German Naval Attaché for the second time in February 1940, had been given explicit instructions to this effect by Grand-Admiral Raeder and repeatedly developed this point with the Vice-Chief of Naval Staff, Admiral Kondô Nobutake, and the Chief of the Naval Affairs Bureau, Admiral Abe Katsuo. (27) Kondô was of the opinion that Japan alone could exert sufficient pressure on the United States to comply and did not believe that the United States had the capacity to fight a war on two fronts. (28)

The situation for the United States and Japan was rapidly transformed by events in Europe and there was speculation on the fate of the Dutch East Indies within a few days of the German attack on Norway. Although the ultranationalist group in the Japanese Navy argued that the opportunity had come to seize the Dutch East Indies and that the opportunity might never recur, Admiral Kondô privately indicated that, while Japan would not tolerate Anglo-American intervention in the East Indies, neither would she attack, as he was certain that that would bring Britain and the United States automatically into a war with Japan at a time when Japan was not yet strong enough to deal with them, mainly as a result of the war in China. (29) One consequence of the German attacks in April and May 1940 on Norway and Holland was the very considerable importance of their tanker fleets denied to Germany and fully committed to the Allied cause. It had been hoped by Admiral Wenneker that it

140

might be possible to charter Norwegian vessels to supply oil from Mexico to Japan, especially as a Mexican delegation had arrived in Japan in late April and agreed the sale of 340,000 tons of oil to Japan. (30) On the other hand, the seizure of oil stocks in the occupied European countries by September 1940 enabled Germany to continue the war with the same level of reserves as one year earlier, with the exception of diesel oil, a fact which was later to be of no small significance for the German Navy's future conduct of the war at sea. (31)

While the Germans were busily engaged in France, the Soviet Union took the opportunity, while Hitler's back was turned, to seize the Baltic states and the province of Bessarabia from Rumania. These moves had extremely important implications for the supply of oil to Germany, which lost the supplies it had been receiving from Estonia and which was threatened by the potential loss of its principal reliable source of oil in Rumania. Its other main source, the Soviet Union itself, could threaten to cut off its exports to Germany at any moment and, as the example of Finland with its valuable supplies of nickel had already demonstrated, strike at the Rumanian oilfields or even the vital iron ore mines of Sweden and Norway if Stalin had a mind to do so. So long as Britain and its fleet remained intact, as it did through the autumn of 1940, and its air force could attack the synthetic oil plants, Germany was effectively forced to contemplate either the Soviet Union or the Middle East as the main attainable locations from which to draw the oil needed not just for the German economy but also, thanks to the greatly expanded territory now under its control, the whole of continental Europe including Italy, which had gratuitously entered the war in June. None of these territories was a significant source of oil, so that Germany had to contemplate in the future providing oil for this whole area, which was estimated to consume a minimum of twenty million tons annually. According to German figures of world oil production for 1940, the Middle East, then only the fourth largest source, could supply only seventeen million tons annually, most of it from Iran which was twice the distance to Berlin as Moscow and over rather more difficult terrain. Given that it might be possible to hope that Britain might oblige by coming to terms with Germany, and thus provide Germany with the access to oil and raw materials essential to preparing a campaign in the east, whereas the Soviet Union had resisted all blandishments to expand southwards to India and the Persian Gulf, Hitler could easily have seen during his weeks of cogitation on the Obersalzberg in July that, with only limited supplies of oil to play with, the Soviet Union with its annual supply of thirty-one million tons of oil, mainly from the Caucasus, was both the more tempting and the more feasible target. (32)

Hitler's economic advisers repeatedly drew attention to the

limitations on military operations against the Soviet Union imposed by oil shortages, which initially suggested that there were adequate supplies for one month of operations. As an experienced front-line soldier, Hitler recognized that in practice it was always possible to forage in enemy territory. The speed of military operations in the west had demonstrated not only that the enemy could be out-manoeuvred and his stocks of fuel and supplies seized to facilitate further advance, but the estimates of the economic planners were not to be trusted any more than the timidity of the generals' esti-mates of the enemy's capabilities. This latter point seemed confirmed by March 1941, when the economic experts discovered that the fuel shortage appeared to be one on paper rather than based on the real situation. (33) It was then stated that reserves of fuel were enough for eight to ten weeks which, *mirabile dictu*, coincided exactly with Hitler's own estimate of how long it would take for the Russians to collapse. Hitler's offensive was aimed primarily at Moscow with provision for a subsidiary drive south to Baku and the oilfields. He recognized that it would not be enough just to capture significant amounts of Soviet territory, but he imagined that the force of the massive blow would be sufficient to resolve the issue. Its failure meant that the combination of synthetic fuel and Rumanian and Estonian imports was inadequate for all the needs of continental Europe, and dictated that operations in 1942 would have to be geared to seizure of the oilfields of the Caucasus. (34)

Having rejected Raeder's alternative grand strategy, Hitler went on to insist that all German resources be diverted to the Russian venture. The Navy's stocks of diesel fuel, already threatened by transfers to the campaign in the west in March 1940, came under fresh threats when decisions were being taken about the allocations of materials for the campaign in the east in the first few months of 1941. The Navy's shortage of diesel fuel was greatly exacerbated by the fact that the heavier quality oils could not easily be produced synthetically and half of the Navy's requirements had to be imported. This meant that the loss of imports from the Soviet Union after June 1941 would hit the Navy harder than the other services. A second very serious blow to the Navy's fuel supplies lay in the demands put forward by the Italian Navy at a meeting between Admirals Riccardi and Raeder at Meran, when it was claimed that without fuel from Germany their fleet would be immobilized by July 1941. Although Hitler had already rejected the Italian demands for fuel, channelled via the Foreign Ministry, Raeder decided that it was absolutely essential to maintain pressure on Britain in the Medi-terranean in order to relieve pressure on German surface and sub-marine operations in the Atlantic and North Sea. (35)

A third factor affecting the German Navy's fuel position was the decision issued by Keitel on 12 March 1941 for German merchant ships in the Far East to be despatched to Europe with cargoes of natural rubber, stocks of which on hand were estimated to be sufficient only for five months' consumption. This involved a very substantial effort of organization which depleted German stockpiles of fuel in Japan and Shanghai from 41,000 tons in September 1940 to only 14,000 tons a year later, when nine blockade-running vessels had been despatched to French ports. This meant that operations in the Indian and Pacific Oceans by armed merchant cruisers had to be drastically curtailed from the summer of 1941. A tanker sent from Europe to Japan with fuel to replenish these stocks was sunk by the enemy in December 1941, so that for subsequent operations by German naval vessels in the Pacific, it became necessary to depend on the provision of fuel from Japanese stocks once the remaining small amounts of fuel from Latin American countries brought on returning Japanese vessels in oil drums had been exhausted. (36)

By the autumn of 1941, it became evident that as a result of the campaign in Russia continuing contrary to Hitler's expectations, the war on two fronts was having a serious effect on the oil supply of the three services. The Navy's reserves of crude oil were virtually exhausted by October and less than half the monthly consumption (118,000 tons) was being replaced from synthetic production. Extraordinary measures were consequently necessary to save the situation and this was starkly posed in terms of either reaching the Maikop fields (which would in any event take at least six months to bring back into operation) or severe cutbacks in consumption, preferably by the Army and Air Force. (37) Inevitably, however, the Navy, as the least influential of the services, bore the brunt of this cutback: this involved introducing an immediate suspension of operations by heavy units which were estimated to consume 72,000 tons of oil monthly and servicing the requirements of the U-boat fleet, estimated at 20,000 tons monthly by January 1942 and regarded as the best value for expenditure in the future constrained circumstances. (38)

* * *

In the course of the period from July 1940 to October 1941, the Japanese Navy's calculations of future strategy had been greatly affected by the tightening raw-material supply situation. The German victories in Europe fundamentally ensured that, if the Japanese Navy decided for war, it would not under any circumstances be likely to be other than as an ally of Germany and Italy. Even if Japan remained neutral, it was fully expected that once the European Axis had been defeated, Japan would be next on the Allied list. The U.S. announcement of an embargo on the sale of machine tools for arms production in June 1940 was not regarded by the Navy as specifically directed at Japan, but it would undoubtedly affect Japan's mobilization preparations considerably. (39) A Naval Staff officer commented on 11 June:

> 'A very serious situation would arise if America also ordered an embargo on oil and scrap metal. He believes that in such an eventuality there would remain no other choice but to occupy the Dutch oil wells by force or, at any rate, opinion in the Navy in favour of such a step is practically unanimous.' (40)

Admiral Kondô pointed to Japan's stronger position in Asia compared to that of Germany in Europe, in that Japan could retaliate against a U.S. embargo by threatening the oil of the East Indies and the rubber and tin of South-East Asia on which the U.S. was partly reliant. He went on to sound a note of caution about oil:

> 'The oil question, on the other hand, is precarious. At present, practically 100 per cent of supplies come from America. If supplies available in Japan (the amount of which he did not reveal, but in general the amount is estimated to be sufficient for nine months to a year) are used up, the situation would be serious as the capacity of the existing refineries is quite insufficient.' (41)

The embargo on the export of aviation gasoline announced on 1 August, was seen as pointedly anti-Japanese in character, but the stockpiles held by the Navy and its own refining capacity meant that it, unlike the Army, would not be seriously affected by the ban. The Navy saw the U.S. failure to intervene in French Indochina as a test of the U.S. will to intervene, but nevertheless decided on negotiations with the Dutch East Indies in preference to the more overtly aggressive posture of the Army in Indochina. The news of the announcement of the Tripartite Pact of 27 September completely overshadowed the U.S. embargo of the previous day on the export of scrap metal, which had reached its high point of about two million tons in 1939. That Japan was being specially singled out by the U.S. authorities became clear when U.S. tankers were chartered to the Soviet Union, but not to Japan. This step made it necessary for the Japanese to employ their own tanker fleet to pick up cargoes of oil and impeded the delivery of their cargoes to Japanese home ports from California and the East Indies, compared to previous years. Since the majority of the European neutrals with sizeable tanker fleets were now British allies and since the United States was able to exert pressure on the Latin American states, it was this factor which began to bite, rather than any other prior to the announcement of the embargo in July 1941.

Japanese-American negotiations began while Foreign Minister Matsuoka was in Europe and, although on his return home he reiterated Japan's support for Germany during the period of incidents between German and U.S. vessels in the Atlantic, the Japanese Navy's spokesmen privately informed Admiral Wenneker

144

that even if it were found to be true that U.S. warships fired first, Japan would not feel itself obliged to enter the war at Germany's side immediately and automatically. It was explained that, while the Japanese Navy was ready for war, the Army had not yet completed its preparations for the capture of Singapore from the landward side. (42) Admiral Wenneker subsequently reported that the Japanese did not anticipate serious objections from the United States and Britain to the occupation of southern Indochina, while the United States appears to have believed that, by freezing Japanese assets and subjecting the export of oil to official permit, it was merely placing Japan on a par with the European Axis. If there remained ambiguities about Japan's future policy prior to the announcement of 26 July, after it nothing could have been more calculated to harden opinion in Japan for war.

It was not until the last week of August that Wenneker received confirmation that the Japanese Army had finally given up any idea of attacking the Soviet Union. The Navy believed that Britain and the U.S.A. would not interfere with the construction of air bases in Indochina or a move by the Army into Thailand. However, the risk of war with the United States would be taken and attacks would be made on the Philippines and the East Indies prior to a blockade of Singapore. The letter from Prince Konoe to President Roosevelt was regarded as the last chance to rescue the situation, but it was expected to be rejected and this would justify the southward advance, probably beginning in October. By this date, however, the military were becoming restive with the government and pointing out that the U.S. conditions on the withdrawal of forces from Indochina and south and central China and from the Tripartite Pact were not negotiable. They demanded that a deadline for the ending of the negotiations be fixed for the end of 1941. The officers of the Naval Staff, unlike Hitler over Russia, were not overly optimistic about the outcome of the war, though they remained confident that they could successfully complete the specific operations planned in the south. With every day that passed, however, the oil stocks were declining. The Navy was firmly convinced that it was not possible to retreat and that a failure to initiate operations would be more disadvantageous for the country than doing so. The situation in the Pacific was coming to a climax and the Naval Staff was anxious to know what the German reaction would be. Admiral Wenneker replied that he could only provide a personal view that, although Germany would not be obliged to declare war on the United States if Japan attacked first, he felt that Germany was as good as at war already.

By the middle of October, the Navy regarded war with the United States as inevitable and the Army's view was that it was impossible to give in to U.S. demands to withdraw from China. By mid-November, it was confirmed that it was now up to Ambassador

Kurusu to make the most of the final negotiating opportunity, but the fact that a ship had been sent to the United States to bring him and members of the Japanese mission in Washington back home indicated that the prospects for a successful outcome were regarded as slight. On 26 November, Captain Maeda Tadashi, the officer in charge of German affairs in the Intelligence Division of the Naval Staff told Wenneker:

'On the basis of an authentic report from Washington, the negotiations being conducted by Ambassadors Nomura and Kurusu, as anticipated, have reached complete deadlock. No one in the Navy believes any longer in the possibility of a peaceful solution. At this point, however, he cannot say at all when the long-prepared and long-planned attack in the south is estimated to begin. The decision is in the hands of his government.

Maeda went on to say that the English are resorting to a new propaganda ploy. In the last few days, a number of lengthy telegrams not in cipher had been sent here by Foreign Secretary Eden to Ambassador Craigie. The telegrams deal primarily with Germany's "hopeless" position. Their specific contents refer to precise statistics about an alleged oil crisis. In Maeda's view, the purpose of these telegrams is to play on Japan's nerves.' (43)

It is quite manifest from German evidence that the British information telegrams were quite correct on the oil problem. However, both Germans and Japanese had good cause to distrust such statements because Eden's previous efforts to play Germany and Japan off against each other over China in the 1930s and again following the German attack on Russia proved clumsy and counter-productive. But even before the decision to attack the Anglo-American states had finally been taken, the Japanese leaders were aware of the fact that Germany was running into difficulties in Russia and had not let such a fact distract them from the decision in the south. The principal objective was the seizure of oil sources in the East Indies and Japan's decision for war was being taken quite independently of the outcome of the war situation in Europe. When Admiral Wenneker tried to put across the arguments then being advanced by General von Bötticher, the German Military Attaché in Washington, to the effect that Japan had nothing to fear from the United States, he was told in unmistakable terms that the Japanese Navy took the opposite point of view and that was why it had been necessary to plan the operations against the Philippines. Von Bötticher had tried to argue that the U.S. policy was nothing but sheer bluff and that Japan, because it had had many years to build up her stockpiles of raw materials, would be in a position to do the U.S. more damage than the U.S. could do to Japan. Although his view that the U.S. could not immediately fight a two-ocean war was shared in Berlin, his economic views were far from credible in the eyes of the military-economic experts.

The Japanese Navy maintained the same line adopted in 1936 about the Soviet Union: there was no guarantee that Japanese intervention in the Soviet Union would be worth the sacrifices, and even if successful, it would not solve the urgent problem of raw material supply. If Japan attacked the Soviet Union, the chances were that Britain and the United States would still intervene in the Pacific and this would involve Japan in a worst-case scenario of fighting all three powers at once, or, if not, then the United States would be quite happy to see Japanese military strength being sapped by the Soviet Union, as was the case already with Germany. A war with the United States would be a long war: Japan might win the first campaigns, but it would be hard to resist the overwhelming economic and technical resources of the United States, as Admiral Kondô had intimated in April 1941. Even if Japan gained all the economic resources of South-East Asia, she would still not be self-sufficient, but they gave Japan a chance that most naval officers thought was worth taking, even if it ended in an honourable defeat. Admiral Yamamoto Isoroku in May 1940 had advocated seizing the East Indies as soon as possible, arguing that the United States, which was bound to be drawn into the war sooner or later anyway, would not be able to dispute control of the Dutch territory at that time and that probably all states would be so exhausted after the war that it would no longer be feasible to reconquer it.

* * *

The lack of secure sources of oil played a structural role in the shaping of the military strategy and external policy of both Japan and Germany in the decade after 1931. Since the bulk of the world's oil resources was controlled by the United States and the Soviet Union, the Axis Powers were bound to come into conflict with either or both states in the long run if they sought to maintain their roles as major powers in the international political system. (44) Ideological antagonism to the Soviet Union was not a sufficient condition for both states to attack that country, as Hitler would have preferred: had there been a substantial source of oil available in Asiatic Russia, the necessary and sufficient conditions for a joint attack on the USSR would have been met. The weakness of the German fleet, combined with the relative inaccessibility of British-controlled sources of oil in Iraq and Iran, were major factors militating against a land-based German attack on the Middle East via North Africa, as advocated by the Japanese. The oil production of the Dutch East Indies and Burma was adequate for existing Japanese requirements. A Japanese attack on the Middle East by land or sea was not within the capabilities of Japanese forces, given the strength of U.S. military capabilities.

147

Japanese leaders had no real desire to strengthen German military capabilities either in the Soviet Union or the Middle East, and would have ideally preferred a stalemate situation which would have enabled them to secure East and South-East Asia against all comers.

The pervasive economic role of the U.S. oil industry and its key relationship to the inter-war economies of Germany, Italy and Japan effectively neutralized the opposition of France and Britain to the resurgence and rearmament of the 'have-not' states during the 1930s. Short-term profit blinded the U.S. oil majors to the ultimate threat to their own financial interests which these states represented, and delayed the growth of political awareness within the United States about the political consequences of foreign economic involvements. Domestic political considerations dictated that economic sanctions by the United States against Germany and Japan proceed by stealth and this surveillance established dangerous precedents for civil liberties in the post-war decades. The United States effectively imposed an embargo on trade with Germany well before Pearl Harbour through informal cooperation with British blockade measures, and gradually extended that embargo to the Latin American states during 1941. These measures, however, were of small economic effect on Germany because the German economy had managed to switch the main weight of its activities from overseas to the continental land mass of Europe. (45) China and the European colonial powers bore the brunt of Japanese expansionism through the refusal of U.S. economic interests to collaborate effectively with federal agencies and with potential allies at an early enough stage to risk confrontation when its adverse consequences would have been far less catastrophic than they need have been.

The moral condemnations of British and French appeasement prior to 1939 can only be tempered by the knowledge that Anglo-French capacity to do economic damage to the fascist states was severely constrained by the external policies of the U.S. oil majors, who could scarcely be expected to respond to the moral suasion of political decision-makers whose fundamental philosophy was based on non-intervention in the affairs of the business corporation. But even if the U.S. oil majors had taken the view of U.S. Treasury Secretary Morgenthau in the summer of 1940 that 'Japan and Germany might be brought to heel if the United States could stop *all* oil exports on grounds of national defense requirements,' it would have had a negligible effect on the German economy. (46) The freezing of German assets on 14 June 1941 was merely a symbolic act which hurt U.S. interests more than German. (47) The subsequent freezing of Japanese assets in July symbolized U.S. acceptance of the view that the have-not states had now been placed in the same moral limbo for future punishment. The intervening German attack on the Soviet Union, as Hitler had predicted, freed

148

Japan in the rear to attack the Western Powers. But, because the Western Powers had made substantial supplies of raw materials and arms available to the Soviet Union, it also lengthened the time it would take the U.S. to be prepared for war in the Pacific in particular.

It was recognized in Japan that the gap between the objectives and the real capabilities of the U.S. was perhaps wider than it would ever be again, and that Japanese strength *vis-à-vis* the United States would decline increasingly from 1942 onward. For Germany, the worsening oil situation meant effectively that, by failing to defeat the Soviet Union as expected in the autumn of 1941, the only alternative source of oil imports outside Europe would be Japan, once the oilfields of the Dutch East Indies had been seized. The Germans certainly attempted to encourage the Japanese to intervene actively in the war from the winter of 1940 and welcomed that intervention for the strategic relief it provided. Japan would almost certainly have fought without its European allies, just as the Western Powers fought a separate, parallel war together with the Soviet Union, but the statement conveyed by Ribbentrop on 21 November 1941 of the German preparedness to enter into a no-separate peace agreement with Japan provided many people in the Japanese government with as much relief as it stimulated righteous anger in the State Department. (48)

As early as 1920, Foreign Minister Tôgô Shigenori had observed as a young secretary in the Japanese Embassy in Berlin that the traditional world order was crumbling even then, when he had said:

> 'Gradually one realises that the Entente is rather weak financially and people are annoyed that America keeps its finger on the purse-strings. America will lose a great deal through its wretched greed.' (49)

Observers of the current scene in the Middle East could be forgiven for harbouring similar sentiments about the Arab oil-producers and their insatiable demands. The Arab oil embargo of 1973 has already indicated that a deliberate denial of essential fuels by states which have far more than they themselves require is a step which can easily ignite a volatile mixture of factors which could prove to be of fateful consequence for the present world order. By comparison with this, the attack on Pearl Harbour could be seen as a significant, but minor precedent. If the leaders of the two superpowers take seriously the prediction that both their countries will be dependent on external supplies of oil by the second half of the 1980s and they find themselves in dispute with Muslim countries which carry out threats to deprive them of that supply, the dangers of a third world war can hardly be dismissed. 'The atmosphere is boiling. It could,' Shaikh Yamani has reportedly stated 'lead to disaster if nothing is done.' (50) Once again the United States faces far-reaching dilemmas over the oil issue, complicated by states which pursue economic deviance and by states which appear to be prepared to follow strategies for violent change in the shaky world order of today.

20

Tradition and Modernity in Japanese Film Propaganda, 'Nippon Nyûsu' 1940-45

GORDON DANIELS

During the first half of the twentieth century the cinema dominated popular amusement in all advanced societies. (1) The power of films to amuse and excite created a new art and a new industry, and the persuasiveness of moving pictures gave them a social and political significance which was recognized by both democratic and totalitarian regimes. In Japan as early as 20 October 1912 the Tokyo police forbade showings of the French film *Jigoma* on the grounds that it might incite crime and disturb social order, and in October 1925 the Home Ministry implemented a nationwide system of film censorship. (2) However, official interest in the cinema was not confined to purely negative precautions. In the interwar years the Ministry of Education took an active role in encouraging documentary productions, while the example of German and Italian film legislation prompted government activity in a wide range of cinematic policies. (3)

In October 1939 a new Film Law was put into effect which made showings of newsreels and documentaries compulsory in all cinemas; and government concern with newsreels soon extended to action to amalgamate the existing Asahi, Mainichi, Dômei and Yomiuri organizations into a single Nippon Nyûsu Eigasha 'Japan News Film Company', which began its operations in April 1940. (4) In its formative period the new company issued three Special Weekly Film Reports, but on 11 June 1940 it issued the first edition of *Nippon Nyûsu*, a regular newsreel which appeared on 254 occasions before the ending of the Pacific War. (5) Besides being projected in all cinemas, *Nippon Nyûsu* was also shown in schools and village halls by travelling film units, and constituted one of the most highly organized attempts at mass cinematic persuasion attempted during World War II. (6) Clearly the organization, methods and motivation of this propaganda were in no way traditional, but an examination of the content of this major voice of official opinion may reveal the relative balance of tradition and modernity within the rhetoric of Japan's wartime administration. Such an examination may also indicate something of the broader blend of illusion and reality which characterised thought and action in wartime Japan.

Nippon Nyûsu began its first regular issue with a sequence of the emperor, in a limousine, emerging from his palace for a visit to the Kansai to visit ancestral tombs. (7) This was during the much publicized celebrations of the 2,600th anniversary of the Imperial Household, and might well be seen as a symbol of tradition effectively used in preparation for total war. On several later occasions the emperor was depicted attending grand Shintô festivals for the war dead at the Yasukuni Shrine (8), but for the most part the emperor appeared like any other head of state in time of war, in military ceremonies which had little connection with tradition or any form of religious activity. Attendance at numerous army parades, waving to happy crowds after the fall of Singapore, and a visit to Tokyo University to stimulate science and learning were typical of the emperor's cinematic appearances, but as the war gathered momentum he disappeared from the screen for substantial periods. He appeared in no major new role until the spring of 1945. (9) At this time he was shown visiting the ruins of Tokyo after the worst American incendiary raid of the Pacific war.

It could be argued that the role of imperial princes, as projected by *Nippon Nyûsu*, had more traditional parallels. They visited conquered territories such as Java and the Philippines, which recalled the significant symbolic activities of princes in the civil war of 1868. (10) Yet even these activities, looked at in wide perspective, are somewhat difficult to distinguish from the acts of western royalty in time of war. If a certain distinctiveness remained, it lay perhaps in the formality, and safety, of the situations in which princes were depicted. There appeared little attempt to identify such personages with combat. Instead they were associated with the restoration of law and order when the fighting was already over. In fact, the most overtly traditional projection of the Imperial Household had preceded the war, in the celebration of the archaeologically and historically bogus 2,600th anniversary of imperial rule. At this time newsreels showed monuments being unveiled, military reviews, and mass displays of traditional martial arts. (11) Yet, ironically, the two most genuine celebrations of imperial tradition which were depicted during the years 1940-45 had little connection with mass mobilization—or the notion of the imperial state in arms. Traditional performances and ceremonies were mounted to commemorate the anniversaries of Shôtoku Taishi's death and the Taika reforms, but in view of their archaic and peaceful character, these events could contribute little to the atmosphere of modern international combat. (12)

Scenes of shrine construction, ceremonies for the dead, and Shintô priests at various national celebrations gave a somewhat traditional dimension to weekly cinema bulletins (13), but though the ever recurring Yasukuni Shrine festivals had no exact parallels in the West, they clearly had a significance for government and citizens which was social and psychological as well as religious. Nonetheless, Shintô ceremonial was at times filmed in imaginative ways to add a pseudo-religious cachet to political or strategic objectives. Shintô shrines had already been constructed in Korea as part of the general policy of assimilating colonial territories, and this example was clearly developed in the prologue to the Pacific war and the conflict itself.

In autumn 1940 cameramen visited the Palau islands where several hundred citizens were involved, with official leadership, in the dedication of a Southern Ocean shrine symbolising the empire's southern advance. (14) Shintô construction in Shônan—the renamed Singapore —also received considerable film attention. (15) Yet certain Shintô ceremonies resembled those of the peaceful post-war period. When the railway tunnel across the Shimonoseki straits was finally completed, there were Shintô rituals, but these were hardly the main focus of contemporary celebration or cinematic interest. (16) As the war reached its military climax, and Japanese military and economic success appeared in graver doubt than at any previous time, aspects of Shintô did appear more frequently on Japanese screens. In 1944, when the mobilization of the inhabitants of Saipan was presented, a child was described as praying fervently to the war god Hachiman and there were Shintô overtones to the extensive depiction of suicide units and their preparations for attacks on American warships. (17) Yet such religious events, like the *kamikaze* assaults themselves, appear to typify one phase of the conflict rather than the overall mood of film propaganda.

If spirituality is often regarded as the overwhelming feature of much propaganda, its other face, a neglect of science, is often seen as typical of war-time Japan and its conduct of the conflict. Clearly, much scientific research could not be projected to a vast public for simple security reasons, but it may be that the comparative neglect of scientific innovation in Japanese news film represented, albeit unconsciously, the retarded state of Japanese science and a somewhat traditional approach to warfare. Yet science was far from totally absent as a theme in *Nippon Nyûsu*'s coverage of events. Such achievements as the electrical detection of bullets lodged in the flesh of wounded men, observation of an eclipse, the filming of a dog's beating heart and the bringing of protective injections to Burmese peasants indicate that the balance between science and tradition in the delineation of the war was far from simple. (18)

One element in Japanese tradition and history, *sakoku* ('closed-country') isolation, is sometimes assumed to have been revived in the intellectual and political history of the Pacific war. In the sense that Japan was isolated from the major centre of liberal scientific and social innovation, the United States, this notion may have some validity. But this concept of isolation requires careful defi-

153

nition before it can be readily accepted. Throughout the years 1940-43 not only did diplomacy receive as much attention as Shintô or the imperial family in newsreel coverage, but conditions in Europe and Asia were major features of Japanese newsreels. (19) Clearly, the diplomacy which Japanese citizens saw on their screens was scarcely representative.

The Tripartite Pact, the Japanese-Soviet neutrality pact, and negotiations with French Indochina received cinematic attention, as did Japan's treaty with Thailand. (20) That these events were deliberately chosen cannot be questioned, but the desire of most newsreel editors and censors appears to have been to emphasize Japan's position within an alliance rather than her solitary position, her international support rather than her isolation, and this is hardly compatible with a simplified notion of an island mentality. (21) When western affairs almost disappeared from Japanese screens in the closing stages of the war, it was probably due to difficulties of communications and supplies rather than to any pre-modern mentality or antique approach to Japan's international predicament. Evidence for such a view can be found in coverage of German triumphs in the west, the bombing of Coventry, war in the Balkans and contacts by submarine with the Third Reich. (22) Even more surprising was the thoroughness with which fragments of favourable news from Europe were shown, even when they signified a clearly worsening situation. The rescue of Mussolini by the Germans, and German defensive moves in France in the summer of 1944 are but two examples of such information. (23)

If an isolationist mentality was apparently absent from the newsreels' treatment of Europe, it was dramatically lacking in their interpretation of events in East and South-East Asia. What is more, in depicting these regions Japanese film propaganda was emphatically and uncompromisingly modern in most of its content. From its beginnings *Nippon Nyûsu* placed emphasis upon the new order in Greater East Asia and the liberation of Asian peoples from alien domination. This propaganda theme had already been apparent in the creation of the Manchu puppet state, and the activities of its emperor received serious newsreel attention. (24) Perhaps more striking was the considerable coverage given to events in the independent kingdom of Thailand. Her diplomatic negotiations with Indochina, alliance with Japan, and military parades commemorating her revolution received substantial mention. (25)

In dealing with both newly created puppet states and liberated areas *Nippon Nyûsu* also gave vivid expression to the role of local nationalist leaders, local pro-Japanese armed forces and the building of new states and new societies. (26) There was little of the traditional in the tone of such propaganda with its emphasis on medicine, increased production, agricultural improvement and the political mobilization of the local population. (27) At times traditional arts were shown serving a modern purpose, as in the case of touring propaganda theatres in China and Indonesia (28), but when tradition was mobilized in the context of Japan's Asian allies it was often the semi-modern tradition of nationalism rather than anything predating the nineteenth or twentieth centuries. In the case of the Chinese puppet state, not only was there notable commemoration of the centennial of the Opium War and the beginnings of British imperialism, but careful mention was made of the inheritance of Sun Yat-sen, whose close connections with Japan were widely known. (29) In the closing stages of the war the independence given to Burma and the Philippines and promised to Indonesia was emphasized, and Burma's declaration of war on the Allies was also the source of joyful screen headlines. (30)

Yet perhaps the most sustained treatment of Asian nationalism came in the repeated shots of the pro-Japanese Indian nationalist movement in Tokyo, Singapore and Rangoon, with anti-British rallies and extensive footage of the Indian National Army including well armed and uniformed ranks of women. (31) However deceptive and unreal such images may have been, they looked forward, unknowingly, to the political atmosphere of the post-war world and not to any long-honoured element in Japanese tradition.

In their treatment of women in Japan, as opposed to East and South-East Asia, the newsreels provide images which are too varied to be dismissed in clean and simple categories. Clearly, the passage of time and the transformation of total war from theory to practice produced a subtly changing interpretation of women's role. For much of the war a somewhat stereotyped view of women as mothers and members of stoic patriotic societies continued (32), yet Japanese women were depicted in construction corps in New Guinea, and increasingly the role of women in war production came to be a dominant theme in the cinema. (33) By February 1944 Prime Minister Tôjô's appeal to Japanese women to emulate those of the United States in replacing men behind the lines was projected on cinema screens and, in the final phase of the war, women were shown carrying out factory work, and driving and signalling trains in poses and uniforms which clearly had military overtones. (34)

In total, the message of the newsreels is complex and unsteady; with twenty-five hours of film and some 1,000 incidents it could scarcely be otherwise. Yet within them, tradition and stability are less significant themes than change, development and multicultural emancipation. In the final year of war, *Nippon Nyûsu* presented a morose collage of discarded lives and reckless loyalism. (35) Perhaps these brief images expressed an archaic tradition. But overall, Japan's official newsreel challenged Asia's colonial past and foreshadowed its future liberation.

21

Japanese Policies in Burma and Indonesia 1942-45 as a Dependent Variable of the 'Gunbatsu' Phenomenon

LASZLO SLUIMERS

When comparing the reactions of South-East Asian political groups to 'the wise and benign guidance of the Japanese military administration' (1), two kinds of attitudes should be clearly distinguished.
I. In Burma, Indonesia, the urban part of the Philippines and urban Indochina, the elitist political groups or, rather, politicians were inclined to follow Japanese guidance.
II. In the rural Philippines (2) and rural Vietnam, there was a peasant resistance aimed directly at the local elites but, indirectly and even mainly, at their Japanese protectors who, by pacification campaigns, tried to prop up the position of these elites. (3)

Here I am concerned mainly with the first set of attitudes and concentrate on the situation in Burma and Indonesia in order to draw a kind of 'idealtypus' of the Japanese era that to some extent is also applicable to other areas.

Assuming that the South-East Asian politicians were both unprepared to resist the Japanese and in a position to impose their will on the majority of the people, especially in the countryside, through a kind of indirect rule, it is not only legitimate but even crucial to seek to determine the limits of Japanese power. So I depart from the notion of *gunjin bannô* ('the omnipotence of the military') and deliberately put this power question at the heart of my considerations. (4) One might say that, viewed from this angle, the limits to Japanese power were mainly of two kinds.

Firstly, especially at the start of Japanese military operations, there were too few trained Japanese personnel at hand to run any administration whatsoever. As an extreme and almost incredible case, I can refer to the situation in Burma between January 1942, when Lieutenant-General Iida Shôjirô's 15th Army invaded the country, and March 8th of the same year when Iida took Rangoon.

During this period there was no centralized military administration whatsoever. In fact, there was a so-called *Gunseiban* ('Military Administration Squad') under Colonel Nakada Saichirô but this group was charged with recruiting Japanese personnel for the administration, not with administration itself. As a consequence, the occupied territories were subjected to a so-called *Kikan Gunsei* ('Military Agency Administration') run by Colonel Suzuki Keiji's

Minami Kikan ('Minami Agency') and the Suzuki-created Burmese Independence Army, the members of which belonged mostly to Aung San's radical-populist Dobama or Thakin Party. This stop-gap administration was run according to the time-honoured method of the *Chian Ijikai* ('Peace Preservation Association'). (5) When Iida's troops took Rangoon, the *Gunseihan* was renamed *Gunseibu* ('Military Administration Section'). This was run by Colonel Nasu Yoshio. Its personnel was scratched together from Japanese expatriates who, until the outbreak of war, had been employed by the big Japanese trading-firms in Burma and Thailand. Shortly after the occupation of Rangoon Suzuki created the so-called Baho government under Thakin Tun Oke.

The second kind of limit to Japanese power was the faction-ridden nature of the Japanese army. By creating the Baho, Suzuki immediately ran foul of Nasu's *Gunseibu*. The manifest issue was that Suzuki's Baho was called into being on the assumption that Burma was to be granted immediate independence. Nasu, on the contrary, started from the Military Minutes of the Liaison Conference of 20 November 1941 between the Japanese government and Imperial Headquarters. Article 8 of the said Minutes stated *inter alia*:

> 'Native inhabitants shall so be guided as to induce a sense of trust in the imperial forces, and premature encouragement of their independence movements shall be avoided.'

So Nasu pushed to the fore another *kikan*, the *Hiraoka Kikan* ('Hiraoka Agency') which, after having obtained the *Minami Kikan*'s 'concurrence', took over its duties in Rangoon. This step inaugurated a process which led to the disbandment of Baho, the *Minami Kikan*, and the Burmese Independence Army successively. The latter some time afterwards re-emerged as the Burma Defence Army, and the *Gunseibu* became the *Gunsei Kanbu* ('Military Administration Executive') under Iida's chief of staff, Lieutenant-General Isayama Haruki. Thereafter, the *Gunsei Kanbu* sought the support of U Ba Maw's equally populist but less radical Sinyetha Party, consisting of more or less western-trained intellectuals. Under Japanese auspices, Sinyetha and Dobama were wielded into the Dobama-Sinyetha Party, a structure not unlike the *Taisei Yokusankai*, 'The Imperial Rule Assistance Organization', founded in Japan in 1938.

On 1 August 1943 Burma was granted independence, with Ba Maw as head of state and Aung San as commander-in-chief of the army. The reasons for this Japanese step were not far to seek. Not only did the Japanese understand quite well that Burma could not be refused what was promised to India, but they also needed at least a modicum of support from those Burmese elements who were able to fill the gap that had arisen due to the lack of sufficient competent Japanese administrators.

During the remaining two years of the *'présence Japonaise'*, Burmese political life was dominated by the rift between the Sinyetha who dominated the administration and the Thakins who controlled the army. The climax came during the British reconquest of Burma when, in March 1945, the Burmese army changed sides and attacked the retreating Japanese.

In fact, a similar situation developed both in Acheh at the northern tip of Sumatra and in the Deli area just south of Acheh. Acheh's political life was traditionally dominated by a split between the Dutch-supported native heads and the orthodox *ulema* (Islamic scribes) who might be considered the leaders of the people. The younger *ulema* at the end of the Dutch era united in the so-called Pusa Federation. (6) When the Dutch army crumbled under the Japanese onslaught in January 1942, this Pusa prepared an anti-Dutch rising. One of the *ulema*, Haji Abubakar, contacted the Japanese army in Malaya for help. Instrumental in this contact was Major Fujiwara Iwaichi, who had sided with the 'Young Officers' (*seinen shôkô*) in staging the infamous *ni-niroku* assassinations in Tokyo in 1936. (7) After Fujiwara promised help, the rising took place in February. Soon afterwards the Japanese army occupied Acheh, only to push aside the Pusa people and seek the support of the Achenese native chiefs. (8)

In Deli before the war, a member of the *Fujiwara Kikan* went even further and contacted the leftish Gerindo Party, then involved in an agrarian dispute. He told the Gerindo people that, after the Dutch were driven out, the Japanese army would liquidate feudal rights so that land would be freely available. This promise came to nothing. Some months after the Japanese army came in, a rebellion broke out as a result of an agrarian dispute. This revolt was severely repressed by the Military Police (*Kenpeitai*). Manifestly, the leading elements in the Japanese army had ideas different from those of the *Fujiwara Kikan*. (9)

Let us now consider Indonesia's main island, Java, which was occupied by Lieutenant-General Imamura Hitoshi's 16th Army in March 1942. Imamura's chief of staff, Lieutenant-General Okazaki Seizaburô, became *Gunseikan* ('Director of the Military Administration'). One month later Shimizu Hitoshi, an activist of the propaganda department who in pre-war days was associated with Ôkawa Shûmei's *Dai Tôa Renmei*, ('Greater East Asia League'), created the 3A Movement, a mass organization structured in the same way as the *Taisei Yokusankai*. The Indonesian leaders of this movement were associated with the pre-war conservative Parindra Party which consisted to a considerable degree of Javanese civil servants belonging to the *priayi* (*noblesse de robe*) class. (10) Partly because these elements had already lost much of their prestige even before the war, partly on account of the movement's excessive Japanism, but mainly

158

because the 3A Movement was prohibited from engaging in activities in the countryside, the movement came to nothing.

In the meantime, Imamura, after serious rows with Southern Army Headquarters in Singapore, had brought Soekarno, later to become president, to Java from his exile in Sumatra. Not without some resistance from Shimizu's 3A Movement, he, Hatta and two other Indonesian leaders were put at the head of a new mass movement, the Putera. This movement was similarly based on the *Taisei Yokusankai* idea, but differed from the 3A in that, *inter alia*, its leadership was somewhat less Parindra-orientated.

In the meantime, tensions in the countryside grew ever sharper. (11) The big plantations, no longer able to export their produce, started to dismiss Indonesian coolies. Afterwards, the forced rice deliveries and the recruiting of workers had a devastating effect on the situation outside the towns. Partly to prevent Indonesian radicalism from seeping through to the countryside, the head of the General Affairs Department of the Military Administration Executive, Colonel Yamamoto Moichirô, 'ordered the Indonesian leaders to lead this movement more spiritually' (12); that is, he watered down Putera's programme and proscribed it from engaging in activities outside the towns.

This Japanese policy of sealing off the countryside from radical influences emanating from the towns had to be abandoned with the setting up of the Indonesian-officered *Kyôdo Bôei Giyûgun* ('Homeland Defence Volunteer Army': PETA) consisting of sixty-six 'battalions' spread all over Java. The main figure behind this latter development was a captain of the *Beppan* ('Special (Intelligence) Section'), Yanagawa Motoshige, who should be considered a typical 'young officer'. (13) Partly because he understood that the war was not developing favourably for Japan, his efforts to create this army might also have been aimed at soothing Indonesian discontent. Be that as it may, the company and platoon commanders in particular were the nucleus of the *pemuda* ('young men's') elite that gradually became more and more dissatisfied with both the spiritualized (14) Indonesian leaders and the Japanese. Partly to pose a counterweight to Peta radicalism, Putera was dissolved and replaced by a new mass movement, the *Jawa Hôkôkai*. This was led directly by the *Gunseikan*, its local chapters being controlled by Indonesian civil servants. The discontent culminated in the abortive Peta rebellion of 14 February 1945, in Blitar. This rebellion might be regarded as an Indonesian counterpart to the actions of the Burmese army. (15)

When comparing Indonesian and Burmese politics of the period, one cannot but be struck by the similarity between them. What in my opinion is important is that in both countries an *oyabun-kobun* 'boss and henchmen' structure can be discerned. In Burma, Iida and Isayama supported Ba Maw, whereas Suzuki associated himself with

159

the Thakin. (16) In Acheh, the *Gunseibu* supported the native chiefs, whereas Fujiwara backed the *ulema*. In Deli, a similar pattern was to be seen. In Java, Shimizu backed the Parindra, Imamura supported Soekarno, and the *Beppan* (Yanagawa) in fact stood behind the *pemuda*.

When mentioning these names and reading Storry's study of the *shishi* (17), it is immediately apparent that *gunbatsu* ('military cliques') were re-emerging, since the same people who were active in pre-war *gunbatsu* with the rank of major, or at best lieutenant-colonel, now re-emerged in South-East Asia with generals' stars. Iida, Isayama and Okazaki were Sakura-kai members. (18) In pre-war days Fujiwara had sided with the 'Young Officers'. Shimizu was associated with Ôkawa Shûmei, the central figure in the Sakura-kai inspired March Incident of 1931, and Imamura was a well known *tôseiha* ('Control faction') exponent.

It is very difficult to come to any other conclusion than that Terauchi's decree of 1936 proscribing *gunbatsu* was not very effective. The question is why? I think Crowley's pioneer study of Japanese military politics between 1930 and 1938 can provide us with an answer. (19) *Gunbatsu* were in fact nothing but old structural fissions within Japanese society in a military attire. Insofar as the rifts between *gunbatsu* arose from social problems, especially during the crisis of the thirties, corrective measures of the Terauchi brand in fact begged the question and solved nothing. When the Japanese expanded into the south Pacific, an intensification of the *gunbatsu* phenomenon was to be expected, for the simple reason that the local military commands were apt to develop into satrapies resisting Tokyo's interference because the influence of the Foreign Ministry there was too great for the liking of the local military commanders. This whole approach suggests, of course, that the incidents of the thirties in Japan should not be seen as isolated incidents but as outbursts due to secular trends in Japanese society. In this respect even the actions of the Tenchû-gumi during the *bakumatsu* period (1853-68) fit into the picture.

I have to acknowledge that I am here in the rather hybrid position of being both a kind of Japanologist and a kind of South-East Asian expert. In my last capacity I am conscious of begging the question with my assumption that, both in Burma and in Indonesia, peasant resistance to the political elites mostly did not amount to more than local jacqueries. Of course, one has to ask what there is to explain this difference from, for example, the Philippines and Vietnam. A very interesting preliminary approach to this question has been made by the American political scientist Anton Lucas in his analysis of the so-called Three-Regions Incident in northern Central Java during the latter part of 1945 and the first months of 1946, which had its roots in developments during the Japanese era (20); but also, in this case,

160

this incident might be seen as a symptom of perennial trends. (21) Even *gunjin bannô* has its limits. (22)

22

The Beginnings of 'Democratic' Politics — Japan's First Post-War Election Campaign

MICHAEL HAYES

The end of the war in August 1945 was generally seen as providing a fresh start for politics in Japan. Pre-war politicians saw it as an opportunity for them to resume their influential role, partially usurped by the military and bureaucracy, using the traditional methods of politics. The Allies, however, saw it as a chance to create a western-style democracy which would overthrow these established interests. The early reforms of SCAP sought to redress the balance and to create a framework for democratic politics. This work was centred on the election of a new Japanese Diet which would replace the one elected during the war. In due course, SCAP decided that Japan was sufficiently prepared, and the election was set for 10 April 1946. Interest in this 1946 election campaign among the Allies and other foreign observers ran very high because it would show to what extent the Japanese people had accepted the spirit of the SCAP reforms. It seemed essential for the modernizers to strike while the old interests were still stunned, disgraced or disorganized, and so set the stage for new methods, new faces and new ideas.

There were several aspects of the 1946 election campaign which did augur well for the future. One of the most important was the enactment in December 1945 of a new election law. (1) The chief features of this were the lowering of the voting age to twenty and the age for standing for the Diet to twenty-five, the enfranchisement of women, the adoption of the large constituency system, and the introduction of the limited plural-ballot system. (2) The extension of the franchise to include women and young men would more than double the electorate. The large constituency and changes in the voting system were designed to break down the *jiban* ('local basis') of the old politicians. (3) Though drafted without the assistance of SCAP, this law was considered 'epoch-making'. It came in the wake of the liberalizing measures of the Occupation. On 4 October 1945, SCAP issued a memorandum on 'The removal of restrictions on political, civilian and religious liberties' (4) and this led to the freeing of political prisoners, as well as ensuring free speech and association. Efforts were also made to encourage a more independent and objective press. (5)

Probably the most effective of the SCAP attempts to change the

Japanese political scene were the purge directives of 4 January 1946. (6) Former politicians were so decimated that all but 150 candidates in the election were new faces. The Progressive Party, which had been made up largely of former members of the Great Japan Political Association (*Dai Nippon Seijikai*), lost virtually all of its leadership apart from Saitô Takao. Candidates were required first to apply for approval of candidature and then they were allowed to place their nominations. The purge not only deterred those tainted with war guilt from standing but also encouraged many unknowns to attempt election.

Political parties were another aspect which changed dramatically at the end of the war. The first major one to be inaugurated was the Japan Socialist Party (though its official title was the Social Democratic Party of Japan) (7) and it was soon followed by the Japan Liberal Party, the Japan Progressive Party and the Japan Cooperative Party. The Communist Party was by now active as a legal party for the first time. Its leaders Tokuda Kyûichi and Shiga Yoshio were among those released from prison by SCAP's 'human rights' directive of 4 October, and on 20 October the *Akahata* newspaper appeared. By election day the following year, the total number of political parties had reached 363, of which national parties (including the big five) comprised 13, regional parties covering more than one prefecture 10, and parties confined to just one prefecture 340. (8) Though most of these parties were of a decidedly conservative nature, they did give the electorate a choice from all parts of the political spectrum which it did not have before.

SCAP placed great emphasis on raising the political consciousness of the people and this was taken up by the press and, to a lesser extent, the Japanese government. From 12 December 1945 the *Asahi shinbun* ran a long series of round-table talks for politicians of the various parties which asked them the question: 'What do the parties fight for in the coming election?' Other papers did likewise and, as the campaign increased in momentum, the press became more and more assertive. The government, for its part, published pamphlets explaining how a campaign should be conducted under the new election law and what penalties there were for breaking it. (9) The *Tôkyô shinbun* revealed that the Japan Educators' Association on 7 December had sent 50,000 pamphlets on 'How to hold a civic gathering' to cities, towns and villages throughout the country. They also planned to distribute 300,000 pamphlets with titles such as: 'What kind of men should be elected for the coming Diet?', 'Why women have been enfranchised', and 'Why one should not abstain from voting'. (10)

For the first time in Japan, election broadcasting by candidates was permitted, and on 15 February 1946 a spokesman for the Civil Information and Education Section of SCAP explained the regulations for this. (11) Election broadcasts went out three times a day for thirty minutes each over the forty-two broadcasting stations in Japan. Nationwide broadcasts were open only to parties which had candidates in twelve or more prefectures, but all candidates were given equal broadcasting hours in the prefectures where they ran. Accordingly broadcasts began soon after the official campaign was announced on 11 March and politicians certainly made full use of them. The Government Section of SCAP estimated that there were 2,180 minutes of national broadcasts and, in the Kantô area alone, 6,509 minutes of local broadcasts. (12) These figures meant an average of over 300 minutes for each party in the national broadcasts. Undoubtedly campaigning by radio was a major step forward in Japan, but its success was limited by the number of sets available, by the inexperience of the broadcasters (13), and by the time restriction of five minutes per session, which did not allow candidates to give their views in detail or the voter to make up his mind. (14)

Japanese elections before the war had been notorious for the amount of police interference which was allowed, and SCAP was firm in its prohibition of this traditional practice. Indeed, the police kept such a distance from election meetings that candidates complained of the lawlessness of some gatherings. There were occasions of Communist candidates being beaten up by people in the audience before the police arrived on the scene. In general, though, there was approval of the inconspicuousness of the police.

SCAP was also anxious to prevent any election offences by candidates. On 23 March, the Tokyo Police Board announced that after nearly two weeks of campaigning only about ten violations of the election law had been observed in Tokyo and all seemed due to carelessness. (15) At the end of the campaign the *Tôkyô shinbun* was able to report that cases of large-scale bribery and door-to-door canvassing had not been frequent. (16) It attributed this to the multiple-ballot system, the great increase in voters, the awakening political consciousness of the voters, and also to the emergency economic measures which prevented candidates from drawing large sums of money. In fact, money never did play an important part in this campaign. On 22 February SCAP issued an order restricting the amount of campaign contributions which could be given by a third party. (17) In addition, at the beginning of March, SCAP demanded that the candidates and parties report their campaign expenditures and receipts each week to the local governors from the time of the announcement of the election to the election day. The first report was to include all expenses incurred from 1 January 1946. (18) Accordingly, the party campaign funds were open to scrutiny and this perhaps helped to control the *kaban* ('briefcase') aspect of Japanese politics. (19)

So far it has been possible to show that reforms were made which modernized much of the structure of Japanese politics. Yet any lasting success depended on a change in attitude on the part of politicians and on increased political awareness among the people. In the week following the inauguration of the official election campaign on 11 March 1946, the heads of the five major parties issued statements setting forth the party principles which were generally vaguely worded and perhaps reflected the traditional approach to a campaign. They seemed to be playing safe so as not to offend important sections of the electorate.

The *Asahi* gave prominence to these statements, beginning on 13 March with Katayama Tetsu, Secretary General of the Socialist Party. (20) His public pledge to the people exhorted them to choose between socialism or capitalism. He proposed agrarian reforms, so that all would become independent farmers, and the nationalization of the fertilizer industry. There would also be nationalization of certain manufacturing industries and the Socialist principle here would be: 'Increased production of necessities through high efficiency and high wages'. Policy on unemployment was mainly the promotion of public works. The Socialist stand on the Emperor was fairly ambiguous, declaring that sovereignty lay neither with the Emperor nor the people but with the 'nation'.

The next day the *Asahi* carried the Liberal Party statement (21) and on 16 March that of the Progressive Party. (22) Both of these conservative parties stressed 'the protection of the emperor system' as one of their basic policies. The statement of the Progressives was the vaguest of all, but they differed from the Liberals chiefly in seeking stronger state control of social welfare and some moderate form of economic control. On 15 March the *Asahi* carried the Communist pledge to the people, and this concentrated on solving unemployment, food, inflation and industrial problems by popular control. However, it made little mention of the Emperor and merely stressed the need for a popular front to carry out these plans. (23) The last major party programme to appear was that of the Cooperative Party, which also stressed the need for a continuation of the emperor system, but with restricted powers. The party also declared that 'cooperation' was the only way to save the country but did not go into details. The most important aspect of its 'democratic political structure' would be the maintenance of the line of emperors. In economics, the party would like to see important enterprises managed by 'the cooperative society'. (24)

From all this it is easy to see how the party leaders were accused of taking equivocal stands on major issues and of intending to rely on the personal appeal or local support of their recognized candidates to gather votes. Ironically, the one point which could have polarized opinion, the emperor system, did not really become an issue. On 6 March, the government announced the SCAP-inspired draft of the

165

constitution and all the major parties, with the exception of the Communists (who merely placed abolition of it further down their list of priorities), gave it their support, with only minor reservations. (25) Yet the campaign did provide many opportunities for exploring and debating in greater depth the various party policies. In this the newspapers played a leading role. Round-table talks were a frequent aspect of press coverage, and they were held mainly to probe in greater depth the party attitudes to problems such as inflation, unemployment and the future of women. The papers even sponsored highly successful public meetings attended by members of all parties. (26) Nevertheless, the chart published by the *Asahi* at the end of the campaign showed a startling similarity between party programmes. (27)

The campaign did build up momentum, however, and by 25 March the *Tôkyô shinbun* was able to report vigorous activity all over the country, certainly on the part of candidates. (28) The main complaint was not directed at the parties but at the ordinary people's lack of interest. Editorials deplored 'indifference' and appealed to the voter's sense of responsibility. Sunday, 17 March, was predicted to be one of the busiest days, yet a writer in the *Mainichi* told of candidates standing in the snow to make speeches but 'nobody stopped to hear them'. (29) On the same day the *Tôkyô shinbun* attributed the lack of enthusiasm to 'the difficulties of everyday living, the psychological shock of defeat and the undemocratic national character'. (30) Attendance at election meetings was often quoted as an indication of the lack of interest. The *Yomiuri hôchi* reported that in cities, as well as in provincial towns and villages, meetings could 'scarcely attract more than one hundred interested parties'. (31)

Tokyo Police Board figures showed that up to 3 April in Tokyo, where 254 candidates were running, there were only about 150 election meetings per day (120 indoors, 30 outdoors). Audiences ranged from 600-700 for leading figures, to averages of 20 in the daytime and 30-40 at night for ordinary candidates. The number of adjourned meetings in an average day was 40 (30 per cent of the total). (32) The SCAP Government Section estimated that the average attendances of meetings in the Tokyo area was 93. (33) Of course, one of the reasons for the relatively low attendance was the sheer number of candidates. In the previous two elections, the average attendance in Tokyo was 130-140 in 1937 and 74 in the 1942 (*yokusan* '(imperial rule) assistance') election but the number of candidates then was only 68 and 97 respectively. (34)

Despite the election slogan urging people to vote for 'parties rather than personalities', the famous names attracted the crowds and people like Hatoyama Ichirô of the Liberals and Nozaka Sanzô of the Communists never failed to get a good reception. Respected figures such as Ozaki Yukio, the veteran parliamentarian, were urging voters to 'choose individuals without regard for party affiliation, because of the present fragmented state of parties'. (35) Ozaki was to issue this appeal several times, even over the radio. Yet with only 150 candidates who had stood before, it was still possible for newcomers to fight the campaign and win.

A brief look at the campaigns of two successful candidates of the Socialist Party will perhaps illustrate the great contrasts to be seen in this election. Hirano Rikizô was the election manager of the Socialists and of great importance to their electoral machine. He had been elected to the Diet for the first time in 1936. His strength lay in the Kantô area and he had great support among the agricultural associations. Yamanashi prefecture was his *jiban* and from the start there seemed no danger of him not being elected. However, Hirano seemed to value his *jiban* more than his allegiance to fellow party members. He and the other dominant Socialist in Yamanashi were accused of treating a newcomer in the prefecture, fellow Socialist Usui Jirô, as an outsider. (36) The latter complained of not being able to make a joint campaign with the other two, and he was almost expelled from the party because he held a joint meeting on democracy with the Communist Party. (37) Hirano, however, felt so safe in Yamanashi that he only paid it a couple of visits during the campaign and spent the rest of the time campaigning for others around Japan. (38) In due course he was elected with over 100,000 votes.

Yamaguchi Shizue, on the other hand, had a very different experience in her campaign for election in the Tokyo First Electoral District. Not only a new face, but a woman too, she had to work very much harder than Hirano. She was one of the first to make street speeches and soon averaged three or four a day, travelling all over the constituency. (39) Soon she had established some sort of record of about fifty speeches. Novelty in being a young woman candidate no doubt helped her and she got much support from the newly enfranchized women voters. Nevertheless, it was quite a feat for an unknown woman of thirty to take second place in the district, behind Hatoyama Ichirô. Behind her were such well-known names as Nozaka Sanzô and Asanuma Inejirô. She even beat famous women such as Takeuchi Shigeyo and Katô Shizue.

From these examples it can be seen that, though the *jiban* and the cult of personality were still very much alive, it was possible to be elected using the modern methods advocated by SCAP. In certain areas, such as Kyoto, the united front had taken hold and the issues were much more clearly defined. (40) In others established interests sought to cling on by using 'substitute' candidates and traditional ways of getting votes. (41)

Western-style political campaigning did not immediately appear in Japan, though there were indications of increased popular awareness and changing tactics. Tradition is still deeply ingrained in political practices even today, and it would take more than the structures and guidelines created by SCAP to shift it.

SECTION 4

Art
and
Architecture

23

Tradition in Japanese Architecture

ELEANOR VON ERDBERG

In Japanese architecture of today, tradition can hold its own in several different ways. A builder may: 1. copy a historical style; 2. add traditional details to a structure in the style of international modernism; 3. incorporate one or more basic features of Japanese architecture into an otherwise modern building; 4. translate the forms engendered by wooden structures of the framework type into reinforced concrete; or 5. express his understanding and respect for the basic values of Japanese architecture without copying structure or detail.

1. Copying the styles of the past is of least concern to us here, much as it is in evidence throughout Japan—from Tokyo's Kabuki theatre to the Momoyama-style shrines of the Tenri sect. Such buildings do not express the personal style of their architect but, rather, the wish of the institution which the building is going to serve; if this in itself is traditional then it will want this fact to show in the architecture. Others will want their buildings to reflect power and magnificence, or a dignity based on the old spiritual values. How modern architecture encroaches even on these preserves of the traditional is seen, for example, in the Minami Midô Temple in Osaka: the main hall, though built in concrete, is in every way a replica of a *kondô* in a Buddhist temple; but it is approached by passing through a cubic, entirely modern entrance building.

2. Of the numerous examples of single features transplanted from famous old buildings to modern houses, the bold squares on the *fusuma* of the Shôkintei in the Katsura garden are a striking example. Aesthetic as well as practical considerations may prompt the application to modern style structures of details borrowed from traditional architecture. The Yamato Bunkakan museum near Nara, by Isoya Yoshida, may serve as an illustration. It is a low square building with a central courtyard. The outer walls have hardly any windows. These are barred, not by lattice, but by part of the solid wall into which are cut long vertical slits, about 15 cm wide. These effectively keep out too much sunlight or heat. They are copied from the traditional storehouse (*kura*), which did not need much light; the same slits can still be seen on the upper floor of old merchant houses, for example, on Shinmonzen in Kyoto.

171

On the plain, white-washed upper storey of the Yamato Bunkakan these groups of vertical slits form a pattern of dark lines that impart a modicum of tension to the otherwise unbroken stretch of horizontal wall-space. Inside, some of these windows are closed with *shôji* —again an aesthetic delight as well as a practical measure. The first floor has no windows; its grey wall is covered with a 'net' of vertical and horizontal, white, rounded ridges, that form row above row of squares. The effect is one of strength and protection—the same impression as that conveyed by its prototype, the walls surrounding such temple compounds as that of the Chion'in in Kyoto. There is one significant difference: on the old walls the ridges run diagonally, implying that such a wall is not a structure in the strict Japanese sense, for there is no wooden framework. But the Yamato Bunkakan is a structure, albeit a concrete one, that has no visible posts and lintels; yet it is subject to the strictures of the upright and the horizontal. The diagonal has no part in traditional architecture.

3. Many modern-style residences have one Japanese room with *tatami*, *shôji* and *fusuma*—if the owner can afford the extra space. This does not always mean a return to the ancient building codes. Even the most traditionally minded builder must take into account that people and habits have changed. By omitting the *nageshi*, the conspicuous beam which serves as a lintel to sliding doors and is continued all round the room, the architect gains freedom from norms. He may add to the height of *shôji* and *fusuma* (once fixed at 176-178 cm) and adapt them to the higher stature of the present generation. He also has greater freedom in the arrangement of the rectangles of his walls. Thus the helpful calculations, which assured good proportions, are no longer valid in modern domestic architecture. The contemporary builder is free to choose the measurements of the respective parts of a room. What was once securely based on time-honoured rules is now left to personal taste and feeling for proportions—and open to all dangers inherent in the vagaries of such tastes and feelings.

The good architect will instinctively choose the right measurements and proportions, as Maekawa did when designing the Kyoto Kaikan. He will use space and materials unhampered by rules and yet abide by those basic principles of good proportions, that cannot be abandoned with impunity. The Japanese section of the Miyako Hotel in Kyoto by Murano, or the Botan, a club house for teachers of traditional dance by Isoya, show how much can be retained and how much can be thrown overboard—yet both are equally and intrinsically Japanese. On the other hand, when the architect Nishikawa chooses a pattern of zigzagging diagonals for the *shôji* lattice of a 'modern traditional' room, this flight of fancy does nothing but disturb to an unbearable degree the harmony of his rectangles. Tradition may be disregarded but not flouted.

172

One feature in traditional architecture that seems well worth keeping is the close relationship between the framework structure and the wall-openings such as windows and doors. All verticals and horizontals, and thus all the rectangles they create, are connected (exceptions occur in tea-house architecture). A window or a door is not a hole cut into wall; it is securely tied to a post and beam. Openings take up either the full space between posts, floor and *nageshi*; or, if they are smaller than a pair of *fusuma* or *shôji*, two or at least one of their sides touch a post or beam, so that windows and doors are safely attached to the framework outlining the walls. A classical example is the window in one corner of the small room for the storage of musical instruments in the Nakashoin of Katsura; it touches the corner post and the ceiling. Isoya follows this example when designing the outside of Oriental House in Tokyo: the door of a balcony is not in the centre, but propped up securely against one corner post.

Even the basic relation of wall to floor and ceiling may be changed, and yet the traditional details will lose none of their character. Seike, when building a house in Tokyo in 1961, was asked to make use of, and find a suitable place for, a pair of handsome gold-paper *fusuma*, which were family heirlooms. He put them in the Japanese room as closet doors. But contrary to traditional usage he placed them about one foot above the floor, so that they reached right up to the ceiling. This would be safer for them; they were not in danger of being scuffed by people no longer used to the delicate constitution of paper *fusuma*. Yet this is still a room where one sits on the floor; a long, low window runs right along the *tatami* floor; two electric lamps hanging above it also light up the lowest zone of activity. This is a good example of a Japanese room in a modern house; it is not seen as a relic of the past—like a collector's item—but incorporated into the house as a whole and sharing its task of providing space and shelter for the flow of daily life and its activities. Though stressing tradition, it adjusts to the tastes and demands of today. *Shôji* and modified forms of *fusuma* are still used in many buildings, which are not strictly traditional. They have proved their worth; western style doors and windows are not always deemed quite as satisfactory.

One characteristic of Japanese art, and hence also of architecture, is the absence of symmetry. An added traditional effect of the balcony door in Isoya's Oriental House mentioned above is the introduction of asymmetry into an otherwise symmetrically subdivided wall. The wall would have been almost unbearable if the door had been placed in its exact centre. This reminder of the irrationality of being alive is one of the most important traditional factors in modern Japanese architecture.

When western buildings became the fashion, the rigid symmetry

173

and with it the concept of a façade, the strictly arranged pattern of which determined the position of doors and windows instead of taking their cue from them, would have been hard to foist upon the Japanese, had it not been for their Chinese-style architecture, which, basically, is strictly symmetrical. But for the Japanese these buildings were reserved for ceremony, religious or secular. The Japanese house could do without a showy façade. Its outside shapes reflect the needs to which the inside of the house caters: doors and windows are installed wherever passage or light is required. Most modern residences also claim this independence from formalism; their builders are still able to fuse the outer walls, doors and windows of a house —however western in style—into a pleasing pattern of rectangles, large and small, light and dark, balanced but not symmetrical, and to harmonize the various tensions they create. In the wake of the tea-masters, they too look at old farmhouses and make use of the framework patterns, the visible beams and bamboo grilles. To balance them is more difficult than to arrange them symmetrically, but this problem is still solved successfully.

The greatest challenge tradition flings at modern architecture is the roof. Modern western buildings usually have flat roofs; already the second and third generation of twentieth-century architects considers the roof dispensible—it is almost viewed with suspicion. The Japanese have always stressed the roof—and not just in the shape of the spectacular Chinese curved roof. Theirs was a cluster of roofs over a building with irregular groundplan—different heights, angles and sizes, with gables facing in all four directions. Katsura is a well-known example, but any old-fashioned Japanese dwelling illustrates this point just as well. Yet such is the power of the western example that the modern Japanese buildings dispense with the roof almost as readily as those in the West.

Kikutake Kiyonari, when he designed the hotel Tôkôen near Tokyo in 1970, gave this many-storied structure a flat roof and then crowned it with a larger and a smaller pointed roof with concave slopes, but even the larger one does not cover one third of the building. It is obviously not expected to perform the task of covering and protecting; rather, it is an addition that ties the modern hotel to its predecessors in representative architecture. It is a symbol rather than an integral part of the building.

4. Modern architecture all over the world had to adjust to the conditions and possibilities of reinforced concrete. The Japanese had perhaps the least difficulty in translating tradition into modernism as far as material and construction were concerned. Wooden framework and reinforced concrete demand the same kind of structural process; in consequence, the architectural forms they engender must resemble one another. If we compare the Shishinden in the Kyoto Imperial Palace with, for example, Tokyo's Daimaru

built in the fifties at the back of the main railway station, the resemblance is striking. In both instances posts and beams are the architecture; the walls seem to recede; they bear no weight; they seem immaterial behind the web of structural elements, which meet at right angles. The strong but delicate looking tracery of wood or steel forms the same simple pattern of rectangles. Yet this need not be so simple: Kikutake in his Tôkôen hotel varies their shapes and sizes, stressing some, while others are but subdivisions of larger units. This is not a copy of an old building—far from it—yet the similarity of the old and new materials as regards their structural possibilities could not fail to make the modern architect aware of the weight of tradition behind him and of the wealth of suggestions and inspirations it held in store for him.

Japanese tradition has also influenced the architects of the West due to this resemblance between wood and steel construction (among others, the German architect Egon Eiermann). Thus modern-minded architects in Japan found that part of what they could learn from the West was what the West had learned from them; or, at least, that the West had been led to develop forms which are akin to those in Japanese traditional architecture, so that, in some respects, international modern architecture leads the Japanese right back to their own traditions.

5. The great masters of modern Japanese building were well aware of the values of their tradition. Attempts to break away from it had led, in the fifties, to the "New Brutality" in a conscious effort to establish the superiority of mass over structure. This style did not last. In the long run, a Japanese could see no merit in it. The buildings for the Olympic Games by Tange, on the other hand, though possible only in concrete and not resembling anything in earlier Japanese architecture, yet bear witness to its true virtues: they show the forces and tensions and the builder's mastery and technique in holding them together—just as the skill of the master carpenter balanced weight and thrust and joined his wooden posts and beams in intricate joints, so that it was visible and obvious that the whole structure would hold together. The logical relationship between the enclosing structure and the enclosed space is made clear. In this sense Tange's Tokyo cathedral is truly and traditionally Japanese, although the prevalence of the curved line is alien to the image of pure Japanese tradition and even goes beyond the role of the curve in Chinese style buildings. Tange's cathedral does not deny the weight of the building materials, as is the case in Gothic architecture. It rests on the ground; it soars no higher into the sky than the weight and thrust of the structure permits and the interior space demands. In this sensible domination of the static over the dynamic, of rational, man-made order over the vagaries of the imagination—a domination tempered by the acknowledgement

175

of the irrational aspects of human life and nature—lies the strength of Japan's architectural tradition.

Because of this, the Japanese have not given up wood as their most congenial building material. Its growth predicts its destination. Even when cut into shapes of geometric precision, it reminds man of its origins. Man does not wish to forget them. The *tokobashira*, the post of the *tokonoma*, is often a tree-trunk, untouched or sparsely trimmed by the hand and tools of man. It stands in the place of honour as a reminder of the origin of all building. It introduces the element of life and nature into the otherwise austere composition of rectangles that surround a Japanese room. In some modern houses it is even exaggerated to proportions unknown in traditional buildings, the huge, gnarled tree-trunk, for example, that reaches from floor to ceiling in a spacious tea-room designed by Yamawaki. The atrium style court of the Yamato Bunkakan is planted with bamboo. From the galleries, through the glass panes, only their strong, green trunks are visible. They form a forceful pattern of verticals—an almost, but not quite geometric design created by natural shapes, like the window grilles of a tea-house made of bamboo sticks. They divest the courtyard of its barren orderliness; the subtle deviations from straight line and right angle give it a touch of the irrational, which is the essence of life. This is the important lesson taught by Japanese tradition.

24

The Birth and Development of Japanese Buddhist Sculpture

TAKESHI KUNO

In the year 538 A.D., King Song Myong of Paekche, one of the kingdoms of ancient Korea, presented a Buddhist image and sûtras, among other objects, to the imperial court of Yamato, thus officially introducing Buddhism to Japan for the first time. The period from the official introduction of Buddhism to the year 645 is called the Asuka period. During the early part of the period, however, Buddhism was not especially widespread in Japan, although immigrants from the Korean peninsula privately worshipped the faith.

In the latter part of the sixth century, one of the powerful clans of that time, the Soga clan, built the Asuka-dera in the Asuka district and thereby established the first full-fledged temple in Japan. Temple architects, tile craftsmen, and bronze casters, too, were invited from Paekche to work on the project. The Asuka-dera was completed toward the end of the sixth century, and the Shaka (Sâkyamuni) statue that is the temple's main object of worship—a gilt bronze statue close to three metres in height—was completed in the beginning of the seventh century.

Later, fostered by imperial patronage, Buddhism flourished in the Nara area: temples were constructed by members of the imperial family and powerful clans, and Buddhist images were widely produced. Of these temples, the Hôryûji is the most important. Shôtoku Taishi, who greatly encouraged the spread of the Buddhist faith, had the Hôryûji built around the year 606 in Ikaruga, the site of his own residence. The seventh-century Kondô ('Golden Hall') and five-storied pagoda still stand today, and there also exist a number of Buddhist images that date from the first part of the seventh century. The main object of worship of this temple is the gilt-bronze Shaka Triad, which was completed in 623 by the sculptor Tori Busshi as a votive offering for Shôtoku's peaceful repose after his death.

In the treatment of the body and the rendering of the drapery, both the early seventh-century Shaka of the Asuka-dera and the Shaka Triad of the Hôryûji have elements in common with Chinese Northern Wei sculpture of the later Yun-kang and early Lung-men caves. Therefore, it was formerly believed that the sculptural style

177

of Northern Wei had been transmitted to Japan by way of Korea. However, Paekche, the kingdom which had introduced Buddhism to Japan, traditionally paid tribute to the Chinese southern dynasties, such as Southern Ch'i and Liang, rather than to the northern dynasties of Northern, Eastern, and Western Wei. Records indicate that sculptors of the southern dynasty of Liang had been invited to Paekche.

In recent years, Buddhist sculpture of the Southern Ch'i and Liang dynasties have been discovered in China's Ssuchuan Province. Gradually, it is becoming clear that Japanese Buddhist sculpture of the Asuka period is more closely related to the sculpture of the southern dynasties than to the sculptural style of Northern Wei. The stone sculpture excavated in Ssuchuan Province, such as the Amitâyus (Wu-liang-shou) inscribed with the date Yung-ming first year (483) of the Southern Ch'i dynasty and the Sâkyamuni stele inscribed P'u-t'ung fourth year (523) of the Liang dynasty, hint at the origins of the sculpture of the Asuka period.

The sculpture of the Hakuhô period (645-710) falls into two categories, separated chronologically by the reign of Emperor Tenchi (662-671). The first part of the Hakuhô period still shows lingering vestiges of the Asuka style but, in the second part, the transmission of the Sui and T'ang styles led to the appearance of a sculptural mode that is a harbinger of the sculpture of the Tenpyô period.

Typical examples of early Hakuhô sculpture are scarce, but the standing gilt-bronze Kannon in the Kanshinji and several of the gilt-bronzes included among the Shijûhattai-butsu ('Forty-eight Buddhist images') are believed to have been produced during this period. In comparison to the sculpture of the Asuka period, these statues are characterized by a certain amount of modulation in the rendering of their bodies: their chests are expanded, their waists are constricted, and their hips are wide. Also, most of the statues of the Asuka period are provided with so-called mountain-shaped crowns (yamagata hôkan), but the early Hakuhô images wear diadems with three plaque-like ornaments placed in the centre and to the left and right (sanmen hôkan) and their bodies are festooned with jewel chains. These characteristics have something in common with the sculpture of Northern Ch'i and Northern Chou in China, indicating that around the middle of the seventh century new continental styles were transmitted to Japan.

The Miroku (Maitreya) in a contemplative pose in the Yachûji inscribed with the date Tenchi fifth year (666) is also constricted at the waist and wears a richly ornamented triple-plaque diadem. The hem of the drapery of this statuette is decorated with a pearl-strand motif which originated in Persia. This motif is believed to

178

have been transmitted to China during the Sui dynasty and sub-sequently found its way to Japan.

In 685 (Tenmu 13), an imperial edict was issued stating that every household must erect a Buddhist shrine and install a Buddhist image and sûtras within. There are numerous small gilt-bronze statuettes dating from this period, since small-scale images suitable for private household shrines were widely produced. Many of the childlike statuettes among the Forty-eight Buddhist Images are thought to have been made at this time.

However, as early as the reign of Emperor Tenmu (673-686), statues with a distinct sense of volume were produced, such as the Kôfukuji Buddha head and the seated Miroku Butsu in the Taima-dera, which clearly display Sui and T'ang influence. It also appears that the mature style of early T'ang reached Japan during the reign of Empress Jitô (686-697).

There are those who have maintained that the Yakushi Triad in the Yakushiji was produced during the eighth century, but the theory that the triad was cast during the reign of Empress Jitô has gained strength in recent years. The mature treatment of the bodies of the Yakushi Triad, the rhythmic tribhanga pose of the bodhisattvas Nikkô and Gakkô, and the fluid rendering of the drapery excite wonder. In the scant half-century since the Asuka period, the emergence of sculpture of this quality was possible perhaps because the images that served as models and the sculptors themselves were different in nature from those of the Asuka period.

During the Tenpyô period (710-794), an element of nationalism was added to the character of the Buddhism of the preceding period, and the concentrated energies of the nation went into the construc-tion of temples and the production of images. In this period of concentrated national effort, Buddhist sculpture attained maturity, both technically and stylistically, and Japanese sculpture marked its classical age.

At the beginning of the eighth century, the capital was transferred from Fujiwara-kyô to Heijô-kyô (Nara), and the great temples estab-lished in the vicinity of Fujiwara-kyô, such as the Daianji, Kôfukuji, and Yakushiji, moved to the new capital. Moreover, Emperor Shômu issued an edict ordering the construction of provincial monasteries and nunneries. In Nara, Shômu decreed the construction of the Tôdaiji, whose central object of worship was the colossal Vairocana Buddha which measured fifteen metres in height. His successor, Empress Kôken, ordered the construction of the Saidaiji. Thus, the Tenpyô period was one that witnessed the unprecedented flourishing of Buddhist art, centering on the capital in Nara, under the protec-tion of successive rulers.

Buddhist sculpture was produced in great quantities as envoys to China and monks who went to China to study brought back knowledge of the high T'ang style. With the start of the Tôdaiji project, which was begun at the behest of Emperor Shômu in 743 (Tenpyô 15), a special bureau for the construction of the Tôdaiji was established, and the sculpture was executed by many craftsmen working in the sculpture studio within this bureau under a division-of-labour system. The sculpture studio received as many as five hundred orders during its busiest periods.

The Buddhist sculpture of this period, however, was not all produced in this type of government-sponsored studio. In the Nara capital and elsewhere, there were independent sculpture workshops that satisfied private demand. Moreover, from around this time, apart from the professional craftsmen, there were monks who sculpted Buddhist statuary. For example, at the beginning of the eighth century, Shami Tokudô carved the central image of the Hase-dera out of a sacred tree. Also, the *Nihon Reiiki* records the fact that a monk named Kanki produced Buddhist statues.

The majority of sculptors of the eighth century, however, were the descendants of immigrants, as was the case during the Asuka and Hakuhô periods. Kuninaka-no-Muraji Kimimaro, who was responsible for the successful completion of the colossal Vairocana in the Tôdaiji, Shôgun Manpuku, who sculpted the Ten Great Disciples and the Eight Demonic Guardians in the Kôfukuji, and Shihino-Muraji Kimimaro and Kochi-no-Obinari, who made the *jôroku* Kannon in the Ishiyama-dera, were all descended from immigrants.

A wide range of sculptural techniques was in use during the Tenpyô period. The principal sculptural media were bronze, dry lacquer, and dry clay, but silver and gold images were also produced. A silver statuette still extant today is the Nirmâna Buddha in the crown of the Fukûkenjaku Kannon in the Hokke-dô of the Tôdaiji. Most of the remaining examples of dry lacquer sculpture that date to the first half of the period have been made by the hollow dry-lacquer process. In the latter half of the period, however, wood-core dry-lacquer statuary also appears. The wood-core dry-lacquer technique consists of carving the greater part of the image in wood, covering the wooden core with hemp cloth coated with lacquer which was then allowed to dry, adding the details in lacquer mixed with wood shavings, and finally applying the colouring or gold leaf. Also, clay tiles stamped with images, bronze repoussé plaques, and stone sculpture were widely produced. Such a variety of techniques was not to be seen before or after this period.

Extant examples of gilt-bronze sculpture include the Tôdaiji Buddha-at-birth and meditative bodhisattva and the Yakushi Nyorai statuette said to have been deposited within the statue of Yakushi Nyorai in the Saien-dô of the Hôryûji. Major extant examples of hollow dry-lacquer sculpture include the Fukûkenjaku Kannon, Bon-ten, Taishaku-ten, and Four Guardian Kings in the Sangatsu-dô of the Tôdaiji, the Ten Great Disciples and Eight Demonic Guardians in the Kôfukuji, and the Roshana Butsu in the Tôshôdaiji. Wood-core dry-lacquer sculpture is represented by the Eleven-headed Kannon in the Shôrinji and the Eleven-headed Kannon in the Kannonji. Extant examples of dry-clay sculpture include the Four Guardian Kings in the Kaidan-in of the Tôdaiji and the Twelve Guardian Generals in the Shin Yakushiji. The statues of the Zutô in Nara are examples of the stone sculpture of the period.

The sculptural style of the Tenpyô period developed under the influence of the T'ang style that was transmitted to Japan around the middle of the Hakuhô period. The Tenpyô style is characterized by a somewhat more intellectualized conception of the body and the countenance in comparison to the sculpture of the preceding period. Accordingly, Buddhist sculpture in general exhibited a realistic style of clarity and refinement that was widely appreciated during this period. The treatment of the body and countenance no longer possessed the childlike quality of the Hakuhô period and instead reflected the features of a mature adult. Tenpyô sculpture, too, includes images that convey a sense of great suffering. The figures of the heavenly deities are usually rendered full of movement.

The century between the transfer of the capital to Heian-kyô and the termination of the practice of sending envoys to China in 894 (Kanpyô 6) is called the Early Heian or Jôgan period. It should be noted, however, that opinions differ as to precisely when this period ended. From a stylistic point of view, the term 'Early Heian period' is sometimes extended into the middle of the tenth century, that is, until the advent of the Wa-yô or Japanese style of sculpture.

At the outset, Emperor Kanmu refused to allow the great temples of Nara to move to the new capital, and the Tôji (Kyôôgokokuji) and the Saiji (no longer extant) were newly constructed to the east and west of the Rashômon, one of the main gateways of Heian-kyô, to preserve the peace of the city. Subsequently, the Heian capital gave birth to a new culture, spurred on by the new forms of Buddhism introduced by Saichô and Kûkai. Saichô expounded the Tendai doctrine from the Enryakuji on Mt. Hiei, while Kûkai first built the Shingon-in in the Tôdaiji, then gradually began to increase the influence of the esoteric Shingon sect through the Kyôôgokokuji and the Kongôbuji on Mt Kôya.

Affected by these developments, sculptural styles and techniques underwent changes. The foremost direct cause was the abolition of the government bureau for the construction of the Tôdaiji and the Hokkeji at the end of the Nara period. The process of sculpting the images, which had been accomplished by numerous craftsmen through a division of labour, was altered. This was one reason behind the rapid emergence of wood sculpture which had previously been overshadowed by the government studios during their period of glory. Although the government studios were abolished, not all of the artisans who had been employed there sought to change their professions.

Looking at extant examples of Early Heian sculpture, two categories can be discerned: dry lacquer-related wooden sculpture and pure wooden sculpture. The former are descended from the dry lacquer sculpture of the Tenpyô period and are wooden statues that have been finished using lacquer in a supplementary fashion. Examples of this technique include the Five Bodhisattvas, the Five Great Myôô, the Four Guardian Kings, and the three Shintô deities in the Lecture Hall of the Kyôôgokokuji; the seated Amida Nyorai in the Lecture Hall of the Kôryûji; the Five Great Kokuzô Bosatsu in the Jingoji; the Nyoirin Kannon in the Kanshinji; and the Five Dhyâni Buddhas in the Anshôji. Many such statues were commissioned as votive images by members of the imperial family and monks of the Shingon sect who were disciples of Kûkai.

The other category, that of pure wooden sculpture, can be further divided into three types. The first of these can perhaps be called plain wood sculpture, statues that are referred to as 'wood sculpture' in records of the time. These statues are carved out of a single block of wood and are left plain without the addition of colour. Examples include the standing Yakushi Nyorai in the Jingoji, which was the votive offering of Wake-no-Kiyomaro, and the seated Yakushi Nyorai in the Shin Yakushiji. Such statues may well belong to the tradition of the independent Buddhist sculptors of the eighth century. The second type of pure wooden sculpture is the polychromed type, which nonetheless displays sharp carving. The third type is the *danzô* or sandalwood sculpture, which developed under the influence of sandalwood sculpture brought from China. Extant examples of polychromed sculpture include the standing Yakushi Nyorai of the Gangôji, the Eleven-headed Kannon in the Kôgenji, the Jizô Bosatsu in the Hôryûji, and the statues of Shaka Nyorai, one standing and one seated, in the Kondô of the Murôji. Typical examples of *danzô* sculpture are the Miroku Bosatsu in the Murôji, the Eleven-headed Kannon in the Hokkeji, and the Miroku Butsu in the Tôdaiji. These two categories of wooden sculpture developed stylistically through a mutual interchange of forms in the latter part of the ninth century.

The sculpture of the beginning of the Early Heian period only rarely provides examples that possess the refinement and clarity of the Buddhist sculpture of the eighth century. Pronounced in volume, solemn images with an element of mystery began to proliferate. Statues with heavy physiques, strongly squared shoulders, thick

182

waists, and bulging thighs were widely produced. In the latter part of the ninth century, however, the forms become gradually less marked in volume and the features once again become refined. The *honpa-shiki* ('rolling-waves style') drapery pattern, which was originally associated with pure wooden sculpture, also begins to appear in dry lacquer-related wooden sculpture, such as the Miroku Butsu in the Jison-in dated Kanpyô fourth year (892). In addition, wooden statues carved to reveal the beauty of the wood itself at times have been provided with dry-lacquer accessories, such as the snail curls attached to the head of a statue. In time, the two types merged and flowed into the *Wa-yô* current of the Fujiwara period.

During the Fujiwara period (894-1185), Japanese sculpture freed itself from Chinese influence, and an indigenous style was perfected that was suited to the tastes of the aristocracy of the period. The tenth century, which corresponds to the first half of the Fujiwara period, serves as a prelude to the development of the *Wa-yô*. The Yakushi Triad in the Jô-Daigo of the Daigoji, dating to the first part of the Fujiwara period, still exhibits lingering traces of the style of early Heian. However, the Amida Nyorai in the Iwafune-dera, which is inscribed with the date Tengyô ninth year (946), displays a distinct roundness in the rendering of the face and the body, even at this early date. At the same time, there are still many statues that remain faithful to the older style, such as the Yakushi Triad in the Lecture Hall of the Hôryûji, which is believed to date from the first year of Tenroku (970).

Upon entering the eleventh century, however, there are statues such as the Fudô Myôô in the Dôshû-in of the Tôfukuji dating from Kankô second year (1005) and the seated Yakushi Nyorai in the Kôfukuji dated Chôwa second year (1013), which display signs of the Japanized style. In particular, the Fudô Myôô in the Dôshû-in represents the angry form of the deity, but nonetheless reflects the milder sentiments of the Fujiwara aristocracy. The true *Wa-yô*, however, was not to be perfected until the advent of the sculptor Jôchô, who was active from the early to the middle part of the eleventh century.

Jôchô assisted his father Kôshô in sculpting Buddhist statuary for the imperial court and the Fujiwara clan, and he was later to become even more active than his father. For his distinguished services in sculpting images for the Hôjôji, he was awarded the ecclesiastical rank of *Hokkyô*, an unprecedented title for a sculptor, and he later advanced to the rank of *Hôgen*. Formerly, Buddhist sculptors, being artisans, had been relegated to a low social ranking, but the honours conferred upon Jôchô contributed to the raising of their status, and the names of sculptors began to appear in the inscriptions on statues.

Jôchô is also regarded as the founder of a new sculptural technique. This technique, known as *yosegi-zukuri* (joined wood-block construction), consists of carving the main portions of a statue, that is, its head and trunk, in several blocks of wood which are then joined together. Ever since the seventh century, there had been examples of statues composed of several blocks of wood, such as the meditative bodhisattva in the Chûgûji and the central cores of wood-core dry-lacquer statues, but the blocks were assembled at will and not often according to fixed rules. Jôchô devised a systematic method of assemblage that enabled several sculptors to work simultaneously on the carving of a single statue. Also, in order to cope with the large number of commissions for sculpture from the aristocracy, guild-like associations of sculptors were formed. In time, sculpture studios were established by craftsmen such as Jôchô's son Kakujo, and Chôsei, Jôchô's foremost disciple, and these studios regarded Jôchô as their principal forebear.

A genuine example of Jôchô's work extant today is the Amida Nyorai in the Phoenix Hall of the Byôdô-in, which was sculpted in 1053 (Tengi 1). The proportions of this image are regulated, the chest has a sense of capacious breadth, the height of the folded legs is relatively low, the drapery folds are arranged perfectly, and the statue as a whole is carved with fluid strokes. The countenance of this work is solemn, yet gentle, in accordance with the refined sensibilities of the Fujiwara nobility. Records of the period indicate that Jôchô statues were used as models by other sculptors, who worked according to the measurements of Jôchô statues and attempted to approximate these measurements as closely as possible.

After Jôchô, Chôsei strove to further the Japanized sculptural style. Extant works by Chôsei include the Nikkô and Gakkô and the Twelve Guardian Generals in the Kôryûji, all of which display a high degree of refinement. Also, works such as the Amida Nyorai in the Hôkaiji, the Kutai Amida Nyorai statues in the Jôruriji, and the Amida Nyorai in the Hôkongô-in are all post-Jôchô but are faithful to the Jôchô style. These statues are evidence of the gradual standardization of the style.

In the midst of the proliferation of the Jôchô style, a new style appeared in the middle of the twelfth century in the form of the Amida Triad in the Chôgakuji, which is inscribed with the date Ninpyô (1151). The style of this triad differs from the Jôchô style, and the statues exude a strong sense of willpower. This triad is noteworthy also in the fact that the eyes have been inlaid with crystal (*gyokugan*). The rendering of the drapery is unlike that of the Jôchô style and is instead complex and unrestrained. It is likely that the style of this triad was influenced by newly introduced

184

foreign elements, and this is, in time, related to the development of Kamakura period sculpture.

The sculpture of the second half of the Heian period reflected the refined sensibilities of the Fujiwara nobility and was somewhat feminine in character but, in contrast, the Kamakura period (1185-1392) witnessed the production of numerous forceful, masculine sculptural works. During this period, Buddhism became wide spread among the general populace and, as a result, Buddhist sculpture was provided with readily comprehensible, realistic elements. This tendency was further fostered by the influence of the art of the Sung dynasty, which was eagerly imported at that time. The sculptor who perfected the new Kamakura style was the famous Unkei.

Unkei was the son of the sculptor Kôkei and began to sculpt from an early age. Kôkei is well known as the sculptor of the Fukûkenjaku Kannon and the Six Patriarchs of the Hossô Sect in the Nan'en-dô of the Kôfukuji. An early work by Unkei is the Dainichi Nyorai in the Enjôji in Nara, which was sculpted in 1176 (Angen 2) when he was about twenty-five years old, under the guidance of his father Kôkei. In the firmly rendered cheeks and body of the image, one can sense the youthfulness of the sculptor. His next work, the Amida Nyorai in the Ganjojû-in, was commissioned by the feudal lord Hôjô Tokimasa and completed around 1186 (Bunji 2). The imposing figure, the features that inspire faith, and the free-flowing drapery are new elements that did not appear in previous sculpture. Unkei's late works, such as the Miroku Butsu and the Muchaku and Seshin in the Hokuen-dô of the Kôfukuji represent the epitome of the Unkei style and reflect the inner depths of the human spirit.

Along with Unkei, Kaikei contributed to the development of the style of the Kamakura period. Kaikei is believed to have been a disciple of Kôkei, and an extant early work of his is the standing Miroku Bosatsu in the Museum of Fine Arts, Boston. This statue had been kept in the Kôfukuji, and the postscript of a sûtra that had been deposited within the statue indicates that it was carved around 1186 (Bunji 2). Kaikei's style, unlike that of Unkei, retains the element of elegance inherent in Fujiwara sculpture, and many of his statues possess very beautiful features, as can be seen in the Jizô Bosatsu of the Tôdaiji. From the fact that Kaikei adopted the name An-Amidabutsu, statues with gentle features are generally said to belong to the An-Ami style.

After Unkei's death, his style was carried on by his sons Tankei, Kôben and Kôshô. The Senju Kannon in the Main Hall of the Renge-ô-in is Tankei's major work and displays masculine strength. Tankei also sculpted the Bishamon-ten in the Sekkeiji; in the movement of the figure one can sense the influence of his father Unkei, but the

185

features are calm. The Kichijô-ten that stands beside this statue manifests the influence of the art of the Sung dynasty. The Ryûtô-ki and Tentô-ki, the lantern-bearing goblins in the Kôfukuji, were sculpted by Kôben in 1215 (Kenpô 3) and are famous for their humorous depiction. The Kûya Shônin statue in the Rokuhara-mitsuji is the work of Kôshô which depicts the monk Kûya, who was active during the tenth century, walking the streets chanting the name of the Buddha Amida, and is a masterpiece of naturalistic carving. Jôkei, who sculpted the Niô (Two Deva Kings) in the Kôfu-kuji, can be regarded as one of Kôkei's foremost disciples. These forceful, muscular images hint at the reason behind the support given to the Unkei school by the newly risen warrior class, with which support this school overpowered the conservative sculptors of the En and In schools, which had been influential during the late Fuji-wara period, to become the dominant school. These Niô statues also have very lifelike inlaid crystal eyes.

During the Kamakura period, as part of the trend towards reviving older styles, copies of the Shaka Nyorai brought from Sung China to the Seiryôji by the monk Chônen in the tenth century and imitations of the Amida Trinity in the Zenkôji were produced. The former are represented by images such as the Seiryôji-style Shaka in the Daienji in Tokyo and the Shaka Nyorai in the Tôshôdaiji, and major extant examples of the latter are the Zenkôji type Nyorai images in the Engakuji in Kanagawa prefecture and the Ankokuji in Hiroshima prefecture.

Also, during the Kamakura period, statues were frequently carved unclothed, the so-called *rakei-zô*, so that they could be clothed in actual garments. A typical example is the Benzai-ten in the Tsuru-gaoka Hachiman-gû in Kamakura, which was made to be dressed in actual robes and hold a real *biwa*. These unclothed statues can also be regarded as the product of Sung influence.

During this period, a number of outstanding portrait statues were produced. Masterpieces among these include the statue of Chôgen Shônin in the Tôdaiji and the Uesugi Shigefusa statue in the Meigetsu-in. The Shigefusa portrait is novel in that it has been sculpted as a lay image in official court dress with individualized features.

Having attained remarkable heights during the Kamakura period, Buddhist sculpture was produced in vast quantities during the Muro-machi period (1392-1573), but the previous styles were only copied without the addition of any new elements, and sculpture gradually declined. Looking at this development in terms of the history of Buddhism in Japan, the rise of the Zen sect, which did not require the worship of images, contributed to this decline. In sculpture as in painting, the characteristics of the Buddhist art of the period are revealed in the portraits of the Zen patriarchs. An image of the patriarch or founder was always enshrined in temples of the Zen sect. Zen portrait statues were realistic depictions of the individual subject, a technique already present during the preceding period, manifesting the character of the subject in the Zen manner. Leading extant examples are the Musô Kokushi in the Zuisenji, the Motsugai Oshô in the Fusaiji, the Yuigen Oshô in the Hôkaiji, the Tômyôenichi Zenji in the Hakuun-an, and the portrait of Ikkyû Oshô in the Shûon-an.

During the Momoyama (1573-1615) and Edo (1615-1868) periods, generally speaking, Buddhist statuary and portrait sculpture became stereotyped and lost their creative energy and vigour. Buddhist sculpture of these more recent periods reveals two currents. The first consists of both the sculptors who boasted descent from illustrious sculptors dating back to Unkei and who carved and repaired statues for the court, the shôgunate, or the various large temples in Nara and Kyoto, and the journeymen sculptors who lived in Kyoto or Edo and carved statue after statue in the older styles. The second consists of monk-sculptors who travelled over the countryside making statues at the request of the humble people they encountered.

The former current includes Kôshô, the sculptor of the Yakushi Nyorai in the Kondô of the Kyôôgokokuji which dates from the Keichô era (1596-1615). He was a master sculptor of this temple and was also called the twenty-first generation Jôchô; his extant works are faithful to the classical style. His son Kôyû's works are more stereotyped and uninspiring. In contrast, works by the monk-sculptors in the latter category exhibit a freedom of carving that is unfettered by the shackles of tradition. For example, Enkû travelled over the entire country and left novel Buddhist and Shintô carvings in the holy mountains and sacred places in each district. Mokujiki Myôman journeyed through the countryside in the same manner, carving statues as he went. Jizai Hosshi's works can be seen in the Tôhoku region, and Mokujô left his carvings in the southern Hokkaidô peninsula. Also, Hôzan Tankai was inspired by intense religious belief to carve images, and Shôun Genkei carved the statues of Shaka and the Five Hundred Rakan (*lohan*) in the Rakanji in Meguro singlehandedly. Tankai's works often show a new interpretation of older traditional images. The works of Genkei manifest the obvious influence of Ming sculpture. Takamura Tôun emerged from among the journeymen sculptors to pass on this tradition to the Meiji period (1868-1912).

Apart from these developments, in the early seventeenth century, Handôsei carved the statues in the Manpukuji on Mt Ôbaku. It is also important to note that Handôsei transmitted the baroque-like sculptural style of late Ming to Japan and exerted considerable influence on the sculptural style of the period.

187

Literature, Theatre and Language

25

The 'Other' Tradition — Modern Japanese Literature and the Structure of Literary Life in Tokugawa Japan

EKKEHARD MAY

In discussing Japanese problems, it is becoming more and more modern to speak of 'tradition'. Modern Japanese literature, whose deep roots in tradition really are of great interest both for Japanese and western scholars, is no exception.

For a Japanese intellectual who studies the history of literature or history of thought, the search for elements of tradition often means the quest for 'genuine' Japanese elements, sometimes perhaps as a compensation for western literary tradition which is—whether rightly or not we cannot discuss here—felt and thought to be an overwhelming one, especially in the field of prose fiction. For the westerner, on the other hand, it is of great importance to trace back the tradition to gain first of all an exact understanding of the literary works themselves and, secondly, to be ready for an adequate aesthetic evaluation in the context of the development of Japanese prose and prose fiction. Therefore, the aspects of 'tradition' in literature and the scholarly approach towards them may differ considerably between Japanese and westerners.

What is indicated by the expression 'tradition' in Japanese literature? The stage performance of old texts like those of Nô, Kyôgen or Kabuki has certainly to be mentioned, as has also the continued use of old poetic forms like tanka (waka) and haiku. But normally, if we speak of 'tradition' in literature—in the Japanese as in any other case —we mean the thematical, stylistic, and formal relations of modern literature (modern prose fiction) with works of the past.

But perhaps more important than such superficial relationships as themes, topics and motifs is the persisting preference for certain patterns of the narrative, for example, in the preference for adding episodes rather than building up a complexly structured story with a climax and a definite end. References to such connections with the past as well as relations to old themes and motifs are described in the recent book by J. Thomas Rimer, *Modern Japanese fiction and its traditions*. (1) The tenor of this study and that of an earlier article by M. Ryan, 'Accommodated truth' (2), is to trace the relations between traditional prose forms like *monogatari*, *setsuwa*, and *zuihutsu* on the one hand and modern prose fiction on the other.

It is certainly beyond question that there are connections and relations between these very oldest and very youngest forms of prose in Japan. Associations of this kind can easily be detected in the works of many modern writers, and they show the extent to which modern Japanese literature has stayed Japanese in its inner structure while the outer shape has been modernized, that is to say, westernized. Tracing such connecting lines creates indeed a deeper understanding of modern prose fiction and provides criteria for their evaluation. But the question remains whether relating the oldest prose forms—the *monogatari* and *uta monogatari* of the Heian period (794-1185), the *nikki* of the Heian and Kamakura (1185-1392) periods, and the *zuihutsu* of the Kamakura and Muromachi (1392-1573) periods—to the modern prose fiction is really able to show all elements of the latter's obligation to the past.

In studies of the type described above there seems to be a curious gap in the argumentation, as the Tokugawa period (1615-1868) with its huge literary production is scarcely mentioned, and this gives the questionable impression that the remoter periods had imposed a stronger influence on modern literature than the immediately preceding period of 270 years, with its flourishing culture of the book which was printed in enormous quantities for the first time. In order to understand and to evaluate modern literature in its full sense it is necessary to include another tradition in our consideration, namely, the tradition of the peculiar patterns of literary life and publishing conditions, the character of the reading public, and the literary market. In these patterns of the literary and publishing life of the Tokugawa period, especially of its latter half, can be found so many surprising similarities and correspondences to modern 'literary environment' that they cannot be overlooked.

How can we specify these similarities, and upon what are they based? The following are, I suggest, the main points of relevance.

1. The existence of a *broad market* able to absorb enormous quantities of prose fiction, above all of a light, entertaining kind.
2. The prose works—or short units of them—can easily be published *in prompt reaction to the predilections of the reading public*: in the Tokugawa period in the form of *sôshi* ('booklets'), and in modern times in a similar way in magazines and newspapers.
3. This results in a permanent and strong demand for new works of prose fiction. The writers are often forced by the publishers (and of course by economic reasons) *to produce constantly a remarkable output* of literary works.
4. The custom of writing long works of prose fiction in the form of a succession of short, not too closely related parts, and to produce sequels according to the demands of the reading public and publishers. Long works of fiction are *not simply published in serialized form but written in the course of publication* and

192

even very famous authors (like Takizawa Bakin in the Tokugawa period or Matsumoto Seichô in modern times) have no
alternative but to write the serials of two or more novels *simultaneously*.

These conditions lead to a very particular structure of the story
told and, on the other hand, such narrative structures perpetuate the
patterns of usual publishing practice. The special character of the
prose fiction of the later Tokugawa period is determined by *the
absence of a dichotomy of fiction as art and fiction as entertainment*.
The romance or the novel were not yet recognized as a species of
literary art and so the whole corpus of prose fiction was exposed to
the mechanism of supply and demand, a mechanism we are accustomed to attribute only to light fiction (*Unterhaltungsliteratur*). I
would prefer to call this kind of fiction by the German word *Marktliteratur* ('literature for the market', *shijô bungaku* in Japanese) to
avoid other terms with negative connotations like *Unterhaltungsliteratur* in German or *taishû bungaku* in Japanese. The works of
Bakin are good examples of this kind of *Marktliteratur*: they ranked
at the top of all works of prose fiction in the later Tokugawa period
in respect of their educational and moral claims and, at the same
time, they were written to appeal to a true mass public. Bakin even
referred to his *yomihon* as *nagusamigusa* ('something for entertainment') and was very anxious about whether they would win public
applause and sell in great numbers of copies.

In modern Japanese literature, too, is now recognized the novel
as an autonomous work of art, but we cannot ignore the fact that
the main body of prose fiction is written for a reading public much
larger than in any western country if expressed as a percentage. In
spite of a venerable tradition dating from the *Genji monogatari*,
prose fiction has never become an isolated, elevated literary art, but
remained a part of daily life, used and consumed freely by a large
public. There are of course writers in modern Japan whose prose
works are of an experimental, elite and exclusive style—for example
Abe Kôbô or Kurahashi Yumiko—but these writers are few in
number and their importance for the whole body of modern
Japanese prose fiction is more highly esteemed in the West, because
these writers appeal to many of our literary predilections and
conventions, than in Japan proper.

Graphic representations inevitably
run the risk of over-simplification
and generalization, but if we were
to try to use them to show literary
situations we would get this diagram for western prose fiction,
with *A* for prose fiction as *art* and
E for prose fiction as *entertainment*,

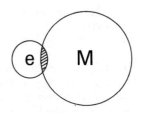

with a small section of overlapping; whereas for Japanese prose fiction we would get this diagram, with *e* for the *experimental, elite* and *exclusive* literature and *M* for the so-called *Marktliteratur*. What can be the reasons for such a peculiar structure of the literary market?

For the Tokugawa period, they can be found in the *early process of the socialization of literature*. The formation and development of a broad market for literary products, especially prose fiction, took place in a remarkably short time. In Europe this process began with the invention of book printing in the fifteenth century and came to an end in the latter half of the eighteenth century, whereas in Japan this process took place, roughly estimated, in an interval of only one hundred years between 1650 and 1750. The process of the socialization of literature in Japan was accompanied by the commercialization of the printed book, a tendency which was accelerated by the emergence of a very popular literature in the first decades of the seventeenth century. In Europe, on the other hand, the early period of the printed book was dominated by works written in Latin, mostly on religious subjects.

The basic condition for the early formation of a genuine book market and of a literature which was suited to commercialization can be found in the development and use of woodblock printing, for this was the ideal method for printing the very complicated 'mixed written style' (*majiribun*) which used both Chinese characters and the phonetic *kana* signs, by offering to the mass of the largely illiterate public an access to the readings (and hence, the meanings) of the characters by showing these beside the characters in tiny phonetic signs called *furigana*.

The literary tradition of the Tokugawa period in which the total production of prose fiction was written for a mass public and represented the main sphere for all literary activities—both in production and consumption—was to last till modern times, and was perpetuated by the custom of publishing works of prose fiction in magazines and newspapers since the beginning of modern Japanese literature in the Meiji period (1868-1912).

The most important works of the outstanding writers were published as newspaper novels (*shinbun shôsetsu*) in several hundred instalments each. This publishing mode strongly influenced the main stream of the Japanese novel in its most sensitive developing phase. The newspaper novel had to be comprehensible for the amorphous mass of newspaper readers, the problems dealt with in the novel had to be actual problems and to be of interest to readers of various social strata. The crucial point is that the newspaper novels which were published between 1890 and about 1920 (for example the main works of Natsume Sôseki) offer the criteria for what is felt and thought to constitute the best examples of prose fiction until the present time.

Japanese studies in the West, and especially those on literature, tend to centre only on the topics which are of interest to Japanese scholars. But the phenomena described above are perhaps of little interest to Japanese scholars, perhaps because they are commonplace and trivial for them. For the westerner, however, it is very important to make clear such basic differences in order to come to a deeper understanding of Japanese literature. In this respect the search for the underlying and persistent structures of the literary life of the Tokugawa period—the 'other' tradition—is surely of use to further studies.

26

Kitamura Tôkoku's Early Years and the Rise of the 'Poet' Concept

WOLFGANG SCHAMONI

The early years of Kitamura Tôkoku (1868-94) preceding his first published work (1889), that is, the years when the foundations of his mind were formed, are attracting a quite exceptional amount of attention in Japan. This is partly due to the discovery of new materials shedding light on Tôkoku's early involvement in the People's Rights Movement (1), but even more to the emotional affinity which some Tôkoku scholars, in the wake of the student movement in the 1960s, have discovered to this author who, facing the defeat of the radical democratic movement and the triumph of the Meiji state, turned from 'politics' to 'literature'.

I intend here (2) to trace the basic line of development in Tôkoku's thought in the crucial years between 1884 and 1890, between his involvement in the People's Rights Movement and his literary debut. This basic line leading to the discovery of the 'poet' concept, seems to me to provide the key to an understanding not only of Kitamura Tôkoku but also of the complex literary landscape of the late eighties as a whole.

Tôkoku's participation in the People's Rights Movement should be seen in its proper perspective: in 1884, when his enthusiasm reached a peak, he was only fifteen years of age. It was, at first, certainly just the usual dream of becoming a 'politician', a dream shared by many young men from samurai families who happened to be in their teens in the early 1880s. In 1884, however, Tôkoku became acquainted with some radical young democrats from Kanagawa prefecture. In 1885 when Ôi Kentarô and his group prepared that rather strange plan for a 'revolution' in Korea (later known as the 'Osaka Incident'), Tôkoku was asked by his radical friend Ôya Masao to join in robberies to procure funds for the 'revolution'. Tôkoku refused. According to a memoir of his wife he told his friend: 'I'm a coward; I want to live a little longer.' (3)

In this way the young Tôkoku began to turn his back on 'politics'. He was not the only one. In the second half of the eighties many other sensitive young men turned away from politics—though usually not as radically as Tôkoku did or was to do during the following years. 'Politics' means here, and this must be clearly understood, not what we today call politics, not a specialized profession promoting certain group interests, but rather concern about the fate of the nation, and saving the nation even at the cost of one's own life. For the young people of the early eighties nearly everything was part of 'politics'. The political radicals in particular—the *shishi* as they liked to style themselves—had no idea of morals or literature or individual happiness independent of 'politics'. For them literature was in fact permissible only in two forms: as occasional poetry in Chinese expressing their own highly traditional emotions and convictions for a circle of friends, or as 'political novels' written for the political enlightenment of the 'uneducated' people. Fundamentally, this treatment of literature was in accordance with the orthodox views of the Tokugawa period (1615-1868).

In 1884-5 Tôkoku himself wrote some Chinese poems and, immediately after his parting from his political friends, he contemplated becoming a 'novelist', in order 'to lead the political movement like Victor Hugo with my weak brush', as he reports in a later letter. (4)

There are very few clues as to what Tôkoku did during the following two years. It is known for certain that he enrolled in September 1885 in the English Department of what is known today as Waseda University (then Tôkyô Senmon Gakkô; Tôkoku had already enrolled in 1883 in the Department of Politics and Economics of the same school). There he became acquainted with Tsubouchi Shôyô who was just publishing his *Shôsetsu shinzui* 'Essence of the novel' (September 1885 - May 1886) and whose novels were beginning to 'rouse the eyes of the reading public in town', in Tôkoku's words in 1890. (5) Tôkoku was also a member of the student club Dôkôkai (6), where Shôyô delivered repeated speeches on his idea of a new literature. It was in those years 1885-1887 that the journal of this club, the *Chûô gakujutsu zasshi*, published important articles by Shôyô, Takada Sanae and Futabatei Shimei. We can therefore say that Tôkoku was living very near to the centre of the emerging new literature.

Shôyô's 'Essence of the novel' was, as is well known, a kind of declaration of autonomy for literature, directed against the older didactic view of literature based on the principle of *kanzen chôaku* 'the encouragement of good and the chastisement of evil', which until then dominated the theory of the novel nearly unchecked (the 'political novel' can be seen as the latest application of this view). It was, however, *not* a declaration of independence. It did free literature from the obligation to teach morals, but it assigned at the same time to literature and in particular to the novel a function of its own, namely to educate the general morality of the individual (though Shôyô emphasizes that, while this is one effect of literature, it should not be the deliberate aim of the author). On the other hand, this idea limited literature to the private,

197

emotional realm from which matters of state were excluded from the beginning. The 'novelist' became an expert on human emotions, on the same level with other specialized professions.

Because there are no documents extant from Tôkoku's hand dating from the period between August 1885 (when he wrote an account of a tour to the top of Mt Fuji which he undertook immediately after his parting from his radical friends) and July-August 1887, it is nearly impossible to determine how far Tôkoku shared this new ideal of the 'novel'. In the above-mentioned reference of 1887 to his earlier intention of becoming a 'novelist' like Victor Hugo, he adds that at that time he did *not yet* think of becoming an artist (*bijutsuka*). This remarks signifies that a certain agreement with Shôyô's idea of the novel as 'art' (*bijutsu*) and a revision of Tôkoku's earlier view of literature had been achieved somewhere between 1885 and 1887.

It was, however, not merely a question of literature. Shôyô's theory of the novel was part of a new view of life, indicating clearly a farewell to the traditional way of life and a progress towards bourgeois society. In a letter of January 1888, Tôkoku notes (looking back to 1885) his disgust with the grandiloquence and the dissolute life style of the political radicals, and already in his account of the tour to Mt Fuji of 1885 there are signs of an emerging criticism of the *shishi* ('patriots'), their ignorance of reality manifest in their rhetorical heroism. (7) Judging from this criticism of the traditional *shishi* mentality it can be guessed that, after 1885, Tôkoku sympathized with the new view of life, whose literary expression was Shôyô's theory of the novel.

In the summer of 1887 a dramatic turn in Tôkoku's life took place, which was to push his view of life and literature still further forward: he fell in love with Ishizaka Mina, three years his elder, who had just graduated from a Christian college in Yokohama. Tôkoku had known her brother, Ishizaka Masatsugu, since 1884, when they were both active in radical political circles (in January 1887, disillusioned with Japan, Masatsugu went to America, where he died in an internment camp in 1944). This love is documented by a number of letters and manuscripts, all from Tôkoku's side, beginning in July or August 1887 with an incomplete draft of a letter to Mina, obviously prior to a declaration of love. This letter contains a fragment of a projected literary work, which relates directly to the concept of the 'poet'. As it is very short I shall quote it in full:

'The dream of the dreaming poet'
(I intend to write separately *The dreaming poet*, where I shall insert this 'Dream of the dreaming poet')
Thus Ôyama Kunizô became successfully a slave of ambition, became completely a servant of pride. One night he fell asleep

beside his desk, making a pillow of Shakespeare's poems. Without his knowing that it was a dream within a dream, suddenly the goddess of literature stood there

extending her hand fairer than a flower
sparkling her eyebrows purer than the moon
and woke him up saying: Kunizô, Kunizô. (8)

This is a very short text, but it contains central elements of a view of literature that was to gain influence among the young during the next ten years, a view of literature that is definitely different from that of Tsubouchi Shôyô, not to mention that of the political radicals of the early eighties: 'literature' is set in opposition to 'ambition' (Tôkoku uses the English word) and 'pride' (*kyôgôshin*) whereas 'poet' (*shijin*) obviously does not designate just a writer of Chinese poems or maybe *shintaishi* 'new poetry', but rather a new quality of writer, united with the name of Shakespeare, one of the 'heroes' of the new view of literature. 'Ambition' was, as is well known, a popular slogan of the early Meiji period well into the People's Rights Movement, and 'ambition' was the main target of Tôkoku's criticism both of the *shishi* and of himself in the following letters. (9) Thus literature is established, not—as it is with Tsubouchi Shôyô—as something different from other professions, but as something radically opposed to the everyday values of Meiji Japan. The source for Tôkoku's first 'poet' reference was in all probability Carlyle's *On heroes, hero-worship and the heroic in history*, which was read by young literary-minded men with growing enthusiasm from the late eighties onwards. It should be noted that Carlyle gives Dante and Shakespeare as the main examples of the 'hero as poet'.

This new view of literature that announces itself in Tôkoku's fragment of 1887 was proposed simultaneously by several young critics in the late eighties. One of the earliest public voices calling for the 'poet' was that of Tokutomi Sohô (1863-1957). In May 1888 he published in his journal *Kokumin no tomo* an article, 'Inspiration', where he declares 'inspiration' to be the pre-condition of any really great work. As examples of 'inspired' works he gives among others Milton's *Paradise Lost*, Victor Hugo's *Les Misérables*, and—strange to say—the pyramids of Egypt and the Great Wall of China. Though Sohô does not use the word 'poet' in this article, 'inspiration' is of course a keyword for the new view of literature. Sohô's choice of examples shows, incidentally, that his idea of spiritual greatness was still closely connected to a very material kind of greatness. In August of the same year he developed his idea of the inspired work further in an article 'The poet of New Japan' quoting from Emerson's essay *The poet* and citing Wordsworth, Shakespeare, Milton and Byron as poets. Two years earlier, in July 1887, he had already given hints of this new view

199

of literature in a criticism of the 'political novels' of the day. (10)

This latter article criticizes the 'political novel' for its propagandism—taking Shôyô's side on this point—and, at the same time, the rising realistic tendencies inaugurated by Shôyô. Sohô uses an interesting metaphor here: he urges the man of letters to be not only the mirror but also the lighthouse of society. From his criticism of the 'political novel' it is clear that he does not call for a return to didactic literature. In fact this metaphor of his reminds us of M.H. Abram's book on the romantic theory of literature which bears the title *The mirror and the lamp* (1953)—thus contrasting two metaphors characteristic of the pre-romantic and the romantic view of literature. The change from 'mirror' to 'lighthouse' indicated a shift in interest from the subject-matter of literature and the techniques of its representation to the person of the author, and from the *novel* as the central genre of literature to *poetry*—though 'poet' of course does not mean exclusively a writer of poems. This was a fundamental change in the concept of literature, which did not, however, prevent both concepts, and even the older didactic concept as well, from coexisting inside one person —Tokutomi Sohô, for instance. It is only when we put Shôyô and Tôkoku side by side that we see this fundamental contrast.

In May 1889 Iwamoto Yoshiharu, the editor of the woman's journal *Jogaku zasshi*, chimed in with an article: 'In this vast desert world may there rise a poet!'. In this rather rhetorical piece, containing a long quote from Carlyle's *Essay on Burns*, Iwamoto first gives a vivid picture of the degeneration of the age, of materialism and discord, going on to call for a sort of 'ideal man':

> 'Whereas the hero is a cripple in (all but his) valour (*tan no katawa*), the scholar a cripple in (all but his) brain, the beautiful woman a cripple in (all but her) passion, herdsman and farmer cripples in (all but their) bodies, here we have a man, not in the least damaged, not at all injured, a man that is complete and fully developed. This is the poet.' (11)

In the 'desert' of the present this 'poet' is the embodiment of full humanity, he is the one 'who puts together the cracked world', who 'leads the people back to their common root'. This 'cracked world' where people have lost 'their common root' assumes more tangible form in an article 'On the poet' published in May 1890 by the eminent Protestant leader Uemura Masahisa:

> 'Today the natural world has passed away and the mechanical world has arrived. The age of warriors and nobles is gone and the age of greed and venality is just beginning. Weeping is done with the abacus and laughing is calculated according to one's company. Society is filled with vulgarity and wantonness. Literary men as well as merchants bury humanity (*ninjô*) on the battlefield of competition.' (12)

And Uemura, again, calls in a hymnic voice for the poet to come forth and save this 'miserable Japan'. It may be added that Uemura quotes Carlyle and Matthew Arnold as critics and Wordsworth, Byron and Tennyson as poets.

There were yet others calling for the poet in 1889 and 1890; for instance, Saganoya Omuro and Uchida Roan, who—thanks to their knowledge of Russian literature—gave their idea of the 'poet' a different shade, connecting the 'lighthouse' concept with the 'mirror' concept, the poetic prophecy of a higher truth with the representation of social reality. Fundamentally they are standing on Uemura's and Iwamoto's side (Roan was a contributor to Iwamoto's journal), but, when religion induced Iwamoto and others to fall back on the old didactic view of literature, criticizing the thematic triviality and moral indifference of contemporary literature, it was Uchida Roan who pleaded most passionately for the literature of the age. This antagonism inside the 'poet' camp became manifest already in 1889 and was to develop during the year 1890 into the so-called discussion on the 'complete decay of literature' (*bungaku gokusui*) which in turn developed further into the debate about Yano Ryûkei's novel *Ukishiro monogatari*. (13)

To return to Kitamura Tôkoku: in the letter of 21 January 1888 to Ishizaka Mina he describes himself as having fallen—after his defection from politics—into a cynical escapism from which love and religion (Christianity) saved him, reawakening his passionate concern for society. This concern soon took the form of vehement criticism of the age and its new literature. In a rather sarcastic letter of March 1888 to his later father-in-law, he attacks the new type of author writing novels for profit, the 'middle-class bastard' (*chûto shakai no kuso-dôbutsu*) as he calls him:

'He takes the words "all men are slaves of money", used by a certain scholar to mock the age, as (representing) the truth, and even writing is to him just a way of making money for the moment, even saying compliments is only a means of getting money for the moment. All and everything depends only on money: women love for money, men become blind for money, pleasure exists in money, and sublime ideas are got for money.' (14)

Definitely this is the same sort of reality which Uemura deplores in his article of 1890 quoted above. It is the society 'with Cash Payment as the sole nexus' between man and man, as Carlyle put it. Nobody would have deplored the present in such a way in the early 1880s. Some striking new features in Japanese reality must

201

have come into being, and at the same time, a new responsiveness to this reality. This new reality is represented by the growing number of indigent farmers of the urban poor. The new responsiveness is to be seen in a way as a result of the defeat of the radical wing of the People's Rights Movement in 1884-5, a defeat which turned the eyes away from 'politics' and towards 'society'. The rapid growth of Protestant Christianity in the late 1880s, in itself a result of this change in the intellectual climate after 1884-5, contributed to this tendency. It was in 1888, when the journal *Nihonjin* reported the terrifying working conditions of the mine workers of Takashima near Nagasaki, that social problems caught the attention of the reading public for the first time. In 1889 the journal *Nihon* published eye-witness accounts of the slums of Osaka and Tokyo, and in 1890 the *Kokumin no tomo* began with reports about the European labour movement. On the other hand, philanthropic societies (mainly Christian, but a few Buddhist ones too) started up around 1890. Iwamoto as well as Uemura were prominently active in these movements.

Thus, it is not surprising to find Tôkoku publishing his first articles in 1889 and 1890 in Iwamoto's journal *Jogaku zasshi*. Of five articles published in this journal in 1889 and 1890 three have special bearing on our theme:
1. 'Tôsei bungaku no ushio-moyô' 'Currents of literature today', January 1890;
2. 'Jisei ni kan ari' 'Thoughts about this age', March 1890;
3. 'Nakan ka warawan ka' 'Should we weep or should we laugh?', April 1890.

These articles are filled with vehement criticism of the age and the new literature, in particular the writings of the Ken'yûsha group. On the other hand we find in these articles, supplemented by Tôkoku's diary, the outlines of his concept of the 'poet', which is very near to that advocated by his contemporaries quoted above. Incidentally, Tôkoku uses the term 'poet' (*shijin*) but also 'hero of literature' (*bungaku no eiyû*) and—in a characteristic mistranslation of Carlyle's 'hero as a man of letters'—'hero of letters' (*monji no eiyû*). (15)

Let me summarize what he says about this hero-poet:
1. The poet is deeply concerned about the age he is living in. Contemporary literature, on the other hand, is criticized for its indifference to society and nation. As examples of the poet answering the demands of the age Tôkoku cites Milton, Swift, Victor Hugo and John Greenleaf Whittier. (16)
2. To answer the demands of the age does not mean of course to comply with the tendency of the times. The poet is rather the prophet of a higher truth, and his authority is—to use Tôkoku's phrase—founded 'not on the many blind of one age, but on the infinite, endless future'. (17)

202

3. This poet is formed not by scholarly learning or literary cultivation, but by one deeply moving experience that jolts him out of
the normal rut, thereby transforming him into the poet 'proclaiming
the mystery of the world'. (18) Tôkoku gives Shakespeare and
Saigyô as examples. As to contemporary Japanese literature, he
announces his hope that Kôda Rohan will in future become a true
poet. (19)
4. The poetical work is not an artifact, but flows naturally out of
the life of the poet. So Tôkoku notes in his diary on 4 September
1890 'First of all the poet must himself be a poem'. (20)
   We all know this view of literature: it is the romantic one, which
still influences our way of looking at literature today. To the Japanese the main theoretical 'source' of this 'poet' concept was Carlyle's
Heroes, itself a very late and vulgarized version of the concept,
supplemented by the writings of Emerson, Wordsworth and others.
But the sudden rise of this concept in the late eighties is not to be
explained simply by these 'influences'. René Wellek says quite
correctly, relating to European romanticism, 'Cultural revolutions
of such profound significance are not accomplished by mere import-
ations'. (21) Carlyle among others just helped to verbalize the concept in Japan. But such Japanese advocates of the concept as
Tôkoku, Iwamoto and Uemura always made it clear that their hope
for the 'poet' was related to a strong opposition to *Japanese reality*.
Therefore, the concept can be understood only in terms of Japanese
literary and social history.
   Similarly, of course, the romantic concept of the poet in Europe
was originally not at all as escapist and vague as we are inclined to
think—a result of the diluted form in which it has come down to
us. The rise of this concept in eighteenth-century Europe and about
1890 in Japan is to be seen as a reaction to a similar reality: the
commercialization of culture on the one hand and the social reality
of the new age on the other. Thus Raymond Williams' analysis of
the concept of the 'romantic artist' applies very well to Tôkoku and
his contemporaries:
   'Certainly, in the documents, there are obvious elements of
   compensation: at a time when the artist is being described as
   just one more producer of a commodity for the market, he is
   describing himself as a specially endowed person, the guiding
   light of common life. Yet, undoubtedly, this is to simplify
   the matter, for the response is not merely a professional one.
   It is also (and this has been of greatest subsequent importance)
   an emphasis on the embodiment in art of certain human values,
   capacities, energies, which the development of society toward
   an industrial civilization was felt to be threatening or even
   destroying.' (22)
In a similar way that European romanticism was preceded by

enlightenment which believed in the progress of society by gradual reform (the novel being regarded as an ideal tool for the emotional education of the new bourgeoisie) so in Japan Tôkoku was preceded by Shôyô who tried to *reform* the novel (that is, to bring about the transition from 'romance' to the 'true novel', the novel of manners) as part of an all-round reform of Japanese society in the direction of modern bourgeois (European) society. Tôkoku, however, already perceived the dangers of this new society from the outset. He answered with the utopian alternative: the 'poet' concept, the poet standing with all his idealized characteristics in opposition to the age; for the unity of life and against division of labour, for personal experience against superficial learning, for literature against ambition, for the self against the market.

Thus, Shôyô and Tôkoku represent two alternative ways of coping with the present: reform and utopia. But these alternatives are at the same time two *consecutive stages* of literary history, fundamentally parallel to the rise of the novel in early eighteenth-century England, and to the romantic reaction beginning shortly after the middle of the century respectively. In Japan these two stages followed each other within a very short interval. Tôkoku's first letter to Ishizaka Mina was written only three years after Shôyô's 'Essence of the novel' began to be published, which had in turn followed only about five years after the rise of the 'political novel'. Because these stages of literary development appeared in such quick succession, they seem to be nearly contemporaneous and the logic of their sequence is blurred, but in the light of Tôkoku's early years, it stands out clearly.

Finally, it may be asked, what characteristics set Tôkoku apart from the other voices calling for the 'poet'. Certainly, in 1889-90 he was very near to Iwamoto or Uemura; but whereas the other Christian critics founded their idea of truth ultimately on Christian dogma, returning to positive religious truth when the truth of the poet proved too destructive to civil life, Tôkoku's truth was founded exclusively on what he later called the 'inner life' (*naibu seimei*), i.e. the authority of subjective experiences. For Tôkoku this experience had begun with his love for Ishikaza Mina in 1887, more than two years after the break-down of his earlier 'political' hopes. This experience, which had shoen to him that there was, after all, the possibility of a united, intense life here and now, later prevented him from making a compromise with reality, with the emerging bourgeois society.

It was inevitable, then, that Tôkoku's and Iwamoto's path would eventually lead them apart. Tôkoku did not believe in an easy way of salvation, neither by political reform nor by institutionalized religion. Only in one manuscript, presumably written in 1890, does he still show some hope in philanthropism. Accordingly, his view of reality is desperate, and his image of the 'poet' is characterized by loneliness and isolation. He does not use the lofty rhetoric of Sohô, Iwamoto and Uemura. Let me close with a quotation from his article 'Should we weep or should we laugh?' of April 1890, which shows the darkness and urgency of Tôkoku's thought:

'But people nowadays laugh too easily, weep too easily. If in these days there were somebody who would not weep with the others, who would not laugh with the others, who would grasp in the darkness the wellspring of strength, that would be the highest blessing for the country.' (23)

The Concepts of Tradition in Modern Japanese Literature

IRMELA HIJIYA-KIRSCHNEREIT

In science, things have to be considered over and over again. This is not to say that everybody has to start his investigations at zero. Rather, it means that the scholar constantly has to check his tools. Are they still precise and adequate means for measuring the segment of reality which is the object of his respective field of studies? Or do they need sharpening, readjustment, or even replacement by more adequate tools in order to bring satisfying results?

For the scholar of literature, his tools are his technical terms, the conceptual framework with which he describes, defines, and analyses his object, that is, a text or a certain group of texts as well as their contextual setting. Effective work and useful results require fit and adequate tools and, in the same way, inadequate tools may be the reason for ineffectiveness in literary studies.

Scholars of Japanese literature hardly seem to have felt the necessity to check their tools. With carefree self-assurance they handle an extensive reservoir of literary terms, never doubting the usefulness and meaning of their operations. They are trying hard to ignore the fact that it is the method which produces its object, or, to use the terms of Habermas, they neglect the interrelation of cognition (*Erkenntnis*) and interest (*Interesse*). (1) My calling attention to these problems is not based on a personal predilection for theoretical issues, but rather on my disappointment with scholarly works on a very practical level, and the experience that every attempt to explain their insufficiencies leads to a discussion of the underlying principles guiding the work.

As an introduction to the problem, let me first present an example. On hearing or reading something about Kawabata Yasunari, we are sure to hear the term 'tradition' mentioned before long. Why is it that this association comes to mind so readily? It derives not so much from observation of his literary work as from the author's proclamations about this subject which keep on ringing in the ears of the reading public. He has never left a chance for anyone to doubt his veneration of the Japanese cultural heritage. A writer's opinions, convictions, and theoretical statements, though, are not identical with his artistic achievements, and to see in his eulogy of classical works the most conclusive evidence of his own 'classicality' is simply a logical fallacy. This way of arguing, for all its popularity, is neither clear nor conclusive. In a scientific context, we would at least have to distinguish between statements of a common nature and statements concerning literature, especially those referring to certain works. But even the clearest theoretical statement of a writer concerning his indebtedness in a particular work to a certain traditional technique does not excuse us from scrutinizing the work for ourselves in order to be able to confirm the author's statement, or at least to show how the traditional device functions within the contemporary creation.

Our next task consists in rearranging the relevant considerations in a more abstract fashion and trying to condense them in order to present a limited number of points apt to shed light on some of the diverse layers of the subject of tradition.

Most of what I have to say may sound self-evident but I think this subject important enough to be reconsidered, and we may find in the end that refocusing things can result in better insight and in new ideas. All I want and can do is to present my propositions and to make my contribution to stimulating a discussion of this important concept in the study of modern Japanese literature.

Tradition as 'Japaneseness'

Whereas in the past many a western study on Japanese literature briskly and frankly handled its subject according to European standards of criticism, which the writers probably mistook for internationally valid ones, authors of recent studies and articles have lost much of this naivety. They hasten to stress the importance of a peculiarly Japanese tradition which is at work even in the most recent example of fiction. Such a work, they maintain, has to be judged by its own standards, not by foreign categories. A realization such as this indeed marks a milestone in the study of Japanese literature or, to express it more strongly, I consider it a prerequisite for a serious scientific discussion of the subject. Without insight into the conditions of the formation and reception of a cultural product, without knowledge of what it is meant to be and what are the expectations and standards of the public for whom it was created, how can we hope to appraise it adequately? Thus we can only wholeheartedly welcome new critics raising their voices in condemnation of older practices. One of them is Marleigh G. Ryan, who in an essay on 'Modern Japanese fiction' makes the following severe criticism:

> 'A particular form of imperialism—literary imperialism—has characterized the western observer's approach to Japanese literature.' (2)

We will indeed have 'come a long way' when we stop asking of Japanese fiction 'that it be non-Japanese' (3), although this will only be the starting point for our work.

My basic agreement with the above statement is not diminished by the following considerations. I merely want to call attention to the problem that appealing to Japanese tradition is not necessarily synonymous with giving up the standpoint of what was termed 'literary imperialism'. It could just as well be the seamy side of the matter. Every element in the Japanese work which resists western-trained interpretation can thus be sorted out and labelled collectively as 'belonging to Japanese tradition'.

This way of dealing with the subject often results in exoticising it, a maybe helpless but altogether more honest method, as it admits the strangeness of the matter, while orthodox 'literary imperialists' tend to repress their difficulties.

The danger behind the 'tradition-talk' is therefore that it seems to offer a handy and neat stop-gap for the 'imperialistic' viewpoint, a convenient way out in case interpretation problems can no longer be ignored. Tradition becomes a synonym for 'Japaneseness', a quality which is described selectively to the extent that it can be made out and named, at best resulting in a wild enumeration of genres and styles which form a jumble evoking all kinds of associations. In a scholarly context at least, it thus becomes indispensable to specify which elements of the native heritage are involved lest the 'tradition-talk' lose its meaning and become a mere word-shell empty of contents. The danger, though, of falling into a trap should not be underestimated.

Sensibility, 'mono no aware' and other pitfalls

In many cases, the 'Japaneseness' alias the 'traditional' flavour of the works under consideration is identified as a special sensibility, a quality detected in practically all 'things Japanese'. No example will be necessary to demonstrate the popularity of this term, I suppose, as anybody who has read introductions or studies on Japanese fiction or poetry, tea-ceremony, gardening, cooking, film, drama or any other discipline will be thoroughly familiar with it. A comparison, however, is likely to reveal that there is 'sensibility' and 'sensibility'. To some it may designate a Japanese sense of beauty and thus correspond to the *Nihonjin no bi-ishiki* or similar expressions which are so popular in Japanese studies. In other cases, sensibility refers to a psychological fact stemming from a narcissistic disposition as when Dennis Keene writes about Shiga Naoya. According to Keene, the 'limitations of the sensibility', which might produce moving effects in short works, become apparent in his novel *An'ya kôro*, where the author's persona becomes repugnant in its 'petty egotism'. (4) Yet in contrast to many authors who feel their job is done by mentioning the term, leaving the task of deciphering its precise meaning to the reader, Keene offers an interesting explanatory model by linking the personal fact to one aspect of Japanese aesthetics:

'...the egotism is a direct consequence of the style, is, indeed, the style itself. A literary (sic) sensibility that is concerned with what is motionless, with life seen at those privileged moments when time is seen to have stopped (and one must note that this is the traditional sensibility in Japanese literature), must turn in upon itself, must become progressively smaller and seemingly trivial, when it uses a literary form whose ambition is to give a total description of human experience.' (5)

This is to me one example of not walking into the trap. There is a great danger, however, of falling victim to the convenience of a term like 'sensibility' which, because it is widespread and familiar, seems to offer no problem, but which in cases of unspecified usage degenerates into a mere synonym of 'tradition' or 'Japaneseness' and thus becomes meaningless.

To avoid the vagueness of a 'rubbery' term like sensibility, many scholars take refuge in the vocabulary of Japanese aesthetics which has the advantage of covering a smaller semantic scope and of offering the chance to describe Japanese literature in its own terms, as it were. Here, the concepts of *mono no aware* and *mujô* come to mind most readily. But the descriptive value of applying them to contemporary works is more often than not disappointing. The main reason for this surely lies in the slipperiness of *mono no aware* itself, so that I am sometimes almost painfully touched by the efforts to prepare this elusive concept to fit into a well-turned argument—assuming the author even bothers to explain his usage of the term.

One of the Japanologists I know who has been most seriously engaged in making *mono no aware* productive for the analysis of modern literature is J. Thomas Rimer in his *Modern Japanese fiction and its traditions*. (6) Yet even his repeated and very serious discussion does not leave us completely satisfied. His definition—or better, circumscription—can naturally not be more precise than the most clear-cut usage of the concept in the past, but why not give it up altogether if it proves of no good use? Clinging too pertinaciously to *aware* may well block our vision of the fact that the same things can be expressed much more concisely and efficiently in a *literatur-wissenschaftlich* way lacking the fussiness of manipulations with speculative terms. I can therefore only presume that Rimer, had he not felt obliged to resort to these 'traditional' concepts again and again, would have been even more successful in describing the effect of certain literary devices. (7) Instead of partly paraphrasing the respective scenes in order to incorporate his *aware* notion however cleverly, an analysis in terms of point of view or changes in perspective, the value system in the work, or types of symbolization—to name only a few of the many reliable instruments modern literary studies are equipped with—would have resulted in a delineation much more precise, without depriving the original of its fascination and charm. (8)

There is one more danger in the use of these common concepts which has to be realized in order to be avoided. It is the danger of ahistoricity. Everything can be compared with everything in the hands of a skilful and well-versed scholar who draws our attention to parallels in works which are centuries apart. The result may be very surprising and even witty and it is certainly fun to read. For example, I enjoyed Rimer's tracing Abe Kôbô's novel *Hako otoko* 'The box man', written in 1973, back to Kamo no Chômei's *Hôjôki* 'Account of my hut', a diary from the early thirteenth-century. (9) The question, nevertheless, remains as to whether these analogies might not be purely accidental and whether the meaning and implications of the hermit's existence in the past and in the present context can be regarded as identical. It certainly will not be an easy job to inquire into questions like these; not to pose them, however, means to deprive the works of their historical roots, to ignore their dependence on the epoch in which they were created.

Another example may illustrate this statement. Eleanor Kerkham, in a lecture on 'The classic and the contemporary in modern Japanese fiction', points out Buddhist influences in contemporary novels. This leads her to the following observation:

'If in modern Japanese literature we find an author who rejects conventional notions of the secure and happy home, who questions the inherent attractiveness, goodness, or even naturalness of the notions of continuity and permanence in family relationships, who doubts the value of private property or material goods, then I think we can say that that author is dealing in the modern context with what has traditionally been seen as a Buddhist theme.' (10)

Although we have to concede that in order to make her point clear, general statements like this might suggest themselves, its weakness is conspicuous. To detect Buddhist influence in all kinds of criticism of society or petty bourgeois life, in forms of escapism as well as in anti-materialist attitudes, seems almost obsessive and far too undifferentiated. Even if she could prove that Buddhist thought is in fact the basic motive behind all these different literary themes and materials, she would have to explain the meaning of Buddhism in contemporary society, which is bound to differ from that in earlier centuries. Otherwise her interpretation would tear the literary works out of their historical context and grant them a dubious quality of timelessness, reducing their contemporary character to mere decoration, a superficial flair to barely hide the fact that Japanese art has been saying the same thing for centuries. But suppose this were true—the ways of saying it must then have differed as much as the periods themselves. Let us pause here for a moment, as we seem to be drifting into a whirlpool of very complicated issues. It is the problem of the interrelationship between the message and the form which is peeping from behind these questions. Unfortunately we cannot dodge this issue, but we might well approach it from a different angle.

Tradition and modernism

Though we have been talking about the concept of tradition all the time, we still have not made it clear what is to be understood by it. According to Structuralist theoretics—and most scholars seem to agree with them on this point—literary tradition means the total of valid aesthetical norms and values. (11) To me, this definition seems to be too unpractical, although it sounds very consistent and consequent. In practical usage, however, in order to describe the extent to which a certain work of art conforms to or deviates from given norms, it becomes necessary first to define the system of aesthetic rules. This, on the other hand, requires a previous analysis of a whole number of earlier artistic productions, but what about the presupposed but missing framework of norms?

In order to avoid this vicious circle I would propose to regard as tradition only those rules and concepts which the literary work in question refers to distinctly and traceably. (12)

In dealing with this subject, it is of vital importance to realize that there are a great variety of ways in which a given work, group of works or genre can relate to tradition. Thus it does not suffice to say that there is a reference to tradition—this would be only part of the necessary information. We always have to specify in which way the reference works. There are two main categories: affirmative or negative reference, but these two abstract positions encircle a wide scale of possibilities. By way of direct or indirect quotations, allusions and serious or humorous imitations or other literary means, the relationship with the past can manifest itself in numerous forms. Respectful veneration of the heritage, resulting in stylization and/or 'Epigonentum', to name only two possible courses of formation, is as imaginable as the free use of elements of tradition for innovative purposes or sharp criticism in the form of parody or travesty.

The fact that a literary work relates to tradition, therefore, does not allow the conclusion that it is not progressive or updated, although mentioning the term in its English or Japanese form (*dentô*) invites connotations of 'conventionality'. Referring to tradition is not opposed to being modern, it does not even exclude avantgardism. The relationship between *dentô to kindai* 'tradition and the modern' —to quote the title of a book by Kuwabara Takeo (13)—is a very complex one. Not opposition but rather a kind of mutual inclusion would come close to a rough description, or, to be a little more precise, they imply each other on a conceptual level in the sense that tradition always relates to a certain historical stage which embodies the modern, while, on the other hand, 'modern' can be realized only in relation to the 'traditional'. In practice, this means that a contemporary artist can be modern in the sense of innovative only to the extent that he is aware of his tradition.

On a different level, we could then distinguish 'tradition-conscious' or simply 'related to tradition' from traditionality, which would indicate an affirmative relationship towards heritage without providing any information regarding its degree of modernism. These points may require some explanation.

Intention and effect

Why do we stress that 'tradition-consciousness' is something quite different from conventionality? Let us first consider an example from European literature.

James Joyce's famous novel *Ulysses* evokes its relation to tradition by its very title. Allusions to Homer and Shakespeare occur so frequently throughout the text that if we regarded it according to popular Japanologist standards, we would have to call it highly traditionalistic. In reality, however, *Ulysses* turns out to be downright revolutionary, and this to a substantial degree is due to its very usage of traditional elements. By projecting these allusions to the classics onto the everyday life in Dublin, Joyce 'perforates the illusionary seclusion of realistic presentation', but at the same time the numerous realistic details of everyday life are being fed back into the Homeric allusions, and thus, 'the relation between the past and the present ceases to appear as being one of ideal and reality'. (14)

We can conclude from this observation that it is not the traditional element *per se* but the way in which it is used, the intention and its effect (15), which is the decisive factor in determining the traditionality as well as the modernism of a work of art.

This statement draws our attention to a fact of a more basic nature in the study of literature which, because it is ignored all too often by Japanologists, deserves to be mentioned here. It is the fact that a certain literary device, e.g. a motif or a technique, is not coupled to a fixed meaning but can be used in different ways. To determine its semantic function, therefore, requires a contextual analysis. This may sound very commonplace, but the practice of Japanese-literature studies reveals the assumption that a given motif etc. is restricted to one meaning to be very widespread indeed. (16) Yet for the sake of justice, we should not conceal that the same holds true for much of non-Japanese and non-Japanologist research. (17)

The consequences of this finding would be to realize that a lot of

212

detailed analysis is necessary in order to make meaningful statements on the relation between literature and its traditions. Not much knowledge is necessary to state that Akutagawa refers to all kinds of periods and genres in his literary creations. The real job has to start here—in analyzing the function of these references. To use another example: practically every Japanese reader will see that the title of Nosaka Akiyuki's recent book *Shishôsetsu* (18) (meaning something like 'Death-novel') alludes to the genre of *shishôsetsu* ('I-novel'), and as the author is Nosaka, everybody will take this reference as ironical. Therefore, it will not bring any new information to verbalize this assumption in a study. Scholarly curiosity will question intuition and lead to a substantiated confirmation, or to a refutation of the impression of irony in case this should turn out to be nothing but a surface phenomenon.

The conscious and the unconscious
The proposal, presented earlier in this paper, of regarding as tradition those elements which a literary work refers to distinctly and traceably, may be thought to be limited to conscious reference only. It is important, therefore, to stress the point that unconscious reference is implied as well. An author may well be aware of only a segment of an element of tradition while his artistic production bears traces of a complex network of supports from the past. He may not even acknowledge his reference to tradition at all, honestly thinking that he has created something completely new, as is the case with the generation of creators of the *shishôsetsu*, which I attempted to show in a paper entitled 'Innovation as renovation'. (19) The phrasing of the title is to indicate that what was consciously undertaken as an overcoming of common native literary conventions by means of references to European authorities, eventually and inadvertently, so to speak, resulted in a revival of traditional patterns. My treatment of the subject will, I hope, also have made it clear that the delineation of unconscious relations to tradition has nothing of the arbitrariness about it that sceptics might suspect.

Let us return once more to the theoretical side of the matter. Tradition as a process of appropriation of the past works on a conscious as well as on a subconscious level. In any case, selection is its prerequisite. To quote Hans Robert Jauss:
'...standards of past art which are transmitted to the present without further thought, cannot be compared to a snowball which carries everything with it; rather, they are subject to the economy of constant abbreviation, simplification and suppression of heteronomous elements which is characteristic of all canonization.' (20)
In an analogous way to the selection active in tradition, our interpretation has to be guided by restriction to the possibilities

213

inherent in the historical horizon (21) which we are going to reconstruct. Thus our analysis can neither pin the meaning of a textual fact down to one single interpretation, because this would ignore the basic quality of artistic products, the multi-functionality of its elements; nor should we aim at describing every possible way of interpretation. The purpose of philological research should lie rather in a description of the spectrum of possibilities which a work offers to readers in a certain period, be it the one in which the book appeared or any later stage. Through the meticulous reconstruction of the 'horizon of expectation' we will manage to avoid the arbitrariness that unhistorical treatment is likely to result in, and we will be able to distinguish adequate interpretations from those based on personal predilection which reads facts into a work which would not withstand deeper investigation.

Literary and extra-literary norms
The last aspect on which I want to focus is the fact that the concept of tradition consists of a complex ensemble of literary and extra-literary norms. Philosophical, ethical or social postulates are as important as purely literary allusions. Most studies on the subject of tradition in Japanese literature do not bother to separate these aspects. (22) A closer look at scholarly works which treat the aspect of tradition would, however, reveal that the majority of the elements named are of a non-literary nature. Be it the special attitude towards nature which is seen as linking contemporary and pre-modern literature or the retreatism of Abe Kôbô's hero mentioned by Rimer, be it the peculiar sentimentalism, the frequently observed fatalism, the theme of 'wasted effort' (23), or an ideal like *muga*—all these elements are primarily non-literary patterns, although on a secondary level they may have merged into a certain genre to manifest themselves in the form of a specific motif or style.

The advantage of differentiating literary and extra-literary aspects will become apparent when we present an example. Let us once more return to one of those images so central in the study of Japanese literature—the concept of *mono no aware*. The difficulties in defining it stem from attempting to tie it to literary facts, but there is no single motif, technique, or genre which could unequivocally represent it, as *mono no aware* is traceable in fiction, poetry, and drama alike. My suggestion would be to interpret it as an 'affective pattern' (*affektives Schema*) manifesting itself in a raised affective receptivity, functioning as a filter in the perception of reality. This pattern is preferably coupled with certain objects, for example, nature, and the coupling has not experienced much change throughout the centuries. The 'affective pattern' appears in literature in the form of a 'cultural action pattern' (*kulturelles Handlungsmuster*). (24) By means of this delineation, sorting out the different literary and non-literary levels, we will obtain a much deeper insight into the process of tradition. My sketch of *mono no aware*, for example, may be too rough to eliminate the uneasiness that scholars of literature feel in regard to conventional demonstrations of the concept in Japanese literature, but I hope that I have succeeded in outlining the importance and value of a more differentiated procedure.

In closing, let me show how this method works, taking as an example the problem of tradition as it poses itself in the case of *shishôsetsu*. The traditionality of this genre is taken for granted by the reading public, critics and scholars alike, but when it comes to explaining it, the statements become strangely vague. Usually, scholars resort to sweeping assertions or they make associations, however faint, with a variety of works and genres. Not only the *Genji monogatari*, mediaeval diaries, and works by Saikaku are invoked as predecessors, but also *waka*, *haiku*, the Nô, and Buddhist tales of renunciation. If we try to argue exclusively on a literary plane and to find a common denominator of all the different styles and historical stages embodied by these genres, we will at best end up in formulating a quality which is so universal that it will sound nonsensical. But if, on the other hand, we scrutinize the genesis of the *shishôsetsu*, we will find out that its authors neither intended to perpetuate traditional literary conventions nor did they consciously refer to any pre-modern genre. Yet even the authors themselves subsequently sensed a close relationship with earlier native literature. Tayama Katai was among those who voiced this impression most clearly. (25) How can we harmonize these seemingly contradictory findings?

First, we will apply the distinction of conscious and unconscious dependence on tradition explained earlier in this paper. The second step will consist in determining the 'channel' by which tradition influenced the *shishôsetsu*. More than any fact in native literature handed down to the originators of the *shishôsetsu*, it was a complex set of socio-cultural, that is, extra-literary, patterns which gave a definitely 'traditional' flair to this genre. The influence of pre-modern patterns of perception and action transformed into literature worked as an agent in providing its apparently most characteristic features. This is, as I see it, the reason for the (unadmitted) helplessness of conventional historical 'explanations', and at the same time it serves to resolve the puzzling contradictions presented above. Tradition, in the form of elements of the cultural code, having entered a literary genre which was actually meant to break conventional rules, is present in the *shishôsetsu* in such an obvious way that even the authors themselves cannot fail to detect it.

In order to describe the relationship with the mentioned predecessors via extra-literary 'channels', vague hints will not suffice. We will have to state clearly which element of the cultural code

215

we detect in a certain group of texts, as these are likely to differ according to the genre. Not all of the extra-literary norms that set the tone in mediaeval diaries will appear in *shishôsetsu*, and the ratio of literary and extra-literary norms will also vary. In *waka* or *haiku*, for example, where a whole set of strict poetic rules determines the artistic creation, the literary tradition will outweigh the extra-literary one, while other genres with less ballast of technical restrictions leave more room for elements of the cultural code to enter. We can also imagine, however, that there are overlappings which would explain the variety of genres associated with *shishôsetsu*. One of these junctions is the concept of *mono no aware*.

This abstract and schematic model may well provoke debate. Of course, I realize that it is not a sufficiently full or satisfying explanation of this aspect of the *shishôsetsu*, but at least we can consider it as the skeleton. By adding flesh and muscles, that is, a consideration of the contemporary literary scene, the socio-political conditions, the individual disposition of the author, and the mechanism of interplay between author and reading public, we can come closer to a complete and finished picture of a historical stage in the complicated process of tradition in modern Japanese literature.

28

Tradition in the Popular Novel 'Rangiku Monogatari'

MIKOLAJ MELANOWICZ

In his 'Junbungaku to taishû bungaku' ('Pure literature and mass literature') (1), Teruoka Yasutaka writes that contemporary Japanese readers read novels as a mental recreation without much ado about classifying a novel as a work of 'pure literature' or 'mass literature', in clear contrast to the pre-war situation, when modern *taishû shôsetsu* 'mass novels' or rather 'popular novels', won considerable acclaim.

This state of mind of the average reader finds expression in Shin-chôsha's Shinchô Gendai Bungaku collection in eighty volumes, for this comprises 'pure literature' and popular literature too, including as it does the works of such 'mass writers' as Matsumoto Seichô, Itsuki Hiroyuki, Minakami Tsutomu, and Shiba Ryôtarô.

This promotion of mass literature deserves our attention and brings us necessarily to the study of Japanese modern 'popular literature'. Thus, the main aim of this paper is to grasp the basic features of the popular novel, taking as an example the *Rangiku monogatari* (1930) by Tanizaki Jun'ichirô.

As the last part of his *Manji* was being published, on 18 March 1930, Tanizaki started to publish a new novel in the evening edition of the *Asahi*. This was a 'mass' novel, as he called it, in accordance with the custom of those days which used this term for new popular literature. The work was *Rangiku monogatari* 'The tale of the scattered chrysanthemum flowers', a historical novel to which the introduction, containing Tanizaki's explanations of his intention and creative motives, had appeared a few days previously, on 14 March. He announced that the novel is placed in Muromachi times, during the rule of the three shôgun Ashikaga Yoshitane, Yoshizumi and Yoshiharu. The title was meant to suggest times of war and skirmishes (*ran* 'scattered' or 'troubled'). He also mentioned that the Ônin civil war (1467-77) led to the total destruction of Kyoto and that, after it was over, the conflicting parties continued their struggle for power in the provinces. This was the beginning of the *Sengoku jidai*, the civil-war period. As Tanizaki stressed, nothing of note was taking place in the capital, nor were there any heroes of importance. He therefore drew attention to events only marginally noted in the chronicles. His reason was not so much to uncover new facts or documents, but rather to develop his creative fantasy in an area where he would not find himself up against the historians. (2) In his desire to avoid such political centres as Kyoto and Kamakura which have been described in detail, Tanizaki picked on the Chûgoku provinces as the scene for his work.

It is interesting to dwell, for a moment, on the reasons why Tanizaki called his *Rangiku monogatari* a 'mass novel' (*taishû shôsetsu*), that is, a story addressed to the mass reading public and based on accepted rules, conventions and frameworks. (3) In the epilogue to an edition of the collected works of Tanizaki (4), Itô Sei explains it by indicating that in 1925 the so-called mass novels first appeared in the dailies. These differed in quality from earlier 'vulgar' or popular stories (*tsûzoku shôsetsu*), and their appearance coincided with a sharp increase in the circulation of the *Asahi* and *Mainichi*, which were widely read among the intelligentsia. In effect, circulation jumped from under one-hundred thousand to several hundreds of thousands. The circulation of various weeklies and monthlies also expanded rapidly, all of which led to a rising demand for popular novels, easily understood and, at the same time, having interesting stories and of some literary and cognitive value. This demand was catered for by writers who delved into historical chronicles for their inspiration. They employed modern techniques required by popular-novel writing, a good literary language and, as a result, won a wide reading public who first encountered their works in the mass printed media. Nakazato Kaizan, for instance, wrote and for many years published successive instalments of his well known novel *Daibosatsu tôge* 'The pass of the Great Buddha' (1913-21), which was published as a mass-edition work in 1927. No less fame was gained from *Akô rôshi* 'The homeless warriors of Akô' (1927-28) by Osaragi Jirô, *Nangoku taiheiki* 'Southern chronicle of the grand peace' (1930-31) by Naoki Sanjûgo, and *Naruto hichô* 'The mysterious scroll of Naruto' (1926-27) by Yoshikawa Eiji, the great writer of historical novels who was to gain even greater renown later in his career.

It was during this formative period of the Japanese mass novel, that two principal trends in Japanese literature became visible—that of proletarian literature on the one hand, and of modernism, that is to say, the 'neo-sensualist school', on the other. At the same time conflicting views were aired on the meaning and function of literature. At one extreme, the role of ideology in art was defended and, at the other, 'artism', ignoring what interests the reader. The mass novel, backed by the press, gained rapidly in popularity. Only the critics refused to recognize it, a fact to which Tanizaki drew attention in an article 'Naoki kun no rekishi shôsetsu ni tsuite' 'On Naoki's historical novel' (5), commenting ironically that mass literature had expanded so greatly mainly due to the critics totally ignoring it. (6) He also mentioned how greatly he was struck by

218

H. Sienkiewicz's *Quo vadis*, and that he would be extremely happy should he himself prove able to write a novel of similar worth based on Japanese motifs. (7)

He also stated that the historical novels of those times by Naoki and Osaragi were not inferior to so-called serious or high literature. They too contained a most praiseworthy knowledge of their periods and used earlier literary forms. In *Jôzetsuroku* (8), Tanizaki gave high praise to the multi-volume *Daibosatsu tôge* by Nakazato Kaizan, giving rise to much surprise among the critics who, in principle, recognized only three literary trends: the political (proletarian), the impressionist (the 'I-novel') and the aesthetic (modernism). Tanizaki noted the great danger inherent in these trends in weakening the ties with the reading public, and threw his authority into the defence of the popular novel, which had been so slighted by the critics, recognizing that the contemporary novel cannot afford to forget the mass public.

This type of fiction had served the public well in the Tokugawa period (1615-1868) and should serve it no worse today. For this purpose, as Tanizaki saw it, it should assume the features of a *monogatari* 'tale' (9), by which he primarily had in mind its transparent fictional structure. Such a form often requires greater literary qualifications and experience than is generally realized. From the very beginning of his career Tanizaki would have nothing to do with naturalistic and impressionist literature (the 'I novel') nor with similar trends. Hence his statements that such tendencies are but a preparatory stage for real, 'mass' literature. To some extent Tanizaki felt the stage of popular literature which ensued after World War II to be that of the so-called *chûkan shôsetsu* 'intermediary novel', which took into account the public's secondary and even higher education. Hence, from what has been written above, it can be deduced that *Rangiku monogatari* arose from Tanizaki's polemical attitude to the contemporary state of affairs in literary circles.

Rangiku monogatari consists of eight separate chapters, each of which is sub-divided into several sections, but without sub-titles. The first chapter, a kind of introduction, as it were, has the narrator describing the exotic features of Japan's trade with mediaeval China, ghost ships and pirates. He tells of a Chinese merchant Chang who, in the Eishô era (1504-20), set out for Muronotsu in Japan's Harima province to purchase the favours of Kagerô, a famous courtesan there, a woman of exceptional beauty who was the uncrowned queen of that port. He carried on his great ship a valuable mosquito net of the very finest weave, packed in a small golden box. When he was in the Inland Sea he got into a small boat and rowed toward the port accompanied by a guide. All trace of him then vanished.

In Chapter Two, entitled 'The two samurai', the scene is transferred to Kyoto. Two samurai, Kume Jûrôzaemon who is in the

219

service of the Akamatsu family, and Numata Shôemon who serves the administrator (*daikan*) Urakami Kamon no Suke of the Akamatsu family, set out to search for beautiful women for their masters, who have been rivals for years. The two travel separately, and although they meet each other often during their travels, they avoid all conversation so as not to betray the purpose of their journey. In the end, however, they do sit down to a long talk, which is the most interesting section of this chapter. The highly humorous dialogue of the two, each of whom senses the other's purpose but does not speak of it directly, is pursued in the style of the mediaeval theatrical Kyôgen farces and the *sewamono* ('domestic plays') of the Kabuki theatre. In the end they both end up in Kyoto where each, on his own, searches for a beautiful woman. The life of the capital, much dilapidated by the wars, is presented as on an illustrated scroll.

In Chapter Three, 'Notes on sea islands', the plot is taken back to the Inland Sea with its many inhabited and uninhabited islands. The narrator's point of observation, however, is different from that in Chapter One. He now looks, as it were, from the perspective of the Karani group of islands, not far from Muronotsu port, where pirates have been very active. The morning after the Chinese merchant has set out for shore, his boat is found empty on the open sea. No trace is found of the merchant or his guide Urume, the courtesan Kagerô's servant. Meanwhile preparations are under way in the port for the grand holiday of *Kozatsuki* 'Little May'. Tension appears among the population of the port city as an announcement is made that the Chinese golden box, mentioned earlier, must be delivered to a certain place at a pre-determined moment of the holiday. The mood of mystery and apprehension thickens, enthralling both the port inhabitants and the reading public.

The next chapter entitled 'The swallow', brings the scene back to Kyoto where acquaintance is made with a conjurer and magician called Gen'ami, among whose onlookers the two samurai again meet. Each is convinced that he is near the end of his task and each proceeds in secret to look over the women they have chosen. It later turns out that they have fallen victim to a band of robbers who take advantage of the naivety of these provincial rustics who have come to Kyoto in search of aristocratic women who have lost their husbands in the war. Luckily, both samurai escape with their lives, but they have to begin their search anew. After numerous adventures they both set out for home with their trophies. As both the ladies concerned have their faces veiled, it is not known which is the more beautiful and, thus, which of the two men will outdo the other.

The narrator then changes the scene to Muronotsu during the holiday, to which all the local feudal lords, samurai, pirates in disguise and various entertainers have flocked; the queen of the port, the courtesan Kagerô, is also expected to make an appearance.

The colourful ceremonies and rites last one week, after which word has it that the Chinese golden box has been found. Those who had intended to return home decide to stay on and even new arrivals are noted. As it turns out, the mosquito net in the golden box is in Gen'ami's possession. As his reward he wins Kagerô, who had earlier promised that she would belong to the man who would bring her the Chinese treasure. But the marriage does not take place, for the port is overrun by the pirates. Chapter Seven sees the two lords, Akamatsu Kazusa no Suke and Murakami Kamon no Suke, resigning from any competition over Kagerô, whom they suspect of being in league with the pirates. So they set out for home, having been informed that their servants have returned with beautiful women for them.

Again the scene changes, together with the narrator's perspective. The two samurai again occupy the front of the stage, after which a comparison of the two ladies' beauty takes place before the two young lords. Kochô, the girl brought for Kazusa no Suke wins, for the other has a red and swollen nose. It later transpires that this is the work of Gen'ami, who was paid by Jûrôzaemon to touch her nose with a leaf from the lacquer tree.

The last chapter sees the narrator diverting attention from Oshio castle in Harima province and the love-making of Kazusa no Suke, to a description of the intrigues which lead up to the abduction of Kochô by Kamon no Suke. The story ends with Kazusa no Suke swearing to kill his rival and to regain Kochô.

This tale of beautiful women, located in a time of civil war and in the colourful surroundings of the islands of the Inland Sea, threatened by pirates, attracts attention by the enormous diversification of fantastic events which take place on a number of mutually intersecting planes. A woman of quite unearthly beauty links together several stories of a Chinese merchant, pirates, a conjurer, intrigues within the Akamatsu family and robbers in the capital. True, she rarely appears as a forefront figure but her presence can be sensed throughout the tale.

This woman is a magic force acting behind the scenes, an object of desire, rivalry and the cause of bloody events. The suggestion would seem to be that women stand behind history as such, but Tanizaki has no intention of proving his point. Nor can one detect attempts to create any fresh form of expression or to present new aspects of man and his destiny. There is no place in this story for new concepts or for reinterpreting traditional forms. That, in any case, is not what a popular novel is about. The most important issue in the majority of such literary works is the plot, with 'real' figures, facts and events assuming primary significance. The *monogatari* principle of time flowing along a single line is accepted here, with events taking place in chronological order though without a

221

consistent narrative perspective being maintained. Indeed it is this lack of unity of time and the resulting absence of a single, unified perspective which would seem to be the *monogatari*'s basic classical feature.

The *Rangiku monogatari* also presents many differing narrative styles. These vary from that of the first chapter, in which the description is that of an omniscient narrator, looking from a timeless perspective, without any clear motive within the novel's subject matter, to a narrowing of this perspective and a focusing of attention on the two samurai during their travels. The description changes into a narration and then into a dialogue typical of farces based on situational comedy. The remaining course of events is that of fairly schematic scenes, the structure and motivation of which are not always acceptable, though typical of adventure stories. It is this unevenness of style which is also characteristic of popular literature. Hence, one cannot assess this novel by the same standards as 'high' or, as the Japanese call it, 'pure' literature (*jun bungaku*).

This is a story written for entertainment, with its literary values constituting no more than an additional encouragement to read the book. The principal attraction it offers is to lead the reader into little-known mysterious and exotic events, using simple language. The term 'simple' here signifies the use of correct words and sentences which are generally acceptable among the reading public and which are void of all experimental tendencies. It is the poetics of the work which are stressed—the composition of the work as a whole and of the chapters, the structure of the narrator's approach, of time and plot—all these diverge little from what the average reader expects from a writer and what he is accustomed to, in the way of treating a tale as the reflection of 'real' events. Those events are accepted as 'real' which proceed and are resolved in accordance with generally accepted principles of valuation, within the norms of common sense, and within the basic longings to satisfy one's curiosity. What is looked for, therefore, is to define those value judgements which are comprehensible to the widest possible readership. The public finds satisfaction in associating with what is familiar and, even in the case of foreign settings, in experiencing standards of behaviour and artistic ideals which do not worry it with novelties but refer to familiar traditions.

Hence the author's relationship to literary and extra-literary traditions in this popular novel lies in his selection of widely accepted patterns, without any attempt at fresh suggestions as to how they could be employed. The author simply implements accepted literary conventions without any attempt to present a new view of the world, as is the invariable goal of more ambitious works. Tanizaki makes the fullest use of existing literary means, without consideration for time or types, as long as they serve his ultimate purpose. Obviously, such a work brings nothing new to the poetics of serious literature. What is new is the events and the way in which they succeed one upon the other, even though they are constructed within the 'good old' patterns.

Rangiku monogatari is a 'mass', popular, novel not because it presents events from history and national legends which are known or assumed and, hence, comprehensible to all, but because it uses generally accepted and respected literary models, free of creative reflections and processes which assume the necessity of formal novelties in the area of language, style and the presented world of the writer. Let it be stressed once more that this is a popular novel because it employs generally comprehensible language and conventions, without setting itself any ambitious aims of searching for the truth of Man, his world, or of truth as such. One could say, even, that it uses literary tradition for the purpose of popular consumption and not for any evident creative or cognitive purpose.

29

A Dialogue between Modern Poetry and *Haiku* — the Bashô Poems of Hoshino Tôru

EDUARD KLOPFENSTEIN

Japan has an outstanding poetic tradition, but it consists almost entirely of very short lyrical verses (*tanka*, *haiku*) and is characterized by an extraordinarily limited range of forms and modes of expression. By way of contrast, the 'new poetry' (*shintaishi*) has broken through such limitations. It has enlarged the possibilities in form and subject-matter to such a degree that · we are tempted to speak of a revolutionary development. On the whole, the contrast between old and new, between the periods before and after that of Meiji (1868-1912), seems even more striking in the field of poetry than in the other literary genres. Modern poetry therefore furnishes a unique example of the break with tradition.

It is not my intention to attempt a general answer to the question of how traditional elements have been preserved in this new development, or how they are reintroduced and in what way they manifest themselves at later times. I would simply like to draw attention to one contemporary poet, Hoshino Tôru, whose work has a bearing on the present theme and who seems to me to represent a certain trend within the past ten or fifteen years.

Hoshino was born in 1925 in Ibaragi prefecture. He still lives there, and is professor of English literature at Ibaragi University in Mito. He has published translations of poems by John Donne, essays by T.S. Eliot, as well as aesthetical and philosophical writings of a number of other English-speaking authors. His own development as a poet is rather unusual. It seems that for a long time he exclusively dedicated himself to *tanka* poetry. After the war he was for some years a member of the Araragi group. In 1955 he was among the editors of the journal *Ibaragi kajin*. Later on he founded his own *tanka* journal and published a *tanka* collection. By the beginning of the sixties he had thus firmly established himself as a *tanka* poet.

At about the age of forty, it appears that he suddenly abandoned the classical form of *tanka* and moved towards contemporary poetry. At first he was active as a critic and theorist. Between 1967 and 1969 three volumes of *shiron* ('essays on poetry') were published, the first significantly entitled *Shi to shinwa* 'Poetry and myth'. He was in fact deeply concerned with the question of the nature of myths, and of the origins and primeval forms of poetry. In 1970, his first collection of new-style poetry appeared, bearing the Latin title *Personae*. In this collection, as well as in his second one, *Kachô* of 1974, he tried to treat historical or mythical figures and personalities as poetic subjects. Thus we find Columbus next to Ôgetsu-hime, the deity of cereals and food mentioned in the *Kojiki*, Isis and Dionysus next to Bashô, and the *Man'yôshû* poet Ôtomo no Yakamochi side by side with Robin Hood and Saint Theresa.

After 1974, Bashô imposed himself as a theme in the mind of the author. In the first collection, there was one Bashô poem, in the second there were already five, and Hoshino then decided to write a whole cycle, which was published in 1976 as *Bashô yonjûichi hen* 'Forty-one Bashô poems', by Kasama Shoin.

These poems all have the same form and about the same length. They are prose-poems of fifteen to twenty lines each, which aim at ending with a *haiku* by Bashô. This form, as Hoshino himself points out, 'has its origin in the desire to revive if possible the old pattern of *chôka* and *hanka* ('verse and counter-verse') in modern poetry.' As a result, Hoshino attaches to his own longer poem (*chôka*) a *haiku* by Bashô as a counter-verse (as a *hanku*, as it should be called here), thus forming an analogy to one of the oldest patterns of poetry in the *Man'yôshû*.

In his postscript, the author gives the following account of his relationship to Bashô:

'Originally, I did not experience any great affinity to *haiku* and *haibun* literature, and I was, so to say, a person of rather *tanka* constitution. That is why I did not have any special interest in Bashô. But when I was working on the chapter 'Vigorous style' in my treatise about 'Primeval poetic images', the antennae of my interest accidentally picked up the first *haiku* from *Nozarashi kikô*. Some time later, I realized that this same *haiku* was placed as a motto on the title poem of Murano Shirô's collection *Sôhaku na kikô*. Accordingly, as my imagination was stimulated by these more or less chance encounters, I wrote my first Bashô-poem against the background of this *Nozarashi haiku*. At that time, of course, it never occurred to me that I would once write a whole cycle of Bashô poems.

'With a certain interest in Bashô, which lingered on from my first to my second collection, and the formal conception embodied in the *chôka/hanka*, which left a kind of resonance even after the second collection, these two components worked together and gradually formed within me the intention to write a whole cycle of poems. In the course of writing these poems, one after the other, this intention gave way to the wish that the cycle should cover the whole life of Bashô. Unnecessary to say

225

that this wish exceeded my capabilities.

'I do not have the least knowledge of the so-called Bashô scholarship. I have never even thought of doing research work on Bashô. Therefore I am an absolute amateur. A book I have used, as an amateur, and that only to write the poems, which is to say in a completely wilful manner, is *Bashô* by Yamamoto Kenkichi. This not only gives a glimpse of what Bashô scholarship may be, but the exact analytical approach of the author permitted me, the amateur, to freely develop my imagination. I am deeply grateful for this. In the same wilful manner, I used *Bashô monogatari* in three volumes by Asô Isoji. This book gives the facts of Bashô's life and of his literary activities in a well-ordered manner, and it was very useful to me as, figuratively speaking, it brought my imagination to a full stop.'

Thus went Hoshino's postscript. It is of special importance that his encounter with Bashô was both an accidental one and that of an amateur. In writing his poems he therefore had something in mind, other than to add a new commentary to the many existing ones on Bashô.

Now, what does such a Bashô-poem look like? As an example, let us look at Number 15 of the collection.

This poem takes its cue from the following *haiku*, drawn from Bashô's travel diary *Sarashina kikô*.

Mi ni shimite	'Through and through
daikon karashi	the sharpness of the radish goes
aki no kaze	and the autumn wind'

In the early autumn of 1688 Bashô travelled from Nagoya eastwards through the Kiso valley to Sarashina in the vicinity of Nagano, wanting to enjoy the full moon on the Obasute mountain. As the name implies, this mountain was connected with a very old legend about the casting out, the 'throwing away', of an old woman into the wilderness. The mountain was also a well known place for contemplating the moon, especially during the eighth month, in early autumn. All this can already be found in ancient sources such as the *Yamato monogatari*, the *Kokinshû*, the Nô *Obasute* etc. Bashô himself was thus retracing the steps of a time-honoured tradition. Somewhere near this mountain he wrote down the *haiku* mentioned above.

The *haiku* itself is also deeply influenced by tradition. It contains *kigo* 'seasonal word(s)' for autumn, here *mi ni shimite*; and the entire expression *akikaze mi ni shimite* 'the autumn wind goes through the body', corresponding to the first and third lines of the *haiku*, can already be found in a *tanka* by Fujiwara Shunzei (or Toshinari). Bashô adds only the sharpness of the radish as a new element. But with this new element he combines in a typical *haiku* manner impressions belonging to different levels of sensorial perception. There is the chilliness of the autumn wind (touch), the sharpness of the radish (taste) and, as a hidden allusion, the whiteness of the radish (sight) which traditionally corresponds to the colourlessness or whiteness, as it is called, of the autumn wind. All this should be kept in mind when we now look at the poem of Hoshino.

BASHÔ 15

Climbing step by step the moon grew whiter   climbing step by step the moon grew whiter and whiter   more and more the moon looked like a slice of white radish   he (Bashô) was on his way to the top of the Obasute moùntain   straying through the darkness of the Kiso valley   disturbed by the voice of the old woman   he yet thought of casting off everything he wore on his way to the top   everything he wore?   nay, rather the whole paper-garment   his Self   there was no more suitable place than the Obasute mountain to cast one's Self off in such a way   for to join the lineage of vagrants   to join the lonely whispering of the outermost twig   there was perhaps no better way than to cast off one's Self here and in such a manner   to cast off one's Self   yet to cast off one's Self, unsubstantial as it was, quite unlike the old woman in the dark   to cast it off as if it were as substantial as she   this, after all, was mere toying with metaphors   this, after all, meant nothing less than ending up in the trap of self-hypnosis   and to avoid this trap on his way upwards   he had to be silent, obstinately and with determination   not like the old woman in the dark   but to climb in determined silence   climbing step by step the moon grew whiter   climbing step by step the moon grew whiter and whiter   and whenever the whiteness of the moon increased, he went one step into the white space   the gloomy dying voice whispering underfoot   gloomy dying the lonely up and down of the Obasute mountain   into the one slice of the giant radish he went the next step

> Through and through
> the sharpness of the radish goes
> and the autumn wind

As can be seen, Hoshino works mainly with elements already incorporated in Bashô's text, the *Sarashina kikô*. These elements are: the moon, the whiteness, the radish, the Obasute mountain and climbing this mountain to contemplate the moon, the casting out of the old woman and her plaintive voice. This last important theme is emphasized in another *haiku* in the *Sarashina kikô*:

> *Omokage ya*   'The image appears
> *oba hitori naku*   of the lonely crying old woman
> *tsuki no tomo*   companion of the moon'

Another current traditional theme is that of conquering oneself, of casting off one's Self.

However, the manner in which these elements are integrated to form a close-knit system of connections is new. The radish, for example, is now 'cut down' to a round slice of white radish which can be equated with the moon. A new line of thought is initiated by the name of the mountain 'Obasute' (the casting out of the old woman) and leads to the casting off of one's Self. But apart from these new connections, we find only a very few elements not included in the original material, such as modern terms like 'self-hypnosis' (*jiko saimin*) and 'thinking in (or toying with) metaphors' (*hiyuteki shikô*). This is rather exceptional, for in other poems we find more of this kind: abstract nouns and technical terms, foreign words and names such as Don Quixote or Audrey Hepburn.

The stylistic method employed in establishing the above-mentioned unity is the same in all poems. Certain words and themes are emphasized by way of repetition, a repetition that gradually arranges them in slightly different connections, so that a network of interrelated concepts is created. We have the impression of circling within a narrow frame, an impression that is stressed by the literal quotation of the beginning lines in the second half of the poem. In this way, each element bears an emphasis and an intensity beyond its primary meaning. These elements become symbols of a process taking place within an interior spiritual space. We come to realize that somebody is picking his way between two opposing spheres, the darkness of the valley and the plaintive voice representing one sphere, the moon as a white slice of radish the other. The voice of the old woman surely no longer points to circumstances of the legend in the first place, but symbolizes the attachment to worldly things which should be shaken off and left behind. The Obasute mountain, therefore, is the place where one casts off, the only passage-way to the world of the moon, thus apparently indicating the breakthrough to a higher plane of reality, to the true essence of things. Perhaps this is equivalent to what in terms of Zen Buddhism would be called enlightenment, *satori*.

Against the background of this concept, the *haiku*, that is, the counter-verse at the end, becomes open to a really surprising interpretation. In the commentaries on Bashô, the sharpness of the radish is explained as alluding to the season (early autumn), to the troubles of wandering through the rugged and rustic Kiso district, possibly to the state of mind of the author. Now, the sharpness of the radish expresses the force of breaking through to the real, true life, a force that shocks and affects one's whole being to its innermost. There is an element of surprise in this new outlook on a verse of almost three hundred years' standing, and this effect motivates the use of verse and counter-verse.

The way traditional forms and subjects are dealt with in these poems seems to me quite remarkable. Hoshino is steeped in his culture. His knowledge of *tanka* poetry and its classical vocabulary makes itself felt everywhere, and he is at home in different traditions, western and Japanese. But he does not stop at this. He looks at Bashô from an entirely modern point of view. In Bashô he discovers the archetype of the poet's ordeal, timeless and still highly relevant because of his radical rupture and search for a higher level of consciousness. In matters of style, Hoshino evidently displays a sensitiveness trained in contemporary poetry.

It seems to me worthy of note that, in spite of the traditional subject, the author is able to push beyond a purely conservative and congenial attitude to arrive at a masterful and truly creative use of traditional material. Such a relaxed and fertile relationship with one's own tradition can by no means be taken for granted in modern Japan. Following the Second World War, it was for a long time almost inconceivable. It may be taken, therefore, as a symptom of certain changes in the attitudes towards oneself and one's own values, as a symptom of the process of self-questioning, which came into being in the late sixties and the seventies.

30

The Reception of Traditional Japanese Theatre in Europe

SANG-KYONG LEE

Since 1868, when Japan opened her doors to the world again, the theatre of the West has contributed substantially to the development of the modern Japanese theatre. However at the beginning of the twentieth century, people in the West began to realize that the theatre of East Asia, being still very close to the origins of theatrical art, could in its turn help to breathe new life into western theatre. Reform movements sprang up, opposing the traditional classical and naturalistic form of theatre as well as the so-called 'decadent' trends. They extolled the return to the original forms of theatrical art and found the perfect example of an ancient form of theatre, preserved to this day, in the highly refined Japanese Nô play which had never completely grown away from its source, the ritualistic dance.

The first to suggest that Japanese art might serve as a guiding principle in saving western art from degeneration was Ernest Fenollosa. (1) He also translated Japanese Nô plays. After his death his widow, jointly with Ezra Pound, published those translations in 1916, under the title *Noh, or accomplishment: a study of the classical stage of Japan.* The group of people around Ezra Pound cultivated the study of Far Eastern literature. It was here that W.B. Yeats, the Irish poet and dramatist, was initiated into the art of Nô. Later, he himself was to write in this newly discovered style. His plays *At the Hawk's Well, The only jealousy of Emer,* and *The dreaming of the bones* are marked by their strongly symbolic content. Inspired by the Nô play, he used the mask and an orchestra of three musicians in his dance plays. The orchestra not only accompanies the introduction and the final part, but also, as in the Nô play, accompanies and controls the actor's movements throughout the whole performance.

Europe and America became acquainted with Japanese stagecraft through guest performances by travelling Kabuki and Nô troupes. The famous French producer and theatre director Jacques Copeau was fascinated by Japanese dramatic art and experimented with the stage and acting techniques of the Nô theatre at his school in Vieux-Colombier. (2) His pupil, Charles Dullin, too, felt indebted to the Japanese theatre as a guiding element in the renewal of western drama.

What impressed Dullin most about the Nô play was the rhythm and vividness of its presentation, as well as a certain feeling of detachment and objectivity which is induced by the use of the mask. (3) The most famous actor and producer ever to have worked at Dullin's theatre in Paris, Jean-Louis Barrault, on the other hand, was most interested in the unity of dance, music, mime, speech, and song that is to be found in the Japanese theatre. He also admired the spirituality of the Nô experience and its deep symbolism brought about by gestures and stage properties. (4)

In Germany, the influence of the Japanese theatre began to show itself at first in the field of stage techniques. As early as 1896, Karl Lautenschläger, stimulated by the Japanese example, introduced the revolving stage in Munich. (5) In Berlin in 1910, Max Reinhardt adapted another device of the Japanese stage, named the *hanamichi*, literally 'flower path', which leads from the back through the auditorium to the main stage and thus extends the acting area right into the audience. But, above all, the great Austrian director strove to give a new position of significance to the art of dance in the theatre. He produced mimes as full-length plays: for instance, in 1910 *Sumurun* by Friedrich Freksa, whose 'murder scenes Japanese-style' were hailed by the critics (6), and, in 1916, *Grüne Flöte* by Hofmannsthal. For this new type of dance, the traditional dramatic art of Japan has served as a model, especially the Nô play, where dance is not used just as an inserted diversion but constitutes an intensification of the action.

However, not only its theatrical techniques but also the content and structure of the Nô play encouraged creative imitation. When Benjamin Britten, the great British composer who died in 1976, wrote *Curlew River*, he created a modern Nô play, adapted to a European Christian background. His adaptation of the Nô play *Sumidagawa* is amazingly well done. Britten, together with his librettist, Plomer, created two further allegorical plays to be performed in church: *The burning fiery furnace* (1966) and *The prodigal son* (1968). Together with *Curlew River*, these two plays make up Britten's trilogy of religious parables.

Among the German dramatists it was Berthold Brecht who had the closest contact with the theatrical forms of the East. His school operas *Der Jasager*, *Der Neinsager*, and *Die Massnahme* are based on the first part of the Nô play *Tanikô* (7) which he got to know through Arthur Waley's translation. Brecht not only paraphrased Nô plays, but also studied the dramaturgy of the East Asian theatre. As a consequence of his intensive study, there are certain similarities to be found between his plays and the Nô play: Brecht aims at creating a play in epic form, expressing a *Weltanschauung*—this corresponds to the nature of the Nô play. However, Brecht's *Weltanschauungstheater* propagates communist ideology, whereas the

Nô play serves to disseminate the Buddhist doctrine of salvation. They both differ from the classical theatre of Europe, in that their main concern is not the portrayal of an individual fate. In Brecht's plays, just as in the Nô theatre, time and space, events and individual situations are created freely according to the needs of the theatre. This alienation effect, their common characteristic, leads to the spectator's detachment from the happenings on stage and thereby affords him the opportunity to reflect on the deeper meaning of these happenings.

Another element that greatly contributes to the alienation effect is the diminishing of tension. This becomes effective already at the beginning of the performance, when the audience is made familiar with the story of the play, either through introductory words of an announcer (in the Nô play by the *waki* 'the secondary actor') or perhaps through a mime. The chorus, with its comments, also participates in giving information to the audience and thus, too, reduces tension.

A further characteristic, common to Brecht's plays and the Nô theatre, is the element of contrast within their construction. Brecht's characters show almost a balance between good and evil (see, for instance, the characters Puntila and Shen Te). In the Nô theatre, on the other hand, the polarity between Yin and Yang is an important structural characteristic which shows itself especially in the synchronous portrayal of the present and past. However, while in the Nô play thesis and antithesis are finally united in a synthesis, in Brecht's plays the two polarities remain opposed to the end. Furthermore, there are occasional similarities to be observed in the way music and mime are used (for instance, in the scene in *Galileo Galilei* where the black plague breaks out).

Samuel Beckett, the Irish dramatist, states that he has never consciously studied the Nô theatre. (8) Would we be wrong in assuming, though, that he became acquainted with it, at least superficially, through his fellow countryman, W.B. Yeats, on the one hand, and through J. Copeau, on the other? In Copeau's theatre school there prevailed a great enthusiasm for experimenting with the performance techniques of the Nô theatre. However, one thing is certain: Beckett's plays contain significant similarities with the Nô theatre. In addition to those already discussed in connection with Brecht's plays, we find the following: the description of a situation rather than dramatic action; previously determined, stylized movements of the actors; and alienation effects attained through explanatory remarks causing detachment, on the one hand, and through a lack of interrelation between the characters, on the other. In the Nô theatre one finds a different type of unconnectedness causing alienation, namely, the seeming unrelatedness between the character appearing on stage and the person to be represented. At first, there seems to be no connection between the main character of the first part and that of the second; the identity of the two *shite* (or principal characters) only becomes apparent in the course of the second part. The division of Beckett's play, *Endgame*, into three sections, also, is reminiscent of the structure of a Nô play, which is divided into the *Jo* ('introductory section'), *Ha* ('central part'), and *Kyû* ('conclusion'). In a Nô play, the second major section often ends with a mimed dance, accompanied by the chorus, who sings the text. By means of this dance the protagonist relates the gist of the story. In *Endgame* too, the loneliness of man and the futility of his daily activities are impressed once again upon the audience by means of gestures. Beckett's play, *Krapp's last tape*, also contains parallels to the Nô play.

Among the French dramatists, Paul Claudel is one of the outstanding writers of the epic theatre. During his eighteen years of diplomatic service in the Far East, he became thoroughly acquainted with East Asian dramatic art. From 1921-26 he was ambassador in Japan. During this period he finished his main work, *Le soulier de satin*, which already shows the universalistic conception of the world, to become so typical of his style. In the Nô play too, life on this earth and the hereafter, the present and the past, are always viewed in the grand context of their causal relation. There are reasons to suppose that this universalistic approach, characteristic of Claudel's late works, is partly due to the influence of the Nô theatre. In Claudel's plays, just as in the Nô play, only the transcendent gives meaning to the events happening in this world. Similarly, as in the Nô play, language and movement determine the ritualistic character of his late plays. Claudel divides his play, *Le livre de Christophe Colomb* (1927), into two main parts with an interlude—this too is clearly reminiscent of the Nô theatre. Music, dance, and mime play a significant part in his plays; these are also elements of great importance in the Japanese theatre. In his theoretical writings Claudel discusses the Nô theatre very exhaustively.

The French dramatist, Gabriel Cousin, created a modern adaptation of a Nô story with his play *Le voyage de derrière la montagne* (1962). He made use of a legend, widely known in Japan, which Zeami had already utilized for his famous Nô play *Obasute*. In Zeami's play, the basic motive is the ingratitude of the members of a family: an old woman is being abandoned on the Obasute mountain by her nephew, who is also her foster-son, because his wife cannot get on with her. A different version of this legend was treated by Fukazawa Shichirô in his novel *Narayama-bushikô* (1956): hunger and poverty drive the inhabitants of a village to abandon their elders on the mountain. Cousin took up this version and made it the central theme of his play, through which he wanted to draw attention to the problem of hunger in our world. The dramatic structure of the play, as well as some of the theatre techniques, indicate that the author, who had made a thorough theoretical study of the Japanese theatre was in some respects inspired by the Japanese theatre. This shows itself, for instance, in the importance he assigns to music, in the choreographically fixed movements, and in the dialogues between protagonist and narrator, which, in lyrical language, give generously conceived descriptions of situations.

To sum up, I would say that notwithstanding their different social and philosophical backgrounds, the Nô theatre and the modern European theatre have, according to our observations, many common characteristics regarding their basic nature, as well as their forms of expression. To a certain extent, this can be explained as being due to the inspiring effect the Nô theatre has had on the modern European theatre. The Symbolists had already prepared the ground for a readiness to be guided by the ideas of the Nô theatre. They opposed the traditional classical theatre, developed since Lessing's time, but also declared war upon the staging of the illusionist theatre because they were also opposed to any naturalistic tendencies. They advocated the return to first principles in dramatic art and pointed to the mediaeval theatre as a model.

When, at the beginning of the twentieth century, western scholars translated Nô plays, thus acquainting the West with the style and stage techniques of the Nô theatre, the Symbolist dramatists recognized in that theatre the realization of the theatre form they had envisaged. The Nô, which in a long process of development has been refined into a theatrical form of extreme symbolism, does not endeavour to present a realistic portrayal of life on its stage. While it can look back on a long history, it has never lost its connection with its origins, where dance and music played an important part. Furthermore, its lyrical style and elevated language satisfied the demands which the Symbolists made of dramatic art.

31

The Female Impersonators (Onnagata) in the Kabuki Theatre Today

METTE BRANDGAARD

While most western theatre is representational, the classical Japanese Kabuki theatre can be called presentational. In representational theatre the audience and the actors are in two separate worlds; the audience is led to believe that the actors are not actors but actually the persons they are portraying. In the presentational Kabuki theatre, however, the audience is well aware that it is watching actors perform on the stage, and does not feel it strange when the actors sometimes address themselves directly to it, in the middle of the play, introducing a new actor or apologizing for having been away from the stage for a while. There is, therefore, not the same gap between audience and actor often found in the western theatre.

One of the big differences between Kabuki and traditional western drama is the importance of the actor in the Kabuki theatre. He is the axis around which the play revolves. While it can generally be said that in the theatre of the West he is the tool by which the story is told, in the Kabuki theatre the play is the tool he uses to display his acting ability.

Although Kabuki can hardly be termed realistic drama, it is not devoid of realism. The function of realism, however, is different from that of the representational theatre. In the latter, realism is applied to convince the audience that it is watching a real story and not just a play. In Kabuki, realism is applied at certain places as a part of the technique of the performance. A very realistic stage setting or realistic hand-properties will delight the audience, just as certain realistic gestures of an actor will bring applause and shouts of praise when performed skilfully.

In this stylized presentational Kabuki theatre the *onnagata* —female impersonator—is a central element. In Kabuki it does not seem in any way strange that all female roles are played by men. For the acting skills of the *onnagata* provide this theatre with one of its most intriguing assets. With the help of such elements as make-up, costume, facial expressions, body movements and gestures, and voice, the *onnagata* must not *symbolize* a woman, but must create the illusion on the stage that he *is* a woman.

The history of female impersonation in Kabuki dates back to the early seventeenth century, when women were banned from the stage and men started playing female roles out of sheer necessity. The early *onnagata* did little more than perform simple dances on the stage, but during the Genroku era (1688-1703), the art of female impersonation underwent great changes, as greater stress was put on the ability to act, and the audience began to demand more of the *onnagata*. Instead of turning to real life for his models, the *onnagata* now often looked at the art of his predecessors to find the inspiration he needed. In this way the Kabuki 'woman' was born, a figure often defined as a man's ideal picture of a woman. In the Genroku era women members of the audience began imitating the *onnagata*, who thus became the leaders of the women's fashions.

One of the most famous *onnagata* of the Genroku era was Yoshizawa Ayame (1673-1729), whose thoughts about how an *onnagata* should conduct himself, written down in the *Ayame-gusa*, were to have a great influence not only on his contemporaries but on all *onnagata* for the rest of the Tokugawa period (1615-1868). Ayame stressed the fact that if an *onnagata* did not act and dress like a woman off stage, he could never be a real woman on stage. The reason for this was first of all to ensure natural acting on stage, but another reason was to avoid 'confusing' the audience and the *onnagata*'s fellow actors. I quote from Charles J. Dunn and Bunzô Torigoe's translation of *Ayame-gusa* (1): 'The *onnagata* should continue to have the feeling of an *onnagata* even when in the dressing room. When taking refreshment, too, he should turn away so that people cannot see him. To be alongside a *tachiyaku* ('male-role actor') playing the lover's part, and chew away at one's food without charm and then go straight out on the stage and play a love scene with the same man, will lead to failure on both sides, for the *tachiyaku*'s heart will not in reality be ready to fall in love.'

The *onnagata* of the post-Genroku period were probably even more aware of their art than their predecessors had been, and they did much to develop it. New roles for the *onnagata* were created, and many of the plays from this period have some of the best *onnagata* figures of the Kabuki repertoire. It was important that an actor decided as early as possible, preferably while still a young boy, whether he wanted to be a *tachiyaku* or an *onnagata* actor, as the training was very different for each. If he chose to be an *onnagata* actor, dancing lessons were of the utmost importance, and he had to learn the correct gestures and movements. Learning to manipulate the often very heavy and long costumes also demanded many years of practice. Furthermore it was necessary that the voice be trained to give the right *onnagata* voice.

By the end of the Tokugawa period the art of the *onnagata* had come a long way since its beginning more than two centuries earlier. From being merely a good-looking and graceful dancer, the *onnagata* became an actor who devoted his whole life to the difficult and serious task of portraying the women of Kabuki. The influx of ideas from the West in the years after the Meiji Restoration of 1868 affected the Kabuki theatre, which now found itself face to face with the theatrical forms of the West.

The ban on female performers was now lifted, and many people felt that now there was no longer any use for female impersonators, and this tradition, which during the Tokugawa period had seemed a very natural part of the Kabuki theatre, was suddenly looked upon by some as bordering on indecency. Why should men play the roles of women when there were women to play them? How could an actor be better at portraying a woman than an actress? Questions like these came from many sides, mostly from people who supported a quick modernization of Japan, and who were eager to break with the many old traditions of the country.

When it was seen that the new Shinpa theatre successfully used actresses (as well as some female impersonators), the questions were raised again. It was the first time that any serious thought was given to the role that the female impersonator played in the Kabuki theatre, and many people, actors, playwrights and Kabuki fans, realized what a vital part of Kabuki this tradition was. The *onnagata* had been a part of Kabuki for so long that everyone took them for granted.

Fortunately, however, the *onnagata* survived the crisis of the new times together with the Kabuki theatre itself. A few attempts were made at using actresses in Kabuki, but they were received with so little enthusiasm that the idea was soon abandoned.

Of course, some changes in the *onnagata* tradition were inevitable. The custom of dressing and acting as women off stage disappeared in the beginning of the Meiji period (1868-1912), and more and more actors began to play both male and female roles. Yoshizawa Ayame or any other *onnagata* of the Tokugawa period would not have believed that these dramatic changes could have led to anything less than the downfall of the *onnagata*. In their time *onnagata* had occasionally been successful at playing male roles, but that an actor of male roles could play female roles as well would have been completely beyond their comprehension.

One of the most fantastic *onnagata* careers ever is that of Sawamura Tanosuke III (1845-1878). The story of his life shows an unparalleled dedication to the *onnagata* tradition and deserves to be told briefly here. Already as a child he showed promise of a brilliant future, and before he was twenty, he had won himself a large audience with his superb portrayals in all kinds of *onnagata* roles. In 1865 tragedy struck. During a performance he fell from a prop—a pine tree—onto the stage and injured his right foot. Nothing much was done at the time, and the wound became infected. Two years later gangrene set in and his right leg had to be amputated. Three

237

years later, in 1870, his left leg also had to be amputated. Soon after both his hands were stricken and had to be amputated as well. But Tanosuke continued to act, keeping to roles where he could sit down on the stage and manipulating his *kimono* sleeves in such a way as to create the illusion that his hands were hidden inside them. He died in 1878 at the age of thirty-three. Only an extremely talented and stubborn actor like Tanosuke could have continued on the stage with such odds against him. His life story has for good reasons become a legend in the history of the *onnagata*.

The *onnagata* is as much a part of the Kabuki theatre today as he always has been, but in some ways he differs from his colleagues of the Tokugawa period. As mentioned before, he no longer carries his art of female impersonation with him when he leaves the stage, and the figures he portrays differ in appearance and manner very much from the women of modern Japan. Most of the female figures of Kabuki were created in the Tokugawa period, and they resembled to a certain degree the women of that time. The women of today cannot in any way identify themselves with the women they see on the stage, as could their predecessors.

Compared with the modern theatrical forms, the Kabuki theatre is today a static theatre form. Many Japanese have difficulty understanding its many conventions, for they are more used to the modern theatre. Some of them have never even set foot in a Kabuki theatre, and for these people the female impersonator is a strange and incomprehensible element. But for the many Japanese, young and old, who love and cherish the Kabuki theatre, and who visit it regularly, there is nothing peculiar about the use of female impersonators. It is as natural a part of the theatre as any of the other elements. In the Tokugawa period there were no actresses at all, so no one thought it strange for men to be playing women's roles.

Already in the Meiji period some Kabuki actors, including *onnagata*, starting playing in modern theatre as well as in Kabuki, and when film production got under way in the Taishô period (1912-1926), some actors were tempted to try their hands at that as well. Today quite a number of Kabuki actors are also engaged in other fields of acting. This is mostly true of actors playing men's roles, but the young, promising *onnagata* actor Bandô Tamasaburô (b. 1950) spreads his sphere of female impersonation widely. He has played the leading female roles in the Shakespeare plays *Macbeth* and *Othello*, and is currently on leave from the Kabuki theatre making a film in which he plays the role of a young woman. He has numerous admirers, especially among the younger generation, and his name is a household word. Even people who never attend a Kabuki performance seem to know this young actor. Weekly magazines run articles and feature photographs of him.

Notwithstanding that Bandô Tamasaburô is an extremely talented and promising young *onnagata* actor, one may speculate whether or not he is receiving a little too much attention from the public. One may also speculate whether or not it is a dangerous trend for the *onnagata* tradition when actors like Tamasaburô spread their acting over so wide a field. Can the classical presentational theatre preserve its distinctive character when many of its actors are being influenced by modern theatre?

Undoubtedly the most famous *onnagata* actor of today is Nakamura Utaemon VI (b. 1917). Like Tamasaburô, he plays exclusively female roles, but unlike him, he concentrates his work one hundred per cent on Kabuki. He acts in the pure classical style and seldom experiments with new styles of acting. He presents to the audience the classical *onnagata* figure at its very best. In *The Kabuki theatre of Japan* (2), A.C. Scott calls Utaemon 'the best possible proof that female roles in the Kabuki drama are essentially the creation of the male actor; even if women did play such parts it provides the curious position of women imitating men imitating women, and the probable result would be a degenerate and confused technique.'

The acting of the *onnagata* is so feminine that, watching them on the stage, one must constantly remind oneself that they are men and not women. I have personal knowledge of a foreigner who had heard of the fact that men played women's roles before he attended a Kabuki performance; but when he sat in the theatre, he was convinced that the tradition had been abandoned and that actresses had been introduced, so well did the *onnagata* play.

Today no one interested in the continued existence of the Kabuki theatre is seriously discussing the substitution of actresses for *onnagata*, as some did in the years after the Meiji Restoration. All agree that the female impersonators are indispensable for Kabuki. As mentioned earlier the technique of the actor is an extremely important factor in Kabuki. The *onnagata* roles were created for male actors and have in them elements that give the *onnagata* ample possibilities of showing his technique in female impersonation. These elements would have no meaning if women were to act the roles.

The main question today seems to be whether the standard of *onnagata* acting can continue high, or whether it will deteriorate, either due to lack of interest among young actors in playing *onnagata* roles or due to the influences of modern acting forms. Fortunately, the former seems at least at the moment a minor concern, for quite a few young actors have in recent years proved that they are ready and able to continue the work of their predecessors. As for the latter, the situation is hopeful, for in the more than one hundred years Kabuki has existed together with the modern theatre, it has not proved susceptible to new acting forms.

It is of course impossible to predict what the future will bring, but one can only hope that nothing will ever threaten this magnificent and, for the continued existence of the Kabuki theatre, absolutely essential art of female impersonation.

32

Past is Present in Furui Yoshikichi

MIYOKO URAGUCHI DOCHERTY

Tradition is often implicit in modernity in literature. The deliberate introduction of 'Tradition' in modern literary work has often been practised. Akutagawa and Tanizaki with *Konjaku monogatari*, for example, and' Mishima and Kurahashi introducing Nô plays into their works. The lady author of *Kagerô nikki*, the mother of Michitsuna, is resurrected as an eternal woman in *Kagerô no nikki* by Hori Tatsuo. Kafû discovered a time tunnel in France through to the Edo period in which he immersed himself and his works until his death.

Furui Yoshikichi (b. 1937) describes in one of his works a swamp; a swamp, like the one found in mediaeval literature, in which all forsaken souls squirm. There he exhibits the same kind of approach to 'Tradition' as the writers mentioned above. However, a more marked, more original, element in Furui's work is the way in which he has in some of his novels 'embodied', rather than merely introduced, 'Tradition'.

Tsumagomi 'Wedlock' is here examined to show how this technique of embodiment works, because it is a good example of the way in which 'Tradition' there emerges naturally from within the piece rather than being used as a particular element. It is ostensibly the story of a rather conventional modern situation but, as it progresses, that very situation reveals itself as controlled by the past. A young office worker, Hisao, with his wife Reiko, feature in the story, assisted by an old woman from a nearby village and the couple's neighbours, who are a group of labourers including the young Hiroshi. The story takes place in and around a two-room apartment in a typical dormitory commuter zone on the outskirts of Tokyo, where an ordinary office-worker couple spend another ordinary day. But this is in fact no ordinary matter for a bread-winner like Hisao, who normally never stays at home on weekdays. Battered by the strain of an industrial dispute, he is on sick leave.

The title *Tsumagomi* derives from the wedding song of the god Susanowo no Mikoto and Kushinada Hime in the palace of Suga, the first poem of the *Kojiki* (712 A.D.):

Yakumo tatsu	Where eight clouds rise
Izumo yaegaki	In Izumo an eightfold fence—
Tsumagomi ni	To keep a wife
Yaegaki tsukuru	I'll build an eightfold fence.
Sono yaegaki wo	Ah, that eightfold fence! (1)

In ancient times, the Izumo people sang it to celebrate a wedding. Simple as it may be, love overflows. Hisao and Reiko practised a modern *tsumagomi*. While on sick leave, for the first time in several years, he did not speak to anyone but his wife for a week. Through this unusual practice and through his sharpened nerves, Hisao comes to notice various components of his daily life which have been hidden to him until then, and thus to let us observe those which belong to the past.

The first suggestion that something uncommon has entered his life arises with the appearance of an old woman from the 'pathless summer thickets' (2) at noon on a hot summer day. She makes Hisao and the Japanese reader uneasy by a manner unbecoming an old woman: 'a coquettish smile', 'a startlingly youthful voice' and the manner of speech which is 'the familiar ways of young people'. And yet her unhesitant approach seems 'to envelop an obstinate young man with her benevolence'. (3) Unwittingly, Hisao adopts her manner of speech in his response. To his dismay, she immediately has a grip on him and makes him momentarily wish to be enveloped. She tells Hisao that she will find him a wife provided that he changes his attitude and stops running around. Why should she say this to a married man? A little ripple caused by the question becomes substantial when he finds out that the old woman has talked to his wife, Reiko, in the same vein.

Her entry is that of a survivor from the past. The old woman, is perhaps 'the descendant of a local priestess who used to take charge of bringing young people together in the days when this was still a remote countryside—someone of that kind—she would begin to feel the blood of her ancestors racing through her veins and would busy herself arranging marriages…' (4) and also, 'She would be keeping a sharp lookout for couples who seemed uncertain about their relationship'. (5) This old woman glides in and out of Hisao's life as she wishes for the rest of the day until after he has gone to bed. And both Hisao and Reiko, though unwillingly, are attracted by the woman.

Next to the apartment building stands a detached house which is used by a small construction firm as a dormitory for the half-dozen labourers. The quiet early morning air of the neighbourhood vibrates with the noise they make. In the evening they come home by truck. They thump about in their little house and out in the fields, howling and shouting until they drop off to sleep 'as if a fuse had blown'. (6) Among them is a young boy, Hiroshi, who works himself up to

242

become a fully fledged member of the group. The old woman is trying to shepherd him out of this bad flock as a new recruit to her own honest people's gathering.

After a long day's work at his office desk, Hisao comes back to the little modern flat where his wife quietly waits. It is a typical life-style of a modern man. The immediate surroundings of his residence, however, suggest that the old Japan lingers around him. His flat is not in a *danchi*, a huge self-contained concrete apartment complex. Sharing the same roof with several other flats, it is perched at the corner of fields where a breeze ruffles the yellow ears of rice plant. Here Furui depicts the erosion of old villages and fields by modern Tokyo:

'The houses around this area had been popping up like mushrooms. Instead of spreading gradually out into the field from the main road they were dotted in groups here and there according to the order in which farmers had sold their land.' (7) Hisao observes as he walks along the field: 'Farther down the road on the right was another disorganized new development, more houses crowded together overwhelming the rural scenery. Immediately after a neat row of two-storied houses came a flock of lately built matchbox-sized ones, already looking weatherbeaten... However, once he turned his back to the residential area on the right side of the street, there was a wholly different view. Fields lay spread out in the dusky light just as in the old days'.

The life of Reiko and Hisao is located on the border-line where present-day Japan meets its past. Hisao spends the daytime in the middle of the dusty, noisy metropolis and comes back every evening to his home in idyllic surroundings where a shaman-like woman and modern savages dwell. Rice fields, paddy or unplanted, have been the home of Japanese since the prehistoric Yayoi period, no matter how quickly they are now transformed to modern residential areas. The happy, strong savages, the labourers, are now in aloha shirts and the slaves of the time, but still run about in the fields. A shaman-like woman is also still trying to exert her power over unstable young people, with a certain limited success. Here, then, Furui demonstrates the presence of past Japan as alive as ever, inseparable from the present. The above mentions concerning the presence of the past are the aspects readily discernible to the reader. In the following section we will see the less obvious aspects of the presence of the past which have been incorporated in the story.

First, we will seek it in the senses and sensitivity of the apartment residents toward the outside world, and then in those of Hisao. The couple live in a box-like flat divided from the next flat by proper, though perhaps they may not be concrete, walls. The reader notices that the senses and sensitivity of the apartment residents (including

Hisao and Reiko) towards the outside world are unchanged from the days when only a paper partition divided their lives from those of others. They self-consciously move about in their own house lest outsiders complain. Through having been on constant guard, they have acquired a living style where, in their consciousness, a third party always participates. The expression, 'the smug silence of the neighbourhood' (8) immediately shows how much they are aware of the presence of other people. One night as he returns home, Hisao witnesses one of the men beating up Hiroshi, the young labourer, outside their house. Here Furui describes an apartment block which stands in deep silence, as 'everyone in the building seemed to be straining to hear the sounds that came from the house next door... There was something lonely about (Hiroshi's gasping), against the hush of those who were listening so intently'. (9)

Hisao is always conscious of other people's presence. He can never forget even for a moment that other people share the walls. For him, the silence is impregnated with muffled noise. 'Hunching over in the tub he strained to listen to the sounds from the kitchen. Along with bottles clinking and slippers shuffling across the kitchen floor, and almost as clearly, came sounds from the neighbouring apartments upstairs and down. Low voices would occasionally utter a few distinct words; someone would stand up on the *tatami*, walk around sluggishly, and then sit down again with a thump; here and there the bath water would be running...' (10) Then at night, lying on his bed, Hisao listens to the men rampaging outside their house. 'Sometimes the voices would fade into the distance, as if the shouting came from across a river, but then they would swell up and fill the bedroom...' (11) Reiko is taking a bath. Hisao interprets 'the stealthy sound of running water beyond the closed door of the bathroom', which he could hear 'during the pauses in the bawdy singing', 'as if Reiko was afraid of being overheard by the men'. They may live in a modern flat in the modern age, but their life in it is constantly governed by the same senses and sensitivity which people in the past possessed toward the outside world.

In fact, their married life is a product of a concept of marriage which belongs to the past. A modern man and woman they may be, but the marriage of Hisao and Reiko takes place in a traditional context. It is not their own spontaneous wish and initiative but their senses and sensitivity to the third person that brings Hisao and Reiko together. 'They had talked of making a new life together as husband and wife. Not from attachment to the past—that subtle charm had been squeezed out long ago. There remained only the haunting shame of a couple who had become too intimate, the fear that, if they were to leave each other now, a part of both of them, the shameful part, would split off and go its way alone, and they would be tortured by the nightmare of pursuing it in their imagination forever.' (12)

244

Their marriage began as they had felt ashamed, in other words, self-consciously aware that society was not kindly disposed towards them. Had society readily accepted them as they were or had they been ashamed, the marriage would not have taken place. They would have gone separately, as they planned, on their own ways. Their marriage 'was arranged' following the convention. In their case society was their go-between. They accept it passively and continue it by inertia. 'Now, five years later, after living together without either the usual honeymoon or that first wave of marital boredom, they had become a typical married couple. Seasonal products arrived regularly from Reiko's family in the country.' As Hisao realizes, it lacks 'the energy to support lush growth' (13), an impetus to create their own positive life.

Like many other conventional marriages, theirs is one in which they forego the deep joy of togetherness which springs out from mutually based understanding. Their relationship readily allows an outsider to intrude. In fact, they exist only because the third person enables them to exist. The life of Hisao and Reiko is always a three-some, even when only two of them sit in the room. If not in his mind or consciousness, in the air, he detects the invisible presence of the third party. This Furui describes with the effects of sound. One evening, Hisao 'got up, intending to watch TV until bedtime, opened the door to the inner room—and gasped. The light was out, and their two sets of bedding were already spread out neatly on the floor. But the darkness was throbbing with the bawdy songs of the construction gang. It was hard to tell where the voices were coming from... He only knew that rough voices had filled that empty bedroom'. (14) He allows the third person to come between them too easily. Sometimes it is the old woman, sometimes Hiroshi. Reiko also has this tendency, seeing Hisao as an extension of Hiroshi, an aged Hiroshi. In fact, in their marriage, there exists something like an air cushion between them.

One afternoon, Hisao is looking at Reiko who is sitting beside him. 'At that moment, as he was lying there beside his wife, he felt like a bachelor furtively spying on someone else's household from outside the window.' (15) In another instance, Reiko mistakes Hisao for a stranger when she, on her return, finds a man curled up in bed one afternoon. She says, 'Finding a strange man in our bed with his face buried in our white sheets—somehow I felt I couldn't tell anybody about it'. (16) Hisao thinks, 'If only for a little while, Reiko had found a strange man curled up under a blanket in his apartment, in their very own bed. Yes, once the reality of a husband and wife was ever so slightly disturbed, it was surprisingly fragile. And now that she had had the experience of staring at her husband that way, perhaps there would be other occasions when she would see a strange person in him.' He may in her, too.

245

Hisao is presented as a modern man in the beginning of this paper. Subsequently, however, he is seen as inseparable from the third person as if he does not have an awareness of individualism, a mark of a modern man. Is he in fact then a slave of the past? On the contrary, Hisao has a fervent yearning to exclude the third party from their life. Only he does not succeed. 'Even delirious with a 104 degree fever he was still glossing it over, wanting to avoid dragging in any outsider, wanting to be as free as possible. He thought he had succeeded. But in the meantime Hiroshi had been watching, had run to the clinic for him, had brought him peaches. There were no secrets. A hollow laugh welled up within him and floated lightly to the ceiling.' (17)

In the following section, we will examine Hisao more closely in his relationship with the old woman. When the old woman talks of Hiroshi with a certain patronage, Hisao feels 'oddly envious' (18) of a young labourer who is the object of such concern. Why should he feel so? An answer is to be found in the nature of the old woman. Reiko says of the old woman, 'When you listen to her you begin to wonder who you are yourself'. (19) And Hisao responds, 'I suppose one person was another to her'. Reiko recalls that back in her part of the country, there was someone similar who conducted the role of a kind of shaman. The old woman forms a local group for the unmarried and undertakes the role of go-between. Her aim is to integrate the young people under her eye, to put them into one flock rather than leave them separate. Their individual identity under the elder's protections will be dissolved into a big group. The old woman has not only the power to 'envelop' (20) the young mind, but also to make them (including Hisao) wish to be enveloped. She, by assuming him to be one of the labourers and thus including him among 'you boys' (21), shakes Hisao's self-reliance.

Listening to her lecture, Hisao observes his own posture as he hangs his head before the old woman: 'the posture you held your body in had a strange effect, Hisao thought. At first it only gave an outward appearance; then little by little it brought about the appropriate kind of feeling. Or maybe for a young man to hang down his head before an old person was something that had been handed down generation after generation since ancient times, until it had the power to sweep away minor differences in age and circumstances and attitude. Could it be a kind of slow conditioned reflex? The way the old woman talked seemed to be making him feel a bit dejected'. (22) So, in other words, the old woman represents 'traditional Japan', where the elders with their authority of age and experience reign over the young who, in return, feel well protected if not allowed to be an individual. Hisao, an aged Hiroshi, in some ways represents young or semi-young modern men who, in the bottom of their minds, are still inclined to accept the traditional patronage of the elders, although at the surface level of their consciousness they reject it with disgust, yearning to gain their own self-confidence. Now we turn our attention to Reiko. The question whether she is thoroughly modern or not does not pester Reiko. She is free from the agitation caused by the presence of the past which subconsciously disturbs Hisao. There remains the smooth continuation of tradition in Reiko. Tradition in various shapes interferes with their relationship, and its closeness to Reiko stirs Hisao's irritation. He is supposed to be the person closest to Reiko. And yet the presence of tradition lying so close to Reiko threatens him and shakes his identity as her husband and the master of the house. First, we look at this aspect in Reiko's link with her family and with the home which she shares with Hisao, and then in her relationship with the old woman and the labourers.

Unlike Hisao who is a rootless city man, Reiko has a traditional root: her family lives in the country, where local custom is still regarded as an antonym of modernity. Also, she has her own root, a house, in Tokyo. The house in which Hisao sleeps every night becomes more tangible when he links it with Reiko. 'A box of the peaches had arrived half a month earlier from Reiko's family in the country. Perhaps for that reason Reiko peeled them with an air of authority befitting the mistress of the house. No doubt her mother had peeled peaches for her that same way. Sometimes he had the notion that his life was being sustained by Reiko's peaches.' (23) It gives Hisao 'an odd feeling to think of his wife (as the mistress of the house)—here in a little two-room apartment with no extra space inside or out, no children, nothing to manage but a monthly salary, no ancestral rites to perform'. Nonetheless, Hisao senses her solid existence as the mistress of the house even in her small movements. A grocery man arrives when Reiko is standing at the kitchen counter. 'There was only a short, swaying curtain between the tiny entryway and the kitchen, and the front door had been left open to let in the breeze... Reiko could have given him her order from where she stood, and yet she had quietly asked him to wait a minute, dried her hands carefully on her apron, lifted the lid of a pot and checked the flame, and then walked on around the table toward the entryway. As she stood in the shadow of the curtain for a moment she smoothed her hair with one hand. Then she drew the curtain aside and went out, closing it immediately behind her.' Hisao thinks, 'To the man waiting in the sunshine even the mistress of this cramped dwelling emerged from secluded depths within'.

On another occasion, as he is lying on his sick bed with his wife beside him sorting out the laundry, 'he felt like a bachelor furtively spying on someone else's household from outside the window. Within every window a woman was secluded, staring just as seriously at all the things of daily life, boiling down to an even richer density an existence that had always been denser than a man's. She was boiling it down endlessly. For a time the thought oppressed him. (24) And again: 'Once again Reiko was directing a serious look at one of the peaches and the knife. Once again he felt a slight shiver as he watched her eyes from the side. If that steadfast gaze, and his furtive, undercover, voyeur's gaze... It was hard to understand how husbands and wives could look at each other, could exchange glances day after day'.

Hisao sees a close link between Reiko and Hiroshi: they have both come from the same village back in the country and therefore share the same regional accent.

' "So he really is from the same village, is he?"

"You can tell by listening to him talk."

"Does he know you come from there?"

"I wonder." '

Reiko turned to look out of the window and smiled.' (25) Here Hisao feels himself excluded by the combination of Reiko and Hiroshi. 'It was a smile implying that something deep had been touched on by a person who didn't understand it. In his primary-school days whenever he tried out a new dirty word in front of the girls in his class, they would suddenly look very grown-up and exchange that kind of smile. Being from the same place seemed to yield a similar secret understanding.' Also he finds out that the peaches which sustained him were in fact Hiroshi's gift:

' "Aren't the peaches from your family about running out?"

"They ran out long ago."

Although he had expected that, her brief reply made him feel all the more disappointed.

"Oh...So you bought these at the store?"

Keeping her serious look fixed on the knife, Reiko again replied briefly:

"No, they're the same kind. Hiroshi brought them over." '

These words of Reiko were a revelation to Hisao: 'He felt the taste of the peach in his mouth go sour. Never had he dreamed that he was letting himself be nourished back to health by peaches received from that boy'. And he goes on: 'In the shadow of dark sunglasses, embarrassed eyes seemed to be observing his lewd bachelor's fantasies as he gobbled down a peach that his wife had peeled'.

Next, we will observe how close Reiko is to tradition in the shape of the old woman and the labourers. When Hisao tells Reiko about what the old woman lectured him about, Reiko smiles to herself. Hisao interprets her expression as 'a woman watching a woman's behaviour' (26) and thinks that Reiko is saying in her mind, ' "She's really going at him!" '. He also notices in Reiko's response to his unkind remark about the old woman that Reiko 'had drawn up a woman's line-of-battle'. (27) This discovery of the closeness of

Reiko to the old woman irritates Hisao. 'Reiko looked rather equivocal' (28), talking about the old woman, 'as if she wanted to say something and yet wanted to conceal it'.

Here, Hisao 'began to feel a kind of jealousy', and this introduces
in him a sense of alienation. Thus, in his imagination, 'Two sil-
houettes passed his window, going down that blazing white road on
the embankment. Now and then the two nodded to each other. Each
time they nodded, he felt like a distant stranger. A transient, for all
the world like Hiroshi'. (29) At the end of the story, Hisao listens
from his bed to the voice of the old woman into which that of Reiko
transfuses. 'Gradually, calling Hiroshi's name over and over, that
disagreeably trembling voice (of the old woman) seemed to become
younger and fuller, to take on a sweet, feminine quality.' (30) And
'As Hisao lay there with one arm around her he felt himself yielding
to the illusion that Reiko's voice was still echoing outside, floating
in the darkness beyond the window'.

As we have already seen, the labourers represent the savage, the
caged savage, in the modern age. In their youth, as is shown in
Hiroshi, they are tender, sensitive and sweet natured. As they grow
up, they become battered but still spontaneous and more significantly, gentle. Reiko's link with the savages is depicted in a scene
toward the end of the story when she goes out to empty a garbage
pail late at night. The drunken men who have returned from their
outing offer to empty and clean the pail. Then Hiroshi offers her a
drink. As he is from the same village as 'ma'am' (31), he is in sole
charge of this hospitality. Hisao having followed Reiko's every
movement from his bed, sits up in bed and peers through the little
gap between the curtains. 'There, where the old woman had ha-
rangued him earlier that day, he could see the pale figure of Reiko
sitting on a stone surrounded by a ring of half-naked men. She
seemed thoroughly at ease, taking little sips from a teacup which she
held delicately between her fingertips as if she were at a tea
ceremony.

'Hiroshi was kneeling down before her resting a big bottle of *sake*
against one knee; he was stripped to the waist too and sat there
imposingly waiting on her with elbows thrust out akimbo. The men
encircling them had squatted like children, hunching their bronzed,
sweaty backs. They looked up delightedly as Reiko sipped from the
teacup.' (32) There is a little teasing of Hiroshi from the men Hisao
hears Reiko, sounding embarrassed, joining in to a roar of cheerful
laughter. And then, 'When the laughter died down he could hear her
clear voice saying "Well, good-night. Thanks for everything." All the
men called good-night to her. Their voices were strangely gentle'.
(33) So, Reiko is a goddess for the savages. She has induced their
tenderness. Her gentle acceptance of their hospitality gains their
admiration still more. As she takes a drink, 'The men fell into a

249

fascinated silence. A low, grunting cheer rose like a sigh'. (34)
Earlier, Hisao sees Reiko as a 'docile animal' (35) as he watches her
slowly getting up from the floor. And now Hisao detects 'a playful,
intimate sound' (36) in Reiko's voice, as she talks to the men. Reiko
may be more sophisticated, but she belongs to the family of savages,
and shares the gentleness of the savages.

From the analysis we have made here of *Tsumagoni*, we can see
how the gradual revelation of traditional forces is the point of the
work. Furui shows how the boundary between private life and the
outer world is paper thin. The reader is struck by the fact that the
hero's senses and sensitivity toward the outside world are unchanged
from the days when only a paper partition divided his life from those
of the others. But as we said at the beginning, this story is precisely
set in a typical situation of modern Japan. In Hisao, we have seen a
modern man who, though it may be subconsciously, yearns for the
past. In Reiko, we have observed how much the past is alive within
the mind of a modern housewife. A remnant of the past, senses and
sensitivity toward the outside world, plays the role of go-between in
their marriage. Perhaps in making an analysis of this work of fiction
we are saying something about the nature of Japanese society today.

33

Origins and Development of Science Fiction in Japan

MILENA PARINI

One of the main problems to be faced by those interested in Japanese science fiction (SF) is the lack of critical essays on the subject. It goes without saying that this is also true for other countries, but I believe this is even more relevant for Japan.

Instead of speaking of a single author (who would be, in my case, Hanmura Ryô) or of a single period, I propose to try to give a general survey of the main characteristics of Japanese SF. This outline will start with what I consider to be the beginning of Japanese science fiction and conclude with the time when it officially established itself. By 'established' I mean having a regular publishing market and a number of writers professionally dedicated to it.

I shall avoid discussing, therefore, present-day Japanese SF. It will be obviously impossible to exhaust the subject within the limits given here, but I am happy to discuss a genre undoubtedly relevant in Japanese literature, a genre which up to now has been left in the shade.

And here we meet immediately with the very obvious first problem: when did Japanese science fiction begin? This is a knotty enough question when dealing with western SF, let alone Japanese SF. In fact, critics generally are tempted into discovering the origins of science fiction in early national cultures in the hope of establishing a kind of historical continuity. But this operation ends up by undervaluing the true historical significance. The motive behind this sort of wishful thinking is the desire to grant SF a 'respectability' which main-stream literature has always denied to it. In particular, as far as Japan as concerned, this attitude arises from the desire to free Japanese SF from the suspicion that its origins were too deeply influenced by the first western SF works.

With the intention of regaining this 'virginity' and of steering clear of the years just preceding the Meiji Restoration of 1868, some Japanese critics were able to find a scent of SF even in such early works as the *Kojiki*. Though an exciting prospect, to enter the realm of myth would take us too far astray.

So, to make good use of Japanese critical essays on this subject it is necessary first of all to specify the 'basic ingredients' which constitute a SF literature, for only then shall we be able to find out just where we can put the origins of Japanese science fiction or, at least, to decide on those works that can be considered its true ancestors.

In the first place, as SF literature is characterized by the fact that fantasy gets its plausibility and credibility from science and no longer from spell or alchemy, it is impossible to deny that, in Japan, this mixture of fantasy and science appeared first in the Meiji period (1868-1912). Here it is possible to find works which fully deserve the title of forerunners and sources of inspiration of the SF-to-be (though, of course, we cannot assert that Japanese SF as such made its first appearance in this period).

This said, I think that the history of Japanese SF, from its origins up to its establishment in about 1960, can be divided into three periods, each with different connotations.

The first runs parallel with the Meiji period and is characterized by original Japanese works known as *bôken shôsetsu* 'adventure novels'. Another main feature of the period is the many translations of works by Jules Verne and H.G. Wells. The second period covers the years from Taishô (1912-1926) to the end of the Second World War in 1945 and this is characterized by the slow passage from the *bôken shôsetsu* to the *kagaku shôsetsu* 'scientific novels'. This is the coming into its own of SF as distinct from the already well established *tantei shôsetsu* 'detective stories' and mystery novels. Finally, the third period, from 1945 to 1960, which sees the passage from the *kagaku shôsetsu* to the *kûsôkagaku shôsetsu*, that is the real science-fiction novel.

During the first period, that is, the Meiji period, Japanese scholars seemed completely taken up by the efforts of translating western works. As far as the origins of Japanese SF novel are concerned, it is interesting to stress the fact that Jules Verne's novels represent a relevant part among the numerous and heterogeneous western works translated in the first half of the period. In fact, not only were all his most famous novels translated but, surprisingly, these translations appeared in Japan only ten years after the original editions. This interest in Verne's novels is a constant feature of the years 1878-1896 when, among the translated titles, were *Le tour du monde en quatre-vingt jours* (1); *De la terre à la lune* (2); *Voyage au centre de la terre* (3).

The widespread success of these translations was due to the fact that they dealt in a fantastic way with the scientific reality which the Japanese were just discovering. Verne's success was mostly due to his positivistic view of the future as an endless progress bringing improvements in the standard of life. Meiji Japan was eagerly clutching at western science as the only means for a better future. On the other hand, it is very easy to understand why H.G. Wells's works did not have an immediate appeal (4): he is much more jaundiced and critical towards science and technology, and especially towards the societies-to-be based on them. Besides the works of these two writers (who are regarded as the real forerunners of western SF), utopian novels by other western authors appeared in translation during the Meiji period. These works differed very much in style and aims and it would be difficult to include them in a paper on SF. However, these translations, together with the works of Verne and Wells, represent a relevant spur for those Japanese works which were the forerunners of science-fiction novels. I refer here to such works as *Atlantis* (5) by Ignatius Donnelly (1882), *Le vingtième siècle* by Albert Robida (1884), and *Looking backward* (6) by Edward Bellamy (1888). From these two currents, one more SF centred, the other more utopian, sprang at last the first original Japanese works. They generally deal with the novelties of the machine age to illustrate the future in optimistic terms. Among the works of this kind we can remember *Nihon no mirai* 'The future of Japan' by Ushiyama Ryôsuke, *Nijûsannen mirai ki* 'In twenty-three years' (1886) by Suehiro Tetchô and above all *Ukishiro monogatari* 'The floating fortress' (1890) by Yano Ryûkei.

This last work was published in serial form and describes the adventures of a group of Japanese patriots who dream of performing heroic deeds for their country. For this reason they build a new weapon on an island in the South Seas, and engage in an incredible naval battle with a foreign country, which they finally overcome.

As can be seen from this work, the hints given by the western books led, first, to a Japanese form rich in patriotic fervour and nationalistic dreams. It is interesting to note that Ushiyama Ryôsuke, Yano Ryûkei and Suehiro Tetchô cannot be regarded properly as novelists. Their first aim, in fact, was to use the style of a utopian novel mainly to express their political views and they did not think of themselves as novelists. When speaking about the Japanese novel of that time we must not forget that those were the years of the *Shôsetsu shinzui* 'The essence of the novel' which Tsubouchi Shôyô published in 1885-86. This essay was an attempt to revolutionize the approach to literature but, because of the very theories it supported, it ended up by delaying the appearance of novels which, not being wholly based on reality, were able to go beyond it by means of fantasy.

To return to Verne's influence, Oshikawa Shunrô was the author who took most advantage of the ideas contained in Verne's work, though we cannot regard his novels as true SF but simply as *bôken shôsetsu*, that is, adventure novels, as they were in fact labelled, Nevertheless, his works represent the first step made by Japanese literature towards SF. His masterpiece is *Kaitei gunkan* 'Undersea battleship' and it was published in 1900. The plot describes the imaginary adventures of a young Japanese naval officer with the seas of the world as a background. When we read his novels or short

253

stories now, they seem rather immature and naive but, notwith-standing that, Japanese critics regard them as classics of this literary genre.

The beginning of the second period coincides with the beginning of the Taishô period. In these years, the writers moved slowly away from naturalism and realism and, as a consequence, the works of this period are characterized by a greater liveliness and originality.

In 1917 *Sanjûnen ato* 'Thirty years later' by Hoshi Hajime was published. It was not well received when it first appeared, but it is now regarded as a milestone in the history of Japanese SF. It is the story of a politician who, tired of the world he is living in, leaves it to seek comfort on a desert island. After thirty years he goes back to Japan and realizes that his country and its society have been com-pletely upset by a new and prodigious medicine coming from the stars. This is the heart of a whimsical plot, rich in adventures and amusing ideas (at least for us!)—for example, the description of a plane flying over Mt. Fuji piloted by a charming kimono-clad lady.

Towards the end of the Taishô era a new magazine appeared. This was *Shinseinen* 'New youth' and it specialized in detective and mys-tery stories. From time to time it included stories which hardly belonged to these categories but which can more properly be con-sidered SF-centred stories.

Two stories in particular are noteworthy: *Ren'ai kyokusen* 'Emotion graph' and *Jinkô shinzô* 'The artificial heart' both by Kosakai Fuboku and published in 1926. In the first, the writer imagines that it is possible to explore human emotions thanks to a weird instrument resembling an electrocardiograph. The second story is a continuation of this plot. It deals with the tragedy of the men involved in these new experiments. In fact, because of this instru-ment, they end up by being no longer able to have feelings and emotions.

In 1922 *Kagaku gahô* 'Illustrated scientific magazine' came out. Compared with *Shinseinen*, this magazine was not so exclusively directed at the new generation but, above all, it specialized in scien-tific stories by both Japanese and western authors. Apart from the value of the works published in *Kagaku gahô*, what was relevant here was the popularization of scientific theories and the fact that for the first time the term *kagaku shôsetsu* 'scientific novel' made its appearance. Compared with the previous term *bôken shôsetsu*, *kagaku shôsetsu* represents a very important step forward, in that it helped to clear the confusion that existed among the detective, mystery and SF stories and their writers.

The most important writer of *kagaku shôsetsu* was Unno Jûsa who is considered the true father of Japanese SF. He made his debut as an author in 1930. Because his stories were from the first so different from detective stories they had little success when they first appeared in *Shinseinen*. From 1935 on he wrote mainly novels and short stories for young people. His greatest merit lies in the skill with which he harmonizes the fantastic with the scientific elements. He was a prolific writer and among his works I would like to mention *Kaitei tairiku* 'The submerged continent', *Kasei heidan* 'The patrol from Mars', *Chikyû tônan* 'The theft of the earth', and *Uchû sentai* 'The outer-space squadron'. Unno Jûsa died in 1948, just when the Japanese SF novel was about to assert itself in a stable way.

The third period begins in 1945 when, owing to the defeat and the occupation of Japan by the U.S. forces, Japanese readers came into contact with the latest American and English works. These had gone beyond the classical themes of the space-opera, and had given birth to novels which were the result of the shock of the atomic bomb. That explosion had in fact achieved and even surpassed the most tragic vision of earlier SF writers. When we read these works, we realize that their content has become less superficial and that they have a higher literary value.

The years from 1945 to the end of the 1950s in Japan must be regarded as a period of transition, during which Japanese SF renounces the military-nationalistic ideals of the years before the war and follows the new ideas developed in the contemporary Anglo-American works, though without immediately managing to find a character of its own. The most interesting aspect of this period is nevertheless not so much the new writers or works, as the boom in publishing: in fact it was during these years that an extraordinary number of new magazines and series was produced. Though they did not meet with an immediate success and some of them had a very short life, they bear witness to the liveliness of SF literature and the interest shown in it.

In 1946 the first group of SF writers was formed, the Kagaku Shôsetsu Sôsaku Kai 'The SF Novels Creation Society'. In 1950 Seibundô Shinkosha brought out the Japanese translation of the American magazine *Amazing stories*, keeping the original title. It went out of print after the seventh number, and whereas the American magazine had critical articles on SF as well as short stories, the Japanese version contained only translations of the short stories.

The first specialized Japanese SF magazine appeared in 1954. It was published by Mori no Michi-sa and had the title *Seiun* 'Nebula': it was discontinued immediately after the first number, though it was quite interesting and offered very good translations.

Muromachi Shobô began in 1955 the publication of a series with the title of *Sekai kûsôkagaku shôsetsu zenshû* 'Complete collection of world SF', but it came to an end after the second volume because most people did not even know what *kûsôkagaku* meant. This word, which is now the accepted name for SF literature, was in fact used for the first time here. It is in itself a clear recognition of the fact that the 'fantasy' (*kûsô*) factor was equally as important as the 'science' (*kagaku*) one: from this time the two terms co-exist in harmony.

About this time even the non-specialized magazines began to show an interest in SF, and in a special number of *Hôseki* 'Jewel' entirely devoted to SF, a critical article on the subject appeared for the first time in Japanese. Written by Yano Tetsu, it had the title 'Atarashii Ei-Bei no kagaku shôsetsu' 'The new Anglo-American scientific novel'.

In 1956 Gengensha began another series called *Saishin kagaku shôsetsu zenshû* 'A complete collection of new scientific novels' which was to cease publication after the 29th book. Meanwhile, the adventure of Sputnik I in 1957 caused a big stir and the popular enthusiasm it aroused greatly contributed to the diffusion of works of SF.

In 1957 Hayakawa Shobô published a magazine, *Hayakawa fantasy*, a title later changed to *Hayakawa SF series*. This continued until 1968. Also in 1957 the first 'fanzine' (7), *Uchûjin* 'Cosmic dust' came out. Still on sale today, its promoter, Shibano Takumi, is very active in the field of SF. The importance of *Uchûjin* lies in the fact that its pages were the proving ground for writers who are now the biggest names in SF.

Early in 1960 we find the birth of *SF magazine*, published by Hayakawa Shobô, which succeeded in making itself known as the specialized journal on SF, first of all as the Japanese edition of the American magazine *F&SF* and later as an independent enterprise publishing mainly Japanese works. *SF magazine* is still being published today with ever increasing success.

The year it first appeared marks at the same time the arrival and the real point of departure for Japanese SF. Its steady achievement means that the period of transition is over and that both writers and public have assimilated and elaborated the stimuli received from foreign SF: the former are now ready to create, and the latter ready to receive, original work.

Beginning with the 1960s, Japanese SF is a reality which can no longer be ignored. Its high standard and popularity in Japan qualifies it as a literary genre worthy of the keen attention of the critics.

34

To Restore to Honour a Dishonoured Honorific

PATRICK LE NESTOUR

To restore to honour a dishonoured honorific
The notions of exteriority and non-exteriority, previously defined
(1), apply to the determination of the linguistic person in its
manifold forms, including the so-called 'honorifics'.

Certain uses, particularly of *o-* and *go-* (2), though, do not fit into
this binary framework, and so constitute proclitic particles, similar to
those which evolved in certain languages, such as Hungarian, Ancient
Greek, Romance languages, until they finally attained the rank of
articles, a disturbing similarity, beginning with the fact that a
'definite article' has generally preceded the birth of an 'indefinite
article'.

Like the Japanese system of enclitics (*joshi*, syntagma markers),
the article system (substantive markers) enriches the determination
relationship by sharpening the apperception and the apprehension
of the factual and the virtual with regard to discourse and its protagonists. 'So the further one gets from the elements most necessary to
language, the greater the chances are of finding elements proceeding
purely from the necessities of the mind. It would be easier to do
without the article than without the noun—a fact beyond doubt,
since certain languages do currently get along without one—which
leads to the conclusion that, since it is not in fact so necessary as the
noun, the article might well offer a clearer image of the abstract
requirements of the thinking mind.' (3)

Even before Thomas Raucat's *L'honorable partie de campagne* (4),
and up to the present day, when jokes and cartoons poke fun at
Chinese and Japanese alike, the Honourable This and the Honourable
That have raised many a smile. To play the game, let us suppose that
the expression:

'Achieve your honourable rest!'
would be rendered in Japanese:
'*O-yasumi nasai!*'

In this attempt to find a word-for-word translation, the two words
'your honourable' converge in a single Japanese morpheme: *O-*, the
O- in *O-yasumi!*

The reader will, of course, realize that this is reasoning backwards
but, knowing full well how things stand, he will find it disconcerting

that, when confronted with this *o-*, Japanese and other linguists should have wavered between two assimilations: the one—the 'Honourable'—becoming 'honorific', and the other—the 'Your' —becoming the linguistic person, in its various forms.

In Japanese the two often merge and a single notion is sufficient to cover them both: exteriority. (5)

The utterance:

'*O-denwa des*'!', for example,

so well sums up the syncretism of the notions of honorific and second person, that when translated into English, French, Italian, etc, it can be cut down to one word:

'Telephone!',

which cuts out the difficulty by cutting dead the 'your honourable': only the intonation used, in the form of an 'exclamative morpheme', will carry the exteriority.

And yet, although it is not possible to deny the second person here, inherent in this invitation to go and pick up the telephone, the exteriority which allows the speaker to assert that the call is not for him, it is doubtful whether 'Telephone!' retains much that is honorific.

O-cha o nonde kara...

Let us now leave a dishonoured honorific for an honorific which is no longer held in honour, which has been abandoned by its entourage, robbed of all its honorific lustre, stripped of exteriority.

In saying:

'*O-cha o nonde kara ikimasu yo!*'

meaning in French:

'*Oui, j'irai quand j'aurai pris le thé!*'

I again risk falling into Thomas Raucat's phraseology:

'*Oui, j'irai quand j'aurai bu l'honorable thé!*'

Here, however, as I put aside *L'honorable partie de campagne*, I cannot help drawing a parallel between this *o-* and this particular use of the definite article in French: *o-cha—le thé*.

When dealing with the lexico-grammatical notions which cover definite and indefinite articles, it should be remembered that there are more than two categories of situation to which the use of these articles corresponds; this is why it is preferable to evoke notions of determination and some situations make it necessary to call not only on the notions of 'non-determined' and 'determined', but also, in particular, that of 'surdetermined'.

In the present instance, should *le thé*, in *prendre le thé*, be considered as determined or surdetermined? Let us consider the problem in another way:

'The cat has found a mouse.'

The cat here may be determined by one or several preceding contexts or situations which have, in fact, defined it.

On the other hand, in a family where there is one and only one, 'the cat' corresponds to a whole set of contexts and situations which continually refer to the same cat, unless otherwise indicated by appropriate statements. Having no further need to be determined, the cat is 'surdetermined', as proper nouns are.

But what of the tea in *prendre le thé* and *prendre du thé*—where *du* is simply an indefinite article applied to an uncountable corresponding to *un* in *manger un gâteau*. (It does not appear necessary to allude to *prendre un thé* or *manger du gâteau* at this point).

Prendre le thé constitutes a social act, which is usually performed in the plural, by several people together. The definite article does not indicate that the drinkers are familiar with the tea they are drinking or going to drink: as has been seen, it is the act itself which is familiar, due to its social ritualisation, and it is therefore as a predicate that it is surdetermined.

It is in this akin to the generic, which is most frequently indicated in French by the definite article.

'*Le thé est désaltérant*'. (Compare with English: 'Tea is refreshing'.)

So far, it matters little, moreover, whether 'the tea' means 'the beverage', or 'the light meal taken with tea (*du thé*) in the afternoon', (with or without cakes and biscuits...) although the latter meaning would be hard to find in *o-cha*. (6)

To finish with this tea before it has lost all its aroma, I would hazard the thought, for the want of a more accurate definition, that the article has become fixed in *prendre le thé*, that it is on its way to becoming lexiconized: the predicate, the verbal phrase, forms a whole, in which *le* and *thé* are particularly inseparable, since it is possible to say '*On prend souvent le thé*', but not '*On prend le bon thé*'.

This is the same phenomenon as occurs in *o-cha*, where *o-* and *cha* are also inseparable.

In all honesty it must be pointed out that the order given in Japanese as '*O-cha!*' or '*O-cha o motte irasshai!*', has nothing automatically corresponding to the article *le* in the French, which would range from '*Le thé!*' to '*Du thé!*', or even '*Un thé!*' in a restaurant or café.

The necessary deduction is that all these examples give some idea of the relations that may exist between *o-* and the article in certain languages, but that they are not sufficient to establish an absolute parallel.

Around the problem of 'O-cha', etc...
The study of a linguistic system constitutes a sort of labyrinth, which inevitably presents a number of dead-ends, where research comes up

short and is sometimes content to simply give up a path which appears negligible.

And yet, if one delves more deeply at this point to penetrate the mystery, it sometimes happens that a new path opens up, offering new perspectives.

In Chapter 3 of his study on the honorifics (7), Gary P. Prideaux quotes the phonologist McCawley (8), to obviate the example of *o-cha*:

'Some of the Sino-Japanese forms he mentions are *otya* "tea", *okaasan* "(your) mother", *otoosan* "(your) father", and *daigaku* "university".

'The first three of these forms are used politely and honorifically (with the possible exception of "tea"), and they take the *o* honorific prefix.'

Neither Prideaux nor McCawley knows what to do with this 'exception of "tea"'.

A few lines further on Prideaux just as serenely considers the fact that 'many native forms such as *hana* "flower" also take the *o* prefix', without enquiring whether *o* is as honorific as it is supposed to be.

Prideaux takes tea again in Chapter 4 ('The polite and formal transformations'), this time adding a pinch of salt: 'In the same manner as for the adjective *samu* "cold"→ *osamuu* and *gozaimasu*, the *o* will be added to polite nouns (sic) if used honorifically. Examples are *otya* "tea" and *otomodati* "friend"'. (9)

The problem arises from Prideaux's failing to discriminate between two features that he delineates quite accurately elsewhere: politeness —a question of register—present or not in *o-cha*: (+ Pol) / (* Pol) (10) and exteriority—a question of enunciation—that Prideaux outlined in 1970 under the heading 'out-group' as opposed to 'in-group' and syncretized under the feature '± 1st Person'. (11)

One may therefore compare:

o-cha (+ Pol, * 1 P.) or (* Pol, *1 P.), and
o-tomodachi (+ Pol, − 1 P.) or (+ Pol, * 1 P.), according to the sex of the speaker, etc.

Prideaux, however, does not transformationally consider the existence of *o-* or *go-* where honorificity is irrelevant—if I may use such a term to terminate this disgression.

Demonstrative and article—historical background
Apart from the fact that there appears to be no other explanation for the nature of the Japanese proclitic *o-* when it is irrelevant to exteriority, historical parallels show that it is from such particles as the exteriorising *o-* that definite articles originated in languages where they exist.

This phenomenon is governed by two principles. The first consists in noting that, in these languages, the definite article always appeared before any indefinite article (12), with the result that for a certain time the only opposition that existed was between (definite article + noun) and no article at all, i.e. (zero article + noun).

So far the Japanese pattern complies fully with the general model.

The other constant, as Guillaume so justly put it, resides in the fact that the definite article always stems from a demonstrative, a deictic determiner like itself. Guillaume expounded the problem in his study of the origins of the article, at the same time raising it to a level for which psycho-linguistics should be grateful. With this in mind, it seems worthwhile to quote in full three paragraphs of his preface: (13)

'I. The article is a secondary development of languages—by which it should be understood that the article did not exist at the outset. There was no article in Indo-European: it appears unfledged in Homeric Greek, in the shape of a barely attenuated demonstrative. Furthermore, among modern languages, those that dispense with an article are also those which, on the whole, remain of an archaic type. Russian, in this respect, is a most cogent example. These facts seem to show that *the article is caused by a certain state of language*: it apparently develops from the moment this state is reached.

'II. The article stems from a demonstrative. This is a well-known fact on which it would be superfluous to dwell. The article in Romance languages stems from the Latin *ille*, the Greek article from an Indo-European demonstrative theme **so*, **to*, which after following a different evolutionary process also provided the English and the German articles (cf. V. Henry: *Gramm. compar. de l'allemand et de l'anglais*, pp. 232 & 286).

'From the fact that the article was originally a demonstrative it is obvious that these two categories of word have at least some characteristics in common. The demonstrative, however, is used to narrow down the general idea of the noun to a strictly particular and temporary idea. It therefore follows that the article has a similar type of function and must be seen as *a sign used to pass from a certain generality of the nominal idea to a lesser generality*.

'III. The article begins with an opposition between two demonstratives of unequal strength. This is no doubt the fact which best explains how the article was able to come into existence and acquire a value of its own. In Latin we see the demonstrative *ille* (3rd person) slowly pushed, as it were, outside the demonstrative field proper, by the more direct demonstratives *iste* (2nd person) and *hic* (1st person). The particle *ecce*, which reinforced the demonstrative in Vulgar Latin could but intensify this action.

'In Greek, the demonstratives *ho*, *he*, *to* were reduced to articles when opposed to the reinforced forms *hóde, héde, tóde*, which were much more directly demonstrative.

'The same process came about in English and German. Their articles stem from the Indo-European demonstrative theme **to-*; their demonstratives come from the reinforcement of this theme by an indeclinable particle *-se* (cf. V. Henry: *Gramm. comp. all. angl.* pp. 232 & 286).

'When considered from the point of view of mental necessities, this creation of the article by distribution of demonstratives is only to be expected. Demonstration, taken as a whole, comprises two movements which are bound to contrast: things as shown directly in reality, or indirectly (anaphoric movement) in the memory. As soon as a language has allotted distinct signs to these two movements, it virtually possesses the article.*

'*Some inconsistency in this distribution is liable to occur at first, and even later in certain conditions, with the consequence that the direct demonstrative overlaps the anaphoric demonstrative, thus acquiring a value very close to that of the article.

> e.g.   *Voit sor ces haubres ces oisellons chanter,*
> *Et parmi Saine ces poissonsiaus noer,*
> *Et par ces prés ces flors renoveler.*

                     ('Raoul de Cambrai')
Chanson de geste, 13th century, published by Meyer & Longnon, Société des Anciens Textes, Paris 1882: 6217-20).'

    I now append some remarks arising from these three paragraphs of Guillaume's and, first, his footnote.

'ces' (in footnote)
In spite of its use as a demonstrative adjective in modern French, the *ces* here must be recognized as an article, which did not catch on either. (14) The meaning is therefore:
Voit sur les arbres les oisillons chanter,
'Sees in the trees the little birds singing,'
Et dans la Seine les petits poissons nager,
'And in the Seine the little fishes swimming,'
Et par les prés les fleurs renaître.
'And all over the meadows the flowers blooming again.'

Archaic type (Paragraph I)
Guillaume may be left to bear alone the responsibility for this hasty judgement. Other notions arising from that of 'state of language', would have to be defined in respect to it: 'Primitive language', 'Advanced language', all chargeable with ethnocentrism.

Demonstratives of unequal strength (Paragraph III)
The Japanese model appears to differ somewhat on this point from

the southern European model mentioned by Guillaume. Parallel with the Latin *hic*, *iste*, *ille*, Japanese does have *ko-*, *so-*, *a-* but it is to another opposition that the Japanese of the future would owe the advent of an article.

And yet the opposition $\emptyset + o-$ (*Ext), (that is, opposition between the absence and the presence of *o-* where the notion of exteriority is irrelevant), attests a state of language—in so far as the article is concerned—comparable to the Homeric period in Greek, or the mediaeval period in Latin, where the inconsistency between the demonstrative and the article was such that it was not yet possible to speak of an article or to foresee its advent.

It is also remarkable that at these periods the 'future' article, too, contrasted with the zero form ($\emptyset$).

If one is to speak of 'demonstratives of unequal strength' in Japanese and look elsewhere than in the triptych *ko-*, *so-*, *a-*, it will no doubt be necessary to go back to an early period. It is known that *o-* stems from *oo-mi-*, a compound particle formed with the archaic reading of the logogram for 'big/great', at present read *oo-*, and an honorific particle read as *mi-* and its successive distortions, given in the following table, where the compound particle is shown to be reduced to *o-*, without changing its meaning.

Among the words—mostly substantives—which finally took the prefix *o-*, some had a prefix stemming from *oo-* 'big/great' alone, entirely unconnected with the honorific *mi-*. Round about the tenth century there were hardly more than three such words left; at least this is how they were felt to be, since they were written with a phonetic *o-* and never with the honorific logogram or the full pronunciation of the time, *oFom-*.

It is interesting to note, then, that attempts to explain the presence of this particle meaning 'big/great' make of it a sort of 'embellisher', or 'emphasiser'. When not otherwise specified it is these functions that are often attributed to the ancient prefix *sa-*, sometimes written 'small', as in *sayo* 'the night'. Will it therefore seem odd that, in a previous study (15), I ventured to formulate the hypothesis that this particle *sa-* could have been an unfledged article—like *o-*—which apparently failed to catch on and become fixed? (16)

263

It should also be noted that the three words mentioned above —*omae*, *omashi* and *omono*—whose heritage did not appear to include the honorific prefix *mi-* but only *oo-* 'big/great', nevertheless all signify respectable entities consecrated to a divinity, an emperor or a nobleman.

As for inequality of strength, it becomes obvious whenever applied to a term with or without a particle meaning or having meant 'big/great', and which has finally been used to mark exteriority.

Addendum to Paragraph III
Without leaving Europe, Guillaume could have put forward the example of a non Indo-European language, Hungarian. In agreement with his theory, the Hungarian definite article *az*—or *a* before a consonant—comes from the classical demonstrative *az*, 'that' as opposed to *ez*, 'this'. (17)

Emphasis, politeness, distance and exteriority
The subject of this paper does not imply a complete revision of what has been said and may be said concerning these notions, and even more might be added without quenching our thirst for distinctions to discriminate between them. Nevertheless, in this instance the sociological nature of the Japanese language is such that the origins of a possible Japanese article may show some originality in comparison with other models.

Politeness, consideration and respect are often forms of distance. The use of a different form of language from that of one's interlocutor is indeed a means of marking sociological distance, even segregation, by selective enunciation.

The forms of so-called feminine language can be felt—or experienced—as marks of a class, which would be feminine when used by a woman, or intello-élitist when used by some elderly professor. One relevant example is that of *o-furo*, 'the bath' ('The honourable hot bath', as Thomas Raucat put it), others being *o-hashi*, 'the chopsticks', *o-tomodachi*, 'a (male) friend', 'a (female) friend', '(the) friends', 'some friends' etc.

This leads us to attempt to define the notion of 'distance' by the one formal criterion of the sociological difference in language forms consciously, deliberately used by a male or female speaker in regard to a male or female addressee. With this definition the notion is vague enough to cover differences in register—but not the registers themselves—and most exteriority markers. (18)

Situation and determination
In the individual's notional environment some terms are more familiar than others, in that certain concrete notions are called upon to be used more frequently, more commonly and may in time

264

acquire an abstract character. Examples may be taken from official language, those of State or of Palace. In writing, one may fall back on the expedient of initial capital letters to turn a common noun into an abstract noun, which is all the more like a proper noun as it is often surdetermined. (19) 'The State' is that of which one is a citizen, and 'the Palace' in London would be Buckingham Palace, in Paris *Le Palais de Justice* and in Kyoto 'the Imperial Palace': *Gosho*, word for 'the Place'—cf. French *en haut lieu*.

The examples of surdetermination which abound in the language of all that is sacred, official, or both, often show that the definite article in certain languages coincides with the Japanese prefixes *o-*, *go-* and *mi-*. (20)

By dint of abstraction the generic use of a word is reached—*le bois* (wood) the substance, *oyu*, *l'eau chaude* (hot water)—and by dint of surdetermination forms become fixed: *la Terre*, 'the earth'; 'the Queen'; *le Président de la République*; 'the Emperor'; 'the Mall'; *le Bois de Boulogne*; and 'the Palace', *le Palais* or *Gosho* mentioned above; or again, without capital letters, *l'éternel féminin*; the happy few; *la loi martiale*; the good life; *oshare*, *à la mode*; *osanji* 'the afternoon tea-break'; *okanjoo* 'the bill', etc.

Finally, certain words having irrevocably assimilated the article —or *o-*, *go-* or *mi-*—may become lexiconized. For example, in *le lierre* (ivy), the initial 'l' is a former article: Latin *hedera* → Old French *ierre*, hence *l'ierre*. The same applies to *une lanière* (strap): Frankish *nastila* → Old French *nière*, hence *la nière*.

In words of Arabic origin, the article *al* is obviously not felt to be an article: 'an alezan' (*al hizan* 'the horse'); 'an alcove' (*al qubba* 'the little room', via the Spanish *alcoba*).

What is the value of the article, at once important and minimised, if it can be treated in such a way, and be lost as a relational marker? The same question may be asked about the lexiconized forms of *o-*, *go-* and *mi-*, when, just as in *lierre*, *ierre* no longer has any meaning, in *oya* 'the parents', *o-* and *ya-* 'the house', thence 'the household', are made inseparable graphically in a single logogram which elsewhere means 'familiar'—and orally, since *ya-* alone no longer means 'parents'. The same applies to *go-* in *gohasan*, a term used both in abacus counting, in a phrase meaning 'Erase (and start again)', and more generally in a phrase meaning 'starting afresh'. The word *hasan*, however, no longer exists without *go-*.

Towards a contradictory conclusion
This study is presented with a dual purpose. First, to outline a component analysis of the deictic particles *o-*, *go-* and *mi-* when they appear outside the notions of exteriority (and non-exteriority), in a semantico-syntactic perspective, therefore, but retaining some considerations of a sociological order (politeness, distance, enun-

ciation). Second, to meet the need for hypotheses concerning these particles, *o-* (etc.), which led me to define either the article—others have tried and have perhaps succeeded—or rather the proto-article, an article in the making. Such a definition can only be based on existing definite articles and the demonstratives or other deictic forms of which they are the mutants, the fruit of transmutation through the ages.

The image acquired by mutants in science-fiction is in fact particularly suited to the proto-article. In the course of my association with philologists as anxious as myself to discover the evolutionary process of these entities, I learned that many moons ago, the Swiss Aebischer, a scholar of mediaeval literature (21), quoted by the Finn Väänänen (22), called these mutants, abandoned by their ascendants and descendants alike, 'articloïdes'.

After this avowal of respective paternities, we shall attempt to show how the term helps to avoid certain confusions and how these confusions came about.

The problem in Gothic

The presence of an 'article', *sa-*, in Gothic (nominative feminine *sô*, neutral *thata*), has given rise to diverse and contradictory comments from various grammatical historians. In the 1st century A.D. the Goths left southern Sweden, where they had been since long before the Christian era, and moved south-east, first to present-day Poland, then to what is now southern Russia, and in the 3rd and 4th centuries into the great peninsula known since the Turks as the Balkans, from south of the Danube to the various seas. Among the Goths it was the Wisigoths, enjoying more peaceful relations with Rome, who, under Bishop Wulfila (or Ulfilas) devised a written language called Gothic, the main evidence of which is Wulfila's Bible—4th century—a translation of the New Testament from Hellenistic Greek into Gothic. The arrival of the Huns in 375 prompted the Wisigoths to move on to south-west Gaul, where they established the Kingdom of Toulouse, that lost lamented civilisation destroyed by Clovis in 507 A.D. Thus driven out, the Wisigoths went and founded the Kingdom of Toledo, the principal haven of civilisation in Spain until the Arab conquest in 711.

This reminder of the highlights of Gothic history was intended to show that the bonds between Gothic and the other Germanic languages lie only in their common origin; the definite article in English, German and the other Germanic languages (Scandinavian, Dutch, etc.) and formerly in Old High German, Franconian, Norse, etc, stems from particles akin to the Gothic article *sa*, and not from *sa* itself.

When he treated the particle *sa* as an article (23), Aurélien Sauvageot—who as late as the 1960s had a linguistics class at the

Ecole Nationale des Langues Orientales—was setting himself up in opposition to Streitberg (24), who asserted that 'if by "article" we mean the demonstrative automatically and compulsorily coupled with the noun and which marks the known character of a person or object, then Gothic does *not* have an article'.

In giving this brief definition of the (definite) article, Streitberg is in fact asserting that Gothic does not have a 'definite' article 'the article of the defined'. On the other hand, Sauvageot does not distinguish between the definite article and the article 'well on the way to becoming the definite article'. Why then should we not be content to use the term 'article'—alone, without the 'definite'—as common denominator?

In fact, Sauvageot enumerates a number of occurrences of the particle *sa* in the Gothic translation of the New Testament, comparing its presence or absence with the much more systematic presence of the definite article in Greek: '*sa* does not appear in half the cases where the article appears in the Greek text'. (25) When it does occur it ranges from the demonstrative, introductory spatial deictic, to the forms of 'referant spatial deictic', the definite article and the closely related attenuated demonstratives, with a possible emphatic effect as in: 'What on earth have I done with that wallet?!' meaning 'my wallet', with no opposition to another object (another wallet) and with no notion of near + far.

Whether demonstrative or 'abstract determinative' (26) this spatial deictic in any case 'individualises the substantive, limits its range'. (27) If we are dealing with an 'article' without really being able to qualify it as a definite article, as yet, what about the proto-article? Or, if in this case we have a proto-article, what term should we use to designate the Japanese particle *o-* in which I have so far seen an unfledged article?

The problem in Japanese
Although it only affects a few nouns, the prefix *o-* does show a marked tendency to spread sociologically and lexically. Although it comes from the spatio-enunciative deictic *o-* (like *go-* and *mi-*) marking exteriority, it no longer limits the range of the noun. It is no doubt the elimination of its spatializing function that might prevent *o-* from becoming a proto-article, and *a fortiori* a definite article.

And yet predictions in the linguistic field are not often confirmed by history. If it was *not* this despatialized (or rather aspatializing), but the exteriorising, spatializing *o-*—with *go-* and *mi-*—which finally became the abstract spatial deictic we call article, it would then fit into the framework, the theory set out by Guillaume.

But what is to be done with this *o-* which thus finds itself abandoned yet again? *O-shimai daroo...* ('That'll be the end...(of it)...').

In coming to a conclusion, it might be safer to hazard a middle term which would take into account the methodological principles called upon in the course of this study.

Even the most superficial comparison between French, Italian or German on the one hand, and English on the other, proves that the definite article is not restricted to covering one single notion. (28) A detailed comparative study between languages possessing a definite article would make it possible for all the notions conveyed by the article to be listed.

A pool of cognito-grammatical categories—as universal as possible —would thus be built up. Grammatical in that they would appear morphologically in some languages, and cognitive in their function, each in its own way, and at different levels, thus enriching our knowledge of the diverse modes of apperception and apprehension of the factual and the virtual mentioned at the beginning of this article.

And yet, while this task is far from accomplished, concording phenomena, a connection between coincidences has compelled us to formulate hypotheses. This is why, on the presumption that there is no smoke without fire, I have presumed that certain characteristics, as in numerous cases of surdetermination, should make 'certain' non-dissociative (non-exteriorising) *o*-'s—which already make up a sub-set among the uses of *o*—coincide with 'certain' uses of the definite article, which also make up a sort of sub-set.

If such an analysis comes to anything it will help to provide an answer to the three questions asked here:

1. What notions and relations are included in the set common to the different forms of definite article to be found in all these 'articled languages'?

2. Which other notions would there be outside this common set, assumed by one language or another?

3. To which of these two groups—common set or notions outside it—can we assimilate the notions that subtend the subset of *o*- that has been the topic of this study? (29)

Notes

Chapter 1 MARIA CONSTANZA DE LUCA *Tradition in Modern Japan*
1. Ezra Vogel: *Japan's new middle class*, University of California Press 1963 & 1971, qtd. in Kanô Tsutomu: *The silent power*, Japan Center for International Exchange, Tokyo, 1976 ed., p. 8.
2. R.J. Lipton: 'Individual patterns in historical change: Imagery of Japanese youth', *Comparative studies in society and history* vol. 6, Mouton, The Hague, 1963-4, pp. 370-71.
3. Solomon B. Levine: 'Analyses of social structure in Japan', review article, *ibid.* vol. 18, 1976, p. 120.
4. Robert M. Spaulding: 'Japan's search for cultural identity', *ibid.* vol. 14, 1972, p. 514.
5. Introduction to the 'Esposizione di grafica Giapponese contemporania', Istituto Giapponese di Cultura, Rome, 27 March - 16 April 1976.

Chapter 3 MASSIMO RAVERI *The Rice Ecosystem and Folk Religion in Japan*
1. A. Vayda: 'Introduction', in A. Vayda (ed.): *Environment and cultural behavior*, American Museum Sourcebooks in Anthropology, The Natural History Press, New York, 1969.
2. See the debate between R. Rappaport: 'Ecology, adaptation and the ills of functionalism', *Michigan discussions in anthropology* 2, 1977, pp. 138-90 and J. Friedman, 'Marxism, structuralism and vulgar materialism', *Man* new series, 9, 1974, pp. 444-69; and also J. Friedman: 'Hegelian ecology: between Rousseau and the world spirit' in P. Bunham and R. Ellen (ed.): *A.S.A. Monographs* 18, *Social and ecological systems*, Academic Press, London, 1977, pp. 253-70.
3. *A.S.A. Monographs* 18, op. cit.
4. 'Kainan shoki', and 'Kaijô no michi', *Yanagita Kunio zenshû* vol. I, ch. 1-2, 1962; and 'Yukiguni no haru', *ibid.* vol. II, ch. 1, 1962.
5. 'Ijin sono ta', *Minzoku*, III/6, 1928, pp. 1069-109; and *Nihon minzoku bunka no keisei*, Gendai no Esprit 4 (21), 1966, pp. 191-207.
6. Nakao Sasuke: *Saibai shokubutsu to nôkô no kigen*, Iwanami shinsho 583, 1976.
7. *Shôyôjurin bunka*, Chûkô shinsho 201, 1978.
8. *Nippon bunka no furusato*, Kadokawa Shoten, 1966.
9. See the detailed map in Ueyama Shunpei et al.: *Tsuzuki shôyôjurin bunka —Higashi Ajia bunka no genryû*, Chûkô shinsho 438, 1978, p. 6.
10. H. Conklin: 'An ethnoecological approach to shifting agriculture', *Transactions of the New York Academy of Science*, 2nd Series 17, 1954, p. 133
11. P. Gourou: 'The quality of land use of tropical cultivators', in W.L.

271

Thomas (ed.): *Man's role in changing the face of the earth*, University of Chicago Press, 1956.
12. Sasaki K.: *Inasaku izen*, N.H.K. 147, 1976.
13. C. Geertz: 'Two types of ecosystem', in A. Vayda (ed.): *op. cit.*, p. 6.
14. Tôkyô Daigaku Nansei-shotô Kenkyû Iinkai (ed.): *Ryûkyû no shakai to shûkyô*, Heibonsha, 1965. Yamashita K.: *Ryûkyû, Amami no minkan shinkô*, Meigensho, 1974.
15. Nishitsunoi M.: *Nenjû gyôji jiten*, Tôkyôdô, 1976.
16. E. De Martino: *Il mondo magico*, Boringhierie, Torino, 1973, p. 91.
17. *Waga kuni minkan shinkô shi no kenkyû*, Sôgensha, 1953; and *Folk religion in Japan*, University of Chicago Press, 1968.
18. Conklin: *op. cit.*
19. Near many shrine buildings a miniature hut, the size of a doll's house, marks the site of the future construction while the earth on which it is built 'lies fallow'. See: Jingûshichô (ed.): *O-Ise-mairi*, Daichôkogeisha, 1975.
20. Watabe T.: *Ine no michi*, N.H.K. 304, 1977; see also: G. Crawford, W. Hurley and Yoshizaki M.: 'Implications of plant remains from the early Jômon, Hamanasuno site', *Asian Perspectives* XIX/1, Archaeology and Prehistory of Asia and the Pacific, 1976.
21. Geertz: *op. cit.*, p. 17.
22. R. Murphey: 'The ruin of ancient Ceylon', *Journal of Asian Studies*, 16, 1957, p. 183.
23. Niiname Kenkyûkai (ed.): *Niiname no kenkyû*, Vol. I and II, Yoshikawa Kôbunkan, 1953-55.
24. J. Kreiner: *Die Kulturorganisation des Japanischen Dorfes*, Veröffentlichung zum Archiv für Völkerkunde, Museum für Volkerkunde, Vienna, 1969.
25. Nakao: *op. cit.*, p. 133.

Chapter 4 MARY J. PICONE *Aspects of Death Symbolism in Japanese Folk Religion*

1. Suzuki M.: 'Bon ni kuru rei', *Minzokugaku kenkyû* no. 3, 1972, pp. 180-2.
2. R.J. Smith: *Ancestor worship in contemporary Japan*, University of California Press, Stanford, 1976.
3. Yanagita Kunio (tr. by F.H. Mayer): *About our ancestors*, Japan Society for the Promotion of Science, 1970, p. 55 and passim.
4. *ibid.* p. 116.
5. Smith: *op. cit.*, p. 51.
6. R. Hertz (tr. by R. and C. Needham): *Death and the right hand*, Cohen and West, London, 1960, p. 152.
7. I. Hori: 'Mysterious visitors from the harvest to the New Year', in R. Dorson (ed.): *Studies in Japanese folklore*, Indiana University Press, Bloomington, 1963, passim.
8. D.L. Philippi (tr.): *Kojiki*, University of Tokyo Press, 1969, p. 62ff.
9. Shiratori K.: *Jindaishi no shinkenkyû*, Iwanami Shoten, 1955, pp. 210, 218-20.
10. Philippi: *op. cit.*, ch. 23-4.
11. W.G. Aston: *Nihongi* vol. 1, Transactions of the Japan Society of London, 1896, p. 64; reprinted by Tuttle, Rutland, 1956.
12. F. Bock, *Engishiki* vol. 2, Sophia University Press, Tokyo, 1972, p. 103.
13. Aston: *op. cit.* p. 59; Bock: *op. cit.*, pp. 85-6; G. Kato: *A historical study*

of the religious development of Shintô, Japan Society for the Promotion of Science, 1973, p. 145.

14. I would like to thank here Prof. Tani Yutaka and Dr. Matsui Takeshi who suggested parts of this table.

15. R. Beardsley, J.W. Hall and R.E. Ward: *Village Japan*, University of Chicago Press, 1959, p. 61.

16. Classification by anomalous means of locomotion explains the common radical (142), also present in characters with a negative connotation e.g. *Shun* 'foolish', *Ban* 'barbarian'.

17. The drumbeats are said to weaken the *mushi*. In other rites such as the *Inoko*, children 'beat the boundaries' of the village to chase away insects.

18. W. Lebra: *Okinawan religion*, University of Hawaii Press, Honolulu, 1966, p. 230.

19. M.W. De Visser: *Fire and Ignes Fatui in China and Japan*, Sonderabdruck aus den Mitteilungen des Seminars für Orientalische Sprachen, Berlin, 1914.

20. Fujino Iwatomo: 'Chinese soul-inviting and firefly-catching songs', *Acta Asiatica* 19, Tôhô Gakkai, 1970.

21. D. Bodde: *Festivals in classical China*, Princeton University Press, 1975.

22. H.Y. Feng and J.K. Shryock: 'The black magic in China known as *Ku*', *Journal of the American Oriental Society*, Vol. 55, 1935, p. 1.

23. Bodde: *op. cit.*, p. 100.

24. *ibid.*, p. 2.

25. 'Ch'ih ya', in Feng and Shryock: *op. cit.*, p. 18.

26. Bodde: *op. cit.*, p. 100.

27. In Feng and Shryock: *op. cit.*, p. 5.

28. H. Maspero: *Le Taoisme et les religions Chinoises*, Gallimard, Paris, 1971, p. 366.

29. Fujino: *op. cit.*, pp. 44-5.

30. *Ibid.*, pp. 47-8.

31. The work is by Chang Heng (78-139), qtd. in Bodde: *op. cit.*, p. 101.

32. Fujino: *op. cit.*, p. 41.

33. Ch. 58 on 'Fire' in De Visser: *op. cit.*, p. 81.

34. *Ibid.*, p. 82.

35. J.F. Embree: *Suyemura*, Chicago University Press, 1972, pp. 182-3.

36. See Thompson's historico-demographic study, *Nakahara*, University of California Press, 1977.

37. Kato: *op. cit.*, p. 164.

38. Philippi: *op. cit.*, ch. 41.

39. I. Hori: *Folk religion in Japan*, University of Chicago Press, 1968, p. 125.

40. R. Needham: 'Polythetic classification: convergence and consequences', *Man*, new series no. 10, 1975.

Chapter 5 BRIAN D. MOERAN *Tradition, the Past and the Ever-Changing Present in a Pottery Village*

1. Yanagi Muneyoshi: *Hita no Sarayama*, Nihon Mingeikan, 1955, pp. 10-13.

2. R.P. Dore: *Shinohata: A portrait of a Japanese village*. Allen Lane, London, 1978, p. 65.

3. Onta potters—and only potters—can all recognize one another's work and tell fairly easily who has made what pot.

Chapter 7 JOY HENDRY *The Modification of Tradition in Modern Japanese Weddings and Some Implications for the Social Structure*

1. Robert J. Smith: *Kurusu: the price of progress in a Japanese village*, Dawson, 1978, p. 185.

2. The research was carried out in a district of the city of Yame in Fukuoka prefecture but it was rather rural with 50 per cent full-time farming households. Many of the practices mentioned are regional, but they are interpreted in a regional context.

3. In such a short paper it is not really feasible to discuss the meaning of the word 'traditional', which is taken here generally to have two meanings: first, merely 'ancient', and in this case, I ask how ancient; and secondly, Japanese, as opposed to western, in that a certain thing dates back to pre-Meiji times. The Japanese *dentô* 'tradition' implies a 'handing-down' through generations, which I regard as the strictest meaning even of the English word.

4. Yanagita Kunio (tr. by Charles S. Terry): *Japanese manners and customs in the Meiji era*, Centenary Culture Council Series, Ôbunsha, 1957, p. 174.

5. E.g., Harumi Befu: *Japan, an anthropological introduction*, Chandler Publishing Company, San Francisco, 1971, pp. 48-9; Kamishima Jirô: *Nihonjin no kekkonkan*, Chikuma Sôsho, 1969, pp. 82-3, 144; Richard E. Varner: 'The organized peasant: the Wakamonogumi in the Edo period', *Monumenta Nipponica* vol. 32 no. 4, 1977, pp. 478-81; Theodore Brameld: *Japan: Culture, education and change in two communities*, Holt, Rinehart and Winston, New York, 1968, pp. 58-9; Yanagita: *op. cit.*, pp. 240-41.

6. Fujisaki Hiroshi: *Kankonsôsai jiten*, Tsuru Shobô, 1957, pp. 27-30; Kawashima Takeyoshi: *Kekkon*, Iwanami Shoten, 1954, p. 42.

7. Details of these gifts may be found in my D.Phil thesis, *Changing attitudes to marriage in Japan*, Oxford University, Bodleian Library, 1979, pp. 193-203.

8. Ema Tsutomu: *Kekkon no rekishi*, Yûzankaku, 1971, p. 110.

9. Shimazaki Chifumi: *The Noh: Vol. 1, God Noh*, Hinoki Shoten, 1972, p. 105; cf. Lord Redesdale: *Tales of old Japan*, Macmillan, London, 1908, p. 368, fn.

10. Fujisaki: *op. cit.*, pp. 103-4; Minami Ryôhei: *Konrei-shiki to kekkon no kokoroe*, Taibunkan, 1953, p. 56; Jukichi Inouye: *Home life in Tokyo*, 1911, p. 183; Naomi Tamura: *The Japanese bride*, Harper, New York and London, 1904, p. 48.

11. Further detail is given in Hendry: *op. cit.*, p. 226.

12. Ema: *op. cit.*, p. 169.

13. Keiichi Yanagawa: 'The family, the town and festivals', *East Asian cultural studies*, 11, nos. 1-4, 1972, p. 12.

14. Cf. Inouye: *op. cit.*, pp. 185-7; Takamure Itsue: *Nihon kon'in shi*, Nihon rekishi shinsho, 1963, p. 260.

15. References to descriptions of the ancient versions of the *san-san kudo* and the *ironaoshi* are to be found in Hendry: *op. cit.*, pp. 213, 220-22; e.g. Ema: *op. cit.*, pp. 87-8, 90-91.

16. Yanagita: *op. cit.*, pp. 175, 179-80: Ômachi Tokuzô: 'Konrei', *Nihon minzokugaku taikei* vol. 4, pp. 262-3.

17. Ômachi Tokuzô: 'Kon'in', *ibid.*, vol. 3, pp. 178-89.

18. Cf. for elsewhere in the region, Chikushi Yutaka: *Nihon no minzoku, No. 40 Fukuoka*, 1974, p. 199; Ushijima Morimitsu: *Nihon no minzoku, No. 43 Kumamoto*, 1973, p. 226.

274

19. Yanagita: *op. cit.*, p. 174; Takamure: *op. cit.*, p. 115.
20. Takamure: *op. cit.*, p. 243; Yanagita Kunio and Ômachi Tokuzô: *Kon'in shûzoku goi*, Minkan Denshô no Kai, 1937, pp. 1-2.

Chapter 8 JOHN B. KIDD *Some Considerations of Individuals, Groups and How Japanese Traditions May Affect Decision Making*

1. T. Kuwahara: 'An understanding of the international applicability of the Japanese management system', *Economic and business review* 5, Kyôto Sangyô University, May 1978, p. 22ff.
2. M. Toda: 'Emotion and decision making', *Acta psychologica*, 1980.
3. K.T. Strongman: *The psychology of emotion*, Wiley, 1978.
4. K. Okonogi: 'The Ajase complex of the Japanese', Pt. I in *Japan echo* V/4, 1978; Pt. II in *ibid.* VI/1, 1979. (Original Japanese version: 'Nihonjin no Ajase konpurekkusu', *Chûô kôron*, June 1978.)
5. E. Vogel (ed.): *Modern Japanese organization and decision*, University of California Press, 1975.
6. Tsuji K.: *Shinpan: Nihon kanryôsei no kenkyû*, University of Tokyo Press, 1968.
7. R.E. Ward: *Political development in modern Japan*, Princeton University Press, 1968, pp. 457-75.
8. S. Arai: *An intersection of East and West*, Rikugei Publishing House, 1971.
9. R. Keeney and H. Raiffa: *Decisions with multiple objectives*, Wiley, 1976.
10. D.E. Bell, R. Keeney and H. Raiffa: *Conflicting objectives in decisions*, Wiley, 1977.
11. F.D. Tuggle and F. Hutton Barrow: 'A theory of human decision making', paper presented to the Sixth International Conference on *Utility, subjective probability and decision making*, Warsaw, 1977.
12. A. Newell and H.A. Simon: 'Elements of a theory of human problem-solving', *Psychology review* 65, 1958, pp. 151-66.
13. Surinder Kaur: *Cultural differences in decision making*, MSc in OR dissertation, Aston University Management Centre, 1978.

Chapter 9 KLAUS KRACHT *Traditional and Modern Thought in Japan: Some notes on the problem of continuity and its meaning*

1. Bodo Wiethoff: *Grundzüge der neueren chinesischen Geschichte* (Grundzüge, Bd. 31), Wissenschaftliche Buchgesellschaft Darmstadt, Darmstadt, 1977, p. 67ff.
2. Reinhard Wittram: *Zukunft in der Geschichte. Zu Grenzfragen der Geschichtswissenschaft und Theologie*, Kleine Vandenhoeck-Reihe 235-6, Vandenhoeck & Ruprecht, Göttingen, 1966, p. 39.
3. Nagata Hiroshi: *Nihon hôkensei ideorogii*, Nagata Hiroshi Nihon shisôshi kenkyû vol. 2, Hôsei Daigaku Shuppankyoku, first publ. 1938; Nagata Hiroshi: *Nihon yuibutsuron shi, ibid.* vol. 3, first publ. 1936; Saegusa Hiroto: *Nihon no yuibutsuronsha*, in Hayashi Tatsuo *et al.* (eds.): Saegusa Hiroto chosakushû vol. 3, Chûô Kôronsha, 1972 ed. (first publ. 1956), p. 253-435; Saegusa Hiroto: *Miura Baien no tetsugaku, Baien tetsugaku nyûmon*, in *ibid.* vol. 5, pp. 15-138, 139-244.
4. Fukumoto Kazuo: *Nihon runessansu shi ron*.
5. See, e.g., Takeuchi Yoshimi: 'Kindai no chôkoku' in *Kindaika to dentô*, Kindai Nihon shisôshi kôza vol. 7, Chikuma Shobô 1959, pp. 225-81; Fukuda

Tsuneari: 'Hankindai no shisô', in *Hankindai no shisô*, Gendai Nihon shisô taikei vol. 32, Chikuma Shobô 1965, pp. 7-49.
6.   In *Sekai*; tr. as 'Theory and psychology of ultra-nationalism' in Maruyama Masao (tr. and ed. by Ivan Morris): *Thought and behaviour in modern Japanese politics*, Oxford University Press 1969, pp. 1-24.
7.   Franz Borkenau: *Der Übergang vom feudalen zum bürgerlichen Weltbild. Studien zur Geschichte der Philosophie de Manufakturperiode*, Schriften des Instituts für Sozialforschung, 4 Band, Paris 1934: reprint: Wissenschaftliche Buchgesellschaft Darmstadt, Darmstadt, 1971.
8.   Tôkyô Daigaku Shuppankai, 1976, Engl. tr. by M. Hane: *Studies in the intellectual history of Tokugawa Japan*, Princeton University Press & University of Tokyo Press, 1974.
9.   Cf. Wada Haruki: 'Kindaikaron', *Nihon shigaku ronsô*, Rekishigaku Kenkyûkai and Nihonshi Kenkyûkai (ed.): Kôza Nihonshi vol. 5, Tôkyô Daigaku Shuppankai 1971, pp. 255-82; Hirata Tetsuo: 'Kindaikaron', Rekishigaku Kenkyûkai (ed.): *Rekishi riron, Kagaku undô*, Gendai rekishigaku no seika to kadai vol. 1, Aoki Shoten 1975, pp. 90-113; Kinbara Samon: *'Nihon kindaika' ron no rekishizô. Sono hihanteki kentô e no shiten*, Chûô Daigaku Shuppanbu 1968.
10. For an introduction, see Hans-Ulrich Wehler: *Modernisierungstheorie und Geschichte*, Kleine Vandenhoeck-Reihe 1407, Vandenhoeck & Ruprecht, Göttingen 1975.
11. For a good analysis, see Carol Gluck: 'The people in history. Recent trends in Japanese historiography', *Journal of Asian studies*, 38/1, 1978, p. 25-50.
12. Robert N. Bellah: 'Baigan and Sorai. Continuities and discontinuities in eighteenth-century Japanese thought', in T. Najita and I. Scheiner (ed.): *Japanese thought in the Tokugawa period, 1600-1868. Methods and metaphors*, University of Chicago Press 1978, p. 139.
13. 'Conceptual consciousness is above all based on the differentiation of subject and object. Its aim is clear and distinct ideas about objective reality with as little contamination from subjectivity as possible... Conceptual consciousness wishes to construct a vocabulary and syntax to deal with the exteriority of things, uncontaminated with concerns about inner states and feelings... Through developing our conceptual consciousness we enormously enhance our capacity to manipulate the world... Nonetheless the hypertrophy of conceptual consciousness is a characteristic of modern philosophy in both East and West.' *Ibid.*, p. 143.
14. G. Vico: *Die neue Wissenschaft über die gemeinschaftliche Natur der Völker*, Berlin, 1965, p. 138.
15. See Klaus Kracht: 'Zur Problematik der Endogenese von Modernität in der japanischen Geschichte. Einige Überlegungen unter Berücksichtigung der Struktur der Zeitbegriffe', in Fritz Opitz and Roland Schneider: *Referate des IV. Deutschen Japanologentags in Tübingen*, (MOAG 73), Hamburg, 1978, pp. 77-91.

Chapter 10   EBERHARD FRIESE *The von Siebold Collection of the Ruhr-University of Bochum: An Outline of its History and Problems*
1.   Hans Körner used both archives for his work *Die Würzburger Siebold. Eine Gelehrtenfamilie des 18. und 19. Jahrhunderts: Siebold. Beiträge zur Familiengeschichte* pt I, no. 3, Deutsches Familienarchiv vols. 34-5, Neustadt a. d. Aisch,

1967. On Philipp Franz von Siebold, see pp. 805-939.
2. *Forschungen und Fortschritte, Nachrichtenblatt der Deutschen Wissenschaft und Technik* no. 10, 1 April 1930, p. 141.
3. Kure Shûzô (1867-1932) published his first biography of von Siebold in 1896. In 1926 the second (enlarged) edition was published (with a somewhat irritating pagination: 1-9, 1-12, 1-32, 1-925, 1-8, 1-76, 1-6, 1-26, 1-12, 1-492, 1-31 pages) under the title: *Shiiboruto-sensei: Sono shôgai oyobi kôgyô. Philipp Franz von Siebold, zijn Leven en Werken. Ten herdenking van zijne verdiensten voor Nippon...* A shortened version was published by Heibonsha, Tokyo, 1967 and 1972. A German version of the 2nd. edition was begun by the author and finished by F.M. Trautz (see n. 4), but has not yet been printed.
4. Friedrich Maximilian Trautz (1877-1952), a Japanologist who 'discovered' these papers in the house of Lady Erika von Erhard-Siebold in Breslau (Silesia) on 13 May 1923.
5. This copy, bought for Reichsmark 6,000 in 1927, was used as the master-copy for the reprint of 1930 (see n. 8). It has been missing since 1945.
6. For a description of the only existing catalogues, see n. 16.
7. A photograph of the painting, showing Ph. Fr. v. Siebold, is published in vol. 5 of the reprint of *Nippon: Archiv zur Beschreibung...* (see the following note), between pages 1635 and 1637, fig. no. XXVIII. The original, a present from Graf Alexander von Brandenstein-Zeppelin (1881-1949), a grandson of Ph. Fr. v. Siebold, to the Japan Institute, has been missing since 1945.
8. See *Nippon: Archiv zur Beschreibung von Japan. Vollständiger Neudruck der Urausgabe. Zur Erinnerung an Philipp Franz von Siebolds Erstes Wirken in Japan 1823-1830. In zwei Text- und zwei Tafelbänden. Dazu ein neuer Ergänzungs- und Indexband von Dr. F(riedrich) M(aximilian) Trautz*, Hrg. vom Japaninstitut Berlin, E. Wasmuth, Berlin, Wien & Zürich, 1930-31, vol. 2. The letters shown are the following: Siebold to his mother (undated): 'Theuerster Frau Mutter! Eine Reihe von Hindernissen...' (no. 412?); Siebold to his Japanese wife Sonogi (undated, 1830?): 'Sonogi-sama mata Oine kaai no kodomo no Shiborudo. Watakushi wa shichigatsu nanuka Oranda no minato ni ikari wo oroshita...' (no. 454); Siebold to his family: 'Japan. Dezima den 22ten. Februar 1829, Meine Theuerstein! Meine Abreise von hier nach Batavia...' (no. ?)
9. Genji Kuroda & H. v. Schulz: 'Briefe aus Philipp Franz von Siebold's Nachlass im Japaninstitut', *Yamato*, 4. Jg., 1932, pp. 34-42, 79-90, 153-60. Unfortunately, the registration numbers of the letters are not mentioned. Also, the refound catalogue often does not list each letter separately, and so the identification of most of the lost letters is not possible.
10. See Herta von Schulz: 'Siebold-Gedächtnisausstellung in Leiden vom 4. bis 8. Mai 1932', *Yamato*, 4. Jg., 1932, pp. 116-25.
11. Nichi-Doku Bunka Kyôkai, Nihon Ishi Gakkai, & Tôkyô Kagaku Hakubutsukan (ed.): *Shiiboruto shiryô tenrankai shuppin mokuroku*, 122 pp.; it lists, with short descriptions, 710 exhibits (367 scientific objects, 343 objects of personal interest), lent by some 100 owners.
12. Irisawa Tatsukichi (ed.): *Shiiboruto sensei bunken shûei*, 1936. Among the literature which resulted from the exposition are also the following: *Shiiboruto kenkyû*, 1938, 712 pp., concerning mainly material of the Japan Institute, and *Shiiboruto bunken shûroku* (6 vols. of facsimiles), 1936-41.
13. Accession date: 23 March 1936. 257 items, and 10,300 sheets of rotograph-photostats. Prof. Irisawa Tatsukichi (1865-1938) was chairman of the Japanese-

German Cultural Association Committee for the Investigation of the Siebold Papers (Nichi-Doku Bunka Kyôkai Shiiboruto Bunken Kenkyû Iinkai) at the time, and under his chairmanship the copies were made. (See *Tôyô Bunko jûgonen shi*, 1939, p. 15-16.) It must be said, however, that about 10 per cent of the copied material did not belong to the Japan-Institute Berlin, but to the University Library of Leiden and to the family archive of Mittelbiberach.

14. According to registration papers, by shipment No. 820 (Supreme Headquarters of Allied Expeditionary Forces). Date in: March 1946.

15. Prof. Numata published an essay and a preliminary catalogue of the Bochum Collection in Sept. 1979: 'Nishi Doitsu ni genzon suru Shiiboruto kankei bunken ni tsuite', *Kinsei no yôgaku to kaigai bunshô*. I obtained useful information from a copy he kindly sent me. His essay is the first detailed description of the collection since World War II.

16. *Siebold-Nachlass im Japan-Institut zu Berlin. Erste Erwerbung (E.E.) angekauft am 30.7.1927 von Frau von Siebold-Erhardt* (sic), 93 pp.; last entry dated 1932. This copy belonging to the Tôyô Bunko was made from a catalogue which accompanied the collection to Tokyo in 1934.

17. Photograph in Hans Körner: *op. cit.*, facing p. 808.

18. For their biographies, see Kure Shûzô: *op. cit.*, pp. 659-886.

19. Original in German; see 'Über Ph. Fr. v. Siebolds Reise nach Japan. Mit Briefen aus den Jahren 1822 bis 1827', *Botanisches Archiv* vol. 43, Leipzig, 1942, pp. 492-3. See also J. MacLean: 'Von Siebold and the importation of Japanese plants into Europe via the Netherlands', *Japanese studies in the history of science* no. 17, 1978, pp. 43-79.

20. No. 221 was already discovered by J. Numata in 1974-5 ('Fragment eines Briefes von Ph. Fr. v. Siebold an Fraissinet über die Schildkröte und ihre Bedeutung im Volksaberglauben...').

21. Copy no. 91 ('Dieses Exemplar trägt die Nummer: 91'). Still missing are vols. 1, 3, 5.

22. Ex libris Gustav Jacoby; on the other hand, parts of the original *Nippon: Archiv...* are missing because of wrong binding.

23. Abteilung für Ostasienwissenschaften der Ruhr-Universität Bochum (ed.): *Bochumer Jahrbuch zur Ostasienforschung*.

24. A first short circular was published in the 'Bochum yearbook', vol. 1, 1978 (see n. 23). The Japan Institute marked its property usually by one or two of the following stamps (mostly in red colour):

1. Property stamp for manuscripts: oval, 12 mm by 8 mm, steel (?), 'Japan-Institut Berlin'. A similar stamp, larger in size, was used sometimes.

2. Registration stamp for manuscripts: rectangular, 20 mm by 15 mm, rubber, 'Sieboldiana'; by hand: 'E.E.' and the registration number.

3. Property stamp for books: rectangular, 50 mm by 30 mm (without border), rubber, inscription in 6 lines: 'Institut zur Förderung/der wechselseitigen Kenntnis/des geistigen Lebens/und der öffentlichen Einrichtungen/in Deutschland und Japan/(JAPANINSTITUT)'.

4. Accession stamp for books: rectangular, 35 mm by 31 mm, rubber, 'Japaninstitut Bücherei, Zugang No. ... Dat. ...' (Usually completed by hand. In the case of the purchase of a whole library, the note was stamped; e.g., 'Nachod-B.' i.e. 'from the library of Prof. Oskar Nachod').

25. See *The national union catalog of manuscript collections 1962*, Hamden, Conn., 1964, p. 64, mss. 62-879.

26. The albums were indicated in 1979 in Hong N. Kim: *Scholars' guide to Washington, D.C. for East Asian Studies (China, Japan, Korea and Mongolia)*, Woodrow Wilson International Center for Scholars, Smithsonian Institution Press, Washington, D.C., p. 156, (Collections F 6, no. 11).

27. The original letter is lost but exists as a translation made for Solf by M. Ramming. It is dated 1 May 1935: '...gelegentlich der Rückgabe der Leihgabe ist in Aussicht genommen, dem Japaninstitut Reproduktionen folgender Stücke zum Geschenk darzubringen:...5. Ein Album mit Photographien der Ausstellung...' (pp. 3-4) See *Personal papers of Wilhelm Solf*, fascicle no. 144, sheet nos. 186-9.

Chapter 11 MARGARETHA VAN OPSTALL *A Basis for Modern 'Rangaku' Studies—Dutch Archival Material*

1. Algemeen Rijksarchief (ARA), Prins Willem-Alexanderhof 20, The Hague.

2. Hôsei Rangaku Kenkyûkai and Nichi-Ran Kôshôshi Kenkyûkai.

3. *Japans dagregister gehouden in 't comptoir Nangasackij 1801-1857*, in stencilled form, 1953-67.

4. Hôsei Rangaku Kenkyûkai (ed.): *Oranda fûsetsu-gaki shûsei*, 2 vols., Japan-Netherlands Institute, Tokyo, 1976 and 1979; this is a collection of the 'world news' presented annually by the Dutch factory at Dejima to the Tokugawa shôgunate, 1641-1857.

5. *Dagregisters gehouden bij de opperhoofden van het Nederlandsche factorij in Japan* (vol. I, 6 Sep. 1633-31 Dec. 1635; vol. II, 1 Jan. 1636-7 Aug. 1637; vol. III, 9 Aug. 1637-3 Feb. 1639), Tokyo, 1974-7; and Nihon Kankei Kaigai Shiryô, Selection I, *Oranda shokanchô nikki*, vol. I (in two parts), 1976; vol. II (in two parts), 1975; vol. III (in two parts), 1977 and 1978.

6. On the organisation of the Company in that period, see Pieter van Dam (ed. by F.W. Stapel and W.Th. van Boetzelaer van Asperen): *Beschrijvinge van de Oost-Indische Compagnie*, 7 vols., RGP 63, 68, 74, 76, 83, 87, 97, 's-Gravenhage, 1927-54.

7. Company charter, VOC 1; J.A. van der Chijs: *Geschiedenis der stichting van de Vereenigde O.I. Compagnie*, Leiden, 1857, 118-35.

8. F.W. Stapel and J.E. Heeres: *Corpus Diplomaticum Neerlando-Indicum; verzameling van politieke contracten en verdere verdragen door de Nederlanders in het Oosten gesloten*, BTLV 57, 87, 91, 93, 96, 's-Gravenhage, 1907-55.

9. M. Kanai: 'Nederland en Japan 1602-1860', in M.A.P. Meilink-Roelofsz: *De VOC in Azië*, Unieboek, Bussum, 1976; and M.E. van Opstall: *De reis van de vloot van Pieter Willemsz Verhoeff naar Azië 1607-12*, WLV 73, 74, 's-Gravenhage, 1972.

10. M.P.H. Roessingh: *Het archief van de Nederlandse factorij in Japan 1609-1863*, 's-Gravenhage, 1964.

11. An inventory of the VOC archives is being made by M.A.P. Meilink-Roelofsz; although the inventory is not yet ready, the new numbering is in use.

12. W.Ph. Coolhaas (ed.): *De generale missiven van gouverneurs-generaal en raden aan Heren XVII der Vereenigde Oost-Indische Compagnie* I-VI, RGP 104, 112, 125, 134, 150, 159, 's-Gravenhage, 1960-76.

13. The papers sent over from Asia form one series of the VOC archives, chamber Amsterdam. Every volume, containing papers of more than one office, has a list of contents. These lists are available in typescript in the reading room.

14. See *op. cit.* in n. 10, where the contents have been described systematically,

For a detailed description of the items see: *Historical documents relating to Japan in foreign countries: An inventory of microfilm acquisitions in the library of the Historiographical Institute (Shiryô Hensanjo)* vols. I-III, University of Tokyo, 1963-5.

15. See n. 5.

16. Hirado diary, p. 84.

17. *Register of incoming letters 1633-1639, factory Japan* 277; and *Register of outgoing letters 1633-1639, factory Japan* 483.

18. The report of March and April 1638 (*Generale Missive* I, 701-4) is lost, as are the other papers sent over from Japan in 1638.

19. *Resolutions Governor-General and Council*, VOC 661.

20. *Outgoing letters Batavia*, VOC 862, f. 217.

21. *Generale Missive* I, 701-4.

22. *Outgoing Dutch letters*, VOC 316, f. 261.

23. *30 June 1639*, VOC 863; and *Register... Factory Japan* 277.

24. 1602-1827; there is an inventory in ms.

25. The VOC was taken over by the government in 1795. The following bodies then took care of colonial affairs: Oost-Indisch Committé, 1796-1800; Aziatische Raad, 1800-1806; Ministerie van Koophandel en Koloniën, 1806-7; Ministerie van Marine en Koloniën, 1808-1810; Hollandse Divisie in Paris, 1810-13; Ministerie van Koloniën, 1814-1900; annex Ministerie van Binnenlandse Zaken, 1900-1960.

26. Ministerie van Binnenlandse Zaken, afdeling onderwijs 1825-1918.

27. G.F. Meylan: *Geschiedkundig overzicht van de handel der Europezen op Japan*, no place of pub., 1827.

28. *Archief NHM, jaarverslag factorij Batavia* 1826-7; *Notulen factorij Batavia* 20 April 1827, bijlage 1; and *Rappoert L.N.F. Plate* 167 no. 6.

29. Factorij Japan nrs. 1593-1601; unpublished paper by L.G. Dalhuizen: *De Societeit van Particuliere Handel op Japan*, (wr. Leiden, 1963).

30. Koloniën 2855. Besluiten van gg in rade, 14 April no. 1.

31. W.M.F. van Mansvelt: *Geschiedenis van de Nederlandsche Handel Maatschappij* vol. 2, Haarlem, 1924, p. 384.

32. Ministerie van Buitenlandse Zaken. Correspondence about Japan 1847-62, related to the Dutch efforts to bring the Japanese government to open the country:

    Consulaat-general te Yokohama 1860-70, inv. ms., 30 nrs.
    Vice-consulaat te Nagasaki 1860-1915, inv. ms., 94 nrs.
    Legatie archief Tokyo 1870-90, inv. ms., 58 nrs.

33. Mansvelt: *op. cit.*, p. 385.

34. *Collectie Sweers en Van Vliet*, Inventarissen Rijksarchieven, 1928, pp. 1-37.

35. *Collectie Doeff*, inv. ms., 96 nrs.

36. *Collectie Cock Blomhoff*, inv. VROA 1907, 14 nrs.

37. *Collectie Bezemer*, inv. VROA 1907, 48 nrs.

38. *Collectie Bik*, inv. door J.J.A. Bervoets, Den Haag, 1977, 151 nrs.

39. *Collectie Fabius*, inv. VROA 1913, 1916, 47 nrs.

40. *Collectie Baud*, inv. VROA 1917, 1072 nrs.

41. M.P.H. Roessingh: *Gids van in Nederland aanwezige bronnen betreffende de geschiedenis van Azië en Oceanië tot 1795*; and F.G.P. Jaquet: *Gids van in Nederland aanwezige bronnen betreffende de geschiedenis van Azië en Oceanië, 1796-1949*.

Chapter 12 ALDO TOLLINI *The Landing in Japan of Giovanni Battista Sidotti in 1708*

1. The edicts on the banishment of Christianity started with that of Toyotomi Hideyoshi in 1587, but this was not strictly enforced. After the coming to power of the Tokugawa at the beginning of the 17th century, however, the anti-Christian policy was intensified.
2. The first page of Agustin de Madrid's book says, 'Brief account taken from various papers and documents...', but he does not specify which.
3. Sidotti used for his study the so-called *Kirishitan-ban*, which are books printed with movable type and published in Amakusa, Nagasaki, Kyoto etc., from the end of the 16th century to the beginning of the 17th. The printing was started when the Italian missionary A. Valignano brought to Japan the first movable-type printing machine in 1590. Most of the books printed dealt with the Christian faith or were dictionaries of the Japanese language.
4. See Miyazaki Michio: *Arai Hakuseki no yōgaku to kaigai chishiki*, 1973, p. 206; and Matsuda Kiichi: 'Shidotti no Nihon sennyû', *Daikôkai jidai no Nihon*, no. 3, Shôgakkan, 1978, pp. 130-31.
5. See, e.g., Arai Hakuseki: *Seiyô kibun*, Tôyô bunko, Heibonsha, 1976, p. 3.
6. The ship was a small two-masted reconnaissance vessel (in Spanish, *patache*).
7. *Traslado simple de la informacion que de orden del Superior Governo de estas islas se (?) sobre el viaje que hizo el señor Abad don Juan Bautista al Reyno del Japon*, dated 1709, in the documents of the Casanatense Library.
8. Among western sources, see *Relacion del viage...*, pp. 11-12; and, among the documents in the Casanatense Library, fasc. 1635, *Traslado simple...*, p. 14, and *Declaracion de Joseph Alexandro Juanes (?) de edad de 26 años*, p. 83. Among Japanese sources, see 'Nagasaki chûshin Rômajin no koto', given as an appendix to the ed. of *Seiyô kibun* cited above, pp. 245, 252 and 259. The last two pages report Sidotti's own declaration during his cross-examination.
9. Marcello Mastrilli (1603-37), an Italian Jesuit who arrived in Japan in 1637 and was immediately captured and martyred in Nagasaki.
10. See *Relacion del viage...*, p. 13; *Declaracion del General don Miguel de Eloriaga*, (among the documents in the Casanatense Library), p. 29; and 'Nagasaki chûshin...', *op. cit.*, pp. 262-75. There is a list of Sidotti's luggage, with descriptions of all the contents. The picture of Our Lady is now in the Tokyo National Museum.
11. See *Declaracion de Joseph Alexandro Juanes*, p. 85; and 'Nagasaki chûshin...', *op. cit.*, pp. 240 & 260.
12. On 5 April 1967, Prof. Matsuda Kiichi made an investigation on the spot. The results are published in his *Kirishitan kenkyû dainibu*, Kazama Shobô, 1975, pp. 372-3 and p. 375 n. 5. See also his 'Shidotti no Nihon sennyû', *op. cit.*, pp. 132-6. There are also photographs of the spot where Sidotti is said to have landed.
13. *Traslado simple...*, p. 15; *Declaracion de Joseph Alexandro Juanes...*, p. 84; *Declaracion del General don Miguel...*, p. 29; and *Relacion del viage...*, p. 13.
14. *Breve relazione...*, p. 28.
15. *Ibid.*, pp. 30-31.
16. The time of departure from Yakushima is reported in 'Nagasaki chûshin...', *op. cit.*, p. 242, and *Seiyô kibun*, p. 22.
17. 'Nagasaki chûshin...', *op. cit.*, p. 252.
18. *Seiyô kibun*, appendix, pp. 23-4.
19. 'Nagasaki jitsuroku taisei', *Seiyô kibun*, p. 361.

20. 'Dejima Rankan nisshi', *Seiyô kibun*, pp. 201-2.
21. *Ibid.*, p. 203. The Dutchman was a certain Adrian Dau (Douwe?).
22. *Seiyô kibun*, p. 25, and 'Nagasaki chûshin...', *op. cit.*, p. 257.

Chapter 13 ADRIANA BOSCARO *The Meaning of Christianity in the Works of Endô Shûsaku*
1. In Endô Shûsaku bungaku zenshû (hereafter Zenshû) vol. 10, Shinchôsha, 1975, p. 146.
2. 'Ihôjin no kunô' ('The anguish of an alien'), in *Endô Shûsaku no sekai*, a special issue of the journal *Shinpyô* no. 6, 1973, p. 56.
3. *Gariraya no haru* ('Spring in Galilee'), Zenshû vol. 7, pp. 311-30.
4. 'Ihôjin no kunô', *op. cit.*, p. 57.
5. *Watashi no bungaku*, Zenshû vol. 10, p. 366.
6. *Watakushi to Kirisuto-kyô*, Zenshû vol. 10, pp. 151-2.
8. Takeda Tomoju: *Endô Shûsaku no sekai*, Chûô Shuppansha, 1969, pp. 314-5.
9. 'Kamigami to kami to (H.N. sama)', the first part of 'Hori Tatsuo ron' in *Shûkyô to bungaku*, Endô Shûsaku bunko B 2, Kôdansha, 1977, p. 154.
10. *Chichi no shûkyô haha no shûkyô (Maria Kannon ni tsuite)*, Zenshû vol. 10, p. 180.
11. *Chiisa na machi nite*, Zenshû vol. 6, p. 281.
12. 'Ihôjin no kunô', *op. cit.*, pp. 59-61.
13. It is worth remembering that the Buddhist pilgrims who used to travel from temple to temple wore a straw hat (*sugegasa*) on which were written the characters for *dôkô futari* 'travelling with another'. In this light, the figure of the *dôhansha Iesu* gains particular significance.
14. See T. Ziolkowski: *Fictional transfiguration of Jesus*, Princeton University Press, 1972, in particular chap. 6, 'Comrade Jesus'. Although the maternal aspect of God is not completely new in the long history of Catholicism, I am sure that even Endô must have been amazed at the unexpected words of Pope John Paul I on the subject.
15. *Iesu no shôgai*, Shinchôsha, 1974, pp. 60-61.
16. *Ibid.*, p. 112.
17. *Shiina Rinzô ron*, Zenshû vol. 10, p. 258.
18. Takeda Tomoju: *op. cit.*, p. 164.
19. 'Nihon to Iesu no kao', *Kikan sôzô* I (October 1976), pp. 90-92.
20. Inoue Yôji, theologian and a great friend of Endô's, called by some 'the priest of hope', spent many years studying in Europe and is now the spokesman of the Japanese Church on this problem. He is the author of the very successful *Nihon to Iesu no kao*, which Endô refers to in an article with the same title (see n. 19 above).

Chapter 14 MARGRET NEUSS *On the Political Thinking of Yamaji Aizan (1864-1917)*
1. Margret Neuss: 'Zur Rolle der Heldenbiographien im Geschichtsbild Miyake Setsureis und Yamaji Aizans', *Oriens extremus*, Jg. 25, Heft 1, 1978.
2. Oka Toshirô: 'Yamaji Aizan kenkyû josetsu', *Hokudai hôgaku ronshû* vol. 25, no. 4, 1975, pp. 333-4.
3. Yamaji Aizan: 'Hyôron', *Dokuritsu hyôron*, 3-4, 1910.
4. Irwin Schreiner: *Christian converts and social protest in Meiji Japan*, Berkeley, 1970.

5. Yamaizumi Susumu: 'Yamaji Aizan ni okeru "Kokka shakai-shugi"', *Waseda seiji kôhô kenkyû*, no. 6., 1977.
6. *Ibid.*, p. 128.
7. Oka Toshirô: *op. cit.* and vol. 26, nos. 1, 3, 4, 1976.
8. Yamaji Aizan: *Gendai Nihon kyôkai-shi ron*, Gendai Nihon bungaku taikei vol. 6, 1969, p. 265.
9. Yamaji Aizan: 'Shakai-shugi hyôron', *Yamaji Aizan-shû*, Meiji bungaku zenshû vol. 35, 1965, p. 95.
10. *Ibid.*, p. 96.
11. *Ibid.*, p. 98.
12. Yamaji Aizan: 'Kokka shakai-shugi kôgai', *ibid.*, p. 108.

Chapter 15   JACOB KOVALIO *The Personnel Policy of Army Minister Araki Sadao: the Tosa-Saga Theory Re-examined*
1. See James Crowley: 'Japanese army factionalism in the early 1930s', *Journal of Asian studies*, XXI/3, 1962, pp. 309-26; Fujiwara Akira: *Gunjishi*, 1961, pp. 150-200; Hata Ikuhiko: 'Kôdôha to tôseiha', *Jiyû*, III/5, 1962, pp. 78-90; *Gun fashizumu undôshi*, 1969, pp. 70-125; *Taiheiyô kokusai kankeishi*, 1973, pp. 256-92; Imanishi Eizô: *Shôwa rikugun habatsu kôsôshi*, 1976, pp. 26-130, Matsushita Yoshio: *Gunbatsu kôbôshi*, 1975, pp. 470-92; *Nihon gunjishi zatsuwa*, 1969, pp. 180-210; Ôtani Keijirô: *Kôgun no hakai*, 1975, pp. 140-73, *Gunbatsu*, 1972, pp. 235-79; Ben-Ami Shillony: *Revolt in Japan*, 1973, pp. 87-135; Takahashi Masae: *Shôwa no gunbatsu*, 1974, pp. 170-215; Takamiya Taihei: *Gunkoku taiheiki*, 1951, pp. 136-70, and others.

This paper concerns only the high command of the Japanese Army (ground forces) during Araki Sadao's service as Army Minister. Although the issue of factionalism at the lower levels of the Army is not dealt with here, it should be emphasized that no meaningful connection existed between radical Young Officers' groups like the *seigunha*, for example, and the Araki high command. This statement is accurate notwithstanding the historically correct contention that Araki was extremely popular among many of the members of the Young Officers' groups.

Professor Crowley, in the article mentioned above, has denied the existence of any connection between Young Officers' groups and the two 'factions' in the high command. However, the fact that he has subscribed to the existence of the *kôdôha* and the *tôseiha* in the Araki headquarters makes it possible to include him among the historians taking a strictly factionalistic approach towards the Araki administration.

2. The above five characteristics have been mentioned with different degrees of emphasis, by post-World War II historians, political scientists and writers, some of whom are mentioned in n. 1.

3. The main aspects of Araki Sadao's administration are the subjects of my doctoral dissertation entitled *Araki Sadao, Japanese army factionalism and the Soviet Union*, submitted to the History Department of the University of Pittsburgh.

4. See Crowley: *Japan's quest for autonomy*, 1968, p. 254; Matsushita: *Gunbatsu*, p. 398; Ôtani: *Gunbatsu*, p. 189; Shillony: *Revolt in Japan*, p. 139 and others.

5. See table opposite: *The Araki and Hayashi administrations: High command structure and position shifts.*

6. Obata Binshirô's ouster from central headquarters in the summer shifts of 1933, an issue on which the questions of Araki's personnel policy and that of the attitude toward the Soviet Union converged, has been widely misrepresented after the Pacific War.

Historians, following the factionalistic interpretation of the Araki ministership, usually totally omit the pivotal importance of Obata's forced departure from the General Staff while stressing that of Nagata Tetsuzan, during what James Crowley has called 'the Araki vendetta' against non-Tosa-Saga officers. However, the evidence points in a different direction.

Obata and Nagata, two brilliant young generals, both of whom had been appreciated and promoted by Araki, were banished by him after serving barely one year as section chiefs in General Staff because they became the protagonists of a conflict that emerged in June 1933 during debates on the question of how to deal with the Soviet Union in the future. While Obata favoured the idea of an early preventive war against the Soviets before they became too strong, Nagata opted for concentrating on Manchuria and China prior to waging war against the communist power. The Obata-Nagata controversy that threatened to split the high command ended after Araki sent both officers away from central headquarters. Given Obata's Tosa (Kôchi) origin and, even more, the very close professional and personal relationship that had existed between him and Araki, his transfer from the General Staff can only be taken as an indication of the Army Minister's commitment to regular army discipline. At the same time Obata's ouster seriously weakens the concept of Tosa-Saga bias in Araki's personnel policy. The demotion of Obata, the main advocate of a preventive war against the Soviet Union, provides strong evidence of Araki's opposition to such a war, although most of the high-ranking officers present at the Soviet policy debates were in favour of Obata's view; see Bôeichô Bôeikenshûjo Senshishitsu: *Kantôgun*, 1969, p. 75. Araki's secret proposals at the Five Ministers' Conferences several months later show a similar defensive approach regarding the Soviet Union. Incidentally, Tôjô Hideki, a Nagata supporter, was also moved from his post in the summer of 1933, as is usually mentioned in support of the factionalistic interpretation, but significantly, not to a field command like Obata and Nagata. Tôjô was promoted to major-general and named head of the newly established Section of Military Research. The fact that Tôjô remained in Tokyo in a key position only supports my view that Araki simply sent away from central headquarters the main figures of the Soviet policy controversy and not the leaders of the non-existent competing Control faction.

7. See table opposite.

8. Yamauchi Ichirô: 'Manshû ni odoru danshi', *Nihon kokumin*, Oct. 1932, p. 117.

9. See n. 6.

10. See table opposite.

THE ARAKI AND HAYASHI ADMINISTRATIONS: HIGH COMMAND STRUCTURE AND POSITION SHIFTS

POSITION	NAME, DATE OF NOMINATION, AND PLACE OF ORIGIN		
	1932	1933	1934
Army Minister:	Araki Sadao, Dec. 1931, Tokyo		Hayashi Senjūrō, Jan., Ishikawa
Vice Army Minister:	Koiso Kuniaki, Feb., Yamagata		Hashimoto Tora-nosuke, Aug., Aichi
Chief, Bureau of Mil. Affairs:	Yanagawa Heisuke, Aug., Saga		Nagata Tetsuzan, Mar., Nagano
Chief, Dept. of Mil. Affairs:	Yamaoka Jūkō, Feb., Kōchi		
Chief, Bureau of Personnel:	Yamashita Tomoyuki, Apr., Kōchi		
Chief, Bureau of Armaments:	Matsuura Junrokurō, Feb., Fukuoka		Tada Reikichi, Aug., Tokyo
Chief, Bureau of Preparations:	Uemura Azumahiko, Aug. 1930, Tokyo		Yamaoka Jūkō, Mar., Kōchi
Chief, Dept. of Control:	Hayashi Katsura, Aug. 1930, Wakayama		
Chief, Dept. of Mobilization:	Uetsuki Yoshio, Aug., Tokyo; Inoue Saburō, Aug. 1930, Aichi	Yokoyama Osamu, Aug., Gunma	Tanabe Moritake, Aug., Ishikawa
Chief, Dept. of Mil. Research:	Okamura Yasuji, Apr., Tokyo; Tani Hisao, Aug., Okayama	Tōjō Hideki (continued as *Section* Chief from Dec.), Aug., Iwate	Kudō Yoshio, Mar., Aichi
Chief of General Staff:	Prince Kan'in Sumihito, Dec. 1931		
Vice Chief of Staff:	Mazaki Kanzaburō, Jan., Kōchi	Ueda Kenkichi, June, Osaka	Sugiyama Gen, Aug., Fukuoka
Chief, General Affairs Sect.:	Umezu Yoshijirō, Aug. 1931, Ōita	Hashimoto Toranosuke, Aug., Aichi	Yamada Otozō, Aug., Nagano
Chief, Dept. of Mobil. Org.:	Tōjō Hideki, Aug. 1931, Iwate	Hashimoto Gun, Aug., Okayama	Shimizu Noritsune, Aug., Fukui
Chief, First Sect.:	Furushō Motō, Feb., Kumamoto		Imai Kiyoshi, Aug., Aichi
Chief, Dept. of Operations:	Obata Binshirō, Feb., Kōchi		
Chief, Second Sect.:	Suzuki Yorimichi, Apr., Hiroshima	Isogai Rensuke, Aug., Hyōgo	Ushiroku Jun, Aug., Kyoto
Chief, Third Sect.:	Nagata Tetsuzan, Apr., Nagano	Yamada Otozō, Aug., Nagano	Suzuki Shigeyasu, Mar., Ishikawa
Chief, Fourth Sect.:	Obata Binshirō, Apr., Kōchi; Nishio Toshizō, Apr., Tottori		
Insp. General of Education:	Hayashi Senjūrō, May, Ishikawa		Mazaki Kanzaburō, Jan., Kōchi
Kwantung Army Commander:	Mutō Nobuyoshi, July, Saga	Hishikari Takashi, July, Kagoshima	Minami Jirō, Dec., Ōita
Taiwan Army Commander:	Abe Nobuyuki, Jan., Ishikawa	Matsui Iwane, Aug., Kōchi	Terauchi Hisaichi, Aug., Yamaguchi
Korea Army Commander:	Hayashi Senjūrō, Dec. 1931, Ishikawa		Ueda Kenkichi, Aug., Osaka

Chapter 16 CHARLES D. SHELDON *Some Traditional Factors Affecting Japanese Politics and Foreign Relations in Two Periods of Crisis, 1853-68 and 1931-41*

1. This process, and the increasing difficulties of maintaining the feudal system, are detailed in my chapter, 'The politics of the civil war of 1868', in W.G. Beasley (ed.): *Modern Japan—Aspects of history, literature and society*, London, 1975, pp. 27-51.
2. Marius B. Jansen: 'Tokugawa and modern Japan', in J.W. Hall and M.B. Jansen (eds.): *Studies in the institutional history of early modern Japan*, Princeton. 1968, pp. 317-30.
3. Quoted in Jansen: *The Japanese and Sun Yat-sen*, Cambridge, Mass., 1954, p. 40.
4. Quoted in Masao Maruyama: *Thought and behaviour in modern Japanese politics*, London, 1963, p. 94. In view of the attempt at the war crimes trial in Tokyo (IMTFE) on the part of the defence to establish a favourable interpretation of *kôdô* (the Imperial Way), it is especially interesting to have this use of the term by the principal spokesman of the Imperial Way faction (*kôdôha*).
5. Delmer Brown stresses the importance of fear and feelings of inferiority as factors in the more virulent, irrational type of nationalism which developed in Japan. *Nationalism in Japan—An introductory historical analysis*, California, 1955, esp. p. 5.
6. See C.D. Sheldon: *The rise of the merchant class in Tokugawa Japan*, Russell & Russell, New York, 1973. This is a reprinted edition with a new introduction and an additional chapter.
7. See Ruth Benedict: *The chrysanthemum and the sword*, London, 1947, chap. III, 'Taking one's proper station'.
8. For a recent discussion of various aspects of *ringi-sei*, see Ezra Vogel (ed.): *Modern Japanese organization and decision-making*, California, 1975; and, in this present book, the article by John B. Kidd, pp. 47-53.
9. In the *bakumatsu* period, as Beasley has pointed out (*The Meiji Restoration*, Stanford, 1972, p. 171), 'to be politically active was to act illegally.' This was 'especially true for non-samurai or for those whose samurai status was tenuous,' and their punishments were more severe than for the upper classes.
10. For some details on Saigô's troubles with his *daimyô*, see Beasley: *The Meiji Restoration*, p. 185 and fn., and Masakazu Iwata: *Ôkubo Toshimichi, the Bismarck of Japan*, California, 1964, pp. 57-8.
11. 'Members of the domain (*Chôshû*) conspired with Sanjô Sanetomi to fabricate anti-foreign imperial edicts.' (Sakata Yoshio and John W. Hall: 'The motivation of political leadership in the Meiji Restoration', *Journal of Asian studies* 16, Nov. 1956, p. 45). Illogicality and hypocrisy is revealed when, after Chôshû's expulsion from Kyoto by Satsuma and Aizu in 1863, they complained that these enemies 'were now issuing false edicts in the name of the Emperor.' (Albert M. Craig: *Chôshû in the Meiji Restoration*, Cambridge, Mass., 1961, p. 213.)
12. Craig: 'Functional and dysfunctional aspects of government bureaucracy', in Vogel, *op. cit.*, p. 24, n. 8.
13. *Ibid.*
14. *Thought and behaviour*, pp. 115-28. Such decision-making by subor-

dinates is well documented in such works as Yale Maxon: *Control of Japanese foreign policy—A study of civil-military rivalry, 1930-1945,* California, 1957, and Robert J.C. Butow: *Tojo and the coming of the war,* Princeton, 1961.

15. See, e.g., F. Joüon des Longrais: *L'est et l'ouest, Institutions du Japon et de l'Occident comparées,* Tokyo and Paris, 1958, pp. 143-66, especially pp. 147-8.

16. Blaker: *Japanese international negotiating style,* Columbia, 1977. See also his essay in Robert Scalapino (ed.): *The foreign policy of Japan,* California, 1977.

17. Butow: *Tojo and the coming of the war,* pp. 238-51. Konoe was quoted as saying at the end of the war that 'the government was considered a liar, because no matter what we promised regarding China, final decision on the removal of our troops from China depended on the military. That was one reason why the meeting was never held... I don't blame Roosevelt, in view of our past performance, for his suspicions.' (*Ibid.,* p. 245, fn. 30).

18. Yale Maxon's book (cited in n. 14) is basically a study of these efforts, with much interesting detail.

19. Sheldon: 'Japanese aggression and the Emperor, 1931-1941, from contemporary diaries', *Modern Asian studies* 10/1, 1976, pp. 10-11.

20. Janis, *Victims of groupthink—A psychological study of foreign-policy decisions and fiascoes,* Boston, 1972.

21. On the obstacles in Japan to frank and thorough discussion of fateful issues, Butow comments, 'Such records as are available with respect to the decision-making process reveal that the responses of members of the Japanese government did not always really answer the queries put to them, nor did the conclusions reached in a presentation inevitably correspond with the facts which were offered along the way. One would expect that when such disparities occurred, further questions would be raised to clarify the point in doubt. But apparently that did not necessarily happen—perhaps because putting anyone on the spot was considered a rather drastic thing to do and was commonly avoided.' (*Tojo,* pp. 253-4.) When Ōshima overstepped his authority in attempting to commit Japan to an alliance with Germany, the Emperor insisted that he (and Shiratori, in Italy) be dismissed, but Arita, the Foreign Minister feared for their honour: 'Their statements should be rescinded as having exceeded their authority. However, because of the fear that this would cause blemishes on their honour and lead to other complications...I believe it would be much wiser not to take action against the ambassadors for overstepping their authority.' (Harada Kumao: *Saionji-kô to seikyoku 1950-56,* vol. VII, pp. 335-6.) For details, see Sheldon: 'Japanese aggression,' pp. 13-14. In February 1945, the former Premiers (*Jûshin*) were seen by the Emperor individually, to permit them to speak freely on whether Japan should continue the war. All except Tōjô favoured a negotiated peace, but only Konoe said so. Wakatsuki confessed afterwards, 'I could not say to the Emperor, please surrender'. (Sheldon: 'Scapegoat or instigator of Japanese aggression? Inoue Kiyoshi's case against the Emperor', *Modern Asian studies* 12/1, 1978, p. 27. fn. 40.)

22. Butow: 'The Hull-Nomura conversations: A fundamental misconception', *American historical review,* LXV/4, July 1960, pp. 822-36. See also Hosoya Chihiro: 'Retrogression in Japan's foreign policy decision-making process', in J.W. Morley (ed.): *Dilemmas of growth in pre-war Japan,* Princeton, 1971,

pp. 81-105, esp. 100-105, and Hosoya: 'The role of Japan's Foreign Ministry and its Embassy in Washington, 1940-41', in Dorothy Borg and Shumpei Okamoto (eds.): *Pearl Harbor as history*, Columbia, 1973, pp. 149-61.
23. 'The English-language presentation of Japan's case during the China Emergency of the late 1930s', in I.H. Nish and C.J. Dunn (eds.): *European studies on Japan*, Paul Norbury, Tenterden, 1979, p. 148.

Chapter 17   IAN NISH *An Aspect of Tradition and Modernity: Matsuoka and Japanese Diplomacy at Geneva, 1932-33*
1.   G.R. Storry: 'The English-language presentation of Japan's case during the China Emergency of the late 1930s', in I.H. Nish and C.J. Dunn (eds.): *European studies on Japan*, Paul Norbury, Tenterden, 1979, pp. 145-7.
2.   Unno Yoshirô: *Kokusai Renmei to Nihon*, 1972, p. 233.
3.   Satô Naotake: *Kaisô hachijûnen*, 1963, pp. 278-280.
4.   Harada Kumao: *Saionji-kô to seikyoku*, 1952 vol 2., p. 365.
5.   *Ibid.*, pp. 365-6.
6.   *Documents on British foreign policy, 1919-39* (hereafter *DBFP*), 2nd. series, vol. XI, no. 85; see also no. 252.
7.   Satô, *op. cit.*, p. 280.
8.   *DBFP*, 2(XI), no. 85.
9.   *Ibid.*, no. 103.
10. *Ibid.*, no. 150.
11. Unno: *op. cit.*, pp. 246-7.
12. *DBFP*, 2(XI), no. 217.
13. *Ibid.*, no. 223.
14. *Ibid.*, no. 252, fn. 4.
15. *Ibid.*, no. 305.
16. Unno: *op. cit.*, p. 252; *DBFP*, 2 (XI), no. 374.
17. Ômura Tatsuzô: *Nihon gaikôka no sanbyakunin no jinmyaku* 1974, pp. 116-17; but Sawada Setsuzô in *Matsudaira Tsuneo tsuisôroku* 1961 does not mention this. Sadako Ogata: *Defiance in Manchuria*, Berkeley, 1964, p. 174.
18. Satô: *op. cit.*, pp. 284-5.
19. *DBFP*, 2 (XI), no. 374.
20. *The Times*, 25 February 1933.
21. *Ibid.*, 28 April 1933.
22. Kiyozawa Kiyoshi: 'Advice to representative Matsuoka', *Chûô kôron*, May 1933, p. 187ff. Hosoya Chihiro: 'Matsuoka Yôsuke' in Hayashi Shigeru (ed.): *Jinbutsu Nihon to rekishi* vol. 14, 1966, pp. 180-82.

Chapter 18   BEN-AMI SHILLONY *Traditional Limitations on Dictatorship: The Bureaucracy vs. Tôjô Hideki*
1.   Quoted in Dan Kurzman: *Kishi and Japan*, Ivan Obolensky, 1960, p. 185 n. See also Robert M. Spoulding: 'The bureaucracy as a political force, 1920-1945', in James W. Morley (ed.): *Dilemmas of growth in pre-war Japan*, Princeton University Press, 1971, pp. 76-7; Kentarô Hayashi: 'Japan and Germany in the interwar period', in *ibid.*, pp. 483-4.
2.   Hillis Lory: *Japan's military masters*, Viking Press, 1943, p. 132. See also Takeyama Michio: *Shôwa no seishinshi*, Shinchôsha, 1958, pp. 130-36; Cohen:

Japan's economy, pp. 70-71.

3. For a description of Tôjô, see Jôhô Yoshio (ed.): *Tôjô Hideki*, Fuyô Shoten, 1974; Matsuoka Hideo: 'Tôjô Hideki ron', in Mainichi Shinbunsha (ed.): *Taiheiyô sensô*, Ichiokunin no Shôwa-shi vol. 33, 1967, pp. 243-7; Matsumura Hideyasu: *Sensen kara shûsen made*, Nihon Shûhôsha, 1964; Takamiya Tahei: *Shôwa no shôsui*, Tosho Shuppansha, 1973; Butow: *Tôjô*. Although the standard English translation of *Rikugun Daijin* is 'War Minister', it literally means 'Army Minister'. Japan had no minister in charge of the whole military establishment.

4. *Nippon Times*, 5 February 1943; see also Masao Maruyama *Thought and behaviour in modern Japanese politics*, Oxford University Press, 1963, p. 17 for a similar quotation from the *Asahi shinbun*.

5. *Chian ijihô*, Gendai-shi shiryô vol. 45, Misuzu Shobô, 1973, pp. 646-9; Ohara Shakai Mondai Kenkyûjo (ed.): *Taiheiyô sensô-ka no rodô undô*, Nihon Rôdô Nenkan, 1965, p. 131. There are some differences between the figures of these two sources. See also Chalmers Johnson: *Conspiracy at Matsukawa*, University of California Press, 1972, p. 15.

6. Hayashi Shigeru: *Taiheiyô sensô*, Nihon no rekishi vol. 25, Chûô Kôronsha, 1967, pp. 166-9; Takashi Itô: 'The role of right wing organizations in Japan', in D. Borg and S. Okamoto: *Pearl Harbor as history*, Columbia University Press, 1973, p. 506.

7. Akimoto Ritsuo: *Sensô to minshû*, Gakuyô Shobô, 1974, pp. 149-50; Rekishigaku Kenkyûkai: *Taiheiyô sensô-shi* vol. 4, Suzuki Shoten, 1972, pp. 213-15.

8. Kosaka Keisuke: *Tokkô*, Raifu-sha, 1956. See also Richard H. Mitchell: *Thought control in pre-war Japan*, Cornell University Press, 1976, pp. 19-39, 97-127.

9. Ôtani Keijirô: *Shôwa kenpei shi*, Misuzu Shobô, 1966, pp. 403-73.

10. *Ibid.*, pp. 578-9; Rekishigaku Kenkyûkai: *op. cit.*, pp. 250-52.

11. The Home Ministers of Japan between October 1941 and August 1945 were: Tôjô Hideki (1941), Yuzawa Michio (1942), Andô Kisaburô (1943), Ôdachi Shigeo (1944), and Abe Genki (1945).

12. The commanders of the Military Police between July 1940 and July 1944 were: Hirabayashi Morito (1939), Toyoshima Bôtarô (1940), Tanaka Shizuichi (1940), Nakamura Aketo (1941), Katô Hakujirô (1942), Ôki Shigeru (1943).

13. There were 22 executions in 1941, 11 in 1942, 13 in 1943, 25 in 1944, and 8 in 1945. *Dai Nihon hyakka jiten* vol. 8, Shôgakkan, 1969, p. 448. For details of the Sorge affair, see *Zoruge jiken*, Gendai-shi shiryô vols. 1-3, Misuzu Shobô, 1962; F.W. Deakin and G.R. Storry: *The case of Richard Sorge*, Chatto & Windus, 1966; Chalmers Johnson: *An instance of treason*, Stanford University Press, 1964. Sorge and Ozaki were arrested on 18 October, 1941, sentenced to death on 29 September, 1943 and executed on 7 November, 1944. Two other members of the Sorge ring died in prison.

14. *Sensôchû no kurashi no kiroku*, Kurashi no Techô, 1973, pp. 79-80; Ienaga Saburô: *Taiheiyô sensô*, pp. 244-5; *Nippon Times*, 29 February, 1944.

15. Isa Hideo: *Ozaki Yukio*, Yoshikawa Kobunkan, 1960, pp. 236-40.

16. Imai Seiichi: 'Ôkô shita rotsuna kanshô', yokusan senkyo', *Shôwa shi no shunkan* vol. 2, Asahi Shinbunsha, 1964, pp. 26-35; *Shôgen watakushi no Shôwa shi* vol. 3, Gakugei Shorin, 1969, pp. 208-18.

289

Chapter 19 JOHN W.M. CHAPMAN *Oil, Deviance and the Traditional World Order—Japanese and German Strategies for Violent Change 1931-41*

1. General Friedrich von Bötticher (German Military Attaché in Washington), Telegram no. 3217 of 16.9.1941. (*Oberkommando der Wehrmacht: Wi-Rü-Amt: Wehrwirtschaftsabteilung Vo: Akte 32/44, 'Attaché-Telegramme USA', 1940-41.*) The U.S. National Archives appear to have incorrectly assigned provenance of this file to the German Army High Command's Attaché Section with the file number H27/47A.

2. Cordell Hull: *Memoirs* vol. II, New York, 1948, p. 81.

3. W.P. Bundy: 'Elements of Power', *Foreign affairs* 56/1, October 1977, p. 23.

4. For an interesting explanation of structural causes and economic and military effects on international politics, see K.N. Waltz: *Theory of international politics*, Reading, Mass., 1979, chaps. 7 & 8.

5. See, for example, C.P. Kindleberger: *Power and money*, New York, 1970.

6. The military applications of the internal combustion engine in World War I meant that most of the major powers had converted fleets to oil, and the development of the aircraft and the motorization of armies increased demand for oil fuels. By 1938, about twenty-one per cent of merchant ships had converted to oil.

   In 1914, the United States exported fifty-six per cent of all oil and thirty per cent in 1932, without taking into account the exports of U.S. oil majors abroad. The United States alone provided sixty per cent of all production in 1932.

7. Figures for Japanese imports in I.H. Anderson, Jr.: *The Standard Vacuum Oil Company and United States foreign policy, 1933-1941*, Princeton, 1975, Table B-6. Figures for German imports in: *Oberkommando der Wehrmacht: Wi-Rü-Amt: Akte 66b, 'Wirtschafts- und Rohstofflage im Inland', 1940.*

8. 'Wall Street and the Far East', *Chûô kôron*, September 1975.

9. For further details of the role of Katô, see S. Asada: 'The Japanese Navy and the United States', in D. Borg and S. Okamoto (eds.): *Pearl Harbor as history*, New York, 1973, pp. 225-60: S.E. Pelz: *Race to Pearl Harbor*, Harvard, 1974; J.W. Chapman: 'The transfer of German underwater weapons technology to Japan, 1919-1976', in I.H. Nish and C.J. Dunn (eds.): *European studies on Japan*, Tenterden, 1979, chap. 26; I. Gow: 'Traditional values and technological innovation in a changing military', EAJS Conference Papers, 1979.

10. Voretzsch (Tokyo) Report J. no. 490 of 3.3.1931 to the German Foreign Ministry. (*Auswärtiges Amt: Abteilung IV Ostasien: Akte Po. 2 Japan: 'Akten betreffend Politische Beziehungen Deutschlands zu Japan', Bd. 4, 1929-1932.*)

11. German holdings of gold and hard currencies fell from 2,806 milliard marks in 1930 to 529 milliard in 1933. By the end of 1937, these fell to approximately 70 milliard: *Reichskriegsministerium/W Wi Nr. 300/38 g. Kdos of 1.2.1938.* (*Oberkommando der Marine: Marinekommandoamt/M IV: 'Attaché- und Auslandsangelegenheiten', Heft 3, 1937-38*, pp. 126-34.)

12. See H.A. Jacobsen: *Nationalsozialistische Aussenpolitik, 1933-1938*, Frankfurt-am-Main, 1968, p. 50 n.

13. Statistics about German synthetic production may be found in W. Birkenfeld: *Die synthetische Treibstoff, 1933-1945*, Göttingen, 1964, App. 4 & 6. For German Air Force statistics of Japanese synthetic production, much of it based on German processes and U.S. patents, see *RdL u ObdL/GL-A Rü Nr. 3594/41g*

of 5.1.1942. (*Oberkommando der Luftwaffe: Generalluftzeugmeister/A Rüstung IV: 'Japan. Luftrüstungsindustrie und Fluggerät. Stand März 1942'.*) For planned and actual Japanese figures from 1937 to 1943, see J.B. Cohen: *Japan's economy in war and reconstruction*, Minneapolis, 1949, p. 137.

14. OKM/Skl/Qu A III 1777/41 *Chefs.* of 27.10.1941 to Admiral Fricke. (*OKM: Seekriegsleitung: 1. Skl.: Kriegstagebuch, Teil C IX: 'Versorgungsfragen'. 1939-1942.*) Captain Kojima Hideo, the expert on the German Navy on the Naval Staff, was asked by Rear-Admiral Paul Wenneker, the German Naval Attaché in Japan, on 7 August 1940 what the effect of the U.S. embargo measure would be. He replied 'the Navy has very large reserves so that it would not be seriously affected. It also has at its disposal numerous refineries which can process oil obtained from elsewhere (Sakhalin). On the other hand, the Army has placed huge orders for aviation fuel in America (people speak of 15 million gallons now stockpiled in Pacific ports). The Army therefore should be badly hit by the embargo, especially as it has no refineries of its own. The Navy can be affected by this if it should prove to be necessary to hand over some of its stocks to the Army'. (*OKM: Marine-Attaché Gruppe: 'Kriegstagebuch des Marine-Attachés und Militärischen Leiters der Gross-Etappe Japan/China'. Bd. 2.*)

15. The lack of substantial sources of oil east of the Urals was initially advanced as an argument for a pre-emptive strike by the Japanese Army on the Soviet Far East in view of the need for the Russians to transport it along vulnerable lines of communications from the Caucasus. See von Dirksen (Moscow) Report No. A/971 of 13.5.1933 to the German Foreign Ministry. (*AA: Abteilung IV Ostasien: Akte Po. 3: 'Akten betreffend Politische Beziehungen zwischen Japan und Russland', Bd. 10, 1933.*)

Relations between the Army and Navy became very strained because of differences over strategy and domestic policies between December 1935 and February 1936, when Britain and China increasingly began to be singled out as targets of future operations. Pelz: *op. cit.*, p. 172 notes: 'Although the navy leaders did not spell out their reasons for considering the South Seas important to national defence, it is probable that oil was primary motive. Japan's fleet had been running on fuel produced in the United States ever since the Japanese navy converted its ships to oil in the previous decade. In order to guarantee that the western Pacific would be secure, Japan would not only have to build a great fleet, but would also have to obtain the oil with which to run it'. The Navy's middle-ranking officers repeatedly expressed their antipathy to Commander Wenneker about Army proposals for a pre-emptive strike on the Soviet Union. The quotation is from Wenneker B. *Nr. 237 geb.* of 26.6.1936 to the German Naval Command. (*Reichswehrministerium: Archiv der Marine: M Att: Attaché-Berichte Tokio 1936.*)

16. Anderson, *op. cit.*, pp. 56-91 which concludes: 'The idea of coping with Japan by curtailing her oil supply was not seriously considered again until 1940'. In 1934, the German Secret Military Intelligence Service was informed of Japanese Navy intentions to build up an 'iron reserve' by purchasing some 400,000 tons of oil from Shell and Esso: *Abw. B. Nr. 3790/34/Vb* of 9.9.1934 to Naval Intelligence Section. (*Reichswehrministerium: Archiv der Marine: Akte Vb-29: 'Ölversorgung', Heft 1, 1934-35.*) Commander Vermehren (*Abwehr IVb*) in a minute of 14.6.1937, based on a conversation with E. Hansen of the Waried Tanker Agency of Hamburg, quoted Hansen as saying that 'he does not deny the

fact that a strict interpretation of the American neutrality laws can have a disadvantageous effect on the supply of oil fuel, but does not believe automatically in any general lack of benevolence in U.S. neutrality in the event of war, or at least not in Standard Oil circles. He points in this connection to Standard Oil's continuing supply of the Italians during the Abyssinian War, when the Italians would not have been able to carry out military operations without it'. (*Ibid., Heft 2, 1935-38.*)

17. Wenneker *B. Nr. 279/41 g. Kdos* of 17.4.1941 to German Navy. (*OKM: M Att: 'Japan-Mobilmachung', Bd. 4, 1941*, pp. 11-13.)

18. See German Navy memorandum *1. Skl. I Op 569/40 g. Kdos. Chefs*, undated. (*OKM: Ob. d. M.: 'Persönlich', 1940.*) German cooperation in the field of radio monitoring and deciphering began in the spring of 1934 and by 1939 a dozen French and a dozen British codes could be read. At the height of the Abyssinian crisis, Captain Brenta, the head of the Italian Navy's Signals and Espionage Service, met Admiral Canaris in September 1935 and promised that he would 'do what he could to pass on information about the movement of ships in the Far East if this was of value to the radio monitoring service of the German Navy'. Canaris memorandum *Abwehr-Abteilung (Chef) Nr. 22/35 g. Kdos* of 19.9.1935: see fn. 11, but *Heft 1. 1935-36.* See also G.W. Baer: *Test case*, Stanford, 1976.

19. Lieutenant Derp was sent by the *Abwehr* to Mexico in 1935, following the Navy's war games in the spring of 1934, to investigate the possibility of chartering tankers to supply fuel to German cruisers operating against merchant shipping in the Central Atlantic. He discovered that all charters were arranged via the Baltic Exchange in London on long-term contracts, but when Mexico nationalized the concessions of the oil majors in February 1938, the situation changed for the better and Eversbusch was summoned to Berlin to make appropriate plans in the event of war. CEPSA was taken over by German interests on 31.10.1939 and handled oil from Mexico consigned to Italy during the period of Italian neutrality. The total Italian import figure from Mexico for the period from October 1939 to January 1940 was 307,000 tons.

20. Stoephasius memorandum *OKW/Ausland IVb Nr. 763/38 g. Kdos* of 14.12.1938 to Captain Menzel (*Abwehr I Marine*) and Admiral Canaris. (*OKW/Ausland IV: Akte III-11: 'Niederschriften über Etappendienst', Bd. 2, 1938-39.*) *OKM/3. Skl. FH 4/40 D g.* of 5.3.1940 listed available ships in the various national tanker fleets. It noted that Japanese tanker tonnage was only 429,790, that when British tankers were withdrawn from Far Eastern routes at the opening of war in Europe, their place was taken by Japanese vessels, but that four-fifths of Japanese tankers were confined to coastal trade in the Sea of Japan and between Japan and China. (As fn. 16, but *Heft 4, 1938-40.*)

21. Hertslet was in Washington in early April 1940 before moving on to Mexico, where he arranged the despatch of the motor ship Havelland to Japan with a cargo of oil and raw materials in conjunction with Eversbusch. He tried, but failed to obtain Mexican citizenship and to set up a company to deal with the Mexican government direct. However, President Cardenas, who had been responsible for the annulment of the oil concessions, left office at the same time as Roosevelt was re-elected in the United States. Hertslet appears to have tried unsuccessfully to return to the U.S.A. in December 1940, and was forced to return home via Japan empty-handed. (*AA: Pol I M: Akte Po. 15: 'Agentenund Spionagewesen—Nachrichten', Bd. 18, 1940* and *ibid.*)

22. According to information received from a Japanese steamer captain, U.S. destroyers and patrolling aircraft were carrying out a surveillance off the port of Manzanillo. (*OKW/Ausland IV L B. Nr. 766/40 g. Kdos* of 20.3.1940 (as fn. 20). The German supply ship Columbus was shadowed in the Caribbean by the U.S.S. Tuscaloosa and its position regularly pinpointed by radio, with the result that it was subsequently intercepted and forced to sink itself when a Canadian warship arrived on the scene.

23. Several German agents with sabotage instructions were passed through Japan on their way to the United States. A Baltic German, Baron von Maydell, told the German Embassy in Washington of his instructions at the end of February 1940. The State-Secretary in the Foreign Ministry wired back a reassuring telegram on 12.3.1940 after consultation with Colonel Lahousen, but the matter was reopened by Hertslet in a telegram to Dr. Fetzer of late March. Further reassurance of Foreign Minister von Ribbentrop was conveyed in a letter from Canaris, *Chef Abw I Nr. 24/40 Chefs.* of 25.4.1940 'for the exclusive information of the Foreign Minister', but copied to General Halder, the Chief of the General Staff.

24. *Abwehr I M/West Nr. 1586/40 g. Kdos* of 20.12.1940 to Naval Attaché in Japan; Wenneker *B. Nr. 68/41 g. Kdos* of 31.1.1941 to *OKW/Ausland IV*. (As fn. 17, *Bd. 3.) A. Ausl. Abw. B. Nr. 1437/40 I M West geh. Kdos* of 9.12.1940 to *OKW/Ausland VId.* (*OKW: Ausland VId: 'Akte Sonderstab HWK', 1940-42.*)

25. Anderson, *op. cit.*

26. Admiral Endô claimed that a partial mobilization of the Japanese fleet had been ordered as a result of the worsening relationship with the United States. *OKM/M Att 1071/39 g. Kdos* of 29.11.1939 to Captain Lietzmann, German Naval Attaché in Japan, on discussion between Endô and Grand-Admiral Raeder. Leitzmann received both oral and written warnings of British complaints about the transit of German citizens on Japanese liners on 12.1 and 18.1.1940 prior to the boarding of the Asama Maru.

27. As fn. 14, entries for 26.3 and 28.3.1940.

28. *Ibid.*, entry for 3.4.1940.

29. *Ibid.*, entry for 17.4.1940.

30. Tokyo Embassy Telegram no. 372 of 24.4.1940 to German Foreign Ministry. (*Ibid.*)

31. *OKM/M Wa Wi 21220/40g* of 23.9.1940 put captured stocks at just over 790,000 tons and Navy stockpiles at 1.9 million tons on 1.9.1940, compared to 1.5 million tons on 1.4.1940 and 2 millions on 1.9.1939. (*OKM; 1. Skl.: KTB, Teil C XII: 'Wirtschaftskriegführung', 1939-43.*)

32. *OKW/Wi-Rü-Amt/Wi VIc Nr. 2490/41g* of March 1941.

33. At a top-level conference of military-economic specialists on 28.1.1941, General Halder noted that it was estimated that there would be only one month's operational supply of diesel oil and three months of gasoline. On 14.2.1941, the rubber supply situation was seen as acute and the oil problem worse on paper. General Wagner, the Quartermaster-General of the Army, spoke of Soviet oil exports being down to a dribble, but that aviation gasoline was assured for a year. If no further oil came from the USSR, then there would be sufficient fuel of all kinds for two to two and a half months. *Halder diary*, entries for 28.1, 14.2 and 13.3.1941.

34. Grand-Admiral Raeder had supported the idea of an attack on the Suez Canal, followed by an offensive through Palestine and Syria. Hitler reiterated the

idea of encouraging the Russians to move into Iran and India on 26.9.1940, but by November and December had firmly decided that Germany must strike first at the Soviet Union and then at Britain. At an earlier conference on 21.7.1940 with Raeder, Hitler had pointed to the fact that Russia had no desire to get involved in war with Germany. It was a duty to consider the questions of America and Russia carefully, as these two countries were where Britain's hopes for continuing the war lay. It was in Germany's interest to carry out strategic operations swiftly, but Hitler at that stage saw no urgent necessity for these at that juncture. Raw materials and foodstuffs were in adequate supply. 'The fuel situation,' he added, 'is the most difficult, but not critical so long as Rumania and Russia provide supplies and the hydrogenation plants could be adequately protected from air attacks.' (*OKM: 1. Skl.: KTB, Teil Ca: 'Grundlegende Fragen der Kriegführung , Bd. 1, 1939-1943*.) See also B.A. Leach: *German strategy against Russia, 1939-1941*, Oxford, 1973, pp. 133-50.

35. Only 50,000 tons of diesel fuel, out of the total 790,000 tons of fuel seized in Western Europe in 1940, were added to German stocks, apart from imports from Rumania and the Soviet Union. German Navy stocks amounted to 700,000 cubic metres of diesel oil in January 1940, but this figure had fallen to only 110,000 cbm. by October 1941. The German Navy used a special fuel mixture for its warships, which meant that anyone who tried to order this mixture would be immediately suspected of procuring it for the German Navy. During 1941, consumption levels of diesel greatly exceeded receipts and far-ranging operational plans by the Naval War Staff had to be axed in October 1941 to much more modest levels. The Italian Navy mainly used lighter quality furnace oil and the German Navy agreed in the spring of 1941 to provide amounts from its own stocks of furnace oil to keep the Italian fleet at sea. The Italians estimated their monthly requirements at 140,000 tons and the Germans at 118,000 tons a month, which involved the consumption of 1.9 million tons annually. As with diesel oil, however, consumption during 1941 far exceeded receipts of furnace oil from synthetic, and Rumanian production and German Navy stocks were down to 338,000 tons by October 1941, with the prospect of a maximum monthly receipt of 87,000 tons monthly for both fleets over the succeeding three months. By maintaining operations at previous levels, both fleets could expect to run out of oil by the end of January 1942. The net effect was to lead to a concentration of German and Italian operations on submarine and air warfare during 1942 as the most cost-effective of the choices available within the constraints imposed by the limited oil production.

36. *OKW/Ausland IV Nr. 2208/41 g. Kdos* of 14.8.1941; *Nr. 2890/41 Chefs* of 22.11.1941 and *Nr. 3561/41 g. Kdos* of 29.12.1941; *OKM/1. Skl. Iga 114/42 Chefs* of 13.1.1942.

37. As fn. 14.

38. *OKW/WFSt/L IV/Qu Nr. 002928/41 g. Kdos* of 4.12.1941 (*Ibid.*).

39. As fn. 14. Wenneker-Kojima discussion, 3.7.1940.

40. *Ibid.*

41. *Ibid.*, Wenneker-Kondô discussion, 3.7.1940.

42. *Ibid.*, Wenneker *Tel. Nr. 474/41 g. Kdos* of 9.6.1941 to German Navy stated that the attack on Singapore had been given up. Captain Takada of the Naval Affairs Bureau confirmed that Japan sought complete freedom of manoeuvre in any decision to enter the European war, a position subsequently repeated in the course of Japanese diplomatic negotiations with the United States during the

succeeding months up to mid-November 1941. This lulled Secretary of State Hull into a false sense of security about the alleged meaninglessness of the Tripartite Pact, a position also adopted by P.W. Schroeder: *The Axis alliance and Japanese-American relations, 1941*, Ithaca, 1958. For the Japanese Army's analysis of the oil problem, see the memorandum of 21.1.1941 by the Military Affairs Section of the War Ministry, 'Gaikô tenken ni tomonau ekitai nenryô kyôkû taisaku ni kansuru ken', *Bôeicho: Riku Man Mitsu Dai Nikki*, vol. III, no. 25, 1941. There is a memorandum about the Japanese Navy's oil problem in a letter of 25.7.1941 from Captain Yokoi, Naval Attaché in Berlin, to the German Navy. (*OKM: 1. Skl. IIIa: 'Japan-Kommission'*, *1941*, pp. 238-9.)

43. As fn. 14, Wenneker-Maeda discussion, 26.11.1941.

44. The point has been reiterated in a recent discussion between Albert Speer and Prof. Allan Bullock in January 1980, but Hitler himself made the point with great clarity to General Ôshima Hiroshi on 14.7.1941: 'Seen from our point of view, Russia menaces us in the East, America in the West; seen from the point of view of Japan, Russia menaces in the West, America in the East. Therefore, he is of the opinion that together we must destroy them.' (*The Observer*, 13.12.1980 and *Auswärtiges Amt* memorandum *Füh. 42/41 g. Rs.* of 15.7.1941.)

45. J.B. Bingham and V.C. Johnson: 'A rational approach to export controls', *Foreign affairs* 57/4, Spring 1979, pp. 894-920, claim: 'in retrospect, it is shameful that the United States did not impose an embargo on trade with Nazi Germany until after Pearl Harbour'. The freezing of German assets in June 1941 effectively meant that trade was possible only at U.S. discretion. See A.S. Milward: *The German economy at war*, London, 1965.

46. *Morgenthau diary*, vol. 284, p. 122: memorandum for President Roosevelt of 19.7.1940, quoted in Andersen, *op. cit.*, p. 132.

47. German assets in the U.S.A. were estimated at 120 million marks in 1941; U.S. assets in Germany at 1,700 million: memorandum by Dr. Emil Wiehl, Director of the Economic Policy Department in the German Foreign Ministry, 15.6.1941. (*Auswärtiges Amt: Büro des Staatssekretärs: 'Akten betreffend USA', Mai-Juni 1941*.)

48. General von Bötticher attempted to persuade General Isoda Saburô, Japanese Military Attaché in Washington, that U.S. policy was one of bluff and intimidation and that Japan had nothing to fear from intervention in the war, as a result of the German attack on the Soviet Union and the weakness of the Anglo-American powers. Washington Embassy Telegram no. 3197 of 15.9.1941 on the Japanese attitude to America, which, he argued, was based on an inadequate understanding of industrial developments and was overly influenced by U.S. propaganda (as fn. 1). Bötticher's reports were passed on to General Banzai in Berlin via General Gerhard Matzky, the Chief of the Intelligence Division of the General Staff and a former German Military Attaché in Tokyo from 1938 to 1941. They were also relayed to Admiral Nomura Naokuni, the Head of the Japanese Naval Mission in Berlin by Admiral Groos and to the Military and Naval Attachés in Tokyo. When Admiral Wenneker tried out the argument on Captain Maeda on 13.11.1941 that Japan had nothing to fear from U.S. entry into the war, Maeda replied that the Japanese Navy took precisely the opposite point of view (as fn. 14).

49. *Auswärtiges Amt* memorandum *RM 777/20* of 27.10.1920 on a conversation with Tôgô. (*AA: Büro des Reichsaussenminister: Akte 40, 'Akten betref-*

fend Japan', 1920-1935.) See also S. Asada: 'Foreign Minister Tôgô Shigenori and the Pacific War', EAJS Conference Papers, Florence, 1979.
50. *The Times*, 8.2.1980.

Chapter 20 GORDON DANIELS *Tradition and Modernity in Japanese Film Propaganda, 'Nippon Nyûsu' 1940-45*
1. For a recent brief account of the history of the Japanese cinema, see Liz-Anne Bawden (ed.): *The Oxford companion to film*, London, 1976, pp. 363-5.
2. Kinema Junpôsha (ed.): *Nihon eiga shi*, Seika no eiga sakka 31, 1976, pp. 16-17, 38-9.
3. For the Ministry of Education's interest in the cinema, see Tanaka Jun'ichirô: *Nihon eiga hattatsu shi* vol. 1, 1976 ed., pp. 408-9, and vol. 2, pp. 362-3. German and Italian influences are noted in *ibid.* vol. 3, pp. 14-15.
4. *Ibid.* vol. 3, p. 17, and Mainichi Shinbunsha (ed.): *Nippon Nyûsu eiga shi —Kaisen zen'ya kara shûsen chokugo made*, Bessatsu ichiokunin no Shôwa-shi, 1977, p. 3.
5. Nippon Eigasha (ed.): *Nippon Nyûsu dai-ichigô naishi dai-hyakugô (Nichi-Ei chôsa shiryô dai-isshû)*, 1943, pp. 1-4, and Mainichi Shinbunsha (ed.): *op. cit.*, p. 487.
6. Tanaka: *op. cit.* vol 3, p. 143.
7. Mainichi Shinbunsha (ed.): *op. cit.*, p. 8.
8. E.g., *ibid.*, Newsreel 20 (22 October 1940), p. 35; Newsreel 99 (28 April 1942), p. 204; Newsreel 124 (20 October 1942), p. 240; Newsreel 151 (27 April 1943), p. 292.
9. *Ibid.*, Newsreel 14 (10 September 1940), p. 23; Newsreel 20 (22 October 1940), p. 36; Newsreel 90 (23 February 1942), p. 185; Newsreel 19 (16 October 1940), p. 32; and Newsreel 248 (22 March 1945), p. 478.
10. Nippon Eigasha (ed.): *Nippon Nyûsu dai-hyakuichigô naishi dai-nihyakugô (Nichi-Ei chôsa shiryô dai-nishû)*, 1944, Newsreel 103 (26 May 1942), p. 4.
11. Mainichi Shinbunsha (ed.): *op. cit.*, Newsreel 19 (16 October 1940), p. 32; Newsreel 20 (22 October 1940), p. 36; Newsreel 23 (13 November 1940), p. 44; Newsreel 26 (4 December 1940), p. 5; and Newsreel 15 (15 September 1940), p. 25.
12. *Ibid.*, Newsreel 45 (15 April 1941), p. 106: and Newsreel 244 (1 February 1945), p. 474.
13. E.g., *ibid.*, Newsreel 5 (9 July 1940), p. 17; and Newsreel 53 (10 June 1941), p. 122.
14. *Ibid.*, Newsreel 24 (20 November 1940), p. 46.
15. E.g., *ibid.*, Newsreel 142 (24 February 1943), p. 276.
16. *Ibid.*, Newsreel 224 (14 September 1944), p. 437.
17. *Ibid.*, Newsreel 216 (22 July 1944), p. 421; and Newsreel 252 (9 June 1945), p. 484.
18. *Ibid.*, Newsreel 56 (1 July 1941), p. 125; Newsreel 140 (9 February 1943), p. 272; Newsreel 53 (10 June 1941), p. 122; and Newsreel 124 (20 October 1942), p. 241.
19. For a subject analysis of the contents of *Nippon Nyûsu* 1-200, see Nippon Eigasha (ed.): *op. cit.*, 1943, Contents pp. 1-5; and *op. cit.*, 1944, Contents pp. 1-5. For a simple listing of all newsreels, see NHK Saabisu Sentaa—Bangumi Shiryô-bu (ed.): *Firumu shiryô risto—Nippon Nyûsu hen (1)*, April 1978.

20. Mainichi Shinbunsha (ed.): *op. cit.*, Newsreel 22 (6 November 1940), p. 42; Newsreel 51 (27 May 1941), p. 119; Newsreel 31 (7 January 1941), p. 67; and Newsreel 169 (3 August 1943), p. 327.

21. E.g., the Nanking regime's declaration of war on the U.S.A. and Britain was a headline item in Newsreel 136 (12 January 1943), *ibid.*, p. 262, and the conference of East Asian ambassadors appeared in Newsreel 251 (10 May 1945), *ibid.*, p. 482.

22. E.g., *ibid.*, Newsreel 29 (24 December 1940), p. 62; Newsreel 31 (7 January 1941), p. 68; Newsreel 44 (8 April 1941), p. 104; and Newsreel 161 (6 July 1943), p. 311.

23. *Ibid.*, Newsreel 193 (9 February 1944), p. 367; and Newsreel 211 (15 June 1944) p. 405.

24. The new Asian ideal was implicit in the Greater East Asian Games depicted in Newsreel 1 (11 June 1940), *ibid.*, p. 9. The Emperor of Manchukuo's visit to Japan was shown in Newsreel 3 (25 June 1940), *ibid.*, p. 13, and Newsreel 5 (9 July 1940), *ibid.*, p. 17. His speech on the 12th anniversary of Manchukuo's foundation appeared in Newsreel 225 (21 September 1944), *ibid.*, p. 438.

25. E.g., *ibid.*, Newsreel 36 (10 February 1941), p. 83; Newsreel 82 (29 December 1941), p. 167: and Newsreel 161 (6 July 1943), p. 312.

26. E.g., *ibid.*, Newsreel 107 (22 June 1942), p. 214; Newsreel 113 (5 August 1942), p. 224; Newsreel 166 (11 August 1943), p. 322; and Newsreel 43 (1 April 1941), p. 101. The spirit of the new Asian states was well illustrated in Newsreel 221 (24 August 1944), *ibid.*, p. 431, and Newsreel 226 (28 September 1944), *ibid.*, p. 440.

27. E.g., *ibid.*, Newsreel 141 (16 February 1943), p. 275; Newsreel 168 (24 August 1943), pp. 325-6; and Newsreel 147 (30 March 1943), pp. 284-5.

28. *Ibid.*, Newsreel 44 (8 April 1941), p. 103; and Newsreel 222 (31 August 1944), p. 432.

29. E.g., *ibid.*, Newsreel 233 (16 November 1944), p. 454; and Newsreel 236 (7 December 1944), p. 462. For an account of Sun Yat-sen's links with Japan, see Marius B. Jansen: *The Japanese and Sun Yat-sen*, Cambridge, Mass., 1954.

30. *Ibid.*, Newsreel 165 (3 August 1943), p. 320; Newsreel 166 (11 August 1943), p. 322; Newsreel 176 (19 October 1943), p. 339; and Newsreel 226 (28 September 1944), p. 440.

31. *Ibid.*, Newsreel 116 (25 August 1942), p. 230; Newsreel 143 (1 March 1943), p. 278; and Newsreel 204 (27 April 1944), p. 387. For a study of relations between Japan and Indian nationalists, see Joyce C. Lebra: *Jungle alliance—Japan and the Indian National Army*, Singapore, 1971.

32. E.g., *ibid.*, Newsreel 14 (10 September 1940), p. 24; Newsreel 17 (1 October 1940), p. 28; Newsreel 19 (16 October 1940), p. 33; and Newsreel 20 (22 October 1940), p. 38.

33. *Ibid.*, Newsreel 145 (16 March 1943), p. 282.

34. *Ibid.*, Newsreel 195 (25 February 1944), pp. 372-3; Newsreel 212 (22 June 1944), p. 409; Newsreel 219 (10 August 1944), p. 423; and Newsreel 222 (31 August 1944), p. 432.

35. Cf. *ibid.*, Newsreel 232 (9 November 1944), p. 450; Newsreel 234 (23 November 1944), p. 455; Newsreel 235 (30 November 1944), p. 460; and Newsreel 237 (15 December 1944), p. 464.

Chapter 16   LASZLO SLUIMERS *Japanese Policies in Burma and Indonesia 1942-45 as a Dependent Variable of the 'Gunbatsu' Phenomenon*

1.   László Sluimers: *A method in the madness? Aanzetten tot een vergelijken de politicologische studie van de Japanse periode in Zuidoost-Azie 1942-1945*, Amsterdam, 1978, gives a fuller treatment of the subject in Dutch.

2.   My colleague, Professor Ot van den Muijzenberg, implicitly criticizing earlier views of mine in his Ph.D. dissertation *Horizontale mobiliteit in Central-Luzon, Kenmerken en achtergronden*, Amsterdam, 1973, sharply distinguishes between urban and rural aspects of Philippine politics during the Japanese era.

3.   I have in mind, of course, the Hukbalahap rebellion in the Philippines. See B. Kerkvliet: *Peasant rebellion in the Philippines—The origins and growth of the HMB*, 2 vols., Ann Arbor, 1972, (microfilm).

4.   A failure to do this might be a flaw in the argument of the late Harry Benda's classic *The Crescent and the Rising Sun—Indonesian Islam under the Japanese occupation 1942-1945*, The Hague, 1958. In an earlier work, 'The beginnings of the Japanese occupation of Java', *Far Eastern quarterly*, 1956, pp. 541-60, this author, not without some justification, concentrates on Japanese *Gleichschaltung* measures.

5.   For further details, see Ôta Tsunezô's masterly analysis, *Biruma ni okeru Nihon gunseishi no kenkyû*, 1967. Much to my regret, due to lack of space, I have to abstain from entering into details of the not unimportant and rather unsavoury in-fighting between army and navy components of the *Minami Kikan*, having its origins in developments in Tokyo.

6.   See A.J. Piekaar: *Atjèh en de Oorlog met Japan*, The Hague, 1949.

7.   Interview with Lt.-General Fujiwara in the Ichigaya Kaikan, Tokyo, 19 November 1971. The go-between was his friend, Mr. Sugano, who came to the Dutch embassy some days before. He is in all probability identical with Sugano Kengô, a former 'Young Officer' said to have been involved in a positive action that, due to some misunderstanding, was undertaken with respect to the Chinese warlord Chang Tso-lin and caused him to be liquidated. See Gôtô Ken'ichi: *Hi no umi no bohyô*, 1977, p. 112.

8.   Fujiwara in his *Fujiwara (F) Kikan—Indo dokuritsu no haha*, 1971, scathingly criticizes the *Gunseibu* and *Kenpeitai*, 'not knowing the circumstances', for their attitude in this respect.

9.   A. Reid and S. Shiraishi: 'Rural unrest in Sumatra', *Indonesia* no. 21, Cornell University Press, April 1976, pp. 115-33.

10.   For more details about this period, see my ' "Nieuwe Orde" op Java—De Japanners en de Indonesische elites 1942-1943', *Bijdragen tot de Taal, Land- en Volkenkunde*, Leiden, 1968, pp. 336-67.

11.   For a very delicate description of the atmosphere during the Japanese era, see Murai Yoshinori: *Sunda no siekatsushi*, NHK, 1978, p. 211ff.

12.   Rijksinstituut voor Oorlogsdocumentatie Indische Collectie no. 30897.

13.   See Gatot Mangkupradja: 'The Peta and my relations with the Japanese —A correction to Sukarno's autobiography', *Indonesia*, April 1968, pp. 105-34. Especially among the *Beppan's* expatriate informers, there were many with a populist or even left-wing background, including Machida, the leader of the Japanese community in Bandung. See Gotô: *op. cit.*

14.   The Islamic wing of the Indonesian nationalist movement was spiritualized in approximately the same way as the secular-nationalist wing.

15. See Nugroho Notosusanto: *The PETA Army during the Japanese occupation of Indonesia*, Tokyo, 1979.
16. And even with the radical Kodaw Hmaing subfaction.
17. *The double patriots—A study in Japanese nationalism*, London, 1957.
18. The same applies for Wachi Takaji and Maeda Masami, both *Gunseikan* in the Philippines.
19. J.B. Crowley: *Japan's quest for autonomy—National defence and foreign policy 1930-1938*, Princeton, 1966.
20. Anton Lucas: 'Social revolution in Pemalang, central Java', *Indonesia*, October 1977, pp. 87-122.
21. For Indonesia, see, e.g., Clifford Geertz: *The agricultural involution—The process of ecological change in Indonesia*, Berkeley, 1968, esp. the chapter on the 'Culture system'.
22. I wish to thank my colleague, Gregor Benton M.A., for correcting my English text.

Chapter 22 MICHAEL HAYES *The Beginnings of 'Democratic' Politics —Japan's First Post-War Election Campaign*
1. *Asahi shinbun*, 18 September 1945.
2. See Naimushô (ed.): *Kaisei shûgiin giin senkyo hôreishû*, 1945.
3. For the official explanation of this, see Zenkoku Kanri Iinkai Jimukyoku (ed.): *Senkyo nenkan*, 1950.
4. *SCAPIN 93*, 4 October 1945.
5. E.g., on 26 October 1945, Brig.-Gen. Dyke, Head of Civil Information and Education Section, GHQ, met Japanese newspaper editors to impress on them the importance of this matter.
6. *SCAPIN 548, 550*, 4 January 1946.
7. *Asahi shinbun*, 3 November 1945.
8. Gikai Seiji Kenkyûkai (ed.): *Seitô nenkan*, 1947.
9. Naimushô Keihôkyoku (ed.): *Seitô undô no kaisetsu*, December 1945; and *Shinsenkyohô ni okeru bassoku ichiran*, December 1945.
10. *Tôkyô shinbun*, 24 December 1945.
11. *Asahi shinbun*, 18 February 1946.
12. Government Section, GHQ: *Report of 1946 election*, 23 April 1946.
13. *Mainichi shinbun*, 28 March 1946, stated that radio addresses by members of all parties were 'far from good...grammatically incorrect...and in many instances cannot be understood'.
14. *Tôkyô shinbun*, 25 March 1946.
15. *Ibid.*, 23 March 1946.
16. *Ibid.*, 10 April 1946.
17. *Imperial ordinance* no. 101, 22 February 1946.
18. *Ministry of Home Affairs ordinance* no. 11, 6 March 1946.
19. The expenses of the various parties from 1 January to 10 March were, Progressives: 839,323 yen; Liberals: 821,646 yen; Communists: 597,543 yen; Cooperatives: 215,800 yen; New Japan Party: 79,360 yen and Socialists: 60,508 yen. But the most interesting was the case of the *Junsei Nippon Jiyûtô* ('Pure Japan Liberal Party') which had no receipts and no disbursements (*Yomiuri hôchi*, 23 March 1946).
20. *Asahi shinbun*, 13 March 1946.
21. *Ibid.*, 14 March 1946.

22. *Ibid.*, 16 March 1946.
23. *Ibid.*, 15 March 1946.
24. *Ibid.*, 17 March 1946.
25. *Ibid.*, 8 March 1946.
26. E.g., a meeting for women candidates organized by the *Yomiuri hôchi* and held on 30 March at Hibiya Hall (*Yomiuri hôchi*, 31 March 1946).
27. *Asahi shinbun*, 9 April 1946.
28. *Tôkyô shinbun*, 25 March 1946.
29. *Mainichi shinbun*, 18 March 1946.
30. *Tôkyô shinbun*, 18 March 1946.
31. *Yomiuri hôchi*, 1 April 1946.
32. *Mainichi shinbun*, 5 April 1946.
33. Government Section, GHQ: *Report of 1946 election*, 23 April 1946.
34. E.J. Drea: *The Japanese general election of 1942: A study of political institutions in wartime*, Ph.D. thesis, University of Kansas, 1978.
35. Isa Hideo: *Ozaki Yukio den*.
36. *Asahi shinbun*, 30 March 1946.
37. *Ibid.*
38. Interview with Hirano Rikeizô, 7 March 1979.
39. *Tôkyô shinbun*, 28 March 1946.
40. See Matsuo Takayoshi: 'Haisen chokugo no Kyôto Minshu Sensen' ('The Democratic Front in Kyoto immediately after the war'), *Kyôto Daigaku Bungakubu Kenkyû Kian* 18, Kyoto.
41. One of the most obvious examples of this was in Gunma prefecture, where Mogami Hideko stood in place of her husband, an ex-member of the Diet (*Asahi shinbun*, 25 March 1946).

Chapter 25 EKKEHARD MAY *The 'Other' Tradition—Modern Japanese Literature and the Structure of Literary Life in Tokugawa Japan*

1. Princeton, 1978.   1978.
2. *Journal of Japanese studies* vol. II, 1976, pp. 249-66.

Chapter 26 WOLFGANG SCHAMONI *Kitamura Tôkoku's Early Years and the Rise of the 'Poet' Concept*

1. The discovery of this material is due to several local historians of the Tama district, but particularly to Irokawa Daikichi, who collected his own studies on the Kanagawa People's Rights Movement in *Meiji seishin shi*, rev. ed. 1973; *Minshû kenpô no sôzô*, 1970; and *Meiji-jin*, 1978.
2. This paper is a summary of one chapter of a detailed study of Tôkoku's early years, which is to be published in German.
3. *Tôkoku zenshû* vol. 1, appendix p. 9; other reasons for his refusal (namely his criticism of violence), which he gives later in the letter of 21 January 1888, should be seen rather as a consequence of his conversion to Christianity two years after the parting from his friends. There are, however, signs of a germinating criticism of the radical democrats already in 1885 (see below).
4. Dated 18 August 1887 to Ishikaza Mine, in *Meiji bungaku zenshû* (hereafter *MBZ*) vol. 19. p. 290. This volume gives a more reliable text of Tôkoku's works than the *Tôkoku zenshû* from Iwanami Shoten, but it is not as complete as the latter.
5. *Ibid.*, p. 61.

6. Cf. Kawasaki Tsukasa: 'Tôkoku nenpu, tsuika, teisei', *Nihon bungaku*, February-May 1974.
7. Cf. Satô Zen'ya: 'Fuji-san asobi no kioku—Sono mochiifu to têma', *Nihon bungaku*, Rikkyô Daigaku, December 1971.
8. *MBZ* vol. 29, p. 287.
9. Especially in the letters of 18 August 1887 and January 1888. It should be noted that Kunikida Doppo too began his literary career with a criticism of 'ambition' (December 1889 in Iwamoto's journal *Jogaku zasshi*).
10. The article is 'Kinrai ryûkô no seiji shôsetsu o hyô su', *Kokumin no tomo* (text reprinted in *Kindai bungaku hyôron taikei* vol. 1, Kadokawa Shoten, which also give the text of 'Insupirêshon'; the other article mentioned, 'Shin Nihon no shijin', is not reprinted).
11. *MBZ* vol. 32, p. 27. This idea is directly borrowed from Emerson, who says in his essay *The poet*, 'He stands among partial men for the complete man.'
12. *Kindai bungaku hyôron taikei* vol. 1, p. 144.
13. These interlocking discussions are fully documented in *ibid.* vol. 1.
14. *MBZ* vol. 29, p. 302.
15. *Ibid.*, p. 61.
16. *Ibid.*, pp. 61-2.
17. *Ibid.*, p. 62.
18. *Ibid.*, p. 311.
19. *Ibid.*, p. 310.
20. *Ibid.*, p. 313.
21. *Concepts of criticism*, New Haven and London, 1963, p. 166.
22. *Culture and society 1780-1950*, (London 1958), Penguin ed. 1963, p. 53.
23. *MBZ*, vol. 29, p. 168.

Chapter 27 IRMELA HIJIYA-KIRSCHNEREIT *The Concepts of Tradition in Modern Japanese Literature*
1. See his *Erkenntnis und Interesse*, Frankfurt/M., 1968.
2. 'Modern Japanese fiction: "Accommodated truth"', *Journal of Japanese studies* II/2, 1976, p. 254.
3. *Ibid.*, p. 266.
4. Dennis Keene: 'The Shinkankakuha: A Japanese literary movement of the nineteen-twenties', *Transactions of the International Conference of Orientalists in Japan*, The Tôhô Gakkai 16, Tokyo, 1971, p. 42.
5. *Ibid.*, p. 42.
6. J. Thomas Rimer: *Modern Japanese fiction and its traditions: An introduction*, Princeton, 1978.
7. Behind his resorting to 'traditional' Japanese vocabulary lies, of course—at least partly—the intention to demonstrate the links of modern fiction to the tradition, but I would still maintain that he could have done better without using them as descriptive tools.
8. Lack of space in this paper forbids me to enter into a detailed discussion of this aspect of Rimer's study, because it would require long quotations of the original scene as well as his argumentation. The reader can, however, check my objections with the aid of his index (see *aware* and related terms). A suitable demonstration object for my proposition to replace his 'conventional' explanation by a stricter *literaturwissenschaftlich* analysis—which by way of the isolation of different layers in the work permits a much more differentiated

and subtle treatment—is on p. 31.

9. See Rimer, *op. cit.*, p. 263.

10. 'The classic and the contemporary in modern Japanese fiction: Are Japanese writers changing their perspectives?', *Japan Foundation newsletter* IV/3, 1978, p. 15.

11. See, e.g., Felix V. Vodička: 'Die Rezeptionsgeschichte literarischer Werke', in his *Struktur der Entwicklung*, München, 1975, pp. 60-86.

12. It has to be admitted that my proposition requires 'circular' thinking, too, although I hope it is 'only' a hermeneutic one which should prove not quite as vicious as the one described.

13. *Dentô to kindai*, 1972. In an essay on *dentô* (pp. 236-44), e.g., he stresses the differences between the European and the Japanese notion of tradition.

14. Wolfgang Iser: *Der Akt des Lesens*. München, 1976, p. 137 (my translation).

15. Of these two, the effect is in the end more important, as it can run counter to the author's intention. Literary reception takes the work for what it is, not for what the author wanted it to be. In case of a gap between intention and effect, the possibilities for 'misunderstandings' must lie in the text itself.

16. A discussion of this practice is to be found in my analysis of Mishima Yukio research; see my *Mishima Yukios Roman 'Kyôko no ie'—Versuch einer intratextuellen Analyse*, Wiesbaden, 1976, p. 28ff.

17. See, e.g., Michael Riffaterre who laments what he calls a 'plague of literary criticism': 'the tendency to maintain that a key-word or a repeatedly occurring expression should necessarily have the same meaning for the author at any time once he uses this word again and again like an *idée fixe*', *Strukturale Stilistik*, München, 1973, p. 279 (my translation).

18. 1979.

19. 'Innovation als Renovation—Zur literarhistorischen Bedeutung von Tayama Katais Erzählung "Futon"', *Bochumer Jahrbuch zur Ostasienforschung*, 1, 1978, pp. 348-73.

20. 'Racines und Goethes Iphigenie: Mit einem Nachwort über die Partialität der rezeptionsästhetischen Methode', *Neue Hefte für Philosophie*, 4, 1973, p. 37ff.

21. The term in the form of *Erwartungshorizont*, adapted from Karl Mannheim, is a key-word in H.R. Jauss's *Rezeptionstheorie*, and has by now entered Japanese studies, too. A definition is given in Hasegawa Izumi and Takahashi Shintarô (ed.): 'Bungei yôgo no kiso chishiki', *Kokubungaku kaishaku to kanshô*, special enlarged edition, May 1979, p. 127ff. Kutsuwada is also the translator of Jauss's epoch-making *Literaturgeschichte als Provokation* (1970) (*Chôhatsu to shite no bungakushi*, 1976). An example of the Japanese way of digesting these theories is Hiraoka Toshio: 'Bungakushi kenkyû e no apurôchi', *Kaishaku to kanshô* 1, 1978, pp. 8-47, esp. p. 12ff.

22. The exception which I have come across is Mikolaj Melanowicz: 'Native tradition in the literature of Tanizaki Jun'ichirô', *Studies on Japanese culture* I, The Japan P.E.N. Club, Tokyo, 1973, pp. 346-50.

23. See Rimer, *op. cit.*, p. 79.

24. For a more detailed description, see my Habilitationsschrift *Shishôsetsu —Gattungsgeschichte und Gattungstheorie*, 1979, pt. III, chap. 5.2.2.4.

25. See the quotation, *ibid.*, pt. V, chap. 3.1.

302

Chapter 28 MIKOLAJ MELANOWICZ *Tradition in the Popular Novel 'Rangiku Monogatari'*
1. *Buntai*, vol. 5, 1979, pp. 99-103. See also vols. 6 and 7, 1979.
2. This search for the blanks in historical records which give scope for creative fantasy was commented upon by Tanizaki in the exposition of *Yoshinokuzu*.
3. See, e.g., *Formy literatury popularnej* 'Forms of popular literature', Ossolineum, Wroclaw, 1973.
4. *Tanizaki Jun'ichirô zenshû (TJZ)* vol. 16, Chûô Kôronsha, 1958-60, pp. 282-7.
5. *Bungei shunjû*, 1933-4; reprinted in *TJZ* vol. 22, pp. 87-126.
6. *Ibid.*, p. 98.
7. *Ibid.*, p. 92.
8. *Ibid.*, vol 19, pp. 164-5.
9. See 'Taishû bungaku ryûkô ni tsuite', in the *Ôru yomimono* special edition of *Bungei shunjû*, July 1930; and *TJZ* vol. 18, p. 285.

Chapter 30 SANG-KYONG LEE *The Reception of Traditional Japanese Theatre in Europe*
1. Ezra Pound and Ernest Fenellosa (tr. by Wieland Schmied *et al.*): *Nô—vom Genius Japans*, Zürich, 1963, p. 8ff.
2. Jacques Coupeau: *Souvenirs du Vieux-Colombier*, Paris 1931, p. 99.
3. Leonard C. Pronko: *Theater East and West*, Berkeley 1967, p. 93.
4. Jean-Louis Barrault: *Journal de bord*, Paris, 1961, pp. 70-88.
5. Adolf Fischer: *Bilder aus Japan*, Berlin 1897, p. 190ff., and 'Japans Bühnenkunst und ihre Entwicklung', *Westermanns Illustrierte Dt. Monatshefte*, Bd. 89, 1900-1901, p. 502.
6. Oskar Bie: 'Sumurun', *Die neue Rundschau*, Jg. 21, 1900, Bd. 11, p. 874.
7. The answer of B. Brecht at the hearing of the Committee on Un-American Activities, in B. Brecht: *Die Massnahme. Kritische Ausgabe mit einer Spielanleitung von Reiner Steinweg*, Frankfurt/M., 1972, p. 256ff.
8. In a note dated 2 June 1964; quoted by L.C. Pronko: *op. cit.*, p. 106.

Chapter 31 METTE BRANDGAARD *The Female Impersonators (Onnagata) in the Kabuki Theatre Today*
1. Published as *The actors' Analects*, University of Tokyo Press, 1969, p. 62.
2. Allen & Unwin, 1955, p. 171.

Chapter 32 MIYOKO URAGUCHI DOCHERTY *Past is Present in Furui Yoshikichi*
1. Furui Yoshikichi (tr. by Howard Hibbett): 'Wedlock', in Howard Hibbett (ed.): *Contemporary Japanese literature*, New York, Knopf, 1977, p. 3.
2. *Ibid.*, p. 4. All following references are to this same work, and a page number against a quotation also applies to all following quotations until a new page reference is given.

3. p. 5.	9. p. 8.	15. p. 17.	22. p. 9-10.	29. p. 27.
4. pp. 26-7.	10. p. 34.	16. p. 20.	23. p. 16.	30. p. 40.
5. p. 27.	11. p. 35.	17. p. 21.	24. p. 17.	31. p. 39.
6. p. 6.	12. p. 25.	18. p. 7.	25. p. 18.	32. p. 38-9.
7. p. 29.	13. p. 29.	19. p. 24.	26. p. 11.	33. p. 39.
8. p. 5.	14. p. 35.	20. p. 5.	27. p. 12.	34. p. 38.
		21. p. 6.	28. p. 22.	35. p. 32.

36. p. 38.

Chapter 33   MILENA PARINI *Origins and Development of Science Fiction in Japan*
1.   This novel was translated in 1878 by Kawashima Tadanosuke with the title *Shinsetsu hachijûnichikan sekai isshû*
2.   Translated in 1880 by Inoue Tsutomu with the title *Kyûjûnanaji-nijuppunkan gessekai ryokô*.
3.   Translated in 1881 by Oda Nobuyoshi with the title *Chichû kikô*.
4.   In fact, it came only in 1900, when Kuroiwa Ruiko published *Hachijûmannen-go no sekai*, a translation of Well's *Time-machine*.
5.   This work was translated by Isono Tokusaburô and appeared with the title *Bunmei no daihakai*.
6.   This work appeared in Japan with the title *Hyakunen-go no shinshakai* translated by Sakai Kosen.
7.   This term is formed by the union of the words 'fan' and 'magazine'. It is indicative of a magazine issued and written only by science-fiction fans.

Chapter 34   PATRICK LE NESTOUR *To Restore to Honour a Dishonoured Honorific*
1.   Patrick Le Nestour: 'Determination of linguistic person—subjectless predicates in contemporary Japanese, and the notion of exteriority and nonexteriority', in I.H. Nish and C.J. Dunn (ed.): *European studies on Japan*, Paul Norbury Publications, Tenterden, 1979. (Papers presented to the first conference of the EAJS, Zürich, 1976.) Briefly, a morphological and/or contextual 'mark of exteriority' rules out the possibility of the speaker being the person referred to, and vice-versa, a 'mark of non-exteriority' rules out the possibility of the addressee or a third person being the person referred to. The way this 'third person' is taken into account raises particular problems that are also considered in this study.
2.   The romanised transcriptions correspond to what might be called 'the extended Hepburn system', in which double vowels are used to transcribe long vowels in the text of the article.
3.   Gustave Guillaume: *Le problème de l'article et sa solution dans la langue française*, dissertation for the Diplôme de l'Ecole Pratique des Hautes Etudes, Paris, 1919; Librairie A.G. Nizet, Paris and Les Presses de l'Université Laval, Quebec, 1975.
4.   Gallimard, Paris, 1924; tr. as *The honorable picnic* and reprinted by Tuttle, Rutland, Vermont, 1977.
5.   Le Nestour: *op. cit.*
6.   My thanks to Kawaguchi Junji for these remarks.
7.   Gary D. Prideaux: *The syntax of Japanese honorifics*, Mouton, The Hague, 1970, p. 44.
8.   James D. McCawley: *The accentual system of standard Japanese*, Ph.D. dissertation, M.I.T., 1965.
9.   Prideaux: *op. cit.*, p. 59.
10.   The asterisk (*) indicates that the feature in question is irrelevant. It is not, however, used by Prideaux.
11.   Prideaux: *op. cit.*, p. 30.
12.   On the other hand, in certain languages devoid of a definite article, such as

Russian, an indefinite article may exist, which is the numeral 'one', in the singular only, and which acts as an indefinite article, while 'definite article substitutes' can also be detected. (I wish to thank Igor Arnstam and Christine Saoulski for bringing these facts to my notice.) The same phenomenon is found in Turkish: *bir ev, une maison,* 'a house' (but also 'one house'). On the other hand, in *evler, les maisons,* '*the* houses', *-ler* is not only the plural marker but this plural is usually a 'definite plural'. The bare form, *ev,* expresses the singular as well as the 'collective, indefinite plural': *des maisons,* 'houses'. Louis Bazin: *Introduction à l'étude pratique de la langue turque,* Librairie d'Amérique et d'Orient, Paris, 1968, p. 28.

13. Guillaume: *op. cit.,* pp. 14-15.

14. Cf. with *ipse* and *cil,* n. 16 below.

15. Le Nestour: 'Syntaxe et nature de l'article', *Comptes-rendus du premier colloque franco-japonais sur l'enseignement de la langue française au Japon,* Tokyo, 1970. The theory of the Japanese proto-article, taking the example of *o-hashi* '(the) chopsticks', was also outlined here.

16. Cases of such unfortunate definite articles existed elsewhere; e.g., in Vulgar Latin (*sermo quotidianus*): *ipse vir...,* 'the man...'; and in Old French: *cil oisel...,* 'the birds...'. These are not generic uses. The article *li-* or *l',* on the other hand, can be found concurrently with *cil* to indicate generic, absolute, surdetermined values, as in *le vent* 'wind', or *l'aube* 'daybreak':

> (...) *et le vent moul et delitable*
> 'and the gentle balmy wind
> *si con en printens perdurable*
> as during an eternal Spring
> *que cil oisel chascun matin*
> when (the) birds each morning
> *s'estudient en lor latin*
> do their best in their Latin
> *a l'aube du jour saluer* (...)
> to greet the break of day'

Guillaume de Lorris and Jean de Meun: *Roman de la Rose,* 13th century, Honoré Champion, Paris, 1973, vol. II, l. 8375-78.

17. Aurélien Sauvageot: *Premier livre de hongrois,* Librairie Orientaliste Paul Geuthner, Paris, 1965, p. 125. Sauvageot specifies that in modern Hungarian the article *az* is maintained after the demonstrative: *ez az ember* 'this person'; *az az ember* 'that person'.

18. This might be the time to look for a better term or metaterm than 'exteriority'. These remarks on 'distance'—somewhat sombre as regards the equality and fraternity of mankind—suggest a phenomenon of 'dissociation' when a language form is used with an exteriorising (dissociative) value. Should the negative pole (-Diss) be termed 'non-dissociative' or 'co-sociative' rather than 'associative'? And why not 'ego-dissociative' (+ 'ego-associative'), which would bring in the speaker?

19. The notion of surdetermination has already been touched on above.

20. We saw earlier that *o-* and *mi-* have the same etymology, whereas *go-* is of Chinese origin with a logogram which in Japan may be read in these three ways with possible variants. Generally speaking, *o-* and *mi-* are affixed to native Japanese words, *go-* and its obsolete variant *gyo-* to Sino-Japanese words.

21. Paul Aebischer: 'Contribution à la protohistoire des articles *ille* et *ipse* dans

les langues romanes', *Cultura Neolatina* 8, 1948, pp. 181-203.
22. Veikko Väänänen: *Introduction au latin vulgaire*, Klincksieck, Paris, 1963, p. 130.
23. Aurélien Sauvageot: *L'emploi de l'article en Gotique*, Librairie Ancienne Honoré Champion, Paris, 1929.
24. Wilhelm Streitberg: *Gotisches Elementarbuch*, Carl Winter's Universitätsbuchhandlung, Heidelberg, 1900, pp. 185-186: 'Versteht man unter "Artikel" das gewohnheitsmassig und obligatorisch zugefügte Demonstrativum, dass eine Person oder Sache als bekannt charakterisiert, so hat das Gotisch *keinen* Artikel'.
25. Sauvageot: *op. cit.*, p. 2.
26. *Ibid.*, p. 88.
27. *Ibid.*, p. 90: '...individualise le substantif, en limite l'extension'.
28. For example, *o-cha*, *le thé*: 'tea'—a definite article can no more express the generic here than it can be used in the expressions 'to have/take/drink tea', *prendre le thé*, or 'tea-time', *l'heure du thé*.
29. In conclusion, I wish to thank the following people for the helpful suggestions and comments they have made on various occasions: Igor Arnstam, Claude Buridant, Fujimori Bunkichi, Kawaguchi Junji, Jean-Jacques Origas, P.G. O'Neill, Alexis Rygaloff, Christine Saoulski, and Andrzej Wlodarczyk.

Index

311